Feeding the Green Monster

Also by Rob Neyer

Baseball Dynasties: The Greatest Teams of All Time

Feeding the Green Monster

Rob Neyer

iPUBLISH.com
at Time Warner Books

For information, address iPublish.com, 135 West 50th Street, New York, NY 10020.

⚌ An AOL Time Warner Company

ISBN 0-7595-5028-X

First edition: August 2001

Visit our Web site at www.iPublish.com.

This book is for anyone who has loved Fenway Park,
and isn't ready to see her go.

Contents

Acknowledgments

Four years ago, I received an e-mail from a talented young man named Jay Mandel. He was the first (and still the only) agent to express any interest in working with me. Since then we've done two books together, and I hope we're together for another twenty-two. Or until he gets sick of me calling him to pitch completely non-commercial book ideas.

Jay eventually got this book into the hands of Zachary Schisgal at iPublish, and Zachary's enthusiasm essentially brought it back from the dead.

Shortly after my arrival in Boston, a talented young jazz drummer named Jason Brannon searched me out, and offered to assist me in whatever way I might think necessary. Well, the project I had in mind was an exhaustive search for the origin of the term, "Green Monster." Through no fault of Jason's, we didn't get far with our search, but he proved indispensable in the making of this book, especially as my deadline approached. Besides that he's great company, a welcome commodity when you're a stranger in a strange land.

My mother, Annette Neyer, has always encouraged me. My father, Bob Neyer, has never discouraged me. I'm grateful to both of them, for those reasons and others.

David Schoenfield, my long-suffering editor at ESPN.com, deserves a lot more than the complimentary copy of this book that I'll send him. The care and feeding of Rob Neyer ain't easy (to which any of my ex-girlfriends will happily attest), but David has accepted this thankless chore, with great grace, for nearly four years now.

I'm also grateful to Geoff Reiss, John Marvel, and John Walsh at the Disney Internet Group, for both their indulgences over the years, and their permission to publish a few of my ESPN.com columns in these pages. Chuck Waseleski, Tom Ruane, Pat Quinn, Don Zminda, and Hall of Fame researcher Eric Enders all assisted me with statistical research.

I remain, as always, grateful to Bill James for far too many reasons to list here.

Two radio hosts have been particularly kind to me in recent months, and I'm grateful to ESPN Radio's Bob Valvano and WEEI's Ted Sarandis (along with their producers, Andy Elrick and Chris Eno) for giving me the chance to propagate my wild theories over the airwaves.

I'm a klutz when it comes to computers, yet my professional life revolves around them. So for his help, I'm grateful to Todd Arntson, who was never too busy to figure out which obvious solution I hadn't discovered for myself. John Pastier patiently answered my questions about Fenway Park and its prospective replacements. Nobody knows more about ballpark architecture.

The Boston Red Sox "feature" the highest-priced tickets in Major League Baseball, and I spent the grand total of two thousand, three hundred and seventy-six dollars (not including monies paid to scalpers) for the privilege of watching a pretty good team in what management considers a pretty crummy ballpark. I'd have spent a fair piece more, but for the kindness of friends and strangers who forked over tickets and wouldn't let me pay. In something like random order, those friends and strangers include: Lilia Guerra, Art Martone, Eric Neyer, Mike Slade, Bill Nowlin, Mike Curto, Geoff Reiss, A.J. Preller, Andy Schader, Jon Sciambi, Robert Gilbert, Michael Berman, Mike Kopf, Mark Haubner, Alan Brennan, Adam Kosberg, Jordan Koss, Neal Roper, and Ryan Mulderrig.

Also helpful in acquiring tickets were David Mundo, A.J. Preller, Bill Considine, Tom Nahigian, Rob Mathews, and Jack Howland. Oh, and I shouldn't forget ticket scalpers "Tommy" and "Kevin," who are relative princes among their ilk.

In my various travels during the season, I rarely had to spend money on hotel rooms, and for that I extend heartfelt thanks to Madison Smith, Bruce Feldman, and Alan Schwarz.

Special Awards for Miscellaneous Meritorious Service go to Mark and Meghan Swardstrom, Susan Wolf, Christine Destefano, Steve Schulman, Pete Fornatale, and Allen Barra, for reasons that they know only too well.

And finally, what gratitude I have left must go to Kristien and Micah. In the course of getting this book published, I ran into a real rough patch, a long stretch when it looked like the only people who would read the book would be my agent and my mom. My hopes flagged but my spirits didn't, because I knew that whatever happened to this book, Kristien and Micah would still be in my life.

First Inning

Tuesday, April 11
Opening Day at Fenway Park

In a couple of months I'll be thirty-four years old, and it strikes me, as I sit here in Section 29, Row 13, Seat 10, that a great percentage of those nearly thirty-four years have been spent preparing me for this day.

Opening Day at Fenway Park.

I'm here because I have, since I was a boy, loved baseball more than anything else, and I believe that Fenway Park might well be the best place in the world for a baseball lover to pass his days and his nights.

A couple of weeks ago, *Sports Illustrated*'s cover featured Pedro Martinez, Boston's (and for that matter, the world's) ace pitcher, along with the words, "Why the Red Sox will win the World Series." Heady stuff, but perhaps not so much of a reach, given that the Sox won ninety-four games a year ago and reached the American League Championship Series before bowing to the hated New York Yankees.

It's been eighty-two years since the Boston Red Sox won a World Series.

◆　◆　◆

My "baseball life" began when I was nine years old. After a decade of moving around the Midwest like middle-class American gypsies, in the spring of 1976 my family—me plus my mom, my dad, and my little brother, Eric—arrived in Raymore, Missouri, a small town just a few miles south of Kansas City.

Two things happened that summer: I turned ten, and I fell hard for a baseball team.

We'd moved to Missouri because my dad was starting a new job with a company called American StairGlide (they built chairs that slide up and down rails installed next to stairs). American StairGlide was a subsidiary of Marion Laboratories, which was owned by Ewing Kauffman, who owned the Kansas City Royals. So my dad could get good tickets for the Royals games. That summer, I saw my first major-league game and wound up going to the ballpark seven times. The Royals won all seven of those games. I just knew that I was their good-luck charm.

That same season, the Royals won their first American League West title. In October, I cried when Chris Chambliss—of the Yankees, damn them—hit a game-ending homer to beat the Royals in Game 5 of the American League Championship Series. (A year later, I cried again, this time at Royals Stadium, when they lost *another* decisive Game 5 to the Yankees, *again* in the ninth inning.)

At the same time, my parents were finally ending a lousy marriage, and the daily soap opera of the baseball season was a welcome, stabilizing presence in my life. I have a friend, a brilliant man who has written many books about baseball, whose mother died when he was a boy. He's never told me so, but I suspect that he lost himself in the comforting intricacies of baseball. Perhaps more than any other American sport, baseball has the power to fill a hole in one's life, because, at least for six months, it's so regularly *there*. Nearly every Monday through Saturday, the Royals would be on the radio in the evening. And then Sunday, in the afternoon. One might have to adjust for time-zone differences when the Royals were on the road, of course, but the rhythms of the season were predictable, and they made sense. Unlike the uncertainties of a busted home.

Perhaps that 1976 season, coupled with my parents' divorce, would have been enough to cement my enthusiasm for the Royals. But they won division titles again in 1977 and '78 (and again lost to the Yankees, damn them, in the playoffs both times). Given the general apathy surrounding the Royals these days, it's probably hard for younger fans to believe, but in the late seventies the Royals were immensely popular in the Kansas City area, and for that matter much of the Midwest. For every home game, buses would arrive at Royals Stadium from not only outlying regions of Missouri and Kansas, but also Iowa, Nebraska, even Colorado. If you happened to miss a game, the chances were good that the next person you met could tell you if the Royals had won. It was in this atmosphere that I became fairly obsessed with the Royals.

In August of 1980, I was involved in a fairly serious car wreck. I was fourteen. As my mom tells the story, she drove for three fearful hours in the middle of the night before arriving at the hospital to see me. I came out of unconsciousness for a few minutes. My only words were, "Did the Royals win last night?" (They had lost to the Blue Jays, but eventually reached the World Series for the first time. I was in the left-field bleachers for Game 4, and saw Willie Mays Aikens hit two home runs.)

The next stage of my obsession with baseball began in 1984, when three things happened.

First, I went off to the University of Kansas, and although my apartment was only half an hour from home, it was the first time I'd been away for any length of time, and I was lonely. Shoot, I even missed my mom. Fortunately, a pair of fellows named Denny Matthews and Fred White—longtime Royals broadcasters—would keep me company that fall, as my white-and-blue-clad heroes got themselves involved in a death struggle, ultimately successful, for the American League West title. My roommates and I didn't have a TV, so every night I sat huddled next to the radio as the pennant race turned and twisted to its mysterious conclusion. (There was, of course, no good reason to park myself so *close* to the radio, but it's one of those things you do when you want to be there, but can't be.)

That same fall I joined the History Book Club, and my first selection was *Bums: An Oral History of the Brooklyn Dodgers*, written by Peter Golenbock. With little else to do at night but study and listen to the radio, I devoured *Bums* in two or three days. Or, more precisely, two or three late nights and early mornings. This book inspired what became my fascination with baseball's incredibly rich history. Golenbock, in all honesty, is not a great writer or a great researcher, but he's a great interviewer and he does understand something that has eluded any number of baseball authors: The most interesting thing about baseball is the *voices*. And not only the voices of the players—baseball oral histories had been popular since the late 1960s, when Larry Ritter's wonderful *The Glory of Their Times* made a big splash in the book world—but also the voices of the *fans*, who had hitherto been completely neglected in the literature of the game.

I've never quite understood why authors don't pay more attention to the fans, because it's the fans who see the most. Players, in extreme cases, spend perhaps twenty years with one team. If they stick around as a coach or manager, maybe it's thirty or forty years. Some men have owned the same team for half a century or more. But the fans . . . given that little boys and girls often become enamored of teams when they're five or six years old, and more and more people are living to be one hundred years old or more, we might assume that there are baseball fans with nearly a *century* of baseball memories. Who knows more about a team? Who has more stories to tell? Who has rejoiced and/or suffered more? After reading *Bums*, a little man in the back of my brain resolved that if we ever wrote a baseball book, we'd find a place for the fans.

And third, shortly after finishing Golenbock's book, and being particularly excited about baseball because of the Royals, I stumbled across the *Bill James Baseball Abstract 1984*. I was eighteen years old, and anything seemed possible. Even though I could barely afford to eat—I mean that quite literally, as my food budget was ten dollars per week—there was always something new to read, something new to learn. When ignorant people talk about Bill James, they talk about numbers. That's not quite right. In his annual *Abstracts*, James looked at baseball—and by extension, everything else—from a unique perspective based on a sort of rational iconoclasm. Sure, he used plenty of numbers, but the numbers were nothing more than tools in the employ of something greater. If you were a baseball fan in the 1980s, there was no better place to learn than at the figurative feet of Bill James.

I studied quite a lot of non-baseball subjects my first year in college, but after that . . . look, I'm not accusing baseball of destroying my academic career. Quite likely, if it hadn't been baseball, it would have been something else. Playground basketball, *The New Yorker*, pool halls, pretty girls . . . whatever. Some people just aren't ready for college when they're eighteen years old, and some people are never ready. I fell into the first of those categories, and perhaps both. Without question, though, the particular catalysts of my academic demise were Harry Caray, his son Skip, and Bill James. Many days, I watched the Cubs on WGN, then the Braves on WTBS. And when there weren't any games on TV, I listened to the Royals on the radio and reread my *Baseball Abstracts* yet again.

By the end of my fourth year—notice I don't say "senior year" (it wasn't)—I'd had enough. With the end of the semester approaching, I took a job roofing houses, and when my classmates were taking their finals, I was developing a gruesome sunburn and learning how to use a staple gun. I never got an official notice from the University of Kansas telling me that I was no longer welcome, but I clearly did not belong there.

Thankfully, the roofing job lasted only nine months, at the end of which I stumbled into an incredible stroke of good fortune. Bill James—yes, *that* Bill James, the author of *The Baseball Abstract*—lived not far from me. What's more, we shared a mutual friend named Mike Kopf, who told me that Bill was in the market for a research assistant. And somehow, before I knew it, this college-dropout-turned-roofer was working for Bill James. The one job, among all jobs, that I would have chosen for myself. It's safe to say that I learned more in those four years about baseball, and about writing, than I had learned in the previous twenty-three years (or in the eight since).

The job with Bill led to one thing, then another, until I arrived at—as people love to tell me—"the greatest job in the world." I write about baseball, and people give me money.

◆ ◆ ◆

The Red Sox won their last World Series in 1918.

In 1999, the Red Sox won ninety-four games.

You could argue that they'll be even better in 2000, given that (1) three of their everyday players—the great shortstop Nomar Garciaparra, right fielder Trot Nixon, and catcher Jason Varitek—are still in their mid to late twenties, and thus might be expected to improve, and (2) the Sox have added a much-needed slugger to the lineup, in the person of center fielder Carl Everett.

But while it's true that Garciaparra and Nixon might be better this season, I'm not convinced that Varitek will improve. He's twenty-eight, and his numbers last year were out of character with the rest of his career. As for Everett, his 1999 season—he played for the Houston Astros and came to Boston in an off-season trade—was also out of character. More worrisome is Everett's long history of non-dependability. He turns twenty-nine this summer, and he's never played more than 142 games in a season. Last year, easily his most productive, he played only 123 games. Oh, and one more thing: in 1999, Pedro Martinez went 23–4. Even if he can match last season's amazing 2.07 ERA, will he match that 23–4 record? I think it's unlikely. Bad luck, bad hitting, and his own inability to start more than perhaps thirty-two games will probably conspire to keep him below twenty wins, let alone twenty-three.

For all these reasons and perhaps a few more, I suggested in my ESPN.com column two weeks ago that the Sox would finish third in the American League East, behind not only the Yankees but also the Toronto Blue Jays. And I'm not the only one with some questions about the Red Sox. In the *Boston Globe*'s preview of the 2000 season, four baseball writers—Peter Gammons, Dan Shaughnessy, Bob Ryan, and Larry Whiteside—picked the Yankees first and the Red Sox second. Interestingly, though, all four have the Red Sox finishing a strong second, strong enough to earn the American League's wild-card postseason berth. A bit of wishful thinking, perhaps.

Actually, that's what *Sports Illustrated* says, too. They also rate the Red Sox as just the number-two team in the American League East (behind the Yankees, of course) . . . but number three in the major leagues (behind Atlanta). And I suppose the thinking is that once the Red Sox reach the postseason, the presence of Pedro Martinez will be enough to carry them to the World Championship.

I don't believe in jinxes. But people around here, whether they believe in jinxes or not, do dearly love to talk about them. In response to that *Sports Illustrated* cover, Shaughnessy devoted an entire column to the latest supposed hex. He wrote, "The *Sports Illustrated* cover jinx takes its place alongside the Curse of the Bambino. Black Cat Bookends . . . will contribute to the paranoia and collective angst that pains the soul of Red Sox Nation." What Shaughnessy ignores, of course, is his own literary contribution to the paranoia and collective angst (but hey, a guy's gotta make a living).

Yes, it would be a wonderful story if, as *S.I.* predicts, the Red Sox really do win the World Series, their first since 1918. But as much as I'd love to see the Sox win the Series—God knows their fans have waited long enough—that's not why I'm here.

◆   ◆   ◆

I visited my first major league ballpark—Royals Stadium—when I was nine years old. Believe it or not, I didn't visit my second major league ballpark—old Comiskey Park in Chicago—until I was twenty-four. My "work" eventually led me to a number of stadiums, but for too long Fenway was not among them. It took me thirty-three years, three months, and three days, but I finally made it on September 25, 1999. Fenway had always been exciting and exotic to me, as exciting and exotic to this Midwesterner as Dodge City, Kansas, might have been to a New England lad in the nineteenth century. And there I was, after all those years. And unlike so many things, this experience lived up to my expectations.

A few minutes before game time, the organist was playing in a mysterious sort of way and I thought to myself, "Good, no rock music. The only rock 'n' roll song that should ever be heard in a ballpark was written by John Fogerty."

Moments later, with none of the sound effects and fireworks that you hear and see in some stadiums, the home team popped out of their Lilliputian dugout and trotted to their respective positions. And at that moment, the PA system (bless its electronic heart) began to play "Center Field." It was then that I knew I was in the right place, and I'm only a little embarrassed to admit that I got a little shiver up my spine, and a little moisture in my eyes. Roger Angell once described Fenway as "the best place in the world to watch a baseball game," and I could not have agreed more. I was in love.

It struck me that day that what people say about Red Sox fans, that they know more about the game than fans anywhere else, is true. As I looked around at my fellow spectators when something important was happening or might happen, I saw ninety-five percent of them staring at the field. They were not eating, or drinking, or talking to their neighbor about their kids or their stock portfolios. If they were talking about anything at all—and most apparently couldn't be bothered for something so trivial as conversation—it was why Jimy Williams didn't use a pinch-hitter for Darren Lewis, or whether Pedro Martinez is better than Roger Clemens.

How knowledgeable are Red Sox fans? Here's one example, from my second game at Fenway last September . . . In the bottom of the ninth inning, Orioles manager Ray Miller summoned forty-two-year-old Jesse Orosco from the bullpen. Orosco, by most accounts a decent-enough fellow, was nonetheless greeted by a medium-sized chorus of boos. Why? Because in 1986, then pitching for the New York Mets, he saved Game 7 of the World Series. Against the Red Sox. You tell me, where else in America (or Canada) will the fans boo somebody for something that happened thirteen years ago?

But it really wasn't until my third game—a night game—that Fenway's magic dust settled on me, and I was hooked. I know this will sound sacrilegious to the "traditionalists" (or is it the "purists"? I always forget), but I believe that baseball is a better game at night, when the field is lit up like a stage, and there are fewer distractions for the fans. And this is especially true at Fenway Park where, when it's dark, the green lights that signify balls in the old scoreboard are greener, the red lights that signify strikes are redder, the yellow neon on the fair poles are yellower, and the Green Monster is both Greener and, well, more Monstrous. At night, everything at Fenway stands out in sharper contrast than in the daytime. It's like the difference between wearing my contact lenses and not wearing them. And I always wear my contact lenses.

As John Updike so famously observed, "Fenway Park, in Boston, is a lyric little bandbox of a ballpark. Everything is painted green and seems in curiously sharp focus, like the inside of an old-fashioned peeping-type Easter egg." And I would argue that the park comes into even curiously sharper focus after the sun goes down. Sitting in my seat for a night game at Fenway Park, then, it struck me that everything I've done, all the reading and the work and the skipping of college classes and the neglecting of girlfriends and everything else, all of it served to prepare me for this moment. As much as I might enjoy watching baseball games in Kansas City or Seattle, both cities are relative newcomers when it comes to Major League Baseball. So there's almost always been something missing: a sense of history, a feeling of mass devotion, a singular *focus* that I dearly wish everyone else in the stands would share with me. But in Fenway, all of that *is* there, all of the history and the passion and the focus.

So sitting there in my seat, thinking about flying back home to Seattle in a few days, it occurred to me that *this* is where I should be, and for more than just a few games. Ralph Waldo Emerson—like Fenway Park, a New England native—liked to say that one might find Truth in a blade of grass. But I suspect that if Emerson were still with us, and working on a baseball book, he'd rather spend six months in Boston than in Seattle or Kansas City.

And thus it was, sitting in Seat 5 in Row CC in Box 101 in Section 12, that I decided I should spend an entire baseball season in Boston. That I *must* spend a baseball season in Boston. Six months in Fenway, eighty-one games—what might all of that tell me about not only the Red Sox, but also about being a fan? What might I learn about my obsession with this useless but perfect game?

◆ ◆ ◆

I didn't find an apartment with a view of Fenway Park, but I did pretty well, I think. My address is 111 Park Drive, and it's four short blocks, almost a straight shot, from the front door of my building to Gate D at Fenway. I walk outside, take a left, walk past one building (a halfway house for ex-convicts), then turn left onto Jersey Street. Three blocks later, Jersey crosses Boylston and turns into Yawkey Way. One block later, Yawkey reaches Van Ness . . . and Fenway Park. At a leisurely pace, it's six minutes and 537 steps, from my apartment to the greatest ballpark in the world.

And right across the street from my apartment—I'm on the fourth floor, so I do have a nice view of this—are the Back Bay Fens, a winding, mile-and-a-half-long park that ranks as one of the lovelier jewels in Frederick Law Olmstead's "Emerald Necklace," a system of linked green spaces designed by the architect of New York's Central Park. The Fens are home to a softball field and two basketball courts, but also a large number of small gardens cultivated by neighborhood residents, and a real wetlands that's home to a wide variety of flora and fauna.

◆　◆　◆

So that's how I got here. And today, "here" is a frigid Fenway Park, 46 degrees at game time. Everybody's bundled up, which makes for something of a comical experience in the grandstand, where the seats have been in place since 1934. People in 1934 were built quite differently than people in 2000; we're taller now, and we're wider. And if you're taller than six feet, your knees bang into the seat to your front; if you're wider than a two-by-four, you're going to bump elbows and thighs with whoever's sitting to your left and right. Or as Ray Kinsella says in *Shoeless Joe,* ". . . the seats are much too close together and we are hunched knees close to chins, as if we were passengers in the rear seat of a foreign car." Now toss in the cold weather, with the attendant layered clothing and baggy coats, and when someone returns from a trip to the bathroom or the beer stand, it's like trying to stuff a kernel back into an ear of corn.

Any other day, and it would be too bloody cold for baseball. But this isn't any other day, this is the *first* day. The first Red Sox home game of the season. *Opening* Day. I've read a number of poetic essays over the years, tying Opening Day to such lofty themes as rebirth, and rejuvenation. It's done quite artfully . . . and it misses the point completely. Opening Day doesn't have much to do with a mystical rejuvenation, or even something so pedestrian as springtime. No. Opening Day is plenty significant for the simplest of all reasons . . . *It's the first day of the baseball season.* Or in this case, the first day of Fenway's season. That's quite special enough for 99.9 percent of us.

But even more so than usual, this Opening Day is important to me. I have been thinking and talking about this book for months, yet on a symbolic level this is Day 1 of the project. If I don't get at least one thousand words about Opening Day on my hard drive, I will consider the day a failure. This summer promises to be something akin to a new marriage, both thrilling and terrifying. Thrilling, because I will be living and working in and around Fenway Park, perhaps the best place in the world to do what I love best—watch baseball games. Terrifying, because I'm supposed to produce a manuscript of roughly one hundred thousand words about the experience.

Beginning today, I must produce. Or perish, at least in a limited, professional sense.

I haven't written a word yet, but I've been thinking about this book for months, since I first conceived it last September. A little research here, a few thoughts jotted down there, and just a week ago I was in Seattle for the Red Sox' first series of the season. That was a homecoming of sorts, as I just moved from Seattle to Boston two weeks ago, after four years there. In fact, I've kept my season tickets at Safeco Field, and in a happy coincidence that's exactly where the Sox opened the 2000 season. So just eight days after arriving in Boston, I was on a plane back to Seattle for three games featuring the Red Sox, then one Mariners-Yankees contest.

The Sox lost two of those three games in Seattle, and then they traveled to Anaheim for three games against the Angels. They won only two of their first six games, and both victories came when Pedro Martinez pitched. In the other four games, Red Sox pitchers went 0–4 with a 7.59 ERA. Not a good sign.

Here's another sign that's not so good . . . the Red Sox lineup for today's game:

OPENING DAY LINEUP

	POS	AGE	OBP	SLG
1. JOSE OFFERMAN	2B	31	.366	.377
2. TROT NIXON	RF	26	.354	.464
3. BRIAN DAUBACH	DH	28	.357	.551
4. NOMAR GARCIAPARRA	SS	26	.367	.566
5. TROY O'LEARY	LF	30	.338	.469
6. CARL EVERETT	CF	29	.348	.458
7. MIKE STANLEY	1B	36	.372	.460
8. JASON VARITEK	C	28	.324	.460
9. WILTON VERAS	3B	22	.323	.398

With the exception of Wilton Veras—who is holding down third base only until John Valentin returns from an injury, probably later this month—these are the guys who are being counted on to produce enough runs for the Sox to win ninety-some games.

It's not a great lineup. The stats I've listed here are the most important ones—on-base percentage, and slugging percentage—and they represent each player's career totals entering this season. Garciaparra and Daubach are the only regulars with .500-plus career slugging percentages. And Daubach's career consists of just 120 games, all of them last season. It's unlikely that he's really that good. Essentially, it's a lineup with one superstar in Garciaparra, one star in Everett (though he's only been a star for about a year), and a bunch of guys who might be good. Or might not be.

Today, though, this lineup was just fine. Facing the Twins, who depending on their starting pitcher can look little better than a Triple-A club, the Red Sox scored twice in the first inning, sent thirteen runners to the plate in the second, and romped their way to a 13–4 laugher. I attended the game with my girlfriend, Sarah, her younger brother, and their parents. Sarah and Joseph are both native New Englanders, while their folks are from Cuba. All of them are, of course, rabid baseball fans. Sunday afternoon, I called Sarah while the Red Sox were playing the Angels in California. I asked her if she was listening to the game, and she replied, "No. What's the point? The Sox are horrible."

After five games and four losses, Sarah had given up on them. And she wasn't alone. Baseball fans in these parts are about as moody as a pregnant woman who forgot to eat lunch, and some of them had already given up on this season. But of course, Pedro beat the Angels that afternoon, the Sox are now 3–4 after today's blowout, and the Twins are in town for a couple more days. Hope springs eternal, especially in the spring.

April 12

Walking to the ballpark tonight, I knew it was going to be cold.

I just didn't know *how* cold. Had I known, I might never have left my apartment. Fenway Park or no Fenway Park. Book or no book. I don't believe that baseball is meant to be experienced while shivering and sucking down hot chocolate just to survive, and it was flat-out cold tonight. When the first pitch was thrown, the thermometer registered 46 degrees, the same as yesterday. The difference, of course, is that while yesterday's game began shortly before noon, and warmed up at least slightly, tonight's game began at 7:06 and only got chillier. Oh, and there was also a brisk wind blowing in, straight over the Green Monster and right into my face.

It's been seven years since I tasted meat, and perhaps a dozen years since I've eaten a hot dog. Yet I was sorely tempted in the third inning as I watched a vendor, just a few seats away, flip open the lid of his shiny stainless-steel bin. As he reached in for a dog, steam surrounded his forearm, and then the wiener itself came out, accompanied by its own moist blanket of heat. The guy selling the hot dogs was young but very good at his job, and the entire process, grabbing the bun to handing the completed dog to the customer, didn't take more than about eight seconds. But that was plenty long enough for me to fantasize about how wonderful it would feel to have five or six bites of pure warmth making the journey from my mouth to my stomach. One could, I realized, eat three or four hot dogs in the course of an evening like this one.

I kept score for the first six innings, but finally gave up in the seventh, preferring instead to devote my full attention to keeping warm. Now, one might think that scorekeeping would provide a pleasant diversion from freezing, but I felt significantly warmer after I stopped. Instead, I simply watched the ball game, my hands jammed into my jacket pockets, and concentrated on relaxing my muscles. The game ended just a few hours ago, but already I remember very little about it. After looking at the box score on the Internet, I can tell you that the Red Sox scored five runs in the third inning against Twins rookie Johan Santana, and cruised to a 7–3 win. I can also tell you that Troy O'Leary doubled (and scored) twice in two innings, and that Jeff Fassero picked up the victory despite pitching only five (shaky) innings.

None of that information will reside in my conscious memory. I'm going to remember freezing my ass off tonight, and that's all I'm going to remember.

Yesterday, the Detroit Tigers christened their new "mallpark" with a victory, beating the Seattle Mariners 5–2. But the game featured five errors, some of them due to the extreme conditions: 40 degrees at game time, plus a steady, stultifying drizzle throughout. While nearly forty thousand fans showed up for the inaugural festivities, at least half of them had gone home by the third inning. And that's kind of sad. If baseball players can't feel their fingers, then they shouldn't be on the field. Baseball is, after all, "the summer game."

In the old days, games would occasionally be postponed due to "cold grounds," but that almost never happens anymore. In recent years, only the Chicago White Sox have used this excuse to postpone a game, and only then when the result was a strategic advantage for them. The reason, of course, is money. Postponements can mean, somewhere down the line, doubleheaders, and baseball teams hate doubleheaders.

But baseball should have a rigid rule about frigid weather, something that would dictate postponement if the game-time wind chill is lower than 32 degrees. Or even 40.

That's one simple solution. Here's another. As much as I love baseball, I'd also love to see Major League Baseball cut the 162-game schedule back to 154, like it was before 1961. This would allow the season to start a week later than it does now. Start a week later and avoid early games in the more northern cities with outdoor ballparks, and you eliminate at least some percentage of the freezing temperatures. An alternative would be for each club to play five or six doubleheaders over the course of the season, which would allow the retention of the 162-game schedule *and* an April 10 Opening Day. But you say the word "doubleheader" in the presence of a baseball executive, and he'll make the sign of the cross and back away slowly, because it means a few less dollars.

Billy Herman, who managed the Red Sox in 1965 and '66, once observed of the weather here, "Boston has two seasons: August and winter." That's something of an exaggeration, of course, but everyone I meet tells me that the conditions at Fenway are often brutal in April, and I can't help but think there's a better way.

Thursday, April 13

Baseball is scrambling for a ball yourself. You don't want an autograph; that's like standing in line for gas.
—ex–Red Sox pitcher Bill Lee

After last night's nipple-raising experience, I decided to enjoy tonight's game on television, safe in my toasty apartment. But sometime in the middle of the afternoon, I started thinking . . . *What, are you nuts? You've got a ticket for a great seat at Fenway Park, you live four blocks away . . . and you're going to stay home? What if something great happens? What if Carl Everett hits three home runs? What if Brad Radke throws a no-hitter? What if . . .*

No, of course I wasn't going to stay home. Instead, I went out and bought some long underwear, and by game time I was just as excited to be going to the ballpark as I always am. And it was a good thing I went, because . . . wait, before we get into that, a few words about souvenir baseballs.

You can walk into any good-sized sporting-goods store and purchase an official Major League Baseball baseball for eight or ten bucks. But turn one loose in a ballpark, and you'd think it was the Hope Diamond. I have thought long and hard about this, and I have come to the conclusion that we find baseballs so fascinating because, all of a sudden, this common object, this whiteish sphere with red stitches, has escaped from its natural element. We're fascinated by baseballs for the same reason that we were fascinated, as children, when we spotted our fifth-grade teacher in the grocery store, comparison-shopping as if she were a normal person.

You've seen it. A ball is fouled into your section, and suddenly every adult male within twenty feet wants to see it, fondle it, *just be with it,* as if he'd never held a baseball before. Aside from the sheer surprise of suddenly having this *objet d'heart* in one's very own hands, the only interesting thing about such a baseball is its color, which is something not exactly white. For as every longtime baseball fan knows, before each game the umpires "rub up" each game ball with Delaware River Mud, to remove the slickness, the gloss, thus making the balls easier for the pitchers to grip. Game-used baseballs look dirty because they are. And people are surprised at this discovery. It's sort of like finding a brown egg in a carton that's supposed to contain white ones.

All right, back to the game. Bottom of the first inning. Three-and-two count to Garciaparra. Radke threw a change-up, and Nomar sliced it foul . . . way foul, a liner over the Red Sox dugout. Anybody who's been to Fenway more than a few times knows that a foul ball like this one is likely to hit one of two steel facings below, respectively, the roof-box seats or the roof itself. And if that happens, the ball will carom back into the lower deck.

This ball did indeed *bonk* off a steel facing, and directly toward me. All this takes less than a second, but one second is time enough for any number of reflexive thoughts . . . *that one might come back down, better dump the scorebook . . . it's coming this way . . . damn, a little too high, just over my hands . . . all right, that was moderately exciting, now let's get back to the ball game . . .*

Like anybody else, I pay attention when there's a foul ball heading in my direction. But once it's past me, I immediately give up and focus on the game. So as soon as this ball was gone, I was already turning back toward the infield. But then I noticed a blur of activity just to my right and my front, and suddenly everyone was looking at my feet. I looked at my feet, too . . . and there sat an official Major League baseball, as ripe for the picking as a Maine apple in September.

I reached down, past a small pair of arms that didn't reach far enough, and that ball, until just a few seconds ago an integral part of a *Major League Baseball game*, was mine. Not for long, though, because that small pair of arms was attached to a small girl sitting directly in front of me.

Let me explain . . . For some years now, it has been my position that adults don't have any business with baseballs, at least not if there are children within hailing distance. When I arrive in my seat for a game, I spend a few minutes scanning the fans around me in search of, in no particular order, (1) attractive women and (2) the best candidate for a free baseball, should I somehow find myself in possession of such an orb. Before the summer months, there generally aren't so many kids in the stands, which often makes the decision easy. Once school lets out, though, it's more complicated. Then you have to study not only the kids, but also the parents. If there are different children roughly equidistant from my seat, I try to guess which one of these kids is mostly likely to get whacked around at home. And that's who gets the baseball.

Tonight it was easy. I picked up the baseball, straightened up, and staring me right in the face was that little girl: brown-eyed, round-faced, and gap-toothed, with long hair, the bangs cut across her forehead as straight as a Triple-A pitcher's fastball. I am powerless when it comes to small children and big dogs, so without even thinking about it I handed her the ball, in return for which I received two thank-yous, three big smiles, and a snack to be named later (as it turned out, a handful of popcorn).

We got to talking, me and the little girl. Her name was Tracy, and she was eight years old. Nice and cozy in her bright red winter coat, tights, and purple tennis shoes, Tracy spent the rest of the game clutching her new baseball in one hand and a tiny version of Wally the Green Monster, the Red Sox mascot, in the other. Tracy's favorite player? Why, Nomar Garciaparra, of course.

In Matt Tavares's children's book, *Zachary's Ball*, young Zachary is given a foul ball caught by his father at Fenway Park. As it turns out, the ball has supernatural powers (the full nature of which will not be revealed here), but eventually the ball simply disappears from Zachary's room. Years later, Zachary is walking down Lansdowne Street, behind the Green Monster, during a Red Sox game. Suddenly a baseball arcs over the Monster, settling gently into Zachary's hands. As he turns for home with his prize, Zachary spies a young girl staring at it. At which point . . . He places the ball in her hands and she proclaims it's magic. But Zachary says they're all magic.

◆   ◆   ◆

Making a little girl happy certainly ranks as the top highlight of my evening, but it wasn't the only highlight, as I also got to see Tim Wakefield record his first victory of the season. Pete Schourek started for the Sox, and pitched well enough. When he exited, with two outs in the top of the seventh, Boston trailed Minnesota 3–2. Rich Garces walked the first batter he faced, thus loading the bases, but then El Guapo retired Matt Lawton on a fly ball to escape further damage. (Back in the first inning, after Lawton singled, a young man behind me grumbled to his girlfriend, "The Bad News Twins. A high-school team could beat these guys.")

After the Red Sox tied the game in their half of the seventh, Wakefield trotted in from the bullpen.

That's not exactly accurate. Tim Wakefield does not trot. He jogs stiffly, sometimes accompanied by the strains of "Eight Days a Week" (presumably in honor of his ability to pitch whenever necessary). Slowing down as he reaches the infield dirt, Wakefield hands his warm-up jacket to a batboy, then proceeds to the mound with short, bowlegged strides, calling to mind a semiretired cowboy, determined to rope an ornery old steer after the young ranch hands have all given up.

I've always liked Wakefield, ever since he came up with the Pirates in 1992 and went 8–1 for the pennant-winning Pittsburgh Pirates. He's a knuckleball pitcher, and I like knuckleball pitchers. People sometimes ask me *why* I like knuckleballers, and I've never really come up with a satisfactory answer. But I'm thinking about it tonight, and I suspect it's simply because they're *different*. I can relate to that, because I grew up thinking I was different, too (of course, that only makes me non-different, because nearly all of us grew up thinking we were somehow different from our peers, and of course we were).

That's not the only reason, though. I like Wakefield because we're nearly the same age, he being just six weeks younger than I. I like Wakefield because he bears a mild resemblance to John Cusack, one of my favorite actors. And I like Wakefield because, among the few baseball players that I've interviewed, he was the most gracious and revealing.

Friday, April 14

Shortly before leaving for the ballpark tonight, I got word that Gary Gaetti had retired. This news was not unexpected. Gaetti went hitless in his first ten at-bats, and looked even worse than his batting average. Nevertheless, the news was unwelcome, as I had hoped to see the old warhorse come through with at least a few more big hits before he left the game for good.

Gaetti's presence on the Red Sox roster, it should be said, has always been fairly inexplicable. He's forty-one years old, and, last year with the Cubs, Gaetti batted .204 and posted a pitiful 599 OPS (on-base percentage plus slugging percentage). True, the Red Sox desperately needed a right-handed bat this spring, but when they, alone among the thirty major-league clubs, invited Gaetti to spring training, I assumed it was simply a favor to a grizzled veteran of the baseball wars. But then he got hot in spring training—well, at least warm, .280 with a couple homers in his first nine games—and suddenly Gaetti was given a valuable role on the roster, a role that he pretty clearly was no longer capable of filling with any sort of adequacy.

Now he's gone, and I'll miss him.

Gaetti certainly wasn't a great player, and is distinguished mostly by his longevity. Nevertheless, there are some things that, if you were paying attention, you might remember about him. He hit a home run in his first major league at-bat. He eventually participated in seven triple plays as a defensive player, which is the all-time record. For a while, he sported long, curly (permed) hair, which masked, at least to a small extent, the fact that Gaetti—nicknamed "The Rat" by his teammates—was not the most handsome man who ever played the game. And later on, he apparently had some teammates in Minnesota—Kent Hrbek sticks out in my mind—who did not appreciate their third baseman's God-fearing ways.

Gaetti ranked as one of baseball's better third basemen from 1986 through '88, but in 1989 he seemed to lose most of his ability to hit major-league pitching. After a couple of years with the Angels, Gaetti joined the Royals in the spring of 1993, and, supposedly thanks to a better prescription for his contact lenses, he suddenly began to hit again.

In 1995 I was living in Chicago, where I found myself without regular doses of Royals baseball for the first time since I was ten years old, so on those rare occasions when they did show up on television, I acted like a ten-year-old. I will always remember one evening in particular. I think ESPN's A-game had either been stopped by rain or had finished up a little early, so the network switched to the Royals and Rangers for some "bonus coverage."

With the game tied 5–5 in the top of the eighth, Gaetti stepped to the plate with two outs, runners on first and second, and Rangers reliever Matt Whiteside on the mound. Gaetti was always a free swinger, so Whiteside went fishing with a couple of pitches off the plate. Gaetti wasn't biting, though, leaving the count at two balls and no strikes.

Even in his prime, the key to retiring Gaetti was always the same: get ahead, at which point he'd swing at the weakest shit you can imagine. But get behind Gaetti, and he could hurt you. I didn't see him play often with the Royals, but for that season-and-a-half when he was going good, it seemed like he *never* missed a fastball if he knew it was coming. Of course, I know that this is simply a trick of memory, that Gaetti must have missed any number of down-the-middle fastballs, including some that I witnessed. I will not fall into the same trap as all those people who tell you that Gil Hodges or Tony Perez *always* came through in the clutch.

Nevertheless, on this occasion a small cheer escaped my throat as I cackled to myself, "He's going deep." And that's exactly what he did, driving Whiteside's next pitch, what baseball players call a "cock-high fastball," over the fence in center field. And there was much rejoicing in the land, or at least in my cramped, cluttered apartment in Evanston, Illinois. That's one of my all-time favorite baseball memories, and I'm grateful to the Rat for it. I'm also grateful for the thirty-five home runs Gaetti hit in 1995, for a Royals team that was, otherwise, virtually powerless.

But even more than his home run that I "called," I'll remember Gaetti as the answer to a somewhat obscure trivia question . . .

Who was the last major league player to bat while wearing a helmet with no earflaps?

The following is Rule 1.16(c) from the *Official Baseball Rules* (2000 Edition):

> All players entering the Major Leagues commencing with the 1983 championship season and every succeeding season thereafter must wear a single earflap helmet (or at the player's option, a double earflap helmet), except those players who were in the Major League during the 1982 season, and who, as recorded in that season, objected to wearing a single earflap helmet.

Now, why anyone would choose not to protect his ear from baseballs traveling ninety-plus miles per hour, I haven't the foggiest idea. But a number of players continued to wear the earflap-less helmet after 1982, Gaetti among them.

By 1996, there were only three such players: Gaetti, Tim Raines, and Ozzie Smith. Ozzie retired after the '96 season, leaving only Gaetti and Raines. Raines actually played his last game early in the 1999 season before being struck by Lupus, but he attempted a comeback this spring with the Yankees. Meanwhile, Gaetti was hanging on for dear life in the Red Sox camp. It could have gone either way, but Raines retired and Gaetti made the club.

Earflap or no earflap . . . I know it's a small thing, unnoticed even by some who consider themselves serious baseball fans. But I revel in details like this, and every day I hear from people who share my joy at such things. So let history remember that the earflap-less helmet made its last appearance in Fenway Park on the evening of April 12, 2000, when Gary Gaetti struck out swinging against Twins pitcher Hector Carrasco.

There is one more reason that I regret the passing of Gary Gaetti: He's old. Or at least, he's older than I. And it's always reassuring to know, however many birthdays I've had, that there are still *major league baseball players* who have had more. I was born on June 22, 1966, and so, even after the retirement of Gaetti, I'm still younger than 140 players (give or take a few) currently making big-league meal money. Small comfort, perhaps, but I suspect that the day that number drops to zero will bring my mortality into sharp focus, even more so than my fortieth birthday.

Postscript: The morning after Gaetti hung up his spikes, I spotted my first gray hair while shaving, nestled among its light-brown cousins and happily sprouting next to my left ear. After half an hour of rooting around in my apartment for tweezers, I sent that lonely gray soul to an early, unnatural death. He was just the advance party, though. There are more on the way, just as sure as Gary Gaetti is going to spend most of this summer huntin' and fishin'.

Saturday, April 15

Last night, perhaps missing Gary Gaetti, the Red Sox got hammered by the Oakland Athletics in the first game of a three-game series.

I admire the Athletics, but I really don't like what they mean for baseball. See, the A's are quite likely the future of the game. Most of the Oakland hitters are like heavyweight boxers: They're big, they're slow, and they swing rarely but with deadly intent. And this is the recipe for offensive success early in the twenty-first century. The hitters are bigger (and stronger), while the strike zones and the ballparks are smaller. Speed? Relatively irrelevant. The Athletics have virtually none, but last year they won eighty-seven games, and this year they were my preseason pick to win the American League West.

As a fan of rationality, I'm thrilled to see Oakland succeed, because power and plate discipline are two of the pillars of sabermetrics (**sabermetrics**, *n.* the scientific search for baseball knowledge). But as a fan of baseball, I'm ambivalent at best about the Athletics' success, because Oakland baseball, quite frankly, is boring baseball. It's a bunch of sluggardly sluggers standing around waiting for a pitch to hit over the fence. That's not to say the A's themselves are boring; at this point in baseball history, they're something of a novelty. But if they should win, say, ninety games this year, they will be imitated. And while one team like this might be a novelty, eight or ten would be a blight.

In practice, here's how Oakland baseball works: Last night the Red Sox actually out-hit the Athletics, 12–11, but the A's outscored the Sox 13–6 because they out-walked (8–1) and out-homered (3–0) them.

Today, though, it was almost as if the Red Sox had gotten together after last night's game and said, "Hey, why didn't we think of that?" Because in the first two innings, Boston scored seven runs thanks to five walks and four extra-base hits, and they cruised to a 14–2 laugher behind Pedro Martinez, the best pitcher on the planet. Including the 1999 postseason and a pair of relief outings, here are

Martinez's stats against major league hitters since last August 19 (when he lost to Tim Hudson, today's starter for Oakland):

G	IP	H	K	BB	W-L	ERA
14	94 1/3	45	152	18	11–0	0.76

In none of those fourteen games did Martinez allow more than two runs. In eleven of his twelve starts over this span, he struck out at least eleven hitters (today the streak ended, as Martinez struck out only nine Athletics). At the risk of hyberbole, I think it's safe to say that few pitchers have ever dominated the competition like this over a comparable period of time. Consider that seventeen of those innings came last October against the Indians and Yankees, two of the great offensive teams of our time, and consider that *all* of them came in an era of bloated run production.

Fenway Moment: Back on Opening Day, the first fifteen thousand fans through the turnstiles were rewarded with a magnetic schedule, the kind you slap on your refrigerator as soon as you get home. Late in tonight's game, our local usher sidled over and sort of surreptitiously slipped Sarah and me a pair of the magnetic schedules. We both smiled and said thanks, as if we couldn't live without two more of these things. His response? A smile, and a few words of wisdom: "Them are handy, you can put 'em on the fridge."

Sunday, April 16

Bottom of the ninth, four runs apiece, and leadoff man Carl Everett tattooed a T. J. Mathews pitch into the center-field bleachers. Game over, just like that.

In the old days—hell, just last year—Everett's hit would have been described as a "game-winning home run." No longer. Now it's called a "walk-off homer."

"Walk-off" is not a new term. Then with the Athletics, Dennis Eckersley introduced it to the masses back in the early 1990s, and apparently it goes back further than that, with any number of people eager to take credit for inventing it when they played in high school, etc. I'm not particularly interested in the history, because we're simply never going to have an accurate creation story.

Anyway, despite Eckersley's best efforts—maybe he should have allowed more walk-off homers—it never really took. I read about "walk-off" in a *Sports Illustrated* profile on Eckersley seven or eight years ago, and that was the last I saw or heard of it . . . until last week. Repetition is a powerful force, and last week "walk-off" was all over the place. Or at least it was all over ESPN, and that's where I get most of my baseball news.

DATE	OPPONENTS	SCORE (INNINGS)	HERO (HIT)
APRIL 10	TWINS	6–5 (9)	JOHNNY DAMON (HOMER)
APRIL 11	ORIOLES	7–5 (12)	BRIAN JOHNSON (HOMER)
APRIL 12	ORIOLES	7–6 (9)	REY SANCHEZ (HOMER)
APRIL 13	ORIOLES	6–5 (9)	CARLOS BELTRAN (SINGLE)

To my knowledge, nobody had used "walk-off" to modify anything except a home run until Beltran kept the Royals' walk-off streak alive with his ninth-inning, game-winning single. By that time, the Royals had won three straight games with walk-off homers, and they had become a big story, at least if *Baseball Tonight* is the most important thing in your day. All of this was, of course, a hell of a good time for me, as the Royals generally are given just a few seconds of highlights, and some-times less than that on *SportsCenter*.

Baseball fans are, of course, generally conservative by nature. And that's even true, though to a lesser degree, of the people who read my iconoclastic column on ESPN.com. Most of them didn't mind the use of "walk-off" to describe a game-ending home run. That's a special event (yes, even in today's homer-happy environment), and it deserves a special descriptor. But fans are a bit less sanguine about the use of "walk-off" as a modifier of lesser hits, and I would tend to agree with them. "Walk-off single" just doesn't *sound* right. As I write this, though, the pol-icy at ESPN is to use "walk-off" for any game-ending hit, at least in their "Bottom Line" (the scrolling ticker-type line that runs across the bottom of the screen dur-ing news programs on ESPN, and constantly on ESPN2 and ESPNews). I suspect that this particular policy won't last the summer, because of opposition from viewers and even (I hear) a fair amount of grousing from the ESPN "talent."

Monday, April 17

Patriots Day has a long tradition in New England, where the third Monday in April is a holiday for just about everyone in Massachusetts. In Boston, there are two won-derful traditions that come with Patriots Day: The Red Sox begin playing a baseball game before noon, and somewhere between fifteen and twenty thousand endeavor to run upward of twenty-six miles through the streets of the city and surrounding villages.

The baseball game was yet another frigid affair, and would have been so even if it had started in the afternoon rather than 11:07 in the morning. The pitchers took advantage of the conditions, the two teams combining for fourteen hits but just a single run. Oakland's Gil Heredia tossed seven shutout innings, and then two Athletic relievers finished up with two more, Oakland taking the 1–0 decision.

At the start, I was sitting by myself in the grandstand behind home plate. In the top of the second inning, a young man settled in next to me. With his sensible shoes, pinstriped shirt, and a tie that almost certainly cost more than my jeans, he looked like an extra from *The Boiler Room*. I had to hand it to him, though; he had guts. No coat or gloves, but somehow he stuck it out—with the help of two hot dogs and a container of something that looked vaguely like Asian food—until the middle of the fifth. We conversed twice. Early on, he asked me who was pitching for the Red Sox (Fassero). And later, he asked me why O'Leary wasn't playing (just getting a day off). And then he was gone, back to his warm office, and the comfort of bears and (especially) bulls.

After the game, I hustled down to Kenmore Square, where Beacon Street meets Commonwealth Avenue ("Comm Ave"), a prime viewing point for Boston Marathon watchers. The crowd on the sidewalks was five deep, but I nestled in behind some shorter spectators and had a decent look at the runners going by. From snippets of conversation, I gathered that I'd just missed seeing the three male leaders, who apparently had been bunched together (it would be the closest finish in the race's history).

As a spectator sport, distance races have to rank somewhere between curling and chess . . . unless you know someone in the race, and given that there are 17,741 entrants this year, that would probably describe a lot of the people on the sidewalks. Not me, though. I went because it's something you're supposed to do on Patriots Day: watch the Red Sox, then troop down to Kenmore Square and watch the marathon. I hung around for another ten minutes, long enough to see the two leading women, and then I headed home, visions of a long, hot shower dancing in my head.

After that long, hot shower, I was off to Harvard. Yeah, me and Harvard! The dropout from the University of Kansas! A young man named Gautam Mukunda

(Harvard, Class of 'o1), invited me to speak at something called Current Events Table, at Leverett House, Harvard's biggest residence hall. (The way it's supposed to work, the speaker eats dinner with whichever residents are interested in the talk, and afterward there's a discussion of the subject at hand; in my case, baseball. Unfortunately, due to post-marathon slowdowns in the subway, I was late. By the time I arrived, everyone else had eaten, so for fifteen minutes, twenty-five Harvard brains watched me eat a big salad. Aside from that, it went well. No honorary degree, though.)

Anyway, heading to Kenmore Square to catch my train to Cambridge, I walked past Fenway Park and turned right on Brookline. There, at the intersection of Brookline, Yawkey, and Lansdowne, sits the Cask 'n' Flagon, a large sports bar, and the preferred hangout for serious pre- and postgame drinkers. And just outside the bar, there was a young man sitting on the sidewalk, a large, bleeding gash in the middle of his forehead. A group of bouncers stood around with nothing to do, like vultures who had already eaten their supper. Meanwhile, this poor fellow is sitting on the sidewalk like carrion, his back against the masonry, dazed from his injury and quite likely intoxicated, too.

I slowed down some, not to help or even to sympathize, really, but rather to try and figure out what might have happened. Everyone was pointing at another young man, who had stopped on the sidewalk atop the Mass Pike, and was looking back toward the scene as if slightly surprised by what he had wrought.

Four days ago, returning from the aforementioned trip to purchase thermal underwear, I happened across a young woman who had apparently just been struck by a car. The way she was lying on her side, with her legs crossed and her head resting on her right arm, she looked like she might have been taking a nap on her couch, on a lazy Sunday afternoon. Except it wasn't Sunday afternoon, and she wasn't taking a nap on her couch. She was lying on the street, a few feet from the curb.

It's been at least two years since I've seen anyone in this sort of distress, and now two within a week.

When you live in a city, you're regularly going to see things that make you feel helpless. This, more than the amorphous threat of violence and the occasional rudeness from strangers, is what I find most disturbing about urban life. I suspect that most people are made uncomfortable by feelings of helplessness, and I'd be committing some sin of self-absorption if I thought I was particularly special in that respect. Still, when I see things like this and wish I could help, I occasionally flash back to when I was a little boy, six or seven years old. Things weren't going well for my mother, and occasionally she just sort of collapsed on the bed that she and my father shared, and sobbed. That little boy—who sometimes shadows me still, only to fade away when I turn my head to get a good look—knew he should do something, but of course he had no idea what that something might be. And part of him, I suspect, still wants to help his mommy.

There's an ambulance permanently stationed in Kenmore Square, and I had been wondering why. Now I think I know. In the city, bad things happen to people with disturbing regularity. And once again, there's not a damn thing I can do about it.

Friday, April 21

Today is Good Friday, but it's been anything but a *good* Friday. Last night the Red Sox game in Detroit was postponed due to inclement weather, and tonight it was our turn in Boston. During the day, the temperature was in the 40s and it was too wet for water polo, so I was less than excited at the prospect of another miserable evening at Fenway. On the other hand, tonight's scheduled starter was Pedro Martinez, and I was blessed with one of the best tickets in the house, six rows behind the Sox dugout.

I knew the evening's plans were in danger when, a bit after noon, I turned on The Weather Channel, and the entire state of Massachusetts was covered by various shades of green, the most common being something one might describe as "off-Kermit." In fact, the entire northeast corner of the country was splotched with a swirling, depressing mess that brought to mind Jackson Pollock with a severely limited pallet. There would certainly be no baseball tonight—the game was officially postponed in the middle of the afternoon—and tomorrow's 1:05 start has been pushed back to 3:05, which might or might not be late enough to let this front move through.

If there's any positive at all in this brutal weather of late, it's the prospect of a future doubleheader, a wonderful occurrence made even more wonderful by its modern rarity. Of course, the catch is that you don't want a doubleheader unless the weather's at least tolerable, otherwise you're miserable for eight hours instead of four.

Saturday, April 22

Rain, rain, go away . . .

Not as nasty as yesterday, but plenty nasty enough. The good news? A double-header tomorrow. Even better, it'll be the old-fashioned type of twin bill: one ticket gets you both games, with the second starting thirty minutes after the first. The bad news? The weather forecast for tomorrow calls for a 60 percent chance of more rain. If the Sox don't play tomorrow, it'll end up being thirteen days between home games, leaving me with not a whole hell of a lot to write about in April.

Sunday, April 23

I wish I could report that, after two days of steady rain and zero baseball, the Great Climate Gods had taken their pounds of flesh, and this morning brought sunny skies and balmy temperatures. Alas, 'twas not so. I awoke at ten in the morning and padded over to the window, only to be greeted by a gray sky and damp streets. And The Weather Channel on today's forecast? THIS AFTERNOON . . . CLOUDY WITH SHOWERS AND PATCHY FOG. CONTINUED COOL. HIGH 45 TO 50. NORTH WIND 10 TO 20 MPH. CHANCE OF RAIN NEARLY 100 PERCENT. (I have watched The Weather Channel more often in the month since I arrived in Boston than in my four years in Seattle.)

Meanwhile, on WEEI, Boston's top all-sports radio station, Dick "Monster" Radatz predicted that the Red Sox would get both games in today. At 12:05, an hour before game time, I looked down at the street from my fourth-floor flat, and the first two cars moving down Park Drive had their windshield wipers on the intermittent setting, not a good sign. (Somebody on WEEI said, "It's drizzling here at the ballpark, but don't worry, they'll force this one in.")

By 12:30 the drizzle had turned into something worse (the Monster allowed that it might be a *solid* drizzle), but I left for Fenway anyway because I was supposed to meet Bill Considine, who had my ticket, at 12:40. For some unknown reason, hundreds of people with tickets were actually entering the ballpark, but Bill and I spent the next couple of hours drinking beer as the solid drizzle turned into light rain. Finally, at 2:30 I walked back home; one of the nice things about living four blocks from the ballpark is that if they suddenly decide to start playing baseball, I can be there in five minutes.

They never did decide to start playing. Once the big green mass reached eastern Massachusetts, it just sat here, with Boston at the epicenter, and so the Sox finally decided to give up. That was at 2:45. Unfortunately for those fans who never stopped hoping, the club didn't announce the postponement until 4:27, which meant that some people had been sitting in the stands, watching old baseball video on the JumboTron, for close to three and a half hours. The Red Sox claimed they didn't want to announce anything, anything at all, until the makeup dates were approved by the Players Association. They also claimed that this was done as a courtesy to the fans. The truth, of course, is that the Red Sox, like nearly every other baseball team, think of their fans only when everything else on the "To Do" list has been crossed off.

◆ ◆ ◆

Today marked the first time since 1976 that the Red Sox have lost four straight games to rain (one in Detroit, and now three here). And the postponement of today's doubleheader cost all of us a little piece of history. Pedro and Ramon Martinez were supposed to start for the Sox today, which would have marked the first time brothers started both games of a twin bill since Gaylord and Jim Perry did so for the Indians in 1974.

Worse, this means no Fenway Park baseball until May, when the Sox return from a weeklong road trip.

Tuesday, April 25

Not long ago, the Royals won four straight games in their last at-bat, three of them on walk-off home runs. But they've not won since the last of those four games, and that was ten days and nine losses ago. In geological time, as we all know, eleven days is less than the blink of an eye. Even in human time, eleven days will pass quickly if you're busy and/or having fun. But when your favorite baseball team has not won in eleven days, it's like they haven't won in eleven years. You forget what it *feels like* to win. You wonder if you'll ever win again. You have murderous feelings in your heart for the manager, the pitching coach, the bullpen catcher, and the guy who shines the players' shoes. And you become desperate. The Royals' pitching has been, as it was last year, atrocious. So tonight I decided that the panacea for all the team's woes is a new pitching coach. Not just any pitching coach, though. We need the *best* pitching coach. But unfortunately, the best pitching coach—a compact, energetic man named Leo Mazzone—is gainfully employed by the Atlanta Braves.

My passion for the Royals, I realized tonight, knows no reasonable bounds. It occurred to me that if writing a check for five thousand dollars would bring Mazzone to Kansas City, I would do it. Ten thousand? I would write that check, too.

And yes, I am fully aware that this borders on some sort of insanity.

Fortunately for both my imaginary bank account and my quite-real state of mind, the Royals came back to win tonight, the decisive run scoring thanks to an error by the enemy pitcher in the bottom of the ninth.

Pedro Martinez won, too, upping his record to 4–0 and dropping his ERA to 1.59. And tonight at least, the world seems to make sense again.

Wednesday, April 26

It rained here today. All day. Oh, except for a few minutes in the early afternoon. When it snowed.

Medium-sized flakes drifting down as if they owned the place, late April or no late April, leaving me to thank the schedule-makers for sending the Red Sox to Texas this week.

Speaking of the Sox, this afternoon they destroyed the Rangers, 14–4. And the Royals won yet another game in the bottom of the ninth, their sixth last at-bat victory in their last six home games.

Here's an oddity involving my two favorite teams: the Royals have now stolen twenty-four bases and been caught once; the Red Sox have stolen one base and been caught four times. And for anyone who still thinks that stealing bases is particularly important in the current environment, it's worth noting that the Royals are now 10–12, the Red Sox 11–7.

Saturday, April 29

This morning I was listening to NPR. Or rather, I was sort of half listening, trying to read William Goldman's new book at the same time. The top of the hour rolled around, time for a newsbreak, so I put the book down for a moment. After the big stuff, the announcer told us that New York's mayor, Rudy Giuliani, who has just been diagnosed with prostate cancer, spoke yesterday with New York's manager, Joe Torre, who recovered from prostate cancer a year ago.

My ears perked up. I set down my book and quickly reached for a pencil and a pad of paper, the better to record the Bronx Sage's words, sure to provide guidance not only for Mayor Giuliani, but also for the millions of men who may, one day, face the same illness or something like it.

According to the news—prepare yourself for Enlightenment, Dear Readers—here's what Torre said:

Listen to your doctors.

Wow. No wonder this guy is considered one of the brilliant managerial minds of our time. Sure, "Listen to your doctors" might *sound* simple enough, but the sheer genius of it, the way he was able to distill everything down to just those four words . . . All right, I'll stop with this silliness now. My point is not that Joe Torre is not a wise man. He's managed one of the five greatest teams in the history of the game, and it's getting to the point where we have to consider him a serious Hall of Fame candidate. And I'm sure that Giuliani wanted to talk to him because when something like that happens to you, it's comforting to speak to someone who has been through it, and lived to tell the tale.

No, my point is, why should we give a damn?

Of course, we shouldn't. Nobody should, except Mr. Mayor himself. Yet National Public Radio, quite possibly our most intelligent, substantive, least-pandering national news organization (if a bit hung up on political correctness, Harry Shearer's occasional contributions notwithstanding), felt that listeners around the country simply had to know what Joe Torre told Rudy Giuliani.

And this is, in a nutshell, why people who don't live in New York resent New York sports teams and their fans. Trust me on this, it is *not* because we're jealous of all the success. Last year I co-wrote, with Eddie Epstein (a Baltimore native), a book called *Baseball Dynasties*. Of the fifteen teams we featured, eight hailed from one of the five boroughs: one New York Giants (Manhattan) club, one Brooklyn Dodgers club, one New York Mets (Queens) club, and *five* New York Yankees (Bronx) clubs. And I promise you, there wasn't a single moment when either Eddie or I begrudged the New Yorkers their great successes. What's annoying is when New York is shoved down our throats for no particular reason, other than that it's New York.

And I promise you this, too: Nobody gets more annoyed than Bostonians.

Sunday, April 30

Pedro Martinez didn't have his best stuff today, notwithstanding the seven shutout innings he threw in Cleveland against the Indians, who scored 1,009 runs last year. His stuff was just good enough, the Sox topping the Tribe and Charles Nagy in a tense game, 2–1. As if the good pitching weren't enough to get everyone's nerves on edge, a little beanball war erupted in the eighth inning. First, Martinez threw a pitch high and tight to Einar Diaz in the bottom of the seventh. Diaz had doubled twice earlier in the game, and it seemed like a clear message: Don't crowd the plate.

Top of the eighth, Nagy nailed leadoff man Jose Offerman in the midsection. The benches cleared, order was restored, nobody was kicked out. Bottom of the eighth, Martinez nailed leadoff man Roberto Alomar in the midsection. And after waiting a few seconds, plate umpire Tim Tschida threw Martinez out of the game. It seemed like a fitting end to an appearance in which Martinez spent much of the game glaring at Tschida after borderline pitches were called balls. This marked Pedro's first ejection since September of 1996.

No real harm done, as Derek Lowe came in for the save (though he did permit a solo homer in the ninth).

If you'll indulge me, I'd again like to run Pedro's stats since his last loss, against the Athletics last August.

G	IP	H	K	BB	HR	W-L	ERA
16	108 ⅓	55	170	22	2	13–0	0.83

It would, of course, be fun if he never lost again. Barring that unlikelihood, it'll be fun to see the reaction here in Boston when Martinez finally does lose. Coming into this season, I assumed that Pedro's chances of duplicating last year's 23–4 campaign were akin to the chances that the next Red Sox ballpark will come in under budget. After watching him for a month, though, I'm not so sure. You do need some luck to go 23–4, and you gotta stay healthy. But Pedro seems to be able to do just about whatever he wants. And whatever else happens, the Sox have a shot at the postseason if he goes 23–4 (or thereabouts) again.

Now, for those of you who bought this book thinking it would be about the Red Sox and only about the Red Sox, you have my apologies. Things will get better, I think, but I simply haven't had much material with which to work. The season is nearly a month old, and the Sox have played the grand total of six games at Fenway Park. Still, given that today is the last day of April, I figured this might be a good time to pause, and see where the Red Sox are . . . except they're not really anywhere. Here are the American League East standings at the close of April:

	W-L	GB
YANKEES	15–8	——
ORIOLES	14–10	1 1/2
RED SOX	12–9	2
BLUE JAYS	12–14	4 1/2
DEVIL RAYS	9–15	6 1/2

If you had to summarize the standings in three words, it would be, "We know nothing." The Yankees are, as usual, in first place. But they've done it with smoke and mirrors, outscoring their opponents by only six runs (112–106) through their first 23 games. The Yanks' starting pitching has been inconsistent, aside from Orlando Hernandez, and somehow they've scored only 4.9 runs per game; in the American League, only the Tigers have done worse.

Still, the Yankees are the Yankees, and one must assume that they'll get their shit together, until they don't.

The Red Sox are doing, to this point, almost exactly what I thought they would do. Pedro is fantastic, the rest of the rotation is shaky but not disastrous, and the Sox offense is decent but not outstanding.

The Orioles might be too old, the Blue Jays might be too young, but right now neither club has proven that it's not a contender for at least the Wild Card. And though the Devil Rays are still within shouting distance, they look just the same now as they did a month ago. Crummy.

Getting back to the Red Sox, are they likely to get better? One thing's for sure, they can't suffer any injuries at key spots. If Garciaparra, Everett, or Nixon goes down for any length of time the Sox are in trouble, because the club has no outfield depth and Nomar is irreplaceable. And of course, they're sunk if anything happens to Pedro.

Even barring injury, though, the Red Sox need two things if they're to approach ninety-five wins. They need help in the rotation—a rehabbed Bret Saberhagen and/or hot prospect Sun Kim provide hope—and they need another bat. The Red Sox have two decent hitters playing for Pawtucket—oops, make that *one* decent hitter down in Pawtucket. Outfielder Michael Coleman, who's seemingly been a prospect since Yaz patrolled left field, severely dislocated his left wrist Friday night, and he may not play again this season. That leaves only Dernell Stenson, a left-handed hitting, first-base/DH type. Exactly what the Red Sox need. The problem is that Stenson's batting average (.222) is, at this writing, lower than his weight (230). He's only twenty-one and may well have a bright future ahead of him, but the Sox need help now. Yesterday Manny Alexander DHed against Chuck Finley, and that's just not going to work.

It's clear that the Red Sox simply have to trade for another potent bat. It's funny, though, as much as people decry the paucity of quality starting pitchers in baseball, a number of contending clubs are short a hitter this year. The Yankees, like the Red Sox, could really use one or two sluggardly sluggers. And everybody knows the Mariners have been looking for a left-handed hitter with power since Griffey left for Cincinnati.

Second Inning

Monday, May 1

The Tigers are in town, and it's been so long since I saw a baseball game in person—exactly a fortnight, to be precise—that I broke with personal tradition and got to the ballpark more than thirty minutes early. It was a good thing, too, because this meant I was already in my seat when *she* arrived.

She was of medium height, slender but not worrisomely so, with drawn features but attractive, perhaps best described as a cross between Nicole Kidman and a young Sissy Spacek (with the emphasis on the latter). Not *pretty*, really, at least not from where I was sitting, but close enough that a nice smile could certainly qualify her for that label.

After taking a seat one and a half rows closer to the field than my seat, and one seat over, she unzipped her backpack and pulled out a composition book. Remember them from college? Mottled green, with black tape binding the covers together? This was one of the thick ones: one hundred sheets, two hundred pages. And on the cover, printed in ink on the two lines in the white box, were these words:

BASEBALL JOURNAL

A. MORROW

I don't think I need to tell you that something like this will set the heart aflutter inside someone like me. It is, of course, nearly every (male) baseball fan's dream to meet a woman who also loves the game.

There are two reasons for this.

One, it gives you something to talk about. Most of us, I suspect, have had girl-friends and/or wives who didn't give a damn about baseball. Yet we can't resist calling them to the TV anyway ("Honey, you *gotta* see this play!"). And of course, the good ones come running, because women really are the gentler, more tolerant sex. They'll watch, make some sounds that we don't even notice, and then they'll get back to whatever it was they were doing. But wouldn't it be fun if they really gave a damn, and would curl up on the couch with you and watch all eleven innings of that Tigers-Twins thriller on the satellite?

And two, it means one less excuse for them to condescend. How many of you have heard something like the following: "Why, if you added up the number of hours you've spent in your life watching and listening to baseball games, there's no end to the things you could have done with that time. You could have built a bridge or read all the greatest books."

That's from Douglass Wallop's novel, *The Year the Yankees Lost the Pennant*, and personally I've never had a girlfriend be quite that blunt about it (though I'm told things can change when a girlfriend becomes a wife). Still, I'm pretty sure that some of them were thinking it, as days turned into weeks, weeks turned into months, and months turned into years, with only the winters providing a respite from baseball on the television nearly every night.

Like I said, it's something that most of us fantasize about. But you know what they say . . . Be careful what you wish for.

Ten days ago, my relationship with Sarah ended. She's a wonderful woman, and boy does she ever love baseball: Red Sox season tickets, a working knowledge of baseball history . . . smart, and pretty, too. The whole package, a veritable power-hitting shortstop. Things didn't work out, for reasons that I won't get into here, but I found that I missed those times to myself, heading home from the ballpark or watching *Baseball Tonight* or just checking the scores on my computer without someone looking over my shoulder.

No, that's not why we broke up, but maybe one baseball obsessive per couple is enough. My last girlfriend was (is) passionate about poetry rather than baseball—in fact, she didn't give a hoot about baseball—and I think that's partly why I haven't completely gotten over her yet. Then again, it would have been nice if she had, just once, sat down and watched a few innings with me, asked questions like "Why does the manager wear a uniform?" and "Then why don't they call it the *fair* pole?"

At this point, I've concluded that the ideal mate would not necessarily *love* baseball, but rather would love *me* enough to at least try to enjoy baseball as she does any number of other pleasant diversions. She wouldn't know anything about the Infield Fly Rule, but if it comes up when you're at the ballpark, she'll ask about it, and eventually master the vagaries of the rule because she understands that the Infield Fly is a big part of your life. As sad as that might seem.

So I don't want to talk to A. Morrow, and I don't want to ask for her phone number, and I don't want to take her out for dinner and a movie, and I don't want to father her children. None of that, no way no how.

Still, I can't help but wonder what the *A* stands for . . . Anna? Abigail? Amy? . . . Yeah, Amy. And would it hurt anything, really, if I just struck up an innocent conversation? Hell, it'd be good for the book. Any woman who keeps a "Baseball Journal" must have something interesting to say, right?

All right, who the hell am I kidding? The truth is that before Jeff Fassero's first pitch to Tigers leadoff man Gregg Jefferies at 7:07, I was already wondering which restaurant would be appropriate for our first date, and I was wondering if maybe, just maybe, she reads my column. And I was wishing that my apartment weren't so messy. The truth is that I almost missed Mike Stanley's homer (his third in the last three games) into the Red Sox bullpen, in the bottom of the first, because I was so busy admiring the nape of Amy's neck, her slender shoulders, and the shoulder-length hair that started out mousy brown but became, at least in my mind, closer to auburn as the game proceeded.

So yeah, I gotta talk to her . . . but how to accomplish this Herculean feat? One could, I suppose, just take the empty seat next to "Amy." But what if the owner of that seat shows up? Then it will look like I moved there for the obvious reason. And indeed, four young men did show up, in the middle of the second inning, and occupied the four seats to Amy's right. Now, generally when four Young Men find themselves within striking distance of a pretty (or near-pretty) girl, one or more of them is going to take advantage of this happy situation (you women reading this know exactly what I mean). And once that happens, I'm sunk.

Nevertheless, before long I arrived at a plan. Amy was sitting in Section 70, and in Section 70 the seats face toward second base. Thus, if she wanted to see the batters she had to lean way forward to see past the fellow next to her, who himself was leaning forward to see past the fellow next to him.

I'm sitting in Section 71, which contains a fair percentage of the best seats in the house. Where Sections 70 and 71 meet, just past the photographers' bay beyond the visitors' dugout, the lower stands angle toward the left-field corner. Thus, while Amy is facing second base, I've got this incredible, dead-on view of the pitcher's mound (with the back of Amy's head in the foreground). As it happens, the two seats to my left—more great views—are empty, and remain so through the first few innings.

So all I have to do, without making a big deal about it, is lean down, tap Amy on the shoulder and (in my most non-threatening manner) say, "Hey, these seats back here are open, if you get tired of not being able to see the plate."

Brilliant. And to think I never even graduated from college.

The problem is, I need some room. I'm too self-conscious to try something like this unless there's at least some modicum of privacy. If my mission fails, I'd rather nobody else noticed. So it will take some help from the couple sitting in front of me. Neither of them svelte, thus both were fairly wedged into their seats, so I figured eventually they'd want to stand up and walk around, get a little relief. I'd just have to wait them out, and hope nothing happened with the Four Young Men.

Meanwhile, the Red Sox took a 5–3 lead over the Tigers in the bottom of the fourth. As one mound 'kowski (Dave Borkowski) replaced another (C. J. Nitkowski), the idiots in the center-field bleachers got the wave going. But when it got around to our little section of the ballpark, Amy didn't move a muscle (yet another reason to love her!).

There are many reasons why All-Star ballots should not be distributed this early in the season, and tonight, between the third and fourth innings, I discovered a new one; it gives Four Young Men a good excuse for talking to a young woman. Amy initially turned down a ballot, but when the Young Men realized that she knew more about the candidates than they did, they all started talking to her. Particularly this tall, good-looking fellow with a Roman nose, the kind of fellow who always looks like he just got a haircut three days ago.

Uh-oh.

Still, hope never dies, and mine got real lively in the top of the eighth, when a few of the Young Men stood up and made going-home motions (obscuring my view of two pitches, damn 'em). Unfortunately, good-looking fellow—the only single chap in the group, I gathered—spurned the offer of a ride home from one of his pals, and hung around. With Amy and her new friend sitting there, just one empty seat between them, there was no way they wouldn't really get to chatting. So they did. The wedged-ins in front of me finally left after the eighth, too late to do me any good.

The woeful Tigers wound up getting hammered, 10–6, and tonight I empathized with the losers even more than I usually do. Sitting here in my apartment, I'm glad, or close to glad, that "Amy" and I didn't meet. Yet I suffer the regrets of every person who consistently loses his or her nerve in the face of potential rejection. I'll be thirty-four years old next month, and I have never, not even once, asked a woman I've just met for her phone number.

Game Note: It's been a rough season for those aforementioned 'kowskis. Starter C. J. Nitkowski, moderately famous as the top webmaster among current major leaguers, is now 1–5 with a 7.67 ERA, and there are reports that Boeing might sponsor his next start. Reliever Dave Borkowski coughed up five runs in 3 2/3 innings, and his ERA is a sprightly 21.94. With the help of two more relievers, Tiger pitchers managed to avoid striking out even a single Red Sox hitter, and I can't remember the last time I saw that.

Tuesday, May 2

In about 1890, a group called The American Acclimatization Society released a flock of European starlings, birds native to Eurasia, in Central Park, Manhattan. Why? These misguided fools endeavored to introduce to America every bird ever mentioned in one of Shakespeare's plays. The starling was mentioned only once, but that was enough for the AAS. Here's Hotspur, from *King Henry IV, Part One:*

> *He said he would not ransom Mortimer,*
> *Forbade my tongue to speak of Mortimer,*
> *But I will find him when he lies asleep,*
> *And in his ear I'll hollow 'Mortimer!'*
> *Nay,*
> *I'll have a starling shall be taught to speak*
> *Nothing but "Mortimer," and give it him,*
> *To keep his anger still in motion.*

I, iii, 219–226

What was wrought from that single mention, in one of the Bard's lesser works? A veritable invasion, as starlings quickly spread across the great majority of North America. They have, as one field guide notes, "proliferated at expense of other cavity nesters like bluebirds, woodpeckers."

Seen from a distance, starlings aren't much to look at. They often congregate in large flocks under bridges, highway overpasses and the like, and they've driven out native birds all over the continent. Most ornithologists consider starlings little better than pests, and most bird-watchers (or "birders," as they prefer) consider them worthy of little attention. (And sometimes they're worse than pests. Starlings caused the worst birds-related air disaster in history. On October 4, 1960, an Eastern Airlines L-188 collided with hundreds of starlings shortly after taking off from Boston's Logan Airport. Of the seventy-two people aboard, sixty-two perished.)

But look at a starling from close up, especially in the spring, and you'll be dazzled by its beauty: metallic green feathers on the side of his neck, colorful speckles on his back, a yellow bill. And say what you want about starlings, but they're able to do something brilliantly—fly without mechanical aid, at fairly high speeds—that you and I can merely dream about.

I got to thinking about starlings tonight while watching the Detroit Tigers.

The Tigers aren't much to look at. They entered tonight's game with a 6–18 record, worst in the majors. This, despite a $58 million team payroll that ranks fifteenth (among thirty) in the majors. Their first baseman, Tony Clark, is hitting .115 with no power (and is getting paid four million bucks this season). Their third baseman, Dean Palmer, is serving a suspension and has been replaced this evening by Gregg Jefferies, who probably should be playing Triple-A baseball (or selling insurance) in Nebraska or Oklahoma. (At one point tonight, center fielder Juan Encarnacion made a great throw to third base, in plenty of time to nail Carl Everett trying to advance from first to third . . . except Jefferies was completely out of position, nowhere near the bag. The ball skipped into the Tigers dugout, Everett trotting home.) Detroit's general manager, Randy Smith, couldn't make money running a whorehouse on an army base.

Right now, at least, the Tigers are simply a bad team, if not as bad as their record (nobody is).

But while the Tigers might well constitute the worst major-league baseball team, they also are some of the finest baseball players on the planet. Intellectually, that's easy to understand. There are 750 players in the major leagues right now, and so it follows that the twenty-five men wearing Detroit uniforms tonight are among the eight or nine hundred greatest players on earth. But *visually*, it's difficult to understand that unless you're close to them.

Last night, the Red Sox hit eight ground balls toward third base, which then was manned not by Jefferies, but by a journeyman utility infielder named Shane Halter. Most or all of the plays were "routine" (notwithstanding the fact that Halter made a poor throw after one of those ground balls and was charged with an error that led to a run). At least, they would look routine to anyone sitting more than a hundred feet away. From my vantage point, perhaps sixty or seventy feet away from third base, six of those eight plays looked pretty damn tough. Major leaguers hit the ball hard, and with hellacious spin.

The point being, Shane Halter might not look like much when he's reduced to a cold line of statistics in *The Baseball Encyclopedia*, but like every other major leaguer, his skill and athleticism are mighty impressive when seen up close.

(This is, by the way, true of just about any sport. If you're ever lucky enough to watch a professional football or basketball game from the sidelines, you'll be amazed. As good as TV is, there are some things you just need to see for yourself, up close.)

I believe that every baseball fan should have the opportunity to see a baseball game from a great seat. The Red Sox can talk all they want about "the new Red Sox ballpark" having ten thousand more "great seats," but of course that's just so much claptrap. New ballparks are about premium seating and luxury suites, and if you can't afford either of those you're getting pushed back.

Granted, the fans don't seem to mind; witness the five-year sellout streak in Cleveland's Jacobs Field, where half the seats in the upper deck should come equipped with a telescope. Nevertheless, I believe that baseball teams have a moral obligation to provide a certain level of enjoyment for the people who support them. What's more, a team is more likely to engender long-term loyalty if its fans have seen the action from up close. So here's my proposal. Every team building a new ballpark should set aside two hundred quality, lower-deck seats for each home game. With eighty-one games, that means about sixteen thousand tickets for the complete season. And anyone who owns season tickets in the upper deck should be entitled to trade one of his tickets for one of those quality seats.

Doesn't a person who lays out, say, sixteen hundred dollars for a crummy season ticket deserve to enjoy *one game* from close up? What frustrates me about baseball teams, more than anything else, is their utter inability or unwillingness to consider the basic needs of the fans who can't afford to spend fifty bucks on one ticket.

Wednesday, May 3

Not much scares me. Old age. Public embarrassment. And (as we have already seen) rejection.

Okay, those are three pretty big ones. I guess what I meant is that not many physical things scare me. I can't be bothered to wear a helmet when I'm riding my bike around the streets of Boston (or anywhere else), I think rock-climbing's a blast, and for much of my "adult" life I didn't think to lock the doors at night, even when I lived in the city. Still don't, sometimes.

But after a few games at Fenway, I'm afraid of baseballs.

Let me explain. I've been to hundreds of baseball games, but for the great majority of them I sat either in the press box, or in what you might call nonlethal seats, where even if the ball does somehow reach your level, there's plenty of time to either dodge, or set up for the catch. Sure, I've been blessed with great seats now and again, especially in the last few years. But it's never been a night-in, night-out thing like it has been this season. And when you regularly sit in box seats at Fenway Park, you regularly see line drives whistle into crowds of people, only half of whom see them coming; as Thomas Boswell once wrote of the box seats at Fenway, "Checked-swing fouls arrive at light speed; you're closer to the bat than any infielder."

It's not just Fenway Park, though, and it's not just me. Nearly all of the new ballparks put the fans very close to the action, and some of the older ones have added high-priced seats that do the same. When baseball players and other team personnel request tickets for family and friends, they almost always make sure the seats are behind the screen.

Just last night, a peanut vendor here was nailed in the back of the head by a foul liner. He collapsed like the mascot in *Bull Durham*, then popped right back up and peddled his wares, buoyed by a round of applause from the fans sitting nearby. I'll tell you what, though; I always thought I'd like to sell peanuts or Cracker Jacks or whatever, for one game, just to see what it's like. But I wouldn't do it in the prime seating areas at Fenway, because you spend too much time walking around with your back to the hitters.

Tonight, Tigers right fielder Wendell Magee ripped a line drive in my direction. I was sitting in the fourth row in Section 71, which as you might remember is just beyond the photographers' bay down the left-field line. The baseball landed in the first row, one section to my left, and then bounced incredibly high, and back behind me a good eight or ten rows. Given that bounce, I assumed that the ball had struck the wall in front of the seats, or perhaps the top of a seat.

But then the people sitting in that area began waving their hands, trying to get the attention of someone who works for the club. As people took their seats, we could all see that a man sitting in the front row was now sporting a small gash on top of his head. It was easy to see this, because the top of his head had no hair. And now it had a laceration.

Those waves notwithstanding, no one rushed to assist our unfortunate bleeding fan. This should not have been a surprise, as the ushers at Fenway Park are not, on the whole, a spry group. I swear most of these guys saw Ted Williams play. And I don't mean the old Teddy Ballgame, the burly geezer who talked like John Wayne. I'm talking about The Kid, who weighed 175 pounds dripping wet and batted .406 one season. Before the war. Being an usher at Fenway Park is like being a Supreme Court Justice; the job is yours as long you want it and you're ambulatory. And the latter of those is only a rough guideline.

The sluggishness of stadium personnel resulted in something I'd never seen before. With this poor fellow bleeding and no help in sight, Tigers pitcher C. J. Nitkowski popped out of the dugout, jogged down to Box 72, and delivered a clean white towel to the injured party. I already liked Nitkowski because of his website, and now I like him even more.

Eventually a pair of geriatric ushers did make their way to the first row and led the fan away. He would return in the bottom of the third (just in time to see Jose Offerman draw a walk), with a small, round, flesh-colored bandage covering the wound. It's an amazing thing, when you think about it. A baseball, traveling somewhere in the neighborhood of 90 miles per hour, hits a man flush on his cranium and he appears little the worse for wear.

In fact, to my knowledge, no one has ever, in the long history of the game, been killed by a foul ball in a major league ballpark. So it's not the possibility of death, or even serious injury, that frightens me. No, what really scares me is the public embarrassment (for want of a better description), and the likelihood of missing part of the game.

As for the first of those, I just can't stomach the thought of lying there on the concrete, with all those people watching to see if I bleed, or twitch, or stop breathing. I mean, if a few people around me want to cradle my head or tell me I'll be fine, that's okay. But everyone else, please watch the game and leave me the hell alone, because your stares are not making this better. The second is obvious. If I have to spend twenty minutes in the nurse's office or, even worse, if I get sent off to the hospital for stitches or to get my jaw wired shut, that's time when I'm not watching baseball.

So now, more than ever, I make every effort to see every pitch. I believe I missed two pitches in tonight's game, and both times I was pissed. This season, I *will* train myself to watch every pitch, at least when I'm sitting in harm's way. Because they're not taking me out of Fenway Park on a stretcher.

Then again, not long ago I read a story about a sixty-year-old member of the Fenway Park grounds crew, who died in 1967 while helping unroll the tarp when the skies opened. His widow allowed that perhaps it was fitting that the man died at work, because he had loved that field like it was part of his family.

◆ ◆ ◆

Speaking of mortality, there are two things that make me want to live forever: books and World Series.

I sometimes despair when I realize that, every year, there are many hundreds of great books published that I won't have time to read. And once I'm dead, the situation gets even worse.

Nearly as bad, though, is the realization that, after I'm gone, World Series will continue to be played, and *I won't have any idea who won them.* I do take solace, however, in the fact that I might well live for another sixty or seventy years, and it's unlikely that the World Series, or at least the World Series as we now know it, will still exist by that point.

So I just need to guard against getting skulled by a foul ball before my time.

Thursday, May 4
I'm no hockey fan. I've watched only one NHL game from start to finish in my life, and I've attended only one NHL game (yes, the same one) in my life. So when the

NHL playoffs roll around in April (and May, and June), all it means to me is less baseball on ESPN. The Red Sox were off tonight, so at ten o'clock, I turned on my TV to watch *Baseball Tonight.* Instead, I found a hockey game. The Penguins and Flyers were tied at one goal apiece with just eight minutes to play in the third period, though, so I figured I could wait them out.

If only I knew. Five overtime periods and nearly five hours later—not to mention any number of great saves and near misses—the Flyers finally won the third-longest game in NHL history (and the longest since 1945). And through it all, I sat watching. Why? Because of the certainty that a single dramatic moment was in the offing. When it finally came, I didn't exactly jump in the air and yell hooray, and a few months from now I'll have forgotten who won (let alone who scored the winner), but I'm glad I saw it.

And this points out something I think is lost in this Hitter's Era. When run production is up like it is, it stands to reason that you'll see fewer close games, and the data bears out this theory.

One could, I suppose, argue that with every player a power threat, nearly every game is "close," or at least within a reasonable doubt if the clubs are within two or three runs of each other in the late innings.

I don't really buy that, though. Most clubs have good or great closers, which means that big late-inning leads are fairly safe even now.

When most people think "drama," they think about movies, or TV shows like *ER.* Or soap operas. (I'm fond of arguing that baseball, because it's a daily event, is something akin to a soap opera for men.) But show-business drama is scripted, and there are any number of ways for the drama to be ruined. One of the wonderful things about sports is that it's unscripted, that *nobody* knows what's going to happen next, not exactly.

Friday, May 5

Red Sox manager Jimy Williams fascinates me.

He's got a funny nickname—"One-M Jimy"—and he's got a stock answer— "We're just playing the schedule"—for nearly every question, that stock answer causing amusement if only because of its predictable frequency.

But what's really interesting about Williams is that he seems to care little for convention. Tonight, Derek Lowe is on my mind. Ramon Martinez pitched five shaky innings against the visiting Tampa Bay Devil Rays, Rich Garces followed with a pair of hitless frames, and then Lowe came in to earn the save with two perfect innings. It was Lowe's sixth save of the season, and his fifth two-inning save.

Twenty years ago, this would not have been worthy of note. And twenty years from today, it might only cause yawns. But in the 2000 season, two-inning (or more) saves—I'll call them "long saves"—are news. Here are the ten pitchers who saved the most games last season, along with some related figures:

CLOSERS, 1999

	SAVES	IP	LONG SAVES
MARIANO RIVERA	45	69	1
ROBERTO HERNANDEZ	43	73	0
JOHN WETTELAND	43	66	0
UGUETH URBINA	41	76	1
TREVOR HOFFMAN	40	67	0

I knew approximately what I would see before constructing this table, yet I was surprised to find just how similar the numbers were, with all five of the most prolific closers pitching between sixty-six and seventy-six innings. And only two long saves among them. Now here are Lowe's numbers thus far in 2000, along with his projected stats through 162 games:

	SAVES	IP	LONG SAVES
DEREK LOWE	6	18	5
PROJECTED THRU 162	40	117	32

If Lowe does record thirty-two long saves, or comes close, it will represent something of a milestone in the history of relief pitching. No pitcher has recorded even twenty two-inning saves since 1984, when both Dan Quisenberry (twenty-seven of forty-four saves) and Bruce Sutter (twenty-four of forty-five) did it. These are the only two relievers to record twenty long saves since 1980, with Quiz also doing it in 1982 (twenty-two of thirty-five) and 1983 (twenty-six of forty-five).

In 1998, Red Sox closer Tom Gordon saved forty-six games, and pitched seventy-nine innings in seventy-nine games. Typical closer usage. So I don't think that Jimy Williams is particularly *averse* to convention. Instead, he's letting his personnel dictate his strategy rather than the other way around, which is what you like to see from a manager. Derek Lowe relies on his sinker, and he doesn't employ a "max effort" delivery like many closers do. In Williams's judgment, Lowe is perfectly capable of pitching more than a hundred innings every year, and in fact he threw 109 last season, recording 15 saves (included seven long ones).

What does this give the Red Sox?

It's a simple equation, really. The more innings your best pitchers pitch, the more games you're going to win. If Pedro Martinez could somehow have pitched four hundred innings last year rather than two hundred, the Sox might well have won 104 games rather than 94. And on a relative basis, the effect is even bigger than that for Lowe, because a significantly higher percentage of Lowe's innings come in crucial situations. This is just a guess, but forty extra innings from Lowe might be roughly equivalent to sixty extra innings from Martinez.

Of course, there's a reason why Pedro Martinez doesn't pitch four hundred innings per season, and we might discover that there's also a reason why Mariano Rivera and Ugueth Urbina don't pitch one hundred innings per season. Lowe might break down, and if that happened the Red Sox would be in trouble because they don't have any other relievers who would look good in that role. And Jimy Williams would probably have to come up with some other unorthodox strategy.

All of this points to one of the advantages of being a longtime baseball fan, or at least knowing something of the game's history. Watching Derek Lowe pitch two innings at a time is infinitely more interesting than it might be otherwise, because I know it's both a departure from modern practice and a return to earlier practice, to the days of Rollie Fingers and Goose Gossage.

Peter Gammons claims that "the era of babying your closers is over." I'm not anywhere near convinced of that yet, but it sure is fun to watch the discussion progress, from a great seat in Fenway Park.

As good as Lowe is, he's been matched inning for inning by his primary setup man, right-handed relief pitcher Rich Garces, who also tossed a pair of scoreless innings tonight. What makes this combination truly interesting is the stark contrast presented by the two.

Lowe weighs two hundred pounds (after stepping out of the shower with his uniform on, and marbles in his pockets), but those two hundred pounds are distributed over a lanky, six-foot-six frame. When he pitches from the stretch, Lowe looks like a man peeking around a skinny lamppost. If sportswriters still bothered nicknaming baseball players, Lowe would be "the Blade."

Garces weighs 215 pounds, and those 215 pounds are . . . wait a second, who the hell are we kidding? One of the dirty little secrets about baseball players is that their listed weights often bear little relationship to reality. When Garces reached the major leagues in 1990, he was nineteen years old, six feet tall, and he weighed 187 pounds.

That was ten years ago, and while he's still six feet tall (or close), it's safe to say that Garces has added more than (215 minus 187 equals) twenty-eight pounds in those ten years. Many things are best seen from the stands at Fenway Park, but Rich Garces is not one of them. Even if you're sitting close to the field, as I was tonight, you don't get a true sense of Garces's dimensions. He is best seen on a TV screen, the bigger the better, where he fills more horizontal space than any other pitcher in the game. His head/neck is immense, a singular mechanism that reminds me of a big balloon topped by a baseball cap. Garces's stomach hangs over his belt, but focusing on his belly would be doing him an injustice, because *all* of him is both big and round. It's as if you threw a dart at him, he would pop, like Underdog in the Macy's Thanksgiving Day parade.

So what do hip Red Sox fans (and Peter Gammons) call Garces?

"El Guapo."

The Handsome One.

Saturday, May 6

The crowd outside Fenway today was a little more charged than usual, the way it always is when Pedro Martinez is going to pitch. It's what happens when everyone knows they just might see something special. And we did.

As I've gotten older, I've become a bit more tolerant of human frailties, but at the same time I've become less willing to be inconvenienced by them. So when David, my editor at ESPN.com and also a good friend, still hadn't arrived at one o'clock—five minutes before game time—I wasn't mad at him, but I did decide to leave his ticket at the Will Call window and go in without him. If he figured it out, great. If not, well, we're talking about Pedro Martinez here. But just as I was turning toward the entrance, Dave showed up. And we reached our seats just in time to see Martinez give up a single to Devil Rays leadoff man Gerald Williams. A guy near me said (and I thought), "So much for the no-hitter."

True enough, but there would be other opportunities for excitement.

After Williams reached, Martinez struck out Dave Martinez and Greg Vaughn swinging, and then he got Jose Canseco looking. In the second inning, Martinez struck out Fred McGriff, Vinny Castilla and, after John Flaherty's line-drive single off the Green Monster, Kevin Stocker, too. Two innings, six strikeouts.

When Pedro Martinez or Randy Johnson strikes out six hitters in the first two innings, your mind turns to one number.

20

That's the record for strikeouts in a nine-inning game, and I know a lot of people who can tell you who's done it, and when it happened.

Roger Clemens in 1986.

Roger Clemens in 1996.

Kerry Wood in 1998.

It's just a great number, **20**, both big and round. I'll never forget watching Wood's twentieth strikeout (Derek Bell) on WGN, and I'll never forget the front page of *USA Today*'s sports section the next day, with all twenty of those Ks aligned vertically. Clemens, by the way, recorded both of his twenty-K games while pitching for the Red Sox.

Pedro Martinez, though he owns the major league record for consecutive starts with double-digit strikeouts, has never struck out more than seventeen hitters in a game. So the way he's been going for the last few years, you figure it's just a matter of time.

What made the beginning of this game all the more interesting was Martinez's mound opponent, Steve Trachsel. The last time Trachsel was in the news, it was in 1999 when he had a real good chance of losing twenty games (he lost eighteen). The last time before that, it was in 1998 when he gave up Mark McGwire's sixty-second home run. This year, he's 1–2 with a 6.15 ERA in six starts, which made this game look like a major mismatch on paper. The thing about baseball, though, is that "on paper" doesn't have nearly the same meaning that it does in other sports. Perhaps inspired by Martinez, Trachsel came out in the bottom of the first and struck out all three batters he faced. Thus, the first nine outs of the game all came by way of punch-out.

Even in the second inning, the fans went nuts with each Martinez strikeout, and things only got more exciting as the game continued, Martinez piling them up one after the other while keeping the Devil Rays off the scoreboard.

But while Trachsel couldn't match Martinez in the strikeout department, he would match him, at least, in nearly every other respect. After seven innings, the pitching lines for the two starters were

	IP	H	R	ER	BB	K
MARTINEZ	7	4	0	0	1	15
TRACHSEL	7	3	0	0	3	8

Miguel Cairo led off the top of the eighth and went down swinging. That made sixteen Ks for Pedro, and a new record was still theoretically possible. But Gerald Williams followed with a ground ball to shortstop, and our dream died. Dave Martinez singled, then stole second base on an extremely close play. That brought up Greg Vaughn—who had previously struck out three times on nine pitches—and with a full count he lifted a high foul down the third-base line. A funny thing happens when you're hoping for a big strikeout game. You want foul balls to reach the seats, and if you don't really care who wins, you even want fair balls to become base hits. Martinez and the Red Sox obviously needed an out here, yet I could hear murmurs from fans around me . . . *Get out of play. Go foul, go foul . . .* And that's what it did, dropping into the third row of seats.

So, still alive, Vaughn ripped Pedro's next pitch, a hanging slider, into center field. Dave Martinez sprinted home from second, and the Devil Rays had a 1–0 lead. That was all they would get, and it was all that Steve Trachsel would need. He wound up pitching the best game of his career: eleven strikeouts, complete game, three-hit shutout. And this was baseball at its best, with every single pitch having the potential to turn the game around.

Pedro did pitch a complete game, and matched his career high with seventeen strikeouts. But he wasn't good enough to beat Trachsel, and got stuck with his first loss of the season.

◆　◆　◆

Most games, I write between five and ten little notes for each team, usually relating to locations of hits, defensive misadventures, when the idiots got the wave going, things of that nature. But for the Red Sox today, there is just one note in my scorebook:

    ① WHY NOT PH NOMAR?

I wrote that in the bottom of the seventh, when number-nine hitter Andy Sheets batted with one out, nobody on base and the game still scoreless. Sheets, generally helpless at the plate and specifically hitless in six at-bats this year, was playing shortstop because Garciaparra was a little gimpy with a sore hamstring. But he was available for pinch-hitting duties, as we found out in the bottom of the ninth. With Jason Varitek batting, Garciaparra stepped into the on-deck circle in place of number-eight hitter Manny Alexander. Varitek flied out to end the game, and thus Garciaparra never batted. And I hate it when a manager loses a game with bullets still in the magazine, so to speak.

As further example that Red Sox fans really do know their baseball, there was a smattering of boos when Sheets was allowed to hit in the seventh, and as Gerald Williams was waiting for Varitek's game-ending can of corn, one could hear grumbling from the fans. "Why didn't he use Nomah befouh?" And I was right there with them.

But now, as I look at my scorebook, I understand exactly what Jimy Williams was thinking. Boston's lineup is fairly strong, one through seven. So if he was going to use Garciaparra as a pinch-hitter, it would be in the eighth (Alexander) or ninth (Sheets) spots. Williams hoped that when that happened, someone would be on base for Nomar to knock in. And the eight spot *would* come up again . . . unless Trachsel retired the next eight hitters after Sheets in order, an unlikely occurrence. Yet that's exactly what Trachsel did.

So my respect for Williams grows a bit more. His strategy was solid, but often the players on the field foil even the best strategy.

Retrospective Postscript: On May 11, Steve Trachsel beat the Yankees 1–0, thus becoming the first pitcher in American League history to win by that score in both Yankee Stadium and Fenway Park in the same season.

Sunday, May 7

Dispatch from Box 71: After three or four days of a pleasant spring, summer arrived today, bringing with it muggy air and 91 degrees, just short of the record. Oh, and the ozone level soared to unhealthy levels, too.

This will come off as sacrilegious at best, whiny at worst, but I'm not a big fan of day games under the warm, bright sun. At least not this warm. You wind up sitting in a tepid pool of your own sweat, and if I wanted to do that I'd take more baths. If the weather's nice, night baseball is much preferred, for reasons that I've either listed already or will later. Granted, I could have moved under the overhang and enjoyed today's contest from a nice, cool, shady seat. But when you paid forty-five dollars for a ticket in the fourth row, it's tough to move back to the twenty-fourth.

The Devil Rays grabbed a 2–0 lead against Jeff Fassero in the first inning, and the Sox got one of those runs back in the second. Miguel Cairo led off the top of the third for Tampa Bay, and he pulled a line drive right toward me. From the corner of my eye, it seemed that the woman sitting behind me and one seat to the right wasn't paying much attention, and I just had time for a quick "Look out!" The baseball didn't hit her or me. Instead it rammed into a high-school kid, who tried to make a bare-handed catch. The ball bounced off him, and back a couple more rows. As usual, no one employed by the Red Sox came down to see if anybody was bruised or bleeding.

I keep hammering on this because, in my experience, Fenway Park is unique in this respect. I've seen games in twenty-two other major league ballparks, and in each of those twenty-two ballparks, a dangerous foul ball is quickly followed to its initial impact point by at least one usher, in case anyone needs medical attention. But in Fenway, nothing, at least not regularly. And as it turned out, this young man did need some medical attention. After half an inning of staring at his right hand with a mixture of surprise and fear, like a man fishing for trout who's just hooked a shark, he went to a concession stand and found a bag of ice. I stole glances in his direction every few minutes after he returned, and nearly every time he was focused not on the close game, but rather on trying to act like he wasn't in serious pain. But you could see him thinking, *Shit, it's broken. Shit, it's broken . . .*

He looked like a tough kid. His old man, with a tattoo on his left bicep, looked even tougher. But in the bottom of the fourth, the kid finally gave up trying to act tough. The two of them left, presumably in search of an X-ray machine, and did not return.

◆　◆　◆

Without checking, I'd be willing to bet five bucks that Jimy Williams "loses" his DH more often than any other American League manager.

Let me explain. In American League games, of course, each team is allowed to replace its pitcher in the starting lineup with a non-fielding hitter. A *Designated Hitter*. The designated hitter may later take a defensive position, but if he does so, the team "loses" its DH, and the current pitcher enters the batting lineup in place of the fielder who was replaced by the DH.

The Red Sox are carrying only four outfielders, and today one of them, Carl Everett, was in the lineup as the designated hitter. So when Williams sent up Garciaparra to pinch-hit for center fielder Darren Lewis in the bottom of the eighth, Williams had a choice in the top of the ninth; he could send one of his two remaining utility infielders—Manny Alexander and Jeff Frye—to the outfield, or he could use Everett, who's regarded as an excellent defensive center fielder. Williams went with Everett, and that meant Derek Lowe, in the game to pitch, went into the No. 2 slot in the batting order.

The move "worked" in the top of the ninth. With the Red Sox clinging to a two-run lead, the Devil Rays had a man on second base with two outs. Fred McGriff smacked a low line drive into center field, where Everett gloved the ball for the final out.

Speaking of moves that worked, Garciaparra came through in his pinch-hitting appearance. With two outs in the top of the eighth, and the Red Sox leading 8–7, Jose Offerman doubled. That brought up Darren Lewis's spot, but of course he's a lousy hitter. So in his place, Garciaparra hit a fearsome line drive off pitcher Roberto Hernandez's right elbow. Garciaparra hit the ball so hard that it caromed, on the fly, all the way behind third base, Offerman scoring from third base easily and the Sox eventually taking the 9–7 victory.

Monday, May 8

When Pedro Martinez pitches, a group of high-school kids, who call themselves "Kerrigan's K-Men" in honor of Red Sox pitching coach Joe Kerrigan, affix a giant red K poster on the wall behind them for each Martinez strikeout. As you probably know, the traditional scoring symbol for a strikeout that ends with a called strike three is a backward capital K, like this . . .

| Я |

. . . but a swinging strikeout gets the standard capital K. However, until Kerrigan's K-Men took over the duties, those in the bleachers who posted the Ks weren't always completely accurate. If the first three strikeouts were all swinging, you would *not* see this:

K K K

Rather, you'd see this:

Why? Because the people doing the posting were worried that KKK would offend people. Then, after the fourth strikeout, they would go back and reverse the third K if necessary. Now, you can say what you want about the insouciance that often accompanies youth, but in this case it's welcome. The new K-Men get it right the first time, over-the-top political correctness be damned.

I got that story from a man named Bill Nowlin, my host for the game tonight. Here's another nugget, courtesy of Bill . . . If you want to perform the National Anthem before a Red Sox game, you're welcome to send a tape to the club, and if they like it, you get to sing at Fenway Park. But here's the interesting part: What the fans will hear is that tape you sent. That's right, everybody. While the person or persons you see singing the Anthem really are singing, their microphone is turned off. It's only there to (1) foster the illusion and (2) serve as a backup just in case something happens to the tape.

Bill Nowlin knows, I suspect, more about Fenway Park and its inhabitants than anyone in the world. He's been coming to games here since the 1940s, and well remembers watching Ted Williams ("When he didn't get on base, you were surprised."). But a lot of people can say that. What most people can't say is, "I've coauthored three books: one about Ted Williams, one about the Red Sox, and one about Fenway Park. Another about the people who work at Fenway will be published in the next year or two, and I've done preliminary work on two others."

Sit next to Bill Nowlin at Fenway, and you'll hope for extra innings. Tonight's game, unfortunately, lasted only nine frames, the Sox topping the White Sox, 3–2, in a fairly quick affair, only two and a half hours. (Brian Rose, who got knocked out in the first inning of his last start, saved his job with six strong innings.)

Aside from having seen Ted Williams play many times and cofounding a great record label (Rounder), Bill Nowlin also lays claim to what must be a truly singular distinction. He served as a paid extra during the filmings of both *Eight Men Out* **and** *Field of Dreams*. In fact, when Bill met his wife, he was still sporting the 1919-style haircut that the on-site barber had given him for *Eight Men Out*. Unfortunately for those of us who might like to see Bill on the screen, his face did not survive the cutting-room floors in either movie.

Like most longtime Red Sox fans, Bill spent a significant portion of his youth, misspent or otherwise, in the Fenway Park bleachers.

"When I was in my early teens, we would sit in the back row of the bleachers beyond center field. That was before they added the wall that's behind the bleachers now, so from the back row you could lean over and look down on Lansdowne Street. Well, sometimes we would fill up empty Coke cups with water. We never actually poured water onto people. That wouldn't be nice. But I would spill the water so it splashed maybe ten feet in front of people, just to scare them. A few times, someone would get so mad, they bought a ticket to get into the bleachers and find me. But by then, of course, I was already in a different seat, usually on a bench—back then, that's what the bleachers were—near the visitors' bullpen.

"The strongest memory I have of Fenway, though, is that of the rush I felt so many times entering the park via Gate A, giving my ticket to one of the ticket takers stationed at one of the two doors in the chain-link fence way off to the far right, and then tearing my way up the ramp. This ramp, which led to the very top of Sections Seventeen and Eighteen, has been closed off for the last ten or so years now. Particularly for the first game of the year, or after being away from Boston for a long stretch, I'd charge up that ramp, my heart pumping with effort and expectation until the sight of the green playing field emerged, seemingly spread out for the convenience of my view.

"I never walked up that ramp. I always ran. And in all the years since, I haven't lost the enthusiasm, the need, to be there. Even today, once or twice during the winter I just drive by, maybe browse the souvenirs at Twins Enterprises across the street. Just to pay a visit, just to be close.

"There can never be another Fenway Park."

Tuesday, May 9

Baseball players have a term for what James Baldwin did to the Red Sox tonight.

He stuck the bats up their asses.

Baldwin pitched nine innings, and allowed one walk and three hits, all of them singles. Two of those singles, both off the bat of Trot Nixon, were less than convincing: one a bloop job down the left-field line, the other a piddling grounder up the middle that sneaked through. The only clean hit came in the fifth, when Troy O'Leary shot a liner into center field. When Baldwin got Garciaparra on a double-play grounder to third at 9:27, he completed the first shutout of his career. It took him 127 starts, which probably isn't a record but sure sounds like one.

Baldwin did keep one streak alive, however. He has never, not in those 127 starts or his seventeen relief appearances, started a double play. And he should have started one tonight. After O'Leary's leadoff single in the fifth, Baldwin struck out Everett. The next hitter, Mike Stanley, squibbed an easy grounder back to Baldwin, who turned and threw to second base. Or rather, he threw in the general direction of second. The throw was low and behind shortstop Jose Valentin, the runners ending up on first and second. This would constitute Boston's only true threat in the game, but Baldwin got the next two hitters on routine grounders, thus becoming the first American League pitcher (by a few minutes) to run his record to 6–0.

Three days ago, Steve Trachsel pitched the best game of his life, and now James Baldwin has done the same. I'm sure that, as I write this, Sox fans are burning up the phone lines trying to reach WEEI and complain about the club's lack of scoring punch. Indeed, at 5.3 runs per game the Red Sox currently rank ninth in the American League in run production, and this problem isn't going away. A year ago they finished tenth in scoring, and simply adding Carl Everett to the lineup, as good as he is, can't make a truly substantial difference.

One might take two lessons from this. "The Sox need better hitting" or "They won last year with this offense, so they can do it again." And the truth is that they probably *can* do it again, as long as Pedro is healthy and Joe Kerrigan continues to get good work from over-the-hill starting pitchers, and great work from the bullpen.

◆   ◆   ◆

There are many advantages to living four blocks from the ballpark. Tonight, I found out how wonderful that four blocks can be if you arrive at the ballpark and discover that you don't have a ticket. Actually, I had *a* ticket, just not the right ticket. I made this frightening discovery at 6:55, and found that I could jog home and back in roughly nine minutes. Unfortunately, it took another three minutes to get through the turnstiles and within sight of the field, at which point I'd missed the first two pitches, both strikes thrown from Pete Schourek to White Sox leadoff man Ray Durham.

Sitting to my right tonight were Joan and Douglas. Joan is what young men once would have called "a real looker." Somebody like Joan takes a job in your office, and every man in the place feels like he just won the lotto.

Douglas was nice-looking, too, I suppose. If tall, square-jawed, athletic types are your thing. Anyway, Joan and Douglas constitute the quintessential late-twentieth-century couple. She sells ads for websites, he sells the hardware that allows websites to function. She lives north of Boston, he lives in Philadelphia, and they visit each other two or three weekends every month. Douglas bought six tickets for tonight's game—two for him and Joan, four for a quartet of business associates in town for a training seminar—and he paid a ticket broker $125 per ticket. And it's all tax-deductible.

(That's one of the "problems" that nobody ever talks about, in relation to the rapidly escalating cost of baseball tickets. A high percentage of the good [read: expensive] seats are purchased by companies which are allowed to write off half the cost. That is, if a Boston-based corporation spent $14,580 on a block of four box seats for this season, they'll get back $7,290 at tax time. And where does that $7,290 come from? Yup. You, me, and every other Joe Taxpayer. Now, one can argue over the justice of subsidizing the entertainment of Gillette's employees and clients—I would argue that it's the height of ridiculousness—but there's a practical effect that one can't logically deny. The subsidization of corporate ticket costs means higher ticket prices for everyone who spends his or her own money at the ballpark.)

Wednesday, May 10

When I was nine years old, my Cub Scout pack went to a Royals game on a sunny Sunday afternoon. Our seats weren't good, middle of the upper deck down the left-field line, which is a long ways from the field. Still, I was crestfallen when the father who had driven us—something of a scruffy sort, if memory serves—decided that we should head home after the eighth inning of a close game, "so we can beat that traffic."

I learned a good lesson that day. Listening to the game on the car radio while cruising down the highway, we heard the Royals tie the game in the ninth, and eventually win in extra innings. Dear old dad, with considerable profundity, said, "Hell, if I'd a known they was gonna come back, we coulda stayed."

I don't remember if the phrase "No shit, Sherlock" was then a part of my vocabulary—I think that was added a couple of years later—but it certainly would have applied in this situation. And I resolved then and there, I would stick out every baseball game to the bitter end.

And I have, with one exception. When I was eighteen (legal drinking age then, at least in Kansas), I went to the ballpark with my father and a buddy of his. Much beer was imbibed, and when we left in the seventh, in search of other, more ribald entertainment, I was in no mood to complain. But that was the last time. I've been to three or four hundred games since then, and I have seen the last pitch of every one of them. But tonight, more than at any other time in the last fifteen years, I desperately wanted to give up on a baseball game.

It rained most of this afternoon, and I was hoping for a rain-out because I've got a flight tomorrow morning and, as usual, I've got too many things to do before I leave.

When Ramon Martinez threw his first pitch, the temperature was 50 degrees, the wind was whipping in from the North Atlantic at twenty miles an hour, and there was a fine mist roiling about in the arc lights, like a cosmic dust cloud from an old episode of *Star Trek*. And over the next six innings, it didn't get any warmer, calmer, or drier. Rather, it got colder and wetter, and if the flag in center field showed less wind, it was probably because Old Glory was saturated with water.

It was so cold and so wet that I completely gave up keeping score after the first, though that still left me plenty of time to misspell both Ray Durham (DURHAMAN) and Frank Thomas (THOMASH) in my book. Ramon didn't seem to mind the weather, as he tossed five scoreless innings; meanwhile, the Red Sox scored a run in the first, two in the third, and two in the fifth.

It was in the sixth that Jimy Williams made what I consider his first truly stupid move of this young season. The knuckleball, more than any other, is what they call a "feel pitch," in that a knuckleball pitcher will fail miserably if his fingers aren't in perfect position when the ball is released. So when Williams summoned Wakefield from the bullpen to protect a 5–0 lead in the top of the sixth—Martinez had suffered a slight injury—I groaned to myself. Meat of the White Sox order coming up, and Wakefield probably can't even *feel* his fingers, let alone throw a good knuckleball with them. And indeed, things got ugly real fast. Wakefield allowed four hits, one of them a two-run homer, and by the time Rich Garces entered the game, the score was 5–3 and Chicago had a runner on base. Garces retired Herbert Perry to end the inning, and so the rally ended.

And the game ended just a few minutes later. The Red Sox batted in the bottom of the sixth but didn't score, and finally the umpires halted the game, at least temporarily. And I went home, at least temporarily.

After watching the last twenty minutes of *The West Wing,* I turned on WEEI to see if anyone was seriously considering playing more baseball in the Fens tonight. One caller, Billy from Waltham, was awfully concerned about the Red Sox bench strength, or lack thereof.

"We gotta do somethin' about the bench," he said. "I call 'em 'the Killer Fleas.' *F* is for Frye, *LE* is for Lewis, *A* is for Alexander and *S* is for Sheets."

Billy has a point. Here are stats for the four Red Sox bench players through tonight's game:

	AB	H	W	R	RBI	AVG
JEFF FRYE	35	6	1	3	2	.171
DARREN LEWIS	30	5	4	4	0	.167
MANNY ALEXANDER	35	6	1	5	3	.171
ANDY SHEETS	14	0	0	0	0	.000
TOTALS	114	17	6	12	5	.149

While none of these players are really this bad (nobody is), it was more than obvious that the Red Sox bench was pretty pathetic entering the season. Without checking every team, in fact, it wouldn't shock me at all to discover the Red Sox feature the worst bench in the American League. If one of the regulars goes down, or is ineffective, the Sox simply can't come up with a productive replacement. Not at any position.

The game had been stopped at 9:30, and at 11:18 it was finally called.

The Red Sox hit the road tomorrow, and so do I. They'll be in Baltimore and then Toronto, and I'll be in the great State of Washington, the closest thing to a home that I've got. I think that I'll miss following the Sox in the local papers, and I'll miss watching them on television. But when they're not in Boston, I get lonely, to the point where I want to be somewhere else, somewhere familiar. And if there's major league baseball in that somewhere else—as there will be in Seattle next week—well, all the better.

Monday, May 15

I spent the last four years living in Seattle, and this is my second season as a season-ticket holder. While I profess no great love for the Seattle Mariners, this city has become, in a sense, my baseball home. I've attended perhaps 250 major league games in my life, and nearly a hundred of them were here in Seattle: 79 games at the Kingdome from 1996 through the middle of the 1999 season, and tonight will mark my eighteenth at new Safeco Field.

I moved to Seattle in the spring of 1996; the Mariners played at the south end of downtown Seattle, I lived at the north end of downtown Seattle. Downtown Seattle is a relatively small area, so getting to the ballpark was a snap, a straight shot on the bus or my mountain bike. That first season, I had access to a press pass, and like a little kid with the new sled he'd been wanting since three Christmases ago, I would be at the Kingdome night after night. It wasn't until I moved to Seattle that I was able to see baseball virtually whenever I wanted, so wherever I might end up, this team and this city will always mean something special to me. And as my plane made its approach into Sea-Tac Airport last Thursday afternoon, and we flew over the ballpark, my eyes did get a little misty when I saw the lettering atop the retractable roof:

WELCOME TO SAFECO FIELD
HOME OF THE SEATTLE MARINERS

No baseball Thursday night, though, as the M's were in Oakland for the weekend. So I headed to the Cascades for a few days. No TV or phone line, which meant I had to drive to a gas station three straight mornings for the newspapers to see how my teams did the previous evening.

And that was enough. When I'm in a pleasant place with pleasant people, I can survive quite nicely without ESPN or the Internet, at least for a few days. Perhaps this does mean, as my friend Jim Baker has argued more than once, that I'm not truly obsessed with baseball. If I were really obsessed, Jim says, I'd have been out in the car every night, fiddling with the AM dial in hopes of pulling in something, anything, that would give me the scores of the day's games. Then again, if this were September and the Red Sox or the Royals or the Mariners were in a pennant race, I would likely have spent at least parts of my evenings fiddling with the car radio, if not sitting on a stool in the nearest sports bar. So perhaps I should be classified as a seasonal obsessive.

Whether I'm truly an obsessive or not, I certainly was ready for some baseball after coming down from the Cascades.

Tonight the Mariners hosted the Twins (who, frankly, I saw plenty of back in Boston). After sixteen games of baseball, Friendly Fenway-style, the Safeco experience was jarring. Walk around outside the ballpark, walk around inside the ballpark, gaze out at the field from your seat . . . and one gets an overwhelming feeling of space. It's quite possible to spend three or four hours at Safeco, or any of the other new mallparks and never physically touch another human. This is, of course, almost impossible at Fenway Park, where you're jostled as you enter the ballpark, nudged while in line for a pizza, and bumped from the sides when you're sitting in your seat.

And I'll be honest about this, there is something comforting about all this space. The truth is that it's hard to relax in Fenway Park, at least for someone like me who grew up in the suburbs. There are so many people, and they talk differently than I do, and they're sort of . . . well, you know . . . aggressive, albeit usually in a nice way.

So I can't help but wonder if the appeal of the new parks isn't tied to the fact that most of the people who can afford baseball tickets grew up outside the cities, where every kid has his own room and every family has its own yard.

I have devoted many words to decrying the new ballparks, but they mirror the lives that most of us have made for ourselves. They're constructed of walls designed to hold billboards, and there's so much elbowroom that you almost feel like you're back home in the suburbs.

But just as my seats at Safeco are farther from the field than they were in the Mariners' old ballpark, most of us are farther from our families, farther from where we grew up, farther from our roots. But by God, we have plenty of elbowroom.

Thursday, May 18

"London has Big Ben, Paris has the Eiffel Tower, and Boston has the CITGO sign," is a quote often heard in the Boston area.

—www.citgo.com

I've been in the Boston area for the better part of two months, and I have never heard that quote. And when I first saw the CITGO sign in person, it struck me as a colossal waste of energy, a monument to a bygone era when nobody knew or cared what the burning of fossil fuels does to the air that we breathe.

Tonight, though, I finally "got" the CITGO sign.

If you've ever been to Fenway Park or watched a Red Sox game on TV, you know all about the sign. Though it actually sits atop a building on Beacon Street, a few blocks north of the ballpark, the CITGO sign—a blinking triangle within a blue rectangle, CITGO at the bottom—seems to loom beyond the Green Monster just as the Green Monster looms beyond left fielders.

Built in 1965 (and replacing a City Services sign in the same spot), the CITGO sign was first shut off in 1973, in response to the oil crisis, and remained dark for about a year. In 1979, in response to the same energy crisis that had the sweater-clad Jimmy Carter asking Northeasterners to lower their thermostats to 68 degrees, the Massachusetts State Energy Office asked City Services to shut off the lights again. According to the CITGO website, the sign used only sixty dollars' worth of energy per week . . . but shutting off the lights was not designed to save energy; it was designed to send a message. And despite the end of the energy crisis and the blind optimism that accompanied Ronald Reagan into office, the sign remained dark for four years.

Finally, in November of 1982, workmen arrived at 660 Beacon to dismantle the sign. But before work could begin, the Boston Landmarks Commission stepped in and said it was considering designating the sign a city landmark, as a "prime example of roadside culture." The following January, the Commission declined to give the sign landmark status, reasoning that undue burden would be placed upon the owner, City Services. Nevertheless, a deal was struck, and City Services agreed to refurbish the sign and relight it for three years, at an estimated cost of $450,000.

And during the seventh-inning stretch on August 10, 1983, the CITGO sign was lit once again, to the strains of "You Light Up My Life" pouring from loudspeakers in Kenmore Square. The Sox beat the Rangers 4–2 that night, and the Fenway Faithful went home even happier than usual. The three years, of course, have become seventeen, and it's now hard to imagine anyone turning the lights out.

Learning all this stuff about the big sign gave me an appreciation for it, but I still couldn't help but think that it's something less than a landmark that deserves protection. I mean, a good number of Sox fans are ready and willing to blow up Fenway Park, but they can't stand the idea of losing an energy-gulping advertisement?

But like I said, tonight I got it.

My plane touched down at Logan just before nine o'clock; by 9:20 I was in a cab, headed for home. And heading southwest on Storrow Drive, we came around a curve and there it was, the CITGO sign in all its glory, like a lighthouse guiding old, half-blind fishermen back to port. *If I can just make it to the CITGO sign in Kenmore Square, by God, I could walk home from there.* And while there's no hearth, no loving family awaiting my return, it'll be good to be in my own apartment, with my own TV and my own ESPN and my own Internet connection.

So I can imagine that Red Sox fans have the same sorts of feelings. They come around a corner, see the comforting blue and red lights of the CITGO sign, and they know Fenway Park can't be far away.

A lot happened to the Red Sox when we all were on the road.

Nomar Garciaparra went on the disabled list with the hamstring problem that had been bothering him during the last home stand. His place at shortstop was taken not by one of the Fleas, but by Donnie Sadler, a tiny (flealike?) minor leaguer with great wheels and lousy everything else.

Derek Lowe finally blew a save, getting racked up Tuesday night for three runs in Toronto.

I've saved the biggest news for last . . . The Sox are in first place! Since last Friday, the Sox have outscored their opponents, 46–10, and won five games while losing just one (a one-run loss to the Blue Jays). So now they own a one-game lead over the Yankees!

Third Inning

Friday, May 19

Jeff Fassero was on the Comeback Player of the Year campaign trail tonight, and once again he gave a hell of a stump speech, tossing seven shutout innings against the still-woeful Tigers. Rich Garces did his usual efficient work in the eighth, and then Lowe worked around a two-out single in the ninth to post his ninth save.

Fassero's now 5–1 with a 3.25 ERA.

A year ago, Fassero went 5–14 with a 7.20 ERA for Texas and Seattle.

It is on the left arm of Jeff Fassero that Joe Kerrigan is solidifying his reputation as one of the top two or three pitching coaches in the game, along with Leo Mazzone in Atlanta and Don Gullett in Cincinnati. There are other candidates, to be sure, but these are the names that keep coming up, the guys who are able to seemingly get something out of nothing, or close to nothing.

And nothing is exactly what I thought the Red Sox would get from Fassero this season. In fact, it was their presumed lack of pitching depth that led me to pick the Red Sox (gulp) for third place in the East this year, behind the Yankees and Blue Jays.

After the first five games of the season, I looked like a genius. Pedro blew away the Mariners in the season opener . . . and then the so-called Four Dwarfs who constituted the rest of the rotation—Ramon Martinez, Fassero, Pete Schourek, and Brian Rose—went winless in the next four games. As did the Red Sox, and the fans were already giving up on the season. You want to experience collective fatalism? Hang around Boston some early April when the Sox are 1–4. The second Sunday of the season, I called my favorite Red Sox fan during Pedro's second start.

"You listening to the game?" I asked. (She doesn't have a TV.)

"What's the point? It doesn't matter what Pedro does, nobody else on the stupid team can pitch."

And so it seemed.

Well, as of tonight the Red Sox sport a 3.28 ERA, lowest in the American League. And here's the kicker: Even if you removed Pedro Martinez's phenomenal statistics from the equation, *the Red Sox would still lead the American League in ERA.* Here are the five best ERAs in the league, absent Pedro:

RED SOX	3.93
YANKEES	3.97
WHITE SOX	4.58
INDIANS	4.59
MARINERS	4.75

That's an amazing thing; it really is. But it's really nothing new for Kerrigan's charges. In 1999, they led the AL with a 4.00 ERA. Pedro Martinez, easily the best pitcher in the league, got most of the credit, and deservedly so. But even without Pedro, the Sox would have posted the second-best ERA in the league, behind only the Yankees. And if you'd taken away the Yankees' best starter, then of course the Sox are back on top.

Wait, here's another kicker. Kerrigan's doing all this with a significantly different pitching rotation. Pat Rapp started twenty-six games last year; he's in Baltimore now. Mark Portugal started twenty-seven games last year; he's in the minors now. Bret Saberhagen started twenty-two games last year and pitched brilliantly; he's spent this season on the disabled list and isn't expected back until sometime in June. Tim Wakefield started seventeen games last year; he's started only twice this season.

◆   ◆   ◆

It rained all day, and it was cold all night. Fleece-jacket, long-johns, wearing-gloves-but-my-fingers-are-still-cold cold. I suppose you're getting sick of me whining about the long meteorological nightmare, but this wasn't my idea of spring in New England, everyone's warnings notwithstanding.

Fortunately, baseball has powerful therapeutic powers.

In the fourth inning, Carl Everett just missed a home run on a drive that sent right fielder Juan Gonzalez to the bullpen wall. And in the sixth, Everett drove a ball on the same vector . . . but twenty feet deeper, and the Red Sox had a 2–0 lead. That made the crowd happy and, one inning later, Mike Stanley made me happy. Leading off the bottom of the seventh, Stanley drove a Brian Moehler fastball deep to left field. And as the baseball described its inevitable parabola, it took my spirits with it. The ball dropped gently into the netting above The Wall, like a faithful hound settling in front of the fireplace after a long day of ranging, and I remembered what brought me here.

Later, during a pitching change, the PA system blared "Sweet Caroline," the old Neil Diamond song. Now, say what you want about Neil Diamond, but I would argue that only a strong man will not be cheered by this particular tune, especially when Neil airs out his pipes during the chorus . . .

> *Sweet Caroline*
> *Good times never seemed so good*

The Sox don't play it during every game, but I'm always glad when they do.

Saturday, May 20

Perhaps I'm adopting the habits of Red Sox Nation. The Olde Towne Team sits atop the standings, but I can't help but worry about them. Today they managed just one run against Dave Mlicki and a platoon of Detroit relievers. The Tiger hitters weren't much better, scoring only two runs themselves. But that was enough, as the Sox left two men on base in the bottom of the eighth and went down meekly in the ninth.

◆ ◆ ◆

There were four kids sitting behind me this afternoon. I had them pegged for high-schoolers, but as one ages, one loses the ability to judge those things with any great accuracy; they might be freshman or sophomores at one of the many local colleges. Anyway, they made me feel old, because they did the things that I used to do. Some of the kids really knew their stuff—how to pronounce all the names, which players came from which teams—but they acted like kids nonetheless. One of them (I think his name was Jeff) kept screaming at the players, Tigers and Red Sox alike.

At Sox catcher Scott Hatteberg, who came in batting .162: "One-sixty-two, you're huge!"

At Sox second baseman Jose Offerman, who singled in the fourth to lift his average to .241: "Two-fifty, here we come!"

At Mlicki, who, with runners on first and third in the fifth, tried the ol' fake-to-third-and-see-if-the-guy-on-first-gets-fooled move: "Throw the ball, you pansy!"

At Tigers catcher Rob Fick, who committed a passed ball, also in the fifth: "Thank you, Rob Fick, we love you!"

And finally, at Tigers shortstop Deivi Cruz, who caught a routine pop in the eighth to end a Sox rally: "Deivi Cruz, you suck!"

I don't suppose these various imprecations translate particularly well to paper, but the fact is that some things are funny only when uttered by a young man or an old man, and these are some of them.

Or maybe I enjoyed this bellowing because it's exactly what I used to do at Royals games, when I was in college (and, truth be told, for a few years after).

◆ ◆ ◆

I'm not a big believer in "chemistry" as it relates to baseball. More precisely, I'm a rabid agnostic. It may exist, but none of us are smart enough to know for sure, one way or the other.

But what you'll generally find is that teams that win are said to have good chemistry, and teams that don't win are said to have poor chemistry. The Red Sox are playing well, so of course everyone is talking about their chemistry. Even Jerry Remy, the one-time Sox second baseman who is now one of the better TV analysts around. Yesterday in the *Boston Herald*, columnist Gerry Callahan wrote

"After 25 years in and around the game, Remy says these Red Sox are quickly changing his mind about one thing: chemistry in baseball. . . . 'It's like one big group . . . They just don't care about individual accomplishments.'"

Great. But does all that non-cliquishness translate to success on the field? It's incredibly difficult to find much evidence that it does.

As for the great chemistry that's supposed to result in great effort, I've seen every home game, and my relatively uneducated eyes have spotted at least four instances of poor concentration or lack of effort. On Opening Day, Carl Everett forgot how many outs there were, costing the Sox a run. On two occasions, frustrated Sox hitters didn't bother to run out ground balls.

And today, lack of effort might have cost the Red Sox the ball game.

Going into the bottom of the fourth, the Sox trailed the Tigers, 1–0. In fact, they hadn't had a base runner yet. But Jose Offerman led off with a base hit. After a ground-out sent Offerman to second, the Sox loaded the bases on Trot Nixon's single and Brian Daubach's walk. Everybody moved up a base on Dave Mlicki's wild pitch, tying the game and giving the Sox runners on second and third, still only one out.

That brought up Carl Everett, and the crowd readied itself for yet another big home run. Batting left-handed against the right-handed Mlicki, Everett sliced a fly ball toward the Green Monster, where left fielder Bobby Higginson made a nice catch against the wall, then threw the ball to second base. Daubach, who apparently didn't think the catch would be made, was halfway to third and had to turn around and head back to second base. Unable to beat the ball to the bag, he was out. Double play.

But what of Nixon on third base? He should have been tagging on the play, right? And if he touched the plate before Daubach was out, Nixon's run would count.

Now, this is an almost impossible call for the umpire, assuming that the play is close at all. He's supposed to simultaneously keep his eye on the plate *and* on the play at second base. Like I said, it's almost impossible. I was watching the play at second, but as soon as I saw the "out" call there, I swiveled my head back to the plate, where plate umpire John Hirschbeck had already turned his back to the field, and was gesturing wildly to the press box (where the official scorer sits) that Nixon's "run" was, indeed, not a run at all.

Later, on ESPN, I saw that Nixon simply hadn't run full speed from third base. Daubach took the blame for straying too far off second base, but had Nixon sprinted full bore from the moment of the catch, he certainly would have scored with a step or two to spare. I'm not suggesting that Nixon is some sort of malingerer; in fact, by all accounts he's a habitual hustler. What I'm suggesting is that even hustling ballplayers sometimes forget to hustle. And more generally, there really isn't much difference in effort between one team and the next, especially early in the season when little has been decided.

Teams that win, as the Red Sox have lately, are said to have good chemistry.

Teams that lose, as the Red Sox eventually might, are said to have poor chemistry.

And for the most part, it's all a truckload of tripe.

Sunday, May 21

Detroit's Gregg Jefferies led off tonight's game against Ramon Martinez with a line drive that hooked around the right-field fair pole, which rises to the sky from a spot only 302 feet from home plate. Nobody in Boston calls it the right-field pole, though; here, it's known as "Pesky's pole" (or, less commonly, "the Pesky pole").

That's "Pesky" as in Johnny Pesky (born John Michael Paveskovich, 9/27/19), the same Johnny Pesky who's been employed by the Boston Red Sox for the better part of the last sixty years. He broke into the majors in 1942 and hit .331 as a rookie shortstop. Pesky spent the next three seasons in the U.S. Navy, but returned in 1946 to hit .335. That fall, he was labeled the goat when the Sox lost to the Cardinals in Game 7 of the World Series. Most serious analysts and historians, however, don't believe that Pesky could have made any difference . . . You know what? I'm going to get into this for a moment, so I hope you'll indulge me. Pesky's play in the '46 Series is a key piece of Red Sox lore, and I shouldn't gloss over it quite so quickly.

It's Game 7 of the 1946 World Series. The Red Sox have just scored twice in the top of the eighth to tie the score at three runs apiece, and now the Cardinals are batting. Enos Slaughter singles to center field, but he remains planted on first base when Whitey Kurowski pops up trying to bunt, and Del Rice flies to left. But Harry Walker dumps a soft liner into left-center field, and Slaughter—who was running with the pitch, hoping to steal second—sprints through a stop sign from his third-base coach, all the way home to put St. Louis ahead.

Simple enough, right? Except that's not how most of the men in the press box remembered it. As most of them wrote the story, Sox center fielder Leon Culberson retrieved Walker's hit, relayed the ball to shortstop Pesky . . . who hesitated before throwing home, too late to nab Slaughter. "Pesky holds the ball" remains, after all these years, the epitaph for the 1946 Series.

The problem is, the men in the press box didn't have instant replay to help them out. A careful study of the film, however, reveals that Pesky didn't hold the ball at all. And as Glenn Stout and Richard A. Johnson write in *Red Sox Century*, the best book ever written about the Red Sox,

> The truth is Slaughter's dash surprised *everyone*, including the writers in the press box. The fiction that Pesky held the ball in the first place reveals their stupefaction at the play. In normal

circumstances the hit would have been a single, and in normal circumstances it would have moved Slaughter to third. But this wasn't normal—it was the last inning of the World Series . . . As the grainy film shows, Pesky took the throw with his back to the plate, spun toward third, spotted Slaughter, took a quick half windup, and threw home. Catch to throw takes less than a second. He does not pause or freeze with the ball, although his body language exhibits surprise . . . Pesky, who got all the blame, simply made an average play in a situation that was already lost. Had he eyes in the back of his head and an arm like Bob Feller's, *by the time he got the ball Slaughter still would have scored.*

The first two Red Sox hitters reached base in the top of the ninth, but both were stranded. After winning their first five World Series—the last of them way back in 1918—the Sox had finally lost one. Of course, no one in his right mind would have predicted that they would go the rest of the century without winning another.

Pesky shifted to third base in 1948 and continued to produce—in 1950, his .437 on-base percentage ranked third in the American League—but he got off to a slow start in 1952 and the Sox traded him to Detroit. He played a few more seasons, but injuries severely limited his effectiveness. After retiring as a player, Pesky coached and managed in the Yankees and Tigers organizations before returning to the Red Sox fold, first as manager of their Seattle farm club in 1961 and '62, and then as manager of the Red Sox themselves in 1963 and '64. Pesky got fired, of course—the mid-sixties Sox were a frightful bunch, beyond the help of any mere mortal—and next spent a few years working for the Pirates. He joined the Red Sox again in 1969, and has been with the club ever since, in a variety of capacities. Pesky is now eighty years old, and officially employed as a Special Assignment Instructor (which sounds a hell of a lot like a sinecure to me, but then he's probably earned it).

Now, to the matter at hand . . . The following quote appears in a wonderful contraption called *Fenway Park: A Stadium Pop-up Book*, written by John Boswell and David Fisher:

The bullpen area added to the front of the right field bleachers to provide a closer home run target for Ted Williams is called

"Williamsburg." . . . At one time the right field foul pole was called
"Pesky's Pole" because Johnny Pesky often hit it for home runs. .

It's a wonderful book, because when you open it, Fenway does indeed pop up
before your very eyes. The historical text is somewhat questionable, as evidenced
by the above citation. We're apparently to believe that people still call the bullpens
"Williamsburg," and that "Pesky's Pole" is some sort of verbal relic. The reality is
exactly the opposite. I've been in Boston for two months, and I've yet to hear anyone utter "Williamsburg," but "Pesky's Pole" is murmured throughout the stands,
every time a home run comes near the right-field pole.

The claim that Pesky "often hit [the pole] for home runs" pops up in other books,
too . . . but I wondered, how many times could Pesky really have hit the right-field
pole? After all, you can go through a whole season and never see anybody do it.
What's more, Pesky hit only seventeen home runs in his entire career, and just thirteen of those came as a member of the Red Sox. To narrow it down further, I e-mailed
a friend, Eric Enders at the National Baseball Library in Cooperstown, and asked for
the dates on which Pesky hit home runs at Fenway Park.

There were six.

Now, how many of those six might we realistically expect to have actually hit
the pole? I don't know, either, so I went searching for evidence. Below, I've listed the
dates of those six Pesky-at-Fenway home runs, along with the geographical destina-
tions of each, as reported in both the *Globe* and the *Herald*.

DATE	*BOSTON GLOBE*	*BOSTON HERALD*
8/18/42	"nearness to the foul line"	"barely penetrated the stands"
4/20/46	"into the second or third row"	"a few feet . . . fair"
8/08/46	"three feet inside the foul pole"	"into the right field . . . grandstand"
6/11/50	"into the right field pavilion"	(no specifics)
6/18/51	"a good way beyond the foul pole"	"into the right field grandstand"
8/02/51	"into the right field grandstand"	"into the right field stands"

Six home runs, eleven accounts from a pair of reputable newspapers . . . and not one mention of a baseball *actually hitting a pole*. So the reported origin of "Pesky's pole"? It's a myth. But how did the myth begin?

Pesky was not a particularly small man. At five feet, nine inches and 170 pounds, he was right around average for a ballplayer of his era. But as we've seen, Pesky didn't have much power, only seventeen career homers. (After Pesky's first home run in 1951, the next day's *Globe* referred in jest to "his annual homer.") Given his lack of power, just about the only chance the left-handed-hitting Pesky had for a home run at Fenway Park was to hit a line drive or foul ball down the right-field line, because of course the fence angles out sharply from the corner.

The accounts are clear about this: Pesky never hit a home run into the center-field bleachers, and he never hit one over The Wall in left field. So all six of his Fenway Park homers did land in the right-field seats, which means, by definition, that they didn't come *far* from hitting the pole.

So again, how did the myth begin? Here's what Pesky told Bill Nowlin: "When [ex-Red Sox pitcher] Mel Parnell was here working with Coleman and Martin, broadcasting, there was a ball hit down the right field line, and I guess it won a ball game. Parnell comes on as the jock and he says, 'Johnny hit a few home runs down there. As a matter of fact, he hit a home run to win a ball game for me.' That's how that name began. They started calling it Pesky's Pole. I don't know how long they're going to keep doing that. It's very flattering."

Good story. It does not, however, fit the facts.

Of Johnny Pesky's six Fenway home runs, only one came in a game pitched by Mel Parnell. On June 11, 1950, Pesky hit a two-run shot in the first inning. Parnell started that game for the Sox, but lost when Tigers right fielder Vic Wertz hit a three-run homer in the *fourteenth* inning.

And that was it. So either Pesky's story is off, or Parnell's memory was off. Either way, the mystery lives.

Anyway, Jefferies's brush with Pesky's Pole represented Detroit's only damage in the first inning tonight, but the Tigers scored another run in the second, and then five more in the third to drive Ramon from the mound. Meanwhile, Tigers right-hander Hideo Nomo was befuddling Sox hitters with his made-in-Japan windup and his downward-diving change-up; after five innings, the Tigers led 7–0. The Sox, thanks to the typical great bullpen work, did mount a comeback, but fell short in the eighth when both Daubach and Stanley struck out on full counts, with runners aboard. Final score: Tigers 7, Red Sox 5.

Tuesday, May 23

A few weeks ago, Dave Daley, a writer from the *Hartford Courant,* contacted me about doing a story. I suggested that we attend a Red Sox game, figuring it would be good for the story and I'd be at the ballpark anyway, so it'd save me an hour or whatever. Dave was thrilled, we picked the game . . . and then I utterly, completely forgot about the whole thing.

Yesterday I got a call from Carrie Kreiswirth, who's been running the publicity campaign for *Baseball Dynasties* (the book I recently coauthored with Eddie Epstein).

"So did you and Dave get everything worked out for the game tomorrow night?"

Huh?

"Yup, we're all set." No reason to admit a mistake if you don't have to, right?

A few minutes later, I got an e-mail from Dave. I had sort of assumed that he would call the Red Sox PR department for tickets, and he had sort of assumed that I would call the Red Sox PR department for tickets. So now it's the day before the game, and we don't know how we're getting into the ballpark.

Two tickets together? For a Pedro Martinez start? Fuhgeddaboutit.

On the day of a Red Sox game, especially one like this, the sidewalks around the Sox ticket office are crawling with ticket scalpers, many of them young white men with lithe bodies and short haircuts, looking like they were honorably discharged from the army a few weeks ago. The thing about scalpers is, you don't have to find them, they'll find you. Just walking past the ballpark going about my daily business, I was greeted with "Ay, need tickets?"

Three times.

And if you talk to one scalper, others quickly converge, like crows around a discarded McDonald's bag. I found this out early in the afternoon, when I finally got up my courage and actually went shopping for tickets. This time when a young man asked, "Ay, need tickets" I stopped walking and said, "Yeah, you got anything good?"

"These ah, these ah great seats, should go fer a buck and a quawtuh but you can have 'em fer a buck apiece."

A quawtuh is twenty-five bucks, a buck is a hundred.

Hey, what's a couple of bucks when the greatest pitcher on the planet is going for the Sox?

Only problem was that my new buddy—I'll call him "Kevin"—didn't have the tickets yet. According to Kevin, they were being FedExed from a season-ticket holder in Providence, and they'd be showing up downtown, at South Station, in half an hour. Kevin's boss, a guy named "Tommy," would be going down to pick them up, and did I want to ride along?

Half an hour with a real-live ticket scalper, riding around in a Cadillac on a sunny day? Sounded like fun to me. Because I love these guys, I really do. I mean, on one level they sicken me, because typically their motivation is simple. They want to buy tickets for the lowest price they can, and then sell them for the highest price they can. And if a few lies are told in the process . . . well, sometimes the truth is less important than making a living.

My old man is a born salesman. When he sold cars, sometimes I would hang around the dealership and listen to him and his buddies talking about various schemes that had or hadn't worked out, and I wished I were personable enough, *clever enough*, to be a part of that world. I've seen *Glengarry Glen Ross* five or six times, and I'll probably see it another five or six times because salesmen, forced to make a living with their wits and their mouths, put themselves on the line every damn day. It's not an easy life, and I'm inclined to forgive them their occasional deceits.

Deep down, I suppose I'm drawn to salesmen, especially good ones, because I envy their ability to hide their insecurities and plow through life like they own the world. And also because they seem so different. For me, it's something like hanging around with an African pygmy. Or a Martian.

When Kevin introduced me to Tommy, I could tell that he'd just as soon not have the company, but I was already in the car, and there wasn't really a graceful way for him to get rid of me, given that I'd be forking over two hundred bucks in a few minutes. So off we went, and after a few minutes of chitchat about the weather and his kids, I asked Tommy about what really interested me: his business . . .

In Tommy's world, there are no scalpers. Rather, there are brokers, there are hustlers, and there are diggers.

As near as I can tell, brokers are the guys who actually spend some of their days in the office, and run advertisements in the newspapers. You won't get any surprises from a broker. Call three of them, and they'll quote you essentially the same prices for the same tickets. And don't bother trying to haggle with a broker; this ain't the market scene from *Life of Brian*.

Hustlers are different. They're generally licensed as brokers, too—for tax reasons, if nothing else—but you won't find a hustler sitting behind a desk. Hustlers are out on the streets, doing just that. Tommy's sort of the king of the hustlers around Fenway Park, the younger guys clustered around him like worker bees around the queen (and yes, this simile would work a hell of a lot better if Tommy were a woman, which reminds me that I have *never* seen a woman scalping tickets).

And those younger guys, they're the diggers. They're the ones who prowl the sidewalks around Fenway for hours before every game, looking to (mostly) buy until perhaps ten or fifteen minutes before the first pitch, at which point they're all sell. (Kevin's a digger, though from what I can tell he outranks the rest of the diggers who work for Tommy.)

Of course, Tommy's business mostly involves cash transactions, no receipts asked for or given. I asked him about the IRS.

"Hey, does a waitress report all the money she makes in tips?"

I had to allow that no, most of them don't.

"Don't get me wrong, I pay my taxes. I like to do my part like anybody else. It makes me feel good to pay 'em, you know what I'm sayin'? But I got a wife and two kids, I got a mortgage, I gotta pay insurance. There's just a lotta stuff."

Hey, who am I to judge? I'm sure I forgot to report a few hundred bucks that I won betting against the Vikings last year.

While this conversation was going on, two other things were happening. One, Tommy answered maybe a dozen calls on his cell phone. And two, like any good hustler would, he tried to work me. Something about having promised my tickets to somebody else, and maybe I'd have to give them back, and take a pair not quite as good. Of course, he never actually came out and told me to give them back, just a bunch of hints. I didn't say a word to any of this, and eventually he gave up. I guess possession is nine-tenths of the law, even when you're dealing with the lawless.

You hang around with these guys, and you wonder if they're ever "off." Do they ever stop talking fast, and recalculating the best angle every few seconds? I suppose you'd have to ask one of their wives or girlfriends, but I don't suppose I'll have that chance anytime soon.

Tommy dropped me off three blocks from my apartment with a "Seeya later, buddy," and nary a glance backward. And that's the story of how Dave Daley and I wound up with a pair of tickets in the seventh row behind the Red Sox dugout. And before we find out how Pedro Martinez actually lost a baseball game, here's a story that Dave shared with me . . .

"In 1979, my dad took my brother and me to Fenway Park for the first time. Royals against the Red Sox. I grew up in Hartford and, like my dad, my brother and I were Yankee fans. But on the way to the ballpark, Dad told us we couldn't cheer, couldn't boo, had to wear neutral caps, everything. Fine, dad. We kept our mouths shut. But there was a little kid near us, over in the grandstand behind third base, and he was waving a Yankees pennant around. Well, these guys sitting a few rows behind him, they were going through beer like it was water, and for some reason they had a bunch of balloons. And one of them made a water balloon . . . but with urine. And then he threw it at the kid. I will never forget the stench and the ugliness."

Neither will I, and I wasn't even there.

Okay, about Pedro. He just didn't have it tonight, "it" being what we expect from him. The first two Blue Jays singled, and one of them eventually scored on a wild pitch, Pedro's first of the season. He gave up a couple more singles in the third, and again one of them resulted in a run, this time scoring on a sacrifice fly. Tony Batista led off the third with a homer down the left-field line, giving the Jays a 3–1 lead. Pedro pitched brilliantly after that, but to no avail as the Sox could scrape together just one more run the rest of the way, stranding far too many runners.

Fenway Moment: Blue Jays closer Billy Koch throws as hard as anybody in the game, regularly hitting the upper nineties on the speed gun and occasionally reaching three digits. With the Jays clinging to a 3–2 lead, Koch came in to pitch the ninth. Varitek led off and struck out, but Donnie Sadler and Jose Offerman followed with singles. John Valentin fouled out to the catcher, leaving Trot Nixon for the hero's role. He couldn't play that role, though, grounding the ball right back to Koch. And Koch did something strange. Rather than make the easy toss to his first baseman, Koch sprinted over himself and touched the base to retire Nixon, then pumped his fist in exhilaration.

To which a fan near me responded, at the top of his lungs, "Fuck you, Billy Koch, you fucking faggot!"

Wednesday, May 24

Yesterday in his wildly popular ESPN.com column, Peter Gammons wrote about Fenway Park, the prospects for a new ballpark in Boston . . . and my adopted neighborhood, the Fenway. Here's a sampling of that column:

> The walk the last block up Brookline Avenue to the Fens Saturday morning was a sad reminder of a street gone to seed. . . . There were pizza crusts, condoms, a scattered pile of rock club leaflets, a doughnut, a couple of moldy hot dogs, a pool of vomit . . .
>
> "If the Boston media walked this block every day, they wouldn't be making fun of New York," said a . . . graduate student walking west on the street. . . . Honestly, compare this to Yankee Stadium."
>
> "It is far cleaner," I replied, "around The Stadium."

Frankly, I was offended by some of the things that Gammons wrote. I walk a route past Fenway Park every day, too. And if the streets around Fenway Park really are worse than those in the Bronx, around Yankee Stadium, then I need to have a CAT scan, because that's not what I'm seeing at all. So today, without mentioning Gammons by name, I wrote a column in response . . .

> A year ago, I could not have commented with any particular intelligence on the plight of Fenway Park. A year ago, I lived eight miles from Safeco Field in Seattle, and I used my Mariners season tickets semi-nightly.
>
> That was a year ago. Today, I live four blocks from Fenway Park, and I'm at the park every day the Sox are. So I've seen twenty-three games at Fenway (including three last season), and in the last seven weeks I've talked to scores of baseball fans who grew up loving their Sox. And with the exception of one courageous holdout, every one of those Sox lovers is ready for a new ballpark. Most people will talk about the uncomfortable seats, and if you spend much time in the grandstand, you'll know exactly what they mean.

But do the Red Sox, as so many claim, "need" a new ballpark? Of course they don't. In my mind, to suggest such a thing is fairly preposterous. This season, thanks to the highest ticket prices in all the land and a rabid fan base, the Red Sox boast the seventh-highest payroll in baseball, and the third-highest in the American League. They don't have a particularly lucrative TV deal, but given that Boston is the sixth-biggest media market in the country, I suspect they'll do quite well with their next deal. True, the Red Sox might fall behind as other new ballparks are built, but it's also true that, at least to this point, Sox fans have shown a limitless ability to pony up for tickets. (And by the way, don't think ticket prices will be stabilized by a new ballpark. It doesn't work that way, despite what John Harrington might tell you.)

The Red Sox ranked sixth in American League attendance last year, and will likely do a bit better this year. There are, to be sure, some lousy seats in the place . . . but it's funny, there are fannies in those lousy seats nearly every afternoon or evening. Why? Because Fenway Park is *Fenway Park*, and that's not something you can duplicate with a new building.

Still, the Red Sox and a fair percentage of their fans are sure that they need a new ballpark. The supposed reasons run to the double digits, but what it always comes down to is, "We can't *compete* without a new ballpark."

That's code for, "We can't compete with the *Yankees* without a new ballpark." Yes, even this debate revolves around the Bronx Bombers.

Fenway Park holds 33,455 baseball fans; Yankee Stadium holds 57,546. Metropolitan Boston ranks as the sixth-biggest media market; New York is *the* biggest. Boston is the educational capital of this country, if not the world; New York is the financial capital of this country, if not the world. (And you know which of those comes first in the hearts and minds of most Americans.) We could continue on in this vein, but you get the point.

When it comes to New York, nearly everybody east of the Sierra Mountains has an inferiority complex, but New Englanders got it bad. The truth is that if it meant beating the damn Yankees, most Red Sox fans would happily fork over Old Ironsides to the British, give up their funny accents for a year, and welcome a decade's worth of Nor'easters all in one brutal February.

But at the risk of sounding like an arrogant carpetbagger, I would argue that sometimes the fate of local environments shouldn't be left in the hands of the locals. Ask people who live in the Cascades about old-growth forests, and they'll try to hug you with a chainsaw in one hand and a toy logging truck in the other. Ask Alaskans about offshore oil drilling on the North Slope, and they'll present you with a framed photograph of James Watt shaking hands with Ronald Reagan. Which is to say that sometimes those closest to the situation have little in mind but self-interest. And short-term self-interest, at that. Sad to say, it's probably just human nature.

Am I suggesting that the good people of Massachusetts can't be trusted with the decision on the ballpark? Nope. I'm just saying that Fenway Park is bigger than Boston or Massachusetts or New England. Fenway Park belongs to every baseball fan who thinks the game on the field is more important than a nice view of the city skyline, more important than the number of flush toilets on the premises.

I guess what frustrates me about all the "information" churned out by the propaganda machine, not to mention the columns written by Boston sportswriters, is that it contains so much *noise*. When you're writing about the deficiencies of Fenway Park, don't mention the bathrooms; you wouldn't want to eat supper in one of them, but they're better than what you'll find in most gas stations. Don't complain about the concession lines; they're shorter than what you'll find in some of the gleaming new mallparks. Don't worry about the dugouts and locker rooms; last I checked, the Red Sox weren't having all that much trouble signing players. Don't tell us it's about economic development; any economist not in the employ of a baseball team will tell you that a new baseball stadium adds little or nothing to the local economy. And please, do not curse the neighborhood around Fenway Park, *my* neighborhood. I walk the streets of that neighborhood every day, and I can tell you that they're not so bad at all. And on a game night, those streets are alive with all kinds of wonderful sights and sounds, sights and sounds unique to a neighborhood ballpark in a big city.

This is, in the end, about one thing: making enough money from rich people to keep up with the Joneses. Or, more specifically, the Yankeeses and Orioleses. And you make money from rich people by building them luxury suites and field-level seats, while squeezing out the little guy and the medium guy. For better or worse, that's baseball in the twenty-first century.

So yes, Fenway Park will be gone sometime soon. After a few days or months or years of their usual shenanigans, the politicians will make it happen. In the meantime, I strongly suggest that you walk, run, or fly to Boston sometime in the next four or six years. Because once it's gone, it's gone forever.

That column resulted in a huge amount of e-mail, e-mail characterized by an immense amount of passion. I took an informal poll, just reading through all of the messages I received, and here are the results:

Red Sox fans who want to destroy Fenway: 45
Red Sox fans who want to save Fenway: 31
Baseball fans who want to save Fenway: 26

Below, are a few of the more interesting comments from those messages, absent any editorial comment. . . .

"I read your column about Fenway. Being a native Bostonian living in Cambridge, I must ask this question: Can you give me the number of your crack dealer? Mine just got busted."

"Excuse me for being rude, you pompous arrogant blowhard. You live in Boston for four months and you think you can speak intelligently about what motivates Bostonians?"

"The simple fact is that any fan of the Red Sox who has seen Camden Yards in Baltimore knows that Fenway needs to be replaced."

"I have always believed that everyone is entitled to his opinion . . . until now. Your article is based on no fact, lacks logic and is riddled with lies. Anyone who has attended a game at both Fenway Park and Camden Yards absolutely cannot make the argument that Fenway Park is an adequate ballpark."

"As we say in Boston, "Hey Neyah, your idea is wicked stupid." Your article reminds me of the tourist visiting the poor village; rallying against their cultural advance because it might ruin your island getaway."

And now, the minority opinion, Sox fans who still love Fenway Park and think the old girl's got a few good years left in her . . .

"I'm marking today down in my calendar: May 24, 2000. The first time I've agreed with your column."

"I wrote a forty-page paper on stadium economics during my senior year in college and the one thing that I'd like convey to people is that for every point they can think of that makes financial sense to build a new ballpark . . . there's at least one rebuttal that dismisses the initial point."

"I'm just starting to love you more and more. I'm a fourteen-year-old girl living in Virginia. However, my dad and all his family are from Boston, and I am very proud to say that I highly oppose a new park . . . I realize that sometime or another a new park will be needed, but right now I think the idea sucks."

That's a fairly representative sample, though of course I selected those words that made me laugh, or cry, or laugh and cry. What amused me most about the mail was that a bunch of people essentially wrote, "If only you were really from Boston, you would *know* that we need a new ballpark." Yet, strangely enough, a number of people who *are* really from Boston do think that Fenway should somehow be saved.

I do suspect that some people missed the point of the column, in which I was *not* suggesting that Fenway Park should live forever. Frankly, I don't have any idea if the interior structure will survive another decade. And I don't *know* if it's possible for the Red Sox to survive, financially, in the long run if they don't move. No, my point is that we're not getting good information on these issues. The Red Sox are churning out propaganda, which is nothing less than you'd expect. Unfortunately, a hefty percentage of the media in Boston is parroting the same propaganda, and that disturbs me. (I should say, too, that the Save Fenway Park people aren't above a little propaganda of their own.)

Frankly, at this early point in my New England residency, I consider myself smack-dab in the middle of this debate. I just want good information, but I fear that I'm not getting much of it these days.

Fenway Park is going to be with us for at least a few more years. So it's too early for eulogies or elegies or any other gies. I'm in the middle of writing a book about this season, from the perspective of a guy who loves the game. Nothing lasts forever, much as we might wish otherwise. I'm going to focus most of my attentions this season on the things that make me happy, and the thought of losing the American League's last great ballpark isn't one of them.

◆ ◆ ◆

As if on cue, the Red Sox worked some magic at Fenway Park this evening, magic that simply wouldn't have been quite as entrancing had it come in a twenty-first-century mallpark.

Jeff Fassero started for the Sox, and pitched six shutout innings. In the seventh, though, he gave up three straight hits to start the inning, and all three of the resulting base runners eventually scored. That tied the game at three, as the Sox had scored three times in the first three innings, thanks to Toronto starter Kelvim Escobar's profligate wildness (five walks). Both starters were gone by the eighth inning, and the bullpens took over. That's about when the rains came, and before the ninth could get underway, the umpires ordered the field covered.

I went home to work on tomorrow's column, figuring I could jog back to the ballpark when the skies cleared enough for more baseball. No sooner had I booted up my computer, however, than one of my best friends called. She was going through something of a personal crisis and wanted to know if I could talk.

"Yeah, but I have to warn you, I might have to hang up on you, real sudden-like."

That didn't go over so well, but I explained the situation at Fenway to her satisfaction, and so we got to talking. The whole time, I had the TV turned to NESN, the station broadcasting the game. But I guess I got a little careless, because when I finally hung up the phone after a bit more than thirty minutes and looked at the screen, there was Rheal Cormier finishing his warm-up tosses!

At that moment, I seriously considered watching the rest of the game on TV. After all, besides still being somewhat damp outside, it was cold. And I had a lot of work ahead of me tonight. While I was deliberating, Cormier got a couple of quick outs . . . and that's when I decided to jog back to Fenway Park, thinking to myself, *Jeez Rob, are you out of your thick skull? What if the Sox hit a walk-off homer in extra innings or something?* Actually, I sprinted, so I was out of breath when I reached Gate D . . . where a gatekeeper refused to let me inside the ballpark without a ticket stub. C'mon, man. *It's after eleven o'clock, there are probably five hundred people still here, and you're not gonna let me in?* That's what I was thinking, but I didn't argue much at all, just don't have it in me. Instead, I did what I always do; I avoided confrontation and looked for a back door. Or, in this case, another gate. And Gate A was wide open, so I trooped back inside to find Jays on first and second base. But Cormier escaped the jam, getting Alex Gonzalez on a foul to first baseman Brian Daubach.

In the bottom of the ninth, Daubach came up with two outs and a runner on first base, and hit an absolute rocket to the outer reaches of right field. But the outfielders were playing deep, and Raul Mondesi hauled in Daubach's drive at the base of the fence.

The tenth inning passed uneventfully, both clubs gaining a base runner, but neither of them reaching second base. Same story for the Jays in the eleventh. And then, the home half . . . Donnie Sadler struck out looking. Jose Offerman walked on a full count, but John Valentin popped to second base. Trot Nixon batted next, and when Nixon shot a line drive foul, Offerman injured himself running to second base, and was replaced by Manny Alexander. Then Nixon singled, chasing Alexander to second. As for what happened next . . . Well, I will always treasure the memory of Brian Daubach's walk-off home run, the white sphere describing its arc through the humid night sky before just clearing the Green Monster, and settling into the netting. Say what you want about Fenway, but that moment would not have been the same anywhere else in the world.

◆ ◆ ◆

After the game, I was supposed to meet up with Dan Shulman and Buck Martinez, TV broadcasters for the Blue Jays. Dan e-mailed me a few weeks ago, just to say that he enjoyed my work, and I responded with an invitation to dinner the next time he was in Boston. And he said he'd try to bring Buck Martinez, a catcher with the Royals in the 1970s who now works as Shulman's broadcasting partner.

So tonight was supposed to be the night, but I had no idea if those guys would show up at Pizzeria Uno (just down Brookline Avenue from Fenway), given that the game didn't end until just after midnight. But sure enough, Dan and Buck showed up a few minutes after 12:30, and both were as friendly as can be.

I brought along a book, *Moments, Memories, Miracles*, published in 1992 to celebrate the twenty-fifth anniversary of the Kansas City Royals (yes, the book was published a year or two early; the Royals played their first game in 1969). When it came out, my mom bought me this copy, and got it signed by Frank White, Paul Splittorff, and John Mayberry, a few of the guys from the late 1970s Royals who were always getting beat, generally in particularly heartbreaking fashion, by the Yankees in the playoffs. Anyway, I thought it would be fun to have Buck, a Royal from 1969 through '77, add his signature to the others.

At the same time, it was a little embarrassing. I'm almost thirty-four years old, and ostensibly I'm a professional journalist and something of a colleague (in addition to his work for the Blue Jays, Buck's an ESPN employee). So I tried to cover for myself. As I pulled out the book, I said, "Buck, I hope you don't mind, but I know my mom would be thrilled if you could sign this book for me."

I shouldn't have worried.

Buck snatched the book from my hands, but not due to excitement about adding his signatures to the others. No, instead he wanted to reminisce, flipping through the pages and looking for photos in which he appeared. It was touching, watching the joy in his face with each new discovery. You might think that old ballplayers get tired of reliving the glory days, but most of them don't. I have seen, many times, ex-ballplayers retelling stories that they've been telling for fifty years. And reveling in the retelling.

Buck is certainly more successful as a broadcaster than he was as a major-league baseball player, but after getting back to my apartment, I spent a few minutes leafing through that book about the Royals. And on page 116, I found this testament to the competitive fire that burned—and, if tonight was any indication, still does burn—within Martinez . . .

> You'll recall that in the mid-'70s, several key Royals run producers like George Brett, Hal McRae and Al Cowens all had adopted a hitting style taught by hitting coach Charlie Lau. Each of them stood as deep as possible in the batter's box and dove into the pitch. Well, [groundskeeper George] Toma helped out by laying out the lines for both batter's boxes about two inches further from the mound than actually was allowed. Nobody noticed, until catcher Buck Martinez was traded from the Royals to Toronto and promptly blew the whistle the first time the Blue Jays came to town.

Buck is, after all these years, still a competitor. I suspect that he longs for his younger days, when how well he did his job—catching, throwing, hitting—was the greatest determining factor in his career. In his current job, it's as much about politics as ability. And I could tell, after throwing out for discussion the names of a few of his peers, that Martinez believes he could broadcast any of them under the table. It's refreshing to see such intensity in a man who's fifty-one years old, gives hope to all of us who can't hit a fastball or stick a jumper anymore, but still feel like doing something with our lives.

Thursday, May 25

Tonight's game itself was interesting if you like slugfests, but the Sox were never really in it. The Blue Jays hit three home runs in the first five innings, led 6–2 at that point. They made it 10–2 in the seventh, which made the Sox comeback efforts moot.

There was, however, one last shot for a bit of drama. In the top of the third, Blue Jays left fielder Shannon Stewart blasted a two-run homer into the center-field bleachers. After walking in the fifth (and eventually scoring), Stewart doubled to lead off the seventh (and scored yet again). No big deal. But the Jays batted around in the seventh, so Stewart led off again in the eighth, and hit a slicing liner toward the right-field corner. Donnie Sadler, making his first-ever start in right field, gave chase, but the ball got by him. A fan reached out and grabbed the ball, and the umpire sent the speedy Stewart to third base, judging that he'd have advanced that far absent the interference (most fans think such a play automatically results in a double, but the umpires do have discretion in these cases).

So all of a sudden, Stewart was just one hit away from the cycle. And he already had the three tough ones. Time was against him, though, which left me to root, for the first time this season, against the Red Sox. Because if, after Stewart's eighth-inning triple, just three more Blue Jays could reach base—double plays notwithstanding—then he would bat again. And maybe I'd get to see something I've never seen before.

The next two hitters made out, but Carlos Delgado singled to plate Stewart with Toronto's eleventh run (and Stewart's fourth). Tony Batista grounded into a fielder's choice to end the inning. Batista was batting fifth in the lineup, Stewart first. So if two Blue Jays reached base in the ninth, Stewart would get his chance.

Todd Greene led off the ninth and flied to Everett in center. But Darrin Fletcher tripled! One more base runner!

Jose Cruz followed with a high fly to medium-depth center field. Looked like a routine play to me, and with the slothful Fletcher on third base, I couldn't imagine that he'd try to tag up and try to score.

I was wrong. Fletcher did indeed tag up, and he did indeed try to score.

I couldn't believe it. You've got a seven-run lead, and your first-string catcher is barreling toward a likely collision at the plate? Anyway, Fletcher was out, thanks to a solid throw from Nixon. The inning ended, as did our chance of seeing something memorable.

Toronto's number-nine hitter, Alex Gonzalez, is not a good hitter. With a left-handed pitcher on the mound, the probability of Gonzalez reaching base would have been roughly 30 percent. Next up would have been Stewart, and the probability of him hitting a single would have been approximately 25 percent. Combine those probabilities, and we might conclude that Fletcher's bizarre base running cost Stewart a 7 percent chance of hitting for the cycle, something that's been done just once before in the club's twenty-four-season history.

Friday, May 26

I don't care what anybody says, there is no rivalry on the face of the earth that can compare with the Yankees vs. the Red Sox. Something special happens when these two teams meet—a certain shiver in the air as the home team comes racing out onto the field that turns their uniforms whiter against the greener grass.

—Ed Linn, *The Great Rivalry: The Yankees and the Red Sox, 1901–1990*

Tonight, the Red Sox grabbed first place, beating the Yankees 4–1 thanks largely to Ramon Martinez, who came into the game with an ugly 6.95 ERA but permitted just one run in seven and two-thirds innings.

Today, I lost my scorebook.

I've been thinking about this book as an annotated version of my scorebook. So without anything to annotate, I'm in trouble. True, I can buy another scorebook, but there were twenty-two games in there, twenty-two games that I hadn't necessarily finished writing about. And I've got all sorts of notes scrawled in the margins. While I certainly can write this book without those twenty-two games, and all their attendant symbols and names and notes, I don't relish the prospect.

I started keeping score, as a regular thing, fifteen years ago. When Joe Hitter comes up in the seventh inning, it's nice to be able to see, at a glance, what he did in the first, third, and sixth innings.

But it goes deeper than that. Scorecards are my photo albums. *Actual* photo albums, I've got no use for. I've just never understood the impulse, when on a vacation, to take roll after roll of photographs that suffer badly in comparison to the vividness of my memories of what I saw. And if there's something that I think I'll want to see again, I buy a postcard; the light's always perfect, and whoever took the photo is certainly better at it than I am.

Baseball games are different, though. The beauty of the game is in the details. Here a double, there a strikeout, everywhere something to be recorded. I have seen hundreds of baseball games that I can't recall at this moment, but if I can find a scorecard for one of them, I can at least re-create the memories of being there. All of which is to say, if I'm at a ball game without a scorebook on my lap, I feel like a man sitting in front of a TV without the remote.

Typically, I'll buy the official scorecard sold by the team. Not because it's a great value or a particularly convenient format, but because the official scorecard is something of a historical artifact. A souvenir. Unfortunately, a fair number of teams don't sell stand-alone scorecards for a dollar or so. Rather, they sell programs for three or four dollars, with the same program sold for a number of games. Even more unfortunately, the Boston Red Sox is one of these teams. So what to do? This was the dilemma facing me before the season, and when Opening Day in Seattle rolled around, I still didn't have a solution.

Fortunately, Mike Curto, the radio voice of the Tacoma Rainiers, showed me his scorebook, and I knew I'd found exactly what I needed. Bob Carpenter, a broadcaster for both the St. Louis Cardinals and ESPN, designs and markets his own scorebooks. I went to his website, ordered one that holds a hundred games, and I had it in time for my fourth game at Fenway. It was this scorebook, then, in which I planned to record my first Yankee Stadium game tonight.

But this afternoon, while engaged in conversation with the fellow sitting next to me on the train, I stuffed this same scorebook into the seat pocket in front of me and completely forgot about it. So after pulling into Penn Station and disgorging me, the train continued on its way to Washington, D.C., and it took my scorebook along for the ride.

I do hope to see my scorebook again, though. My name and telephone number are writ large across the back cover, along with the promise of a reward. So we'll see. In the meantime, tonight I kept score in the most rudimentary fashion: in a notebook, like a man actually getting up every time he wants to change the channel.

Now, my first visit to Yankee Stadium.

Actually, I've been here once before. In 1991, Bill James and I traveled to New York for the annual convention of the Society for American Baseball Research. The Yankees were on the road, but I took the subway to the Bronx anyway, just to see the building. A gate down beyond the right-field corner was open. I could see a swath of the field but I wanted more, and so I took a couple of steps toward the inviting grass. Just a couple, because a beefy, blazered security guard suddenly materialized between me and the famous greensward.

"Where do you think you're going?"

"Uh, I just wanted to, uh, see the field."

"You can't do that."

And so ended my first Yankee Stadium experience.

Yesterday in my column, I described Fenway Park as "the last great ballpark in the American League." A few readers, presumably New Yorkers, wrote in to ask if I had somehow forgotten about Yankee Stadium. Let me tell you something. You take away the history, and Yankee Stadium doesn't even rank among the top ten or fifteen ballparks in the majors. It's just not a great place to see a game, not unless you've got great seats.

What a lot of people don't know is that while The Stadium's been around since 1923, what's there now bears very little resemblance to the original House That Ruth Built. In 1973 and '74, the Yankees played their home games at Shea Stadium, while Yankee Stadium was completely gutted and rebuilt.

Can you think of any great ballparks built in the 1970s? Royals Stadium opened in 1973, and it was the state of the art for its time, a relatively intimate, baseball-only stadium, with perhaps the best sight lines of any ballpark to that time, every seat facing second base. But while Royals Stadium contained 40,762 seats, the new Yankee Stadium, by necessity, contained 57,545 seats. And many of those 57,545 seats are far, far from the action.

I had one of those seats tonight. Upper Deck, Box 29, Row L, Seat 12.

Bob Sheppard, the Yankees' public-address announcer, has been performing his duties since 1950. The sound of his player introductions has been described as "the voice of God." But when you're sitting high up, *really high up*, in the upper deck, in the right-field corner, Bob Sheppard sounds like one of the adults in a Peanuts cartoon. I didn't have a program and I don't know which Yankees wear which numbers, so except for a few players with particularly distinctive batting styles—Bernie Williams and Paul O'Neill, for example—for most of the game I had no idea who was batting, because the relevant scoreboard, beyond the center-field fence, was not visible from our seats.

So I cannot endorse the upper deck, or at least not its nether regions. And here's another thing . . . I believe that the dominant color in any baseball stadium should be green, but in Yankee Stadium it's as if the club went out of its way to avoid green. Instead, everything is trimmed in blue. Lots and lots of blue. Hell, I think they'd paint the field blue if they could, and I'm sure that Steinbrenner is pissed that the Merion bluegrass that covers the field isn't actually blue.

In most ballparks, the hitting background—a rectangular space above and just beyond the center-field fence—is green: grass and/or a painted wall. In the old days, many ballparks featured bleacher seats in these spots, but that's no longer acceptable. The new ballparks all are built with solid hitting backgrounds, and the older parks have been retrofitted, Wrigley Field being perhaps the best remaining example.

Anyway, in Yankee Stadium the hitting background is black. Without checking, I would guess that Yankee Stadium is the only major league ballpark in which the color black plays any stylistic role at all. And frankly, it's unsightly, like a once-verdant meadow that has just been laid waste by a forest fire.

One neat thing about Yankee Stadium is its quirky spaces. There's an immense amount of foul territory behind home plate and up past the bases, but that foul territory shrinks to almost nothing roughly halfway into the outfield. You really can't get the full effect on TV, unless there's a blimp shot. Which, of course, is essentially what we had from high in the upper deck.

All of which is to say, I didn't much enjoy the game on the field. My companions, two lady friends, were lively, though, as were the dueling fans—Red Sox partisans chanting "Yang-kees suck!" met with "Nine-teen eigh-teen!" from the Yankee rooters.

Before the game, we took the subway from Manhattan, and not long after you come out of the ground, there's *The Stadium* as you look out the left side of the car.

The anticipation builds, and then you're *there*, at the planetary capital of twentieth-century baseball. It's a stirring experience, and I wouldn't want to arrive at the ballpark any other way.

The train ride from Yankee Stadium to Manhattan *after* the game, though, was something else. First of all, you're packed in your car with scores of baseball fans, most of them pulling for the Yanks but a fair number of Sox fans, too. And they're chanting, the same stuff that we heard in the ballpark, but of course louder since we're in this relatively tiny, enclosed space.

One thing I noticed, the great majority of Yankee fans listened to the Red Sox fans with little apparent rancor, and when we were on the subway I asked a Yankees fan about this.

"That stuff doesn't bother us," he replied, "because we know we'll win."

"You think so? With Pedro pitching Sunday, the Sox have a pretty good shot at winning the series."

"Tomorrow, Sunday, it doesn't matter. In the end, we'll win."

After thinking about it, I realized that he was right. The Yankees probably will win, because they have (arguably) the better front office and (inarguably) virtually unlimited financial means. The Yankee fans, knowing they've got the upper hand, were humoring the Sox fans, like parents chuckling at the silly jokes of their eight-year-old daughter.

Standing there in the subway car, I realized that the 4 train (or the D train) after a big game is perhaps the only place in New York where one can get the same vibe that comes with attending a game at Fenway Park. And that's not a criticism; in the great majority of cities, there's *nowhere* to find that atmosphere, at least not around a baseball game. This particular vibe is the result of jamming passionate people into a space that's slightly too small, and you're just not going to find it anywhere but Boston and New York.

Sunday, May 28

The best game of the season (so far, at least), and I almost missed it. Or at least, I almost missed the beginning of it. My plan was to reach Yankee Stadium approximately half an hour before the first pitch, the better to soak up the pre-game atmosphere. Unfortunately, I . . .

Got on the Number 6 train in lower Manhattan.

Didn't know the 6 doesn't go to Yankee Stadium.

Didn't know I needed to get off at 125th Street and transfer to the 4 train.

I realized my error about three stops too late, and detrained at the Cypress Avenue stop, intending to simply hop a train going in the other direction back to 125th. I suppose a lot of people, even battled-toughened New Yorkers, will tell you that jumping off the subway at any ol' stop in the East Bronx isn't the wisest decision in the world, but hey, we're talking about Pedro and the Rocket here. Took the stairs two at a time up to street level, spent maybe three seconds looking for a taxi—perhaps I should have spent a few more seconds considering the plight of the urban poor, *but goddammit the game starts in forty minutes*—and then I hustled across the street and back down below, to the opposite side of the tracks.

So at 7:30 there I sat, with a great ticket for the biggest game of the season in my pocket, waiting on a nearly deserted platform for a train, a train without a brain that hadn't a care in the world for my evening plans. I waited and I waited, and I waited some more, all the while with visions of the Rocket pitching in my head.

Of course, the train did show up. I didn't do anything else stupid. And thus, I arrived at the gates of Yankee Stadium at 7:58, plenty of time to spare. Still a bit confused about the seating plan, I consulted an usher down the right-field line. Now, if he'd wanted to get theatrical about things—this is, after all, New York—he could have nodded sagely and said, "I think you're going to enjoy your seat, young squire." Like the hotel bellman in *That Thing You Do*.

Instead, he simply pointed to the signs that denote the different sections, and then in the direction I needed to travel: toward the infield. And it took me only a few seconds of walking to realize that my seat would be found directly behind the Yankees dugout. There, in the fourth row, I found that seat, along with Andy, the Harvard law student who sent me my ticket. Andy's great, a Yankees fan since the mid-eighties who hasn't let his favorite team's incredible run of success get to his head. And it was nice to know that these great seats are often used by someone who knows the game, as opposed to the guy behind me who asked his buddy, "So where did Knoblauch come from?"

(Answer: Knoblauch came from the Twins early in 1998, in return for pitcher Eric Milton, shortstop Christian Guzman, outfielder Brian Buchanan, pitcher Danny Mota, and cash. Yeah, I had to look up the details, but anybody sitting in the fifth row for this game, of all games, should at least know that Knoblauch is an ex-Twin.)

It was nice, too, to know that Yankee fans aren't all obnoxious louts. I mean, I already knew that intellectually, but I've never actually sat down and watched a game with one of them. Let alone one of the best games anybody ever saw. Through the first eight innings, how many runners reached third base? One. With one out in the seventh, Trot Nixon tripled to left-center. The Yankee infield converged on the plate—a single run might be quite precious—but Clemens didn't need any help, striking out Brian Daubach (looking) and Nomar Garciaparra (swinging). That top of the seventh aside, there was little sustained drama involving the hitters in more than a bystanding way. But then, the ninth. Oh, the ninth . . .

What happened in the ninth inning could almost as easily happened in the seventh, or in the eighth. But it happened in the ninth, thus lifting tonight's proceedings from good game to *man, what a great game.*

John Valentin led off for the Sox, and tapped a grounder to Chuck Knoblauch. Knoblauch suffered a recurrence of the "yips" lately—the easiest throws to first base suddenly and inexplicably difficult—and he didn't play the first two games of the series. The Yankees said he was injured, and maybe he was. Anyway, Knoblauch completed this play in fine fashion, and was rewarded with not only an assist, but also a fairly rousing show of appreciation from his friends (for today, at least) in the stands. Jason Varitek tried to bunt his way on, but he didn't get the ball close enough to the third-base line, Clemens throwing him out with ease. Two outs, and at this point we're all beginning to wonder if morning baseball is in our future.

But then Clemens ran a pitch high and inside to Jeff Frye, who trotted toward first base after getting plunked . . . But no! Plate umpire Brian Runge is waving off the HBP, then pointing madly at Frye's bat on the ground, telling all of us that before the ball struck Frye, it struck his bat. Foul ball. Frye argued and Jimy Williams argued ("Siddown, Jimy!" one fan behind me screamed), but there was nothing to be done about it. Were this game scripted by some hack TV writers, Frye would have either followed up with a home run, or Clemens, granted the reprieve, would have registered his fourteenth strikeout.

Fortunately, real baseball games aren't scripted, and Frye meted out the best kind of justice, smashing a hot grounder right back to the box. Clemens could have made the play, perhaps *should* have made the play. But he did not make the play, and it is such fractions of inches that often determine victory. As these did. Because

Trot Nixon, he of the seventh-inning triple, batted next. And Nixon creamed one of Rocket's fastballs well into the right-field stands. Two-zip, Red Sox.

(Later, we learned that after Nixon struck out looking in the first inning, Clemens had screamed at him, "Swing the bat!")

Just a few seconds after Nixon's blast touched down, I turned around to look at the crowd. It seemed to me as if perhaps 20 percent of the people were cheering. This was, I suspect, due to a couple of things. One, a lot of people from Boston live in New York. And two, a lot of people from the Dominican Republic live in New York, and they'll pull for the Sox when Pedro is pitching.

Knoblauch led off the bottom of the ninth, and Pedro nailed him. Was it a coincidence that, just a few minutes earlier, Clemens had come inside on Jeff Frye? Does Pedro have so much confidence that he'd happily award the Yankees a base runner in the ninth inning of a 2–0 game? Nah, I don't think so. I think the ball just got away from him. And Knoblauch's a tough character, he probably enjoyed getting plunked. That brought up Jeter, who promptly singled to right field, Knoblauch stopping at second.

Out of the Red Sox dugout popped Jimy Williams, and I was so sure about what would happen next that, on my scorecard, I drew the line that denotes a pitching change. I had no good idea of Pedro's pitch count, but I estimated somewhere around a hundred, given that he'd run very few deep counts, and had faced only twenty-eight hitters to that point. He'd been a bit shaky lately, though, if Tino Martinez's long fly in the seventh and Ricky Ledee's longer fly in the eighth were any indication. What the Sox really needed was a double play, and Derek Lowe—ready to come in at a moment's notice—throws a heavy sinker that results in a lot of double plays.

Say what you want about him, but Jimy Williams is his own man. After a lengthy consultation with his battery, Williams shuffled back to his subterranean lair, never having unsheathed his right hand in the direction of the bullpen. It would be Pedro's game, and he responded by striking out Paul O'Neill with high heat. Next, Bernie Williams, and he shot a fly ball into the right-field corner. Initially, I thought it was gone, and part of me wanted it to be gone. Yeah, I was pulling for the Red Sox, but what a thing to see, a game-winning, three-run bomb in a contest between these ancient adversaries. Nixon flagged down the ball near the warning track, however, with Knoblauch tagging up and advancing to third.

That brought up Jorge Posada, and he missed Pedro's first two pitches by a couple of feet. One change-up and it's over, right? Ah, but this game wasn't prescripted. Posada took a ball. And then, impossibly, Martinez plunked him, too.

So here comes Tino Martinez with the bases loaded. A single probably ties the game, a double probably wins it, and a home run gets you the biggest celebration in the Bronx since last October. By this point, I was hoping for an out, or a home run. This game, it seemed to me, should be decided by the two starting pitchers. Plus, I was drained. After being on edge for eight-plus innings, Bernie's drive to the track had grabbed most of what emotional energy I had left.

I'll be honest with you, after three games at Yankee Stadium, I'm not in love with the place. Yankee Stadium is history: Babe Ruth and Joe DiMaggio and Mickey Mantle and Reggie Jackson, and of course all those World Series. The building itself, though, is not particularly distinguished.

Fenway Park is a *place*: The Green Monster and Pesky's Pole and Lansdowne Street. If a native of Alpha Centauri 4 came to Sol 3 for the express purpose of watching a couple of baseball games but knew nothing of the game's lore, Yankee Stadium would be just another ballpark, albeit a fairly rowdy one, at least in the upper deck. Take our alien to Fenway Park, however, and he'd likely fall in love with not only the building, but the game as well. (Of course, this assumes that he's a slender alien, otherwise he wouldn't fit into Fenway's seats.)

There is one thing that I do love about Yankee Stadium, though, and it's probably not something that you would guess.

I love the clock.

At the top of the scoreboard that's just to the left of straightaway center field, you may always find the time. And not just any old time, but the OFFICIAL TIME. I guess I'm a sucker, but I'm so much more impressed by something labeled "Official" than I would otherwise be.

The time of my life runs according to the baseball season, especially this particular baseball season. So there's the OFFICIAL TIME in big block letters, *my* official time, always available in one's field of vision, just like the pitcher and the hitter. And at 11:08 tonight, a game I'll never forget *officially* ended when Tino Martinez chopped a routine grounder to second baseman Jeff Frye, who—after waiting for Brian Daubach to find his footing, and then the bag—made the routine throw to first base. At 11:08 tonight, I was as happy to love this sport as I ever have been.

◆ ◆ ◆

Aside from the obvious, the difference between Yankee Stadium and Fenway Park is perhaps best exemplified by the relative accessibility to the best box seats, the ones closest to the field.

In Yankee Stadium, there are two levels of security to prevent any lesser-heeled fans from sneaking into the great seats. At the top of each section is an usher, spiffily attired in vest and tie. And these are, for the most part, young men and women in the prime of life (as opposed to the old codgers who haunt Fenway like so many Ghosts of Pennants Blown Past). Also at the top of each aisle is a chain, to prevent any non-accidental spillage.

And the security around the Field Box seats at Fenway? Don't make me laugh. There is no security. In fact, it's considered almost de rigueur to grab the best seats you can, and there are no limits. The ushers do absolutely nothing to discourage this practice, and in fact they sometimes seem almost apologetic when evicting someone. Instead of saying something like, "You're in the wrong seat," an usher is just as likely to say, "I need these two seats." It's a subtle difference, but telling. And the trespassers are not escorted away in shame, but rather are simply expected to find more empties in the vicinity. And sometimes the new seats are better seats. Earlier this season, I watched a married couple in their forties get kicked out of two seats in the fourth row . . . and they ended up sitting, one in front of the other, in the first and second rows, right behind the visitors dugout.

This will almost certainly change when the Red Sox move into their new park. Then, the best tickets will involve Personal Seat Licenses and three-figure face values, and the people who lay out that kind of dough won't enjoy seeing some interloper in their seats when they arrive.

Monday, May 29

Good news! When I got back to my apartment after taking the train from New York to Boston, I had a most welcome message waiting. A young man named Maurice, whom I chatted with for quite some time on the train to New York last Friday, retrieved my scorebook just before an Amtrak employee discarded it. Maurice works in Charlestown, and later this week I'll be able to pick it up at his office.

I'm a lucky guy.

Tuesday, May 30

How small is Fenway Park?

This afternoon, I went to the box office to pick up a ticket for tonight's game. A great one, too: Field Box 51 (as close to the plate as you can get without being behind the screen), Row M (extra legroom). And damned if I didn't run into somebody I know from Kansas.

Sat down a few minutes before the game, and thought the stocky, white-haired man two seats away looked familiar. He was entering the lineups on his scorecard, and I thought I'd sat near the same man, a month or so ago. It was early and there weren't many people around, so I figured I should make an effort to be friendly.

"You come to many games?"

"Yeah."

"Did I see you out here earlier this season, over in Box 71?"

"Nope, I'm in from Kansas City."

And then it hit me . . . *"Jim Carothers?"*

Sure enough, it really was Jim Carothers, an English professor at the University of Kansas. I took a class Jim taught, must have been thirteen years ago, called "The Literature of Baseball." Jim gave me a B in the class, but I did get an A- on my big paper, in which I analyzed Bernard Malamud's *The Natural* and Robert Coover's *The Universal Baseball Association: J. Henry Waugh, Prop.* It's lost to the ages now, but for a long time that paper was the only remnant of my academic "career."

I asked Jim if he still taught "The Literature of Baseball," and he responded with a pretty sad story. It seems that on the last day of class, he would bring in some of his favorite baseball memorabilia. But about ten years ago, something was stolen. Namely, a dinner menu, signed in the early 1950s by a number of Brooklyn Dodgers, including Jackie Robinson. The loss of that valuable family heirloom—his sister got the menu signed on a train—destroyed Jim's enthusiasm for the class, and he hasn't taught it since. People who love baseball tend to think that other baseball lovers are good people, and I suspect that Jim was shocked to find out that all of them aren't.

On a happier note, tonight Jim got his first baseball—a foul liner off the bat of Mike Stanley during batting practice (before I arrived)—at a major league game. As Jim told me this, I was reminded again of my good fortune in acquiring Nomar's foul ball back in early April (and while I know I should have resisted the urge to gloat, I couldn't help but tell Jim all about it).

Jim was fortunate to have finally found a baseball, and I was fortunate to have found a friend, as it would have been a miserable three hours if I'd been alone. The weather wasn't so bad, but Royals (and ex–Red Sox) starter Jeff Suppan was driven from the mound in the third, and the Sox cruised to an 8–2 victory behind Jeff Fassero, who ran his record to 6–1.

◆　◆　◆

With the Red Sox winning and the Yankees losing, the Sox increased their lead over the Yanks to one and a half games. Nevertheless, their pennant hopes took a small blow tonight. In the top of the second, Royals center fielder Carlos Beltran chopped an easy grounder toward third base. John Valentin set up to make the play . . . and collapsed, like he'd been shot. Initially, I thought he'd merely tripped, and I cheered a little as the ball rolled into left field and Beltran trotted to first base. My joy ended quickly, though, when I realized that Valentin wasn't getting up, and must be badly hurt.

He lay on the ground in obvious pain, eventually surrounded by teammates and trainers before being carried off the field atop a groundskeeper's cart. There was no definite word tonight on Valentin's injury, but I'll be surprised if he didn't tear a knee ligament (he supposedly heard a pop). If it's the anterior cruciate ligament, he's done for the season. And the pressure will only increase on the Sox to acquire a solid bat, because neither of Valentin's backups, Wilton Veras and Manny Alexander, can hit their weight.

Wednesday, May 31

I have never felt so miserable after a Royals victory. Hell, I can't remember *ever* feeling miserable after a Royals victory.

Entering the bottom of the eighth, my favorite team owned a 9–2 lead over my second-favorite team . . . and they came too damn close to blowing it. How? Well, Royals manager Tony Muser called on his former (and probably future) closer, a sore-armed right-hander named Ricky Bottalico. Royal fans have taken to calling him Ricky Blow-talico, because he's been horrible since signing with Kansas City before this season. He came into tonight's game with four saves, and four blown saves. Tonight did not, of course, represent a save situation, but he nearly blew it anyway, as the Sox scored seven runs in the eighth. When Troy O'Leary grounded out to (finally) end the inning—he had started the inning with a strikeout—the tying runner was on second base. And I was a lot more pissed off than relieved.

I know that sounds awful, but I should not have been put through the wringer like that. You take a seven-run lead into the seventh, and the tying run reaches second base? I was hoping for just one victory in this three-game series, and I got it . . . yet on my walk home from Fenway, rather than feeling happy about the Royals' win over a superior team, I was happy only because I'd be able to check my e-mail in a few minutes.

◆ ◆ ◆

Jimy Williams got busted tonight. Twice.

In the top of the second, with two Royals on (first and second bases) and two Royals out, Johnny Damon shot a liner down the right-field line, where it bounced once and kicked up toward the padding on the wall. And then it just sort of stopped, as if a fan had interfered. Both base runners scored, and Damon sprinted all the way to third base. Williams wanted the umpires to rule fan interference and send Damon back to second and one of the runners to third, but instead all he got, after a few minutes of vigorous protest, was an ejection.

Here's what the rulebook says about ejections:

> **4.07** When a manager, player, coach or trainer is ejected from a game, he shall leave the field immediately and take no further part in that game. He shall remain in the club house or change to street clothes and either leave the park or take a seat in the grandstand well removed from the vicinity of his team's bench or bullpen.
>
> If a manager, coach or player is under suspension he may not be in the dugout or press box during the course of a game.

The truth, of course, is that no manager is going to put on his street clothes and go sit with the fans in the grandstand. Rather, they hang out in the locker room, or even in the hallway leading to the locker room, and relay instructions to their coaches. What they *don't* do is admit this after the fact, because relaying instructions might easily be interpreted as taking "further part in that game."

Williams admitted it tonight, because he didn't want to leave bench coach Buddy Bailey, who theoretically was running the team, hung out to dry after the

Sox lost a close one. See, after the Sox batted in the seventh inning, Garciaparra and Everett came out of the game. Thus, they weren't available in the eighth when the Sox were mounting their improbable comeback. Varitek batted in Garciaparra's spot, and grounded out. Donnie Sadler batted in Everett's spot, and was hit by a pitch (as it happened, Bottalico's last pitch). After the game, Bailey was circumspect about his role in the decision to yank the stars, saying, "You keep in contact with the manager the best you can during the game," but Williams didn't mince words, saying the decision to remove Garciaparra and Everett was "made by me."

Last season, Mets manager Bobby Valentine was ejected from a game, then returned to the bench wearing a Groucho disguise. For that, he was fined $5,000 and suspended for two games. I think that Valentine got off far too lightly, but the precedent suggests that Williams might be suspended for one game, at most, and fined lightly. After all, this has been going on for a long, long time. As the late, great Leonard Shecter wrote in 1968, "It is a polite fiction of the sport that when a manager is thrown out of a game he ceases managing. In fact, he merely runs the game from some other vantage."

It's an interesting question. When, exactly, during a blowout do you take out your regulars, fall on your collective sword and save the stars for another day? After all, baseball's not a sprint, but a marathon.

Obviously, the answer depends on the score, the ballpark, the team you're playing, and the particular fragility of your star players. If I were Jimy Williams, I'd have done exactly what he (and/or Buddy Bailey) did tonight.

But as we all know, a seven-run lead ain't what it used to be.

Thursday, June 1

Last game of the Royals series, last game of the home stand. My seat was in Row NN, the last of the Loge Box directly up from the inside edge of the visitors' dugout, and at the top of a long aisle. And as I bounded up the steps just a few minutes before game time, I was happy to see that I'd be sitting close to a pair of Royals fans: Steve, the principal of a high school in northwest Missouri, and his son Nikos, who just graduated from college.

Steve was wearing a Royals hat, and Nikos was wearing a Royals hat *and* an official Royals jersey, the blue, "special" jersey that the club wears occasionally. I have one just like it, and when I saw Nikos wearing his, I suddenly regretted not wearing mine. And I didn't wear it because . . . well, because I think men look silly wearing jerseys, and by extension I must look pretty ridiculous wearing mine, too. It looks good on Nikos, but he's still a kid, twenty-two (and could easily pass for eighteen). The last time I wore mine was last September in Seattle, when the Royals were in town. My friend Kyle, also a Royals fan, and I sat in the left-field stands for batting practice, and Jeff Montgomery threw me a baseball.

But while I rarely wear my Royals jersey, sometimes—I feel like a fool, admitting this—sometimes I open the closet and trace my right index and middle fingers over the letters, the Royals written on the front in white satin (or at least something that feels like satin). At those moments, I lament the possible passing of the club, and I worry that someday I'll be left with nothing of my favorite team aside from memories and this jersey that never got dirty.

I've never really been the garrulous sort, but this season I've made some efforts to be a little more outgoing, if only because this book project fairly demands some level of interaction between me and the fans. This time it's easy, though, given the obvious common ground.

Steve, I was happy to learn, appreciates Fenway Park. Last night, he and Nikos, visiting Fenway (and Boston) for the first time, sat in the bleachers, and as Steve told me,"heard the f-word and the s-word more in one game than in all the games I've seen in Kansas City. So yeah, they may get kind of vulgar at times, but they do know their baseball here. I've been to Wrigley Field, but I like the atmosphere here better. I was in Chicago to see the Cardinals last year, and the fans stopped to watch the game when McGwire and Sosa hit, and they stopped to sing 'Take Me Out to the Ball Game.' The rest of the time, it's just drinking beer."

Steve wasn't drinking beer tonight, but he did get up to use the rest room in the third inning, so I started talking to Nikos. Turns out he desperately wants to work for a baseball team. "It's tough getting a job," Nikos said, "but I just can't imagine not being around baseball." I had Nikos write down his e-mail address for me, and promised to put him in touch with at least one of my acquaintances who work for major league clubs (and I did, too).

The three of us had a wonderful time together, thanks to a wild 13–11 Royals victory that saw our team score nine runs in the sixth, and then two runs in the eighth to break an 11–11 tie.

We were joined for the last few innings by Susan. I met Susan last week at the ballpark. At the conclusion of a recent ESPN.com column about Fenway Park, I mentioned where I would be sitting that evening and invited anyone who'd be at the game to stop by and say hello before the game. Seven or eight people did stop to chat, and Susan was one of them. She'd sent me a Royals-related e-mail a few days before, so after actually meeting her and determining that she wasn't some sort of nut, I figured maybe we could be friends.

Susan is pretty and she's a Royals fan, and that's a powerful combination. Let me tell you, sitting next to a curvy, brown-haired and brown-eyed woman while your favorite team is pounding the ol' horsehide leads to a wonderful sense of well-being, whether one senses a pennant contender and/or a hint of long-term compatibility or not. My evening with Susan, the guys, and the Kansas City Royals ranks, at this early stage of the season, behind only the Pedro-Rocket duel among my favorite experiences.

◆ ◆ ◆

Back near the beginning of this book, I testified to the long collective memory of Red Sox fans, and tonight I believe I found another, bizarre example of this.

In the bottom of the eighth, Ricky Bottalico got lit up by the Red Sox, just as he was last night. Jose Santiago trotted in to replace Bottalico . . . and was greeted with a smattering of boos. I asked a few people around me (and later, a few longtime Red Sox fans) why Santiago would elicit such a reaction, but nobody could tell me.

After getting home tonight, I think I figured it out.

In 1966, the Red Sox finished ninth in a ten-team league. But in 1967, they survived an incredible, four-team pennant race that wasn't decided until the season's final day, thus capturing their first American League title since 1946. The '67 season will forever be remembered as "The Impossible Dream."

Well, one of the key players for the '67 Sox was a Puerto Rican pitcher named Jose Santiago, who went 8–0 from July 15 through the end of the season.

Kansas City's Jose Santiago is also a native of Puerto Rico, but he's not related to Boston's Jose Santiago. And I think that the boos tonight were from Red Sox fans who thought, "How *dare* this young whippersnapper have the name of one of our heroes?"

That, Dear Reader, is a long memory.

Saturday, June 3

A beautiful afternoon in Boston, yet I'm glued to the television. Why? Because for the first time, Roger Clemens is pitching against Greg Maddux in a game that counts. Yes, finally something to like about interleague play. Here are the most relevant career numbers for the two pitchers:

	W-L	PCT	ERA	CY YOUNGS
CLEMENS	251–139	.644	3.05	5
MADDUX	228–127	.642	2.79	4

Clemens is No. 1 among active pitchers in victories; Maddux is No. 2. Clemens has won more Cy Young Awards than any pitcher in history; Maddux is right behind. You can jimmy around with the numbers all day long, but good luck trying to figure out which of the two has been the better pitcher. (Maddux's career ERA is significantly better than Clemens's, but of course that's because the former has done all his pitching in the DH-less National League, the latter in the DH-ful American.)

Alas, this matchup, unlike last Sunday night's in New York, didn't quite live up to its billing. Maddux came into this game with a 2.16 ERA for the season, second-best in the National League. But for the first time in his career, he allowed four straight hits to start the game, and had to pitch out of a serious jam just to escape, having permitted just two runs. He gave up three more hits, and another run in the second. Meanwhile, Clemens was even worse, and the Braves grabbed a 5–4 lead in the third on Brian Jordan's three-run homer.

The Braves wound up winning 11–7, neither Maddux nor Clemens figuring in the decision. Some pitcher's duel. But while Maddux might not have won, he did almost strike an accidental blow for Red Sox fortunes, fouling a ball off Yankee catcher Jorge Posada's right knee. Posada left the game with a bruised knee, but is expected back in the lineup Monday. (How bad was Maddux today? In journeyman Chris Turner's first at-bat after replacing Posada, he hit the fourth home run of his major league career.)

Whatever happens tonight in Philadelphia, the Red Sox will still have at least a share of first place when tomorrow dawns.

◆ ◆ ◆

I couldn't bring myself to watch the Sox on TV tonight. It's become painful for me to watch a baseball game played in Philadelphia's Veterans Stadium, what with the sickly green artificial turf, and the lines marking the football field clearly visible. I've been to the Vet, and I think it's the worst "ballpark" I've seen, somehow even worse than the Kingdome.

And it's even more painful for me to watch Tim Wakefield getting roughed up, which is what I've been expecting lately when he pitches. So instead I caught a movie, Woody Allen's *Small-Time Crooks.*

Woody's movies don't generally last long, and this one was no exception. When I got back home, the Sox and Phillies were only in the seventh. Plenty of time, unfortunately, for the Phils to take a 6–2 lead; as my crystal ball foretold, Wakefield did not pitch well. The final score was Phillies 9, Red Sox 3, leaving the American League East standings, as of midnight tonight:

	W-L	GB	RS-RA	PYTHAG W-L
RED SOX	29–22	—	278–201	33–18
YANKEES	29–22	—	246–230	27–24
BLUE JAYS	28–29	4	296–325	26–31
ORIOLES	23–30	7	265–296	24–29
DEVIL RAYS	18–36	12 ½	252–325	21–33

(Next time, by the way, I'll probably drop the bottom two teams from the standings, as it's unlikely they'll play much of a role in the future proceedings.)

It's June and the skies over New England are clear, at least for the moment, so I figure it's okay if we spice things up with a bit of sabermetrics. The fourth column in the table is simply the runs scored and allowed by each club. The fifth is a little trickier, but essentially it describes, thanks to something called the "Pythagorean method," the record of a *typical* team with those same runs scored and allowed totals. Now, I know that many of you will protest, *but the Yankees are not typical.* Everybody likes to think their favorite team is special, and in many respects, the Yankees are. But not in this particular respect. Any team, given a year or three, will eventually win almost exactly as many games as the Pythagorean method says it will.

Anyway, the big news here is that the Yankees are somewhat fortunate to be tied with the Red Sox, as the Sox have scored significantly more runs than their rivals *and* allowed significantly fewer.

There is, of course, a counterargument, which goes something like this: "Eventually, the Yankees will right their ship. And while they have perhaps been lucky to this point, they're in great position to really make hay once the hitting comes around." There's something to this argument, too. Perhaps the Yankees really are baseball's slumbering giants, and their good fortune to this point may well give them a springboard for another big run. After all, last year on June 3, the Yankees were just 30–21, a game and a half behind the Red Sox. And we know what happened next.

◆   ◆   ◆

Quickly, a brief note on the end of tonight's game in Philadelphia . . . With two outs in the top of the ninth, Darren Lewis hit a ground ball up the middle and was called out at first base by umpire Jim Joyce. Lewis—who should have been safe, if you believe the videotape—slammed his helmet to the ground and was ejected . . . from a game that had officially ended when Joyce called him out. This does happen occasionally, and I always wonder, what's the point?

Sunday, June 4

Tonight Carl Everett hit his nineteenth home run, a three-run shot in the third that put the Sox ahead of the Phillies, 5–0. A year ago on this date, when he was with the Astros, Everett had hit three home runs (he finished with twenty-five).

Everett, by the way, is something of a strange duck. He does not, for example, believe in dinosaurs. Or the moon landings. As he told the *Herald*'s Michael Silverman, "I've never seen a *Tyrannosaurus rex*. How do you know those bones are millions of years old? Stuff you can't prove, I don't believe. Like men walking on the moon. I guarantee you none of us have seen a rock from the moon."

It's a sabermetric truism that hitters typically peak in their late twenties, and very few of them get better after reaching that point. But just as Everett doesn't believe in *T. rex*, he probably wouldn't believe in sabermetrics, either, especially if he considered his own career.

Everett turned twenty-nine yesterday, yet this is just his fourth season as an everyday player in the major leagues, and he seems to be getting better with each passing year. Here are his stats in those four seasons, with this year's numbers projected through the full schedule:

	AGE	G	AB	HR	R	RBI	OBP	SLG	OPS
1997	27	142	443	14	58	57	.308	.420	728
1998	28	133	467	15	72	76	.359	.482	841
1999	29	123	464	25	86	108	.398	.571	969
2000	30	150	548	59	96	171	.390	.693	1083

At this point, the only thing that concerns me about Everett is his durability. Another truism of sabermetrics states that players who have been injured in the past will likely be injured in the future. Everett spent a month on the disabled list in 1999, and has never played more than 142 games in a season.

But now that Junior Griffey's in Cincinnati, when Everett *is* in the lineup he's probably the best center fielder in the American League.

◆ ◆ ◆

Everett wasn't quite enough today. After his third-inning homer, the Sox didn't collect another base hit until the tenth, by which time the Phillies had tied the game at five runs apiece, their fifth run coming against Derek Lowe in the eighth. And then they won it in the bottom of the twelfth.

Just more "bad luck" for the Red Sox. Not only did they lose a one-run game, but the Yankees won a one-run game, leaving the Sox a game off the pace. Then again, a cynic, or even a realistic optimist, might suggest that the Red Sox don't deserve to be in first place, given that they've now lost five straight, including three against a team that entered the weekend with the worst record in the National League. And a pessimistic Red Sox fan—you'd be amazed how fast optimists become pessimists around here—might figure we've seen the beginning of the end. Yes, already.

Monday, June 5

Carl Everett hit another home run tonight, his sixth in the last seven games, and this time it wasn't wasted. My man Wakefield tossed a couple of scoreless relief innings, Everett's solo bomb in the top of the ninth gave the Sox a 3–2 lead, and Lowe closed out the Marlins in the bottom of the ninth. Just like the script said, and the five-game losing streak is over.

Even better, the Sox are back in first place! The Yankees lost tonight in Montreal, and once again the ancient combatants are tied atop the standings.

David Cone got racked up yet again—six runs in six innings—and he's now 1–6 with a 6.49 ERA. It's getting to the point where the Yankees have to think about getting him out of the rotation, whether they have a suitable replacement or not.

Tuesday, June 6

There's one image from this evening that will stay with me forever, an image that will eventually, I suspect, come to symbolize my first two months in Boston.

Today, and tonight until early in the morning, we experienced one of New England's famed Nor'easters, relatively common in the winters but exceedingly rare in the summer. In the morning, I woke up to find rain, falling from dark gray skies and propelled by near gale-force winds, pelting my windows. The storm ebbed and flowed, but the wind and rain never did let up much.

On the way to downtown TV studio, where I was to appear on a Fox News program called *Hannity & Colmes*, I asked the cabbie, a Haitian, about the storm. "I've been here for ten years," he said, "and this is the worst I've ever seen in the summer." Driving through the Storrow Drive tunnel, the standing water halfway up the wheels of the cab, I started to worry. But we made it to the studio in fine fashion, half an hour to spare.

I paid the driver, and reluctantly stepped out of the cab and faced the Nor'easter still pounding downtown Boston. And there, on the sidewalk and in the gutter, lay perhaps a dozen shattered, sodden umbrellas, rendered useless like so many fallen young men on Omaha Beach, left where they fell by comrades who figured that taking cover and perhaps surviving the bloody slaughter was the best course of action. I stopped and pondered this scene for all of maybe five seconds, and then I searched out some cover of my own.

Actually, that's a lie. I didn't stop at all, and pondered the fallen umbrellas only *while* I was searching for cover.

◆　◆　◆

After the show I was home lickety-split, just in time to see Derek Lowe put the finishing touches on another one-run victory over the Marlins. The Yankees beat the Expos again, so we're still tied in the East.

Thursday, June 8

On this date, the Sox were supposed to be in the middle of a twelve-game, thirteen-day road trip. But then they lost that entire April series against Cleveland to three days of rain, so the Sox returned to Boston for a single makeup game against the Indians tonight. And lucky us, this one-game home stand featured Pedro Martinez. And not just Pedro Martinez, but *the* Pedro Martinez.

Indians right fielder David Justice led off the top of the fifth and grounded out to second base. The guy behind me said to his besotted buddy, "Maybe I shouldn't say anything, but they don't even have a hit yet. I just noticed that."

It's supposed to be bad luck to talk about a no-hitter until it actually happens, and to this day some broadcasters won't specifically mention a no-hitter while it's in progress. Instead, they'll say things like, "If anyone's driving around near the ballpark, you might want to stop by, because something exciting might happen here tonight." Of course, I don't believe in any of that. If I notice that a pitcher has no-hit stuff in the first few innings, I'll mention the possibilities to whoever's sitting next to me. (Then again, if it's Pat Rapp or someone similarly untalented, and among the outs have been a bunch of atom balls, I might not bother.)

Anyway, it was true. Pedro hadn't allowed a hit. The closest thing to a hit had come in the fourth, when Trot Nixon made a diving catch of Omar Vizquel's fly to shallow right field.

After Justice's grounder, Travis Fryman sent Nixon to the warning track for another fly-out. And that brought up rookie slugger Russ Branyan, who treats each of his swings as if it were his last, and was one of Pedro's three strikeout victims in the second inning. He swung hard this time, as usual, and was rewarded with fly ball that carried over Nixon, and bounced off the warning track and into the visitors' bullpen for an automatic double.

And that was it. No more hits for the Indians, who didn't even get another ball out of the infield until the ninth, after Pedro had departed.

Pedro's mound opponent, Bartolo Colon, wasn't quite as sharp, but for six frames he was sharp enough, tossing a shutout of his own. Carl Everett broke the logjam by leading off the bottom of the seventh with a homer, however, and the Sox tacked on a pair of insurance runs in the eighth. Derek Lowe pitched the ninth for his thirteenth save, and Sox had the W.

◆ ◆ ◆

I sat with Bill this evening, in the first row of the upper box seats, a bit beyond third base and facing straight toward the pitcher's mound. Bill's entertaining as hell, and not only because he eats both the peanuts *and* the shells, crunching them up in one big salty package. Here's Bill . . .

On Mike Stanley: "When Stanley hits a ground ball, it's like watching Tom Berenger legging out that bunt in *Major League*. He runs like my mother on crutches."

On where pretty girls sit: "You know the Sox are doing well when you see the pretty girls in the good seats. I've been here when the Sox were in last place, and then you don't see anybody down here worth looking at."

On Roger Clemens: "Unlike most Sox fans, I like Clemens, but that's tempered by the fact that I know him for what he is, a complete cement-head."

On Jimy Williams: "I like the guy, but if you ask me he's got a bit of the village idiot in him."

On eating the peanuts and the shells: "See, the shells are high in fiber, so that offsets all the fat in the peanuts."

◆ ◆ ◆

Just outside the park after the game, I heard a father and his son talking about Pedro, whose ERA now stands, somewhat improbably, at 0.95.

"Dad, who had the lowest ERA in a season?"

"In 1968, Bob Gibson was 1.05 for the Cardinals."

Actually, it was 1.12, and with the passing of Roger Maris's home-run record, Gibson's mark just might be the most talked-about single-season record out there.

What casual baseball fans don't know, and what even many serious baseball fans understand only vaguely, is just how friendly conditions in 1968 were to the pitcher. I'd like to put this in perspective, and I'd like to do it very carefully because this is one of the most important things you'll read in this book.

In 1968, National League pitchers combined for a 2.99 ERA.

As of tonight, *Pedro Martinez is the only starting pitcher in the American League with an ERA below 3.07.*

Read those last two sentences again. Let them sink in. Now you've got some idea of just how good he's been this season.

For a slightly more scientific approach, we can look at ratios, each pitcher's ERA divided by his league's ERA. Gibson's 1.12 was 37.6 percent of the National

League ERA in 1968. That's quite impressive, one of the better figures you'll see.

At this moment, Pedro Martinez's 0.95 ERA is 19.3 percent of the American League ERA. That ratio is almost twice as good as Gibson's.

If we could somehow transport Martinez back to 1968—what I wouldn't give for a time machine!—and give him that same 19.3 percent ratio, he'd post a 0.58 ERA, which of course would easily rank as the lowest mark in major league history. Do I think that would actually happen? No, I don't. There must be some logical lower limit, and I think 0.58 is below that limit. But it's certainly not unreasonable to suggest that Martinez would have been even better than Gibson, and posted an ERA somewhere below 1.00.

What's really interesting about Gibson's 1.12 ERA, to me at least, is that it's not actually a "record" of any sort. It's not the major league record; that's held by Tim Keefe, who posted a 0.86 ERA in 1880. It's not the so-called "modern" (post-1900) record; that's held by Dutch Leonard, who posted a 0.96 ERA in 1914. It's not even the National League record; that's held by Mordecai "Three Finger" Brown, who posted a 1.04 ERA in 1906.

People remember Gibson's season because he posted the lowest ERA in a long, long time. It was the lowest since Leonard in 1914, and in fact Gibson's 1.12 was the first sub-1.50 ERA since Walter Johnson (1.49) in 1919.

Sunday, June 11

Maybe I should have stayed home tonight, and watched the Yankees and Mets on ESPN. But two of my favorite singers, Aimee Mann and Michael Penn, were playing a show in Boston, at the Berklee College of Music. It started early and it ended early, and since the show was just a hop, a skip, and a jump from the Fenway, and I figured I'd get home in time to see at least the last couple of innings. So as nice as the warm, light rain felt, I stepped lively.

What I didn't know, walking along the edge of the Back Bay Fens, was that the weather system raining droplets on my head was dumping torrents on Yankee Stadium. When I got home, instead of the game, ESPN was showing an old special about the Ted Williams Museum, with a graphic in the corner of the screen telling viewers that the game was being delayed by rain. And a few minutes later, Jon Miller himself appeared, to tell us that the game has been postponed, no makeup date determined.

On a happier note, tonight's postponement makes the Yankees and Red Sox "even" again; that is, for now they're separated by whole games (or in this case, *a* whole game). Had the Yankees played tonight, they would have entered tomorrow's series opener at Fenway either one and a half games or one-half game ahead of the Sox, and no matter what happened the next three days, a tie would have been impossible. But now, the ideal scenario is possible: Red Sox win tomorrow night, leaving the clubs tied for first place entering Tuesday night's game, which pits Pedro against Rocket in a rematch of that classic game of two weeks ago.

Here are the latest standings in the American League East:

	W-L	GB	RS-RA	PYTHAG W-L
YANKEES	33–24	—	287–262	31–26
RED SOX	33–26	1	304–233	37–22
BLUE JAYS	33–31	3 ½	353–362	31–33

Nobody's "luck" has changed much since the last time we checked. The Red Sox have, in every respect save the most important one, played better than the Yankees, and could boast a four- or five-game lead without a lot of planets lining up differently. Instead, they're a game behind, not a good omen more than a third of the way through the season. Because while both teams have a lot of holes—mostly the same holes, in fact—the Yankees are better equipped to fill those holes.

Lately, I've discovered that I have a fairly hefty emotional stake in the Red Sox doing well. As initially conceived, this book wasn't predicated upon a successful season for the Sox, or even a pennant race. But now that the Red Sox have apparently established themselves as pennant contenders, I can't help but hope that they do enjoy a successful season. It would mean a lot to the friends I've made here in Boston, and it would mean a lot next summer when my publisher is trying to sell this book.

But history is littered with the carcasses of decent teams that remained in contention for two or three or four months, only to fall apart—or to be more fair, only to reach their natural level—in August or September. And of course, the Red Sox are famous for such late-summer fades.

Monday, June 12

It's funny, when people find out what I do for a living, they always want to know if I talk to a lot of baseball players, and most of them seem to be a bit disappointed when I admit that I spend very little time hanging around the locker room. These people assume, I suppose, that baseball players are my heroes, and so I'd be eager to spend time with them. But my heroes have always been writers. And tonight, I was supposed to meet two great ones, Kevin Baker and Nicholas Dawidoff. Kevin wrote a wonderful baseball novel, *Sometimes You See It Coming*, and at this writing I'm in the middle of his most recent work, a sprawling historical novel called *Dreamland*. Nick's also an accomplished writer, and his biography of Moe Berg has to rank among the best twenty or so baseball books ever written. If writers were baseball players, Nick would be somebody like Nomar Garciaparra, and I'd be Manny Alexander, or perhaps the kid in Pawtucket who dreams of becoming Manny Alexander. (Kevin's a novelist, so I don't know who the hell he would be.)

Allen Barra is a friend of mine and also a hugely successful freelance writer who knows virtually everybody worth knowing in the business. That includes Kevin Baker and Nick Dawidoff, and the four of us are supposed be going to the game together.

There's just one problem: It's been raining like hell all day long. It was raining on the Amtrak from New England to New York, it was raining on the New Jersey Transit from New York to South Orange (where Allen lives), and it didn't look like it was ever going to stop raining. And this wasn't one of those light, warm, refreshing summer rains, either. It was a cold, malevolent rain, more suited to March or October than the middle of June.

So when I arrived at Allen's house, my spirits weren't exactly jumping for joy. And they stopped jumping completely when I realized that, just as I'd left my scorebook on a train the last time I came to New York, this time I'd left my planner—you know, one of those leather-bound things with a calendar and address book inside—sitting next to a pay phone back in Penn Station. No big deal. After all, I don't really need the phone numbers and addresses anyway, as nearly all of them are entered into the address book on my computer. One problem, though . . . all of my tickets for the Red Sox–Yankees series this week—four for tonight's game, two for Wednesday afternoon—are in that planner, too.

What else could I do, but rush back to Penn Station and hope to get lucky? If the weather allowed, I could still meet Allen and the others at the Stadium.

Taking the train back into Manhattan, just east of Newark we passed a small lake of sorts, bracketed by railroad tracks on two sides, a transformer station on another, and a giant post office on the fourth. Nevertheless, the lake was teeming with avian activity, as I spotted six great egrets, four Canada geese, and two red-winged blackbirds. I had the unoriginal thought that neither the egrets nor the geese nor the blackbirds, occupied with mere survival, gave a wit about my address book, and for some reason this thought cheered me.

That said, I was significantly more cheered to learn, upon reaching Penn Station, that some kind soul had turned in my planner, and my six Yankee Stadium tickets were still within. I do lead a charmed life.

(By the way, this was the second time tonight that I'd been impressed by the kindness of New Yorkers. When I first arrived at Penn Station from Boston, I had to purchase a ticket for the New Jersey Transit train that would take me to South Orange. They've got these handy machines that allow you to avoid standing in line. However, all I had were twenty-dollar bills, and what I didn't know is that the machines dispense only coins as change. My ticket cost six bucks and change, which resulted in a cascade of metal, a few quarters and a passel of new dollar coins. As the man standing next to me said with a twinkle in his eyes, "Sounds like you hit the jackpot."

For some reason I was still clutching all those metallic dollars in my hand as I walked toward the NJT waiting area . . . and I dropped them. All of them. And would you believe it? Complete strangers, close to a dozen of them, went chasing after those dollar coins rolling around in one of the busiest train stations in America. I got every dollar back.)

Not so charmed that I would get to meet Baker and Dawidoff, though. With my tickets in hand, I could have met them, and Allen, at Yankee Stadium. But the Bronx is a pretty good subway ride from midtown Manhattan, and as I stood on the side-walk along Seventh Avenue and let the rain wash away the anxiety that hadn't completely left with the discovery of my (temporarily) lost tickets, I realized that there wouldn't be any baseball tonight, nor would I be meeting any great writers. This rain just wasn't letting up.

I had brought along the latest *New Yorker*, which I started flipping through dur-ing the train ride back to Allen's. And there on page 58 was an article by Nicholas

Dawidoff. Titled "My Father's Troubles," it recounted Dawidoff's relationship with his late father, who suffered from sometimes-debilitating mental illness. I've never had to deal with anything like that, but Dawidoff touched on a number of things that we all deal with, at least if we have parents. And he just writes so beautifully.

Before I knew exactly what was happening, I had tears running down my face. (Fortunately, by then it was after eight o'clock and the train was nearly empty.) I'm not sure what caused the tears. I think my sadness was the result of not getting to meet Dawidoff, and also of realizing that I don't write, and never will write, as beautifully as he does. Or maybe I just needed the catharsis. It was, after all, an emotional day. One minute I thought I was going to Yankee Stadium, the next I thought I wasn't. One minute I thought I had lost my tickets, the next I had the tickets, and the next I realized that the Red Sox would play no baseball in New York tonight.

It was a long, baseball-less day, and I slept well.

Tuesday, June 13

Outstanding with a capital *O*.

What else can you say about the Red Sox bullpen? Tonight in the Bronx, the Yankees drove Brian Rose from the mound in the third inning. They'd just scored their second run of the inning and their third of the game, and they had the bases loaded with one out.

But Hipolito Pichardo came in, and got Shane Spencer to bounce into a double play. And the Yankees would not score again, in fact they would collect just one more *hit* the rest of the way, a harmless single in the sixth. By then the Sox were leading 5–3, thanks to Varitek's two-run homer in the top of that inning, a titanic blast into the upper deck beyond left field.

With this victory, of course, the Sox moved into a tie for first place with the Yankees.

◆　◆　◆

As you know if you've been to New York, it's hard to take three steps without tripping over somebody famous, and the celebrity du soir was Mia Hamm. She and a few of her teammates showed up in the top of the eighth inning and took seats in the first row next to the visitors' dugout, just a few feet away from us. And after the game, Nomar Garciaparra came over and chatted with Mia for a few minutes. I'm told she's married (he's not), so I guess they're just friends.

♦ ♦ ♦

Today a Red Sox fan named Christine forwarded me the following joke, which apparently has been making the rounds but is just now reaching my e-mailbox . . .

On the eve of the big game, a first-grade teacher explains to her class that she is a Yankees fan. She asks her students to raise their hands if they are Yankees fans, too. Not really knowing what a Yankees fan is, but wanting to be just like their teacher, the children shoot their hands into the air like fleshy fireworks. There is, however, one exception: a girl named Lucy.

The teacher asks her why she has decided to be different.

"Because I'm not a Yankees fan."

So (asks the teacher) what are you? "Why, I'm proud to be a Red Sox fan," boasts the little girl.

The teacher is a little perturbed now, her face slightly red. She asks Lucy why she is a Red Sox fan. "Well, my mommy and daddy are Red Sox fans, so I'm a Red Sox fan, too."

The teacher is now angry. "That's no reason! What if your mother and father were both morons, then what would you be?"

Lucy pauses, and smiles. "Then," she says, "I'd be a Yankees fan."

Wednesday, June 14
Writing sometime after two in the morning on June 15, from aboard a train somewhere in Connecticut . . .

Pedro-Rocket II didn't exactly live up to its advance billing. Oh, the score certainly did—2–1, with the Yankees winning this time—and so did Pedro Martinez, who permitted just one run in six innings. But Roger Clemens, after escaping a bases-loaded jam in the first inning, left the game with a strained groin. The Yankee bullpen took it from there, taking a page from the Red Sox notebook and permitting just the single run when Garciaparra homered down the right-field line in the seventh.

The Yanks now lead the Sox by one game.

♦ ♦ ♦

After three days in New York, I'm reminded of an article I read many years ago, in which the author argued that our government would work better if Congress were suddenly transplanted to some Midwestern city, like Kansas City or Omaha. Well, I happen to think that Major League Baseball would work better if it were suddenly transplanted to somewhere, anywhere other than New York City.

If baseball has a big problem, it's money. You can make a list of all the things people complain about—games that last too long, outrageous ticket prices, new "mallparks" financed by reluctant citizens, World Series games that don't even begin until nearly 9:00 P.M. on the East Coast, billboards plastered all over every available space in ballparks, with ads actually on the grass not far off—and they're all tied to money.

Yes, money is the root of all baseball evil. Or almost all of it.

And if U.S.A. really stands for, as someone once suggested, "United States of Advertising," then New York is certainly our capital city. There is, at least in my experience, no place like it. Walk down any busy Manhattan sidewalk, and unless you're looking up at the skyscrapers or straight down at the pavement, you will be targeted by people selling things. Sure, there are the storefronts, many of them with open windows, goods displayed for all to see. And there are also guys on nearly every block, sitting or standing behind card tables, and selling knockoff watches or necklaces or old magazines or children's books or sunglasses or compact discs or just about anything else you might ever want. Use a pay phone, and you'll find yourself staring at an advertisement as you chat away.

It just never stops, and when I'm walking around Manhattan, I find myself dropping into J. Crew or The Gap or Barnes & Noble and buying something, just because I feel duty-bound, as a visitor to the island, to spend a chunk of my money on something I don't particularly need. And perhaps I'm wrong, but I have to think that this rampant commerce has to affect the people who live and work here. What happens, I think, is that good people, people with the best of intentions, come to New York thinking they're going to make it a better place. But frankly, nobody can change New York. It's too big, and it's been doing this for too long. New York will crush any puny human who tries to get in the way. So you give in. When they start talking, in the meeting, about making compromises in the interest of making more money, or perhaps even just completely rolling over in the interest of making more money, you don't say anything. Because that's just the way things are in the United States of Advertising.

Now let's say you're working for Major League Baseball. And FOX or NBC comes to you and says, "Here's a big pile of money for the rights to broadcast the postseason, your annual showcase. The only catch is that every World Series game has to start between 8:30 and 9:00, and so very few children in the Eastern or Central time zones will get to see the games. We *could* start the games earlier, but then the pile of money would have to be just *slightly* less big. So what'll it be?"

And if you're Major League Baseball, you take the big pile of money. *Every damn time.*

Aside from the obvious annoyance factor, the real problem with MLB's efforts to sell everything is simple . . . *Baseball isn't basketball or football.* Basketball and football are about individuals, at least on a surface, marketing-oriented level. If you attend a Toronto Raptors game, you can pretty much count on Vince Carter scoring his twenty points, and throwing down a couple of super-spectacular monsta-dunks in the process. If you attend a St. Louis Rams game, you can count on Kurt Warner tossing a few touchdown passes. But baseball's not like that. Nomar Garciaparra might be the greatest shortstop in the world. Sure, today Nomar hit a home run. But last Thursday he struck out twice and rapped into a double play. If anyone came to Fenway that night just to see Nomar, they would have felt cheated.

Very few came to Fenway to see Nomar, though. They came to see the Red Sox, and baseball. But MLB can't market the Red Sox (that's the team's job), and they don't know *how* to market baseball. And frankly, I'm not sure if they need to market baseball. It's such a great game, I think that it's perfectly capable of taking care of itself. All MLB needs to do is stay out of the way and avoid labor wars. Unfortunately, they're not so great at either of those. And being in New York certainly doesn't help.

Fourth Inning

Friday, June 16

The Fenway bleachers are either the best, or the worst, place in baseball.

— Tom Boswell

If you ever have the chance to sit in Section 35 of the Fenway Park bleachers, do it. You're right behind the pitcher, and you've got as good a view of the strike zone as anybody in the ballpark who's not wearing a uniform. There's a catch, though. If you're at Fenway Park for a game that starts before 7:05, you can't sit in Section 35. Nobody can. If the game doesn't start at 7:05 (or later), the seats in Sections 34 and 35 are covered with tarps. Why? Because 34 and 35 are in straightaway center field, and thus directly in the hitter's line of sight as the pitcher delivers the ball. And hitters, wherever they are, get real touchy when you start messing with what's called the "hitting background." In the great majority of ballparks these days, the hitting background in center field is simply a big green wall, or perhaps a nice green lawn. That's how they build them now. But of course, in Fenway there are still seats out there, which has been cause for concern from time to time.

For many years, the bleachers beyond straightaway center field were rarely used, if only because they were rarely needed. They did serve as "overflow" seats for big games, mostly when the Yankees were in town. The "problem" of the hitting background in Fenway's center-field bleachers was first considered a serious issue in 1969. In 1967, twenty-two-year-old Red Sox outfielder Tony Conigliaro, a budding superstar and a Boston-area native, was seriously injured when beaned just under the left eye by a Jack Hamilton fastball. Conigliaro missed the entire 1968 season, but returned in 1969. And on May 4 at Fenway Park, Conigliaro struck out four times. After the game he complained to the writers, "I couldn't see a curveball out there all afternoon. The glare that comes off the shirts of those fans in the left-hand corner of the center-field seats produces a glare that makes it impossible to pick up breaking balls. It's dangerous, real dangerous. Somebody's going to get killed one of these sunny days. They should do something about it."

So they did. As David Cataneo writes in *Tony C: The Triumph and Tragedy of Tony Conigliaro*, "Not wanting to be responsible for getting their heroic gladiator beaned again, but also not wanting to flush away nine hundred paying customers, the Sox brain trust compromised. They gave that section of the ballpark a cutesy nickname, 'Conig's Corner,' and posted a sign that read: 'Dear Patron, please do not sit in green seat section unless you are wearing dark-colored clothing. Conig thanks you. Management thanks you.'"

Conigliaro hit twenty home runs that season and was named American League Comeback Player of the Year (though he didn't really play all that well), and in 1970 he hit 36 homers and paced the Red Sox with 116 RBI. Yet, for reasons that remain murky to this day, Tony C was traded after the '70 season, and white shirts were once again allowed in the center-field bleachers (Conigliaro's career went straight downhill after he left Boston). According to my research—and my research turned up a fair number of contradictions—Sections 34 and 35 remained open for all games until the late 1990s. Roger Clemens signed a free-agent contract with the Toronto Blue Jays prior to the 1997 season. His first start in Fenway Park came on July 12, in a late-afternoon game. Clemens struck out sixteen hitters, which of course was a lot but not unprecedented for him. That same day, though, Aaron Sele tied his career high with eleven strikeouts, and suddenly people started talking about the background again. And so, since 1998 the seats in Sections 35 and 36 have not been sold for any games starting before five in the evening.

◆ ◆ ◆

You hear a lot of stories about the craziness out in the bleachers, ranging from beach balls and inflatable dolls to clouds of marijuana smoke and drunken brawling. I've witnessed some of this, the beach balls and the brawling, from my box seats prior to this evening. Things were relatively sedate tonight, though. I'm told that most of the shenanigans take place in the spring and the fall, when a lot more students are in town. And if I think back to what I was like in college, that makes a lot of sense.

◆ ◆ ◆

As great as Section 35 is, I have to admit that I didn't take full advantage of my seat tonight. I was too distracted by Susan, who supplied the tickets—which she bought from a coworker named Tax Bob—and sat on my right. This is not a complaint. Given a choice between watching a game by myself (notwithstanding the hundreds of people within earshot) and focusing on the action, or watching a game in the company of someone I like and missing some stuff, I'll choose the latter almost every time.

And like everyone else who's been to a number of games here, Susan's got a great "Fenway story" . . .

"I was here at Fenway with Tax Bob, who I'd just met. We were sitting very close to these seats, here in Section 35 or maybe 36, in the seventh row. I don't remember who the Red Sox were playing, but I do remember that ex–Red Sox player Dave Henderson was playing center field for whoever it was. During the couple of minutes between innings, with Henderson taking his place in the field, there were increased murmurings and some laughter coming from the bottom rows of our section. We looked in that direction and saw articles of clothing flying up in the air, then over the center-field fence and down to the warning track. A woman in the front row was taking off every piece of her clothing and throwing it onto the field. By the time I could tell what was happening, she was only half dressed. I distinctly remember her throwing even her watch over the railing.

"The whole time she was doing this, she had a perfectly blank look on her face, not even the trace of a smile. And she wasn't a teenager or twenty-something working on her first Fenway beer. She had to be in her thirties, at least.

"By the time she was down to her birthday suit, the aisles in our section and the next were full of people trying to get a better look. After noticing the garments on the field, Dave Henderson even glanced up a couple of times with a shocked look on his face. I was getting more and more uncomfortable with the whole scene. And with all of her clothes gone, the woman sat back down, totally naked, on the gross, dirty bleacher seat.

"By now, some security guards were lined against the railing in front of her, seemingly at a loss about what to do. They were probably afraid of getting in trouble if they touched her. Finally, after several long minutes, one of them draped his blazer around the woman and escorted her away. You know how the backs of blazers have those flaps? As he guided her toward the exit, those flaps kept going up in the air with every step. I still have that image in my mind, her mooning the crowd with each step as the flaps went up and down, up and down."

Susan's charms notwithstanding, I did have the presence of mind to watch *Baseball Tonight* when I got home. And joy of joys, I learned that the Yankees lost to the surprising Chicago White Sox, who at 42–24 now have the best record in baseball. That means the Red Sox—jeez, I almost forgot to tell you, they beat the Blue Jays tonight, 7–4—are back in first place, a half-game ahead of New York.

No, I still haven't become a Red Sox fan. And no, I don't root for the Red Sox because I think this book will sell better if the Sox win (though of course, it will). I've never been good at focusing on the future, and next summer (when the book is supposed be published) seems like a long, long ways away. No, I'm pulling for the Sox for two reasons.

One, a lot of people around here have treated me kindly since I got to Boston, and I'd love for them to finally see the Sox win a World Championship.

And two, it'd be history. Like anybody else, I like to be around when stuff happens. The thing about a baseball game is, there's always the potential for something special, whether it's a no-hitter or an unassisted triple play or whatever. But in a larger sense, the Red Sox winning a World Series would certainly rank as one of the biggest stories in a long, long time. And if I were here to see it, I'd have a hell of a story for my grandkids.

Saturday, June 17

Tonight, the fates very nearly played a big joke on the American League East.

The Red Sox trailed the Blue Jays 11–1 in the fifth; the Yankees trailed the White Sox 10–3 in the sixth. And both the Sox and the Yanks almost came back.

It was a hot, muggy day in Boston, and as hot, muggy days often do, this one ended with a hot, muggy downpour. The line of fast-moving thunderstorms hit Fenway at 4:35. The rains stopped at 5:25, Ramon Martinez threw his first pitch at 5:46, and Ramon Martinez gave up a three-run homer to Tony Batista at 6:09, giving the Blue Jays (and ace David Wells) a 3–0 lead in the second inning.

The Jays got to Martinez for four more runs in the fourth, and then Wakefield gave up a pair of two-run homers in the fifth, making it 11–1. At that point, I was questioning my rule about leaving baseball games early. And even after the Sox scored four in the bottom of the fifth to make it 11–5, the game seemed pretty hopeless. But the Sox batted around in the seventh and scored five more runs, the rally climaxed by Jason Varitek's bases-loaded double down the left-field line.

That made the score 11–10, and unfortunately that's where it stayed, as Blue Jays closer Billy Koch pitched two scoreless frames to finish off the Sox. Fortunately, first place remains in Boston's hands, for at least one more day. The Yankees did turn a 10–3 rout into a 10–9 nail-biter—Bernie Williams drove in seven runs—but left the tying runner on second base in the bottom of the ninth.

◆　◆　◆

Koch's performance deserves a few more words, as he just might be the hardest thrower in the American League. I had a great seat this evening, second row behind the visitors' on-deck circle, and from that close I wondered how any hitter could ever make contact, let alone hit the ball hard.

As impressive as Koch was, he would have been significantly less impressive in May than he is now. A few weeks ago, the Red Sox installed a pair of large billboards for Fleet Bank, which happen to incorporate relatively small displays for pitch velocity. For some reason they're often wildly inaccurate, but it's a hell of a lot better than nothing. Last fall, after my first visit to Fenway Park, I wrote a sentimental column about the old place, essentially a mash note to a ramshackle old building. But Fenway fell short of perfection, and one of the missing ingredients was a radar display.

A few Red Sox fans blasted me for suggesting that Fenway wasn't already perfect, but I'm not a knee-jerk preservationist. I think that altering Fenway is just fine, if the alteration serves to make the game more interesting. And pitch velocities are interesting as hell. Tonight, Billy Koch's first pitch registered at 99 miles per hour. Now, I think it's probably safe to say that no pitcher in Red Sox history has ever thrown quite that hard, and the fans were duly impressed. You could hear murmurs of awe from all around. And his seventh pitch, a fastball to Trot Nixon, crashed the three-digit barrier, hitting 100 exactly. More murmurs, a bit louder this time. Nixon struck out on the next pitch, the third he saw, a slider that registered 91 on the speed gun.

Koch really was something. I might have missed something along the way, but I believe that before he entered the game, not one of the six preceding pitchers had reached even ninety miles an hour; the starters, Martinez and Wells, both topped out at 89 with their fastballs. But Koch threw twenty-seven pitches, and only one of them—a rare change-up, to Brian Daubach—registered at *less* than 90. Otherwise, it was all high-90s fastballs and low-90s sliders, both types of pitch practically unhittable, at least tonight.

Sunday, June 18

It never really seemed like the Red Sox were a part of the game this afternoon. Jeff Fassero gave up homers in the first and second innings, the Red Sox couldn't do a damn thing with Blue Jays starter Frank Castillo, and the final score was 5–1, the Jays drawing to within just one game of the Sox in the East standings.

I had good company, though, in the person of Art Martone.

Art is the sports editor at *The Providence Journal*, but as a hobby he writes incredibly intelligent columns about the Red Sox for the *Journal*'s website (ProJo.com). Someone pointed me to his columns a few years ago, and since then we've composed something of a Mutual Admiration Society, though we didn't actually meet (via e-mail) until this spring. When Art found out I would be in Boston this season, he invited me to a game, and today was the day.

Art is forty-five, he grew up in Cranston, Rhode Island, and he attended his first Red Sox game on August 23, 1964 (Yankees 4, Red Sox 3). Art estimates that he's seen approximately 654 games at Fenway Park . . . and he's never caught a foul ball. Thus, it was with some amount of glee that I told him about getting my own foul ball in my sixth game at Fenway. He took it well, I thought. At the least, he didn't growl at me when I asked for his favorite Fenway memory. Art gave me something of an abbreviated version, as we both were too engrossed in the game for good story-telling or note-taking, so later I asked him to e-mail me his memories . . .

"October 1 is a date that drips with meaning in Red Sox lore. In 1967, it was the day they clinched the Impossible Dream pennant. In 1977, it was the day they were eliminated from contention, inspiring (if that's the word) A. Bartlett Giamatti to write his stirring essay 'The Green Fields of the Mind,' in which he famously concluded, 'It breaks your heart. It is designed to break your heart.'

"October 1, 1978, was a drizzly and dismal afternoon in more ways than one.

The Sox were poised to complete their ignoble journey from fourteen and a half games ahead to historical infamy. All that stood between them and the cliff were the Cleveland Indians, who had to beat the Yankees in New York while the Sox were beating the expansion Blue Jays in Boston to force a one-game playoff.

"'To be frank with you,' Carl Yastrzemski would tell a television interviewer later, 'starting today's game I didn't have any hope at all.' Neither did I. In those days the Sox would take the field (to the final lines of 'Take Me Out to the Ball Game,' courtesy of the sublime John Kiley at the organ). As they did, the Fenway crowd—vilified in recent times as self-indulgent whiners fixated on failure—gave the Sox a raucous standing ovation. We're with you, they were saying, and we still love you.

"Tears came to my eyes. It can't end this way, I thought to myself. It can't. Please, I whispered to the heavens, do the right thing. Give them one more day.

"There was a small radio station in New Bedford, Massachusetts, about forty miles south of Boston, that carried the Yankee games, and throughout the stands you could see transistor radios pinned to ears as people strained to catch the scratchy, thin signal. Hope rose when they reported that Andre Thornton had homered off Catfish Hunter, but the Yanks had already tied it by the time the Sox game started. Now, with the Blue Jays batting, there was another stir.

"'Gary Alexander just hit a home run!' shouted a man about ten rows in front of us, turning to face the crowd. 'Indians lead, 3–2!'

"Thornton we could believe. But Gary Alexander?

"Someone nearby stood. This was a time when scatological language wasn't quite as prevalent publicly as it is now, so when he said in an ominous voice, 'If you're bustin' our balls . . .' it was considerably more threatening than it might be today.

"'No! I mean it!' the first man insisted. 'The Indians are ahead!'

"Soon the score was 4–2. Then 6–2. Hunter was gone, and—suddenly, euphorically—the Sox weren't. What had been a funereal atmosphere, framed fittingly by the weather, turned electric. By the time the late innings rolled around, the Red Sox were comfortably ahead and the Yankees irretrievably behind. The season would not end, not yet.

"The Sox of that era would, just before the ninth inning, list the next home game on the scoreboard. And as Luis Tiant began his warm-up tosses, we read:

> *RED SOX*
> *NEXT HOME GAME*
> *TOMORROW VS.*
> *NEW YORK 2:30 P.M.*

"The joint erupted. Tears came to my eyes again. That straightforward announcement, in that context, had more meaning than the half hour's worth of fireworks or 'WE WIN!!!' histrionics or 'Who Let the Dogs Out?' barking that would greet such a victory today.

"Some say all that victory did was set up a heart-crushing defeat the next day, but I've never felt that way. I was never devastated by the playoff loss to the Yankees. It was a great game between two great teams that the Yanks happened to win. No complaints.

"I *would* have been devastated had they never gotten the chance to play. And thus I learned that day that there's always hope, even when things—literally and figuratively—are darkest. Sometimes, justice does triumph.

"Because baseball, and especially Red Sox baseball, is *not* designed to break your heart."

◆ ◆ ◆

Red Sox left fielder Troy O'Leary, batting .211 with five home runs (and zero since May 7) finally went on the disabled list today.

◆ ◆ ◆

Also this afternoon, the Yankees got blasted again by the White Sox, 17–4! They have now been outscored this season, 310–309, a strange state of affairs for a club that (1) won a World Series last October and (2) was expected by many to win another one this October.

But of course, all anybody cares about are the wins and the losses. And based on those, the Yankees remain just a half-game behind the Red Sox, and the Blue Jays are just a half-game behind the Yankees.

And tomorrow night, the Bronx Bombers bounce into Beantown for a four-game series that will, by definition, determine first place at least for a couple of days. As important as this series seems, though, it's only four games, and unless somebody wins all four of them, the effect on the standings is negligible or nonexistent. The most likely outcome of any four-game series between two roughly equal clubs is, of course, a split. And if that happens, then of course the standings won't change at all. The second-most likely outcome is one team or the other winning three of four, but even that results in just a two-game change in the standings.

A four-game sweep by either club is pretty unlikely. In the 1990s, the Sox and Yankees played eleven four-game series; they split four of them, both clubs took three of four three times . . . leaving one sweep. In 1990, the Red Sox took four straight from the Yankees at Fenway (and, later in the season, swept a three-game series at home). The Sox won a division title that season, which I'm sure we'll read about in the newspapers if the Sox do manage to win all four this week. The Yankees, meanwhile, haven't swept a four-game series with the Red Sox since 1986. That was fifteen four-game series ago, and one might argue that the Sox were giving less than their best efforts, as it was the last series of the season and Boston had already clinched the pennant (the Yankees finished second in '86, five and a half games behind the Sox despite the sweep).

Monday, June 19

Before tonight's game, we all were asked to observe a moment of silence for Elizabeth "Lib" Dooley, who died today.

Dooley was eighty-seven years old. She started going to Red Sox games in 1944 . . . and didn't stop until this season. According to Dan Shaughnessy, she attended more than four thousand consecutive home games, which of course makes my attempt at eighty-one straight look awfully puny.

Lib took ill last season, and her last home game was this year's opener. Only in Boston, perhaps, would you find someone who went fifty-some years without missing a game. And perhaps only in Boston would a columnist write, as Shaughnessy did after tonight's game, something like "There must be a hardball god. The Red Sox lost to the Yankees by a score of 22–1 on the day Elizabeth Dooley died."

Yep, 22–1. The day after the Yankees were smashed by the White Sox, 17–4, they turned around and dealt the Red Sox their worst-ever home defeat. Talk about your mismatch . . . It was scoreless after three innings, but then Brian Rose—who must be getting close to losing his job—gave up a three-run homer to Jorge Posada in the fourth. Derek Jeter hit a two-run shot over The Wall in the fifth, and the rout was on. The Yanks batted around in the eighth and the ninth, scoring nine runs (only one earned) off Rob Stanifer and seven (all earned) off Tim Wakefield.

I watched all this from high in the bleachers, courtesy of an Irish fellow named Alan, a reader of my column who e-mailed me an invitation a few weeks ago. Alan's only been in this country for a few years, but he quickly found great affection for both baseball and the Red Sox. As depressing as it was, watching the Sox, and especially Wakefield, get beat up like this, there was something heartening about sitting with someone who fell in love with the game I love, yet under completely different circumstances.

Tuesday, June 20

Pedro Martinez entered tonight's start with a 0.99 ERA, which meant that if he allowed even *one* earned run, this ERA would increase. As it turned out, if he allowed even one earned run, the Red Sox would lose. And he allowed three, each of them the result of solo home runs: Derek Jeter and Bernie Williams lofted balls into the netting in the fourth and seventh innings, respectively, and Paul O'Neill shot a low liner into the Sox bullpen in the eighth. Meanwhile, Andy Pettitte, inconsistent as hell this season, tossed seven and two-thirds shutout innings, and then Mariano Rivera finished up the team shutout.

This leaves the Red Sox a game and a half out, and, with Pedro losing, suddenly that four-game sweep doesn't seem so unlikely at all.

Wednesday, June 21

The Red Sox did away with the possibilities of a sweep tonight, topping the Yankees 9–7 thanks to some exceptionally erratic work by New York's bullpen. The Sox scored twice in the first, then twice again in the sixth, only to see the Bombers grab a 5–4 lead with three in the top of the seventh. But in the bottom of that inning, the Sox sent ten men to the plate, five of them via the free pass, and scored five runs. Bernie Williams got to Derek Lowe for a two-run homer in the top of the ninth, but then Lowe struck out Jorge Posada to end the game, drawing the Sox back to just half a game behind the first-place Yankees, with the Blue Jays lurking just another half-game behind Boston.

Rod Beck, the rotund, long-haired relief pitcher who just a few years ago was considered one of the best in the game, made his first appearance this season for the

Sox. He lumbered in from the bullpen to the accompaniment of "Sweet Caroline," and this was the first time I'd heard the song when the house was full.

It's a different experience at night, with a big crowd. People are happy, some of them have been drinking, and the result is a gigantic public sing-along, especially when the chorus gets to the *ba ba ba*s. And it feels unique, as opposed to "YMCA" or one of the other crummy songs that get played in most of the ballparks (including this one).

Thursday, June 22

Today is my thirty-fourth birthday, and I don't give a damn. I know I'm supposed to feel a little bit older, and perhaps consider, yet again, my mortality. But for me it's just another day, it really is. Now, that's not to say the number doesn't make a difference. It does. But it's not *turning* thirty-four that makes me feel older, but rather *being* thirty-four. So given that I've been thirty-four for only a few hours, I really don't feel any different. Give me another six months of being thirty-four— in six months, I'll be mired in the middle of another cold, dark, baseball-free winter (The Void, as Jonathan Yardley has described it)—and I'll tell you just how old I feel.

It's funny, all day long my friends were asking me what I was doing for my birthday, and they sounded a little sad for me when I told them I was going to the game tonight with a stranger. But I've enjoyed most of the strangers I've met this season, and I can't think of anywhere I'd rather be on my birthday than a ballpark. And Fenway's the best ballpark in the world. (Plus, today Susan treated me to lunch, and then I impressed her with my sketchy knowledge of birds while we walked through the Fens.)

Anyway, just imagine how sorry everyone would have felt for me if they'd known that I ended up going to the game alone. Which I did.

Back in March, knowing that tickets for the Yankees games would be tough to come by, I solicited them on my website. And somewhat to my surprise, a few kind souls responded. Among them was Loren, who in short order sent along a fantastic ticket, which as it turned out was in the third row behind the Sox dugout. I assumed that Loren would be taking the seat next to mine, but nobody ever did take that seat next to mine, which is why I spent most of my birthday alone, or as alone as you can be when there are thirty-three thousand people within hailing distance.

That wasn't so bad, but I did feel a little guilty, or something, when I had trouble staying awake. I only slept for four hours last night. There's nobody sitting next to me. I cannot keep score, because I forgot to bring a pen. And I'm embarrassed to admit that these things, if I let them, would have lulled me to sleep like a three-man tag team composed of Mr. Sandman's bastard triplets. I'm embarrassed because, gosh, I have a great seat for a Yankees game at Fenway Park, with first place on the line! Intellectually, I had that exclamation point, but physically I was an ellipsis.

Except for a few brief catnaps between innings, I did manage to stay awake, so I did see the Red Sox recapture first place in the East. Bernie Williams hit a two-run homer in the first inning, but the Yankees didn't score again. The Sox scored twice in the second and twice more in the third, and they didn't score again either. So that's how it ended: Red Sox 4, Yankees 2. And the Sox grabbed a half-game lead over the Yanks.

It's funny, when the season started my favorite pitcher was Tim Wakefield. However, between his performance and his recent public whining about his role, he just doesn't hold quite the same place in my heart anymore. Of course, it's easy to love Pedro Martinez, but where's the fun in that? It's like falling for the prettiest girl in class, doesn't take any imagination at all. So lately, my favorite pitcher is Petey's big brother.

Ramon Martinez came into tonight's start with a 6.08 ERA, but the fans haven't turned on him yet. This is partly because he's Pedro's brother and partly because he's won five games while losing only four, but I think maybe there's something else going on. Ramon carries himself with more quiet dignity than perhaps any player I've ever watched. His countenance is exactly the same whether he's just given up seven runs in three-plus innings, as he did five nights ago, or he's pitched one of his best games of the year, as he did tonight.

Nomar Garciaparra, everyone's favorite non-pitcher, got an especially rousing hand when he came up to bat in the sixth inning. Why? He doubled his first two times up, so on the auxiliary scoreboards down the left- and right-field lines, the fans now saw this:

AB	AVG	BALL	STRIKE	OUT
5	.400	0	0	0

Yes, Garciaparra (who wears number 5 on his back) was hitting .400, a fairly amazing accomplishment for this point in the season, even if he did spend two weeks on the disabled list. Garciaparra made outs in his next two at-bats, dropping him to .396, but I know that his flirtation with the magical mark will result in a modest deluge of e-mail, the great majority of it from young Red Sox fans, wondering if *he's the guy* who can become the first major leaguer to hit .400 since Boston's own Ted Williams in 1941.

I know I'll get this deluge, because it happens every summer. In 1999, it was Blue Jays third baseman Tony Fernandez, who was hitting .401 as late as June 27, only to slump badly in the second half and finish at .328 (baseball men were so impressed, Fernandez is playing in Japan this season).

So no, Nomar Garciaparra's not going to hit .400 this season, or any other season. Nobody's hit .400 since 1941, when Ted Williams hit .406. And no *right*-handed hitter has hit .400 since . . . geez, it's been so long that I gotta look this up . . . since 1925, when Rogers Hornsby hit .403.

◆ ◆ ◆

Standings after tonight's action:

	W-L	GB	RS-RA	PYTHAG W-L
RED SOX	37–31	—	342–292	39–29
YANKEES	36–31	1/2	343–324	35–32
BLUE JAYS	39–34	1/2	407–421	35–38

Amazing what a 22–1 game can do, huh? Now the Red Sox and Yankees are both almost exactly where they should be, leaving only the Blue Jays as Pythagorean anomalies. And they suffered a few blowout losses earlier, and might really be about as good as their record. These three clubs, it seems, truly are evenly matched. So the pennant will, I suspect, go to the team that's either the healthiest, or the most able to get help from outside the organization.

The Blue Jays, easily the youngest team in the hunt, are likely to be the healthiest of the three. And the Yankees, easily the richest team in the hunt, are likely to be the ones who can go out and get what they need. So where does that leave the Red Sox?

You guessed it. Third place.

Saturday, June 24

I've missed just one Society for American Baseball Research convention since 1990, and thanks to a quick three-game road trip to Toronto for the Red Sox, I don't have to miss this year's gathering in West Palm Beach.

Pro Player Stadium, home of the Florida Marlins, isn't as bad as I thought it would be. I mean, it's pretty obviously a football stadium with a baseball field wedged in somewhat awkwardly, and everything's orange and blue and dark orange and teal, but Pro Player does have its charms. They do a pretty good job with the scoreboards, and I appreciate the display listing the velocity and type of every pitch.

Have you seen that episode of *The Twilight Zone* called "It's a Good Life," wherein Billy Mumy's character, a monstrous eight-year-old named Anthony, is able to simply "wish" things away? At the beginning of the story, we learn that little Anthony has wished Peaksville, his hometown, into space. Or perhaps he's simply wished away the rest of the planet. Either way, the effect is the same; beyond the town's borders, simply nothing.

Well, that's what Pro Player Stadium feels like after dark, as if the ballpark is in the middle of a great void, and if you jumped off the edge you'd fall through space for eternity. This is not an entirely unpleasant feeling. I've never understood this recent fascination with skylines when new ballparks are designed. Hell, I'm here to watch a baseball game. If I want to look at buildings, there are far better places to do it than from inside a ballpark. Skylines are, in my opinion, an unnecessary distraction. In fact, among the many wonderful things about old Tiger Stadium, the most wonderful was the feeling of isolation one got there. Double-decked and completely enclosed, Tiger Stadium allowed nothing from the outside world into its baseball world. And that's how I prefer things.

The rest of the SABR guys—many of whom I consider friends, although I see them just once a year—and I saw a good game tonight. Florida's Preston Wilson and Derrek Lee both homered twice, and the Marlins scored five runs in the eighth to beat the Cubs, 7–4.

Sunday, June 25

My seat today was so fantastic that I presumably violated some subsection of the journalism ethics rulebook to get it (a member of the Marlins' radio crew offered, and I accepted). I was, if you can believe this, sitting just a few feet from the Cubs dugout, with a great view *into* the Cubs dugout. It's a perspective that is available in few other ballparks.

When you're sitting this close to the players and the coaching staff, you can learn some fascinating things about nicknames.

Mark Grace? Gracie.

Brant Brown? Brownie.

Jeff Huson? Hughie.

Glenallen Hill? Hillie.

Joe Girardi? Jo-Jo.

Okay, so maybe the nicknames aren't so thrilling. What's better is the proximity to the coaches, specifically Cubs pitching coach Rene Lachemann, who spent the entire game standing up in the corner of the dugout, so close that we could have carried on a conversation with him, without even raising our voices. And in fact, that's what an obese fellow sitting behind us did.

Even though Lachemann's the pitching coach, he seemed to most enjoy yelling to the Cub hitters, "Get a strike and hit it hard!"

Except it didn't quite sound that way. In practice, all baseball coaches run their words together for the sake of brevity, so Lachemann's imprecation actually sounded like this:

getastrikeandhititithard

Lachemann saved his best material for late in the game. In the bottom of the eighth, Marlins center fielder Preston Wilson missed what was, apparently, a hittable pitch, the result a high pop-up to the second baseman. Immediately after making contact, Wilson flipped his bat high in the air before jogging toward first base.

I'm not exactly sure why—it might have something to do with Wilson's slow trots around the bases after each of his two home runs last night—but Lachemann took extreme umbrage today, letting loose with a torrent of, well, of something . . . *Hey, what the fuck is that? Jiminy Christmas! What, are you going into the Hall of Fame? Call me for the induction ceremony.*

He proceeded in this vein for some time. The only thing we could figure is that Lachemann considered Wilson's display a sign of disrespect to the pitcher (Cubs reliever Steve Rain, also cleverly known as "Rain Man").

You can get up close and personal with the players from these seats, too. In the top of the second, Jeff "Hughie" Huson struck out looking, and was not happy about this. He didn't get in the umpire's face, but he did say "Fucking *bullshit*," as he walked away. Then he stopped walking, finished stripping off his batting gloves, and announced to nobody in particular, "That was *not* a fucking strike."

When Huson went to the on-deck circle in the fourth, my friend (and ex-roommate) Dave—who's a world-class smart-ass—said, "Hey, Jeff, watch the potty mouth this time." Huson looked up just as Dave was looking away, saw me looking at him and mumbled, "Go fuck yourself." So today I achieved a lifelong dream, being sworn at by a real major leaguer for something I didn't even do. And a moment later, Huson himself achieved a lifelong dream; he tripled.

Another odd thing about sitting so close, of course, is that not only can you hear the players and coaches, *they* can hear *you*. Now, in my younger days I used to heckle fairly often, but it was done primarily to amuse myself and (I hoped) the people sitting around me. But when you're sitting thirty feet from home plate, the batter will hear you, no matter what they might say.

And I think that maybe, just maybe, I had a small effect on the game today. Sitting so close to the plate, I couldn't help but notice that Sammy Sosa takes way, way too long to get ready to hit. Before each pitch, he digs in with his back foot, and *then* he steps out of the batter's box, takes a few practice swings, stretches his neck, does a few deep knee-bends (or whatever), before finally taking his position in the box.

Every pitch, this same foolishness.

So after a bit of this, I started yelling. First at Sosa ("Get in the box, Sammy!" and "Play ball!"). And when that didn't work, I started yelling at plate umpire Eric Cooper ("Come on, Coop! Get him in the box!"). Yes, I know this was not the most imaginative material, but in my defense, I'm long out of heckling practice.

Cooper never did discipline Sosa, (who went zero for five, and twice struck out on sliders in the dirt even though I warned him, quite audibly, what was coming the second time). But in the top of the eighth, Glenallen Hill pinch-hit for Henry Rodriguez. And when Hill took his time getting back in the box after going oh-and-two, Cooper motioned to pitcher Armando Almanza to go ahead and bring it. Hill jumped back in the box at the last possible second, took a defensive swing . . . and singled down the right-field line, pulling the Cubs to within a run, at 7–6. One batter later, they tied it on Jose Nieves's sacrifice fly, and eventually the game went to extra innings.

In the bottom of the tenth with one out, left-handed-hitting Cliff Floyd came out of the Marlins dugout to pinch-hit for the pitcher. In response, Cubs manager Don Baylor summoned left-hander Felix Heredia from the bullpen. And then, *BOOM*, the game was over, as Floyd drove Heredia's first pitch well over the fence in right field.

Heredia is a slight man, probably speaks little or no English, and at that moment he was probably feeling like the smallest man in Florida, if not the world. He stood on the mound for a moment, staring at the spot where Floyd's blast landed, and then he trudged to the dugout with a look of bewilderment on his face, like someone who's just been hit by a car but hasn't quite registered what happened. He sat down at the edge of the bench, and as his teammates filed past on their way to the locker room, nobody paused to give Heredia a pat on the knee or a word of encouragement.

Nobody except one.

Jeff Huson.

◆ ◆ ◆

Another day, another one-run loss for the Red Sox in Toronto, as Pedro Martinez gave up three home runs for the second straight start. One of them came with a runner on base; believe it or not, it's the first time he's permitted a homer with somebody aboard since September 24, 1998 . . . 325 innings ago.

After the game, Pedro said some truly bizarre things, the *most* bizarre being, "I'm glad I gave up five runs." Near as I can tell, he's tired of everyone assuming he's perfect, and he's hoping that this game will convince them otherwise.

Brian Rose finally got demoted to Pawtucket, after yet another poor outing Saturday night. Taking his place on the roster? Twenty-seven-year-old slugger Israel Alcantara, who is leading the International League in both home runs (22) and RBI (53). He's a bat, and the Sox could sorely use such a beast these days.

Remember when the Boston Red Sox were supposed to be the best team in the American League, if not the best team in the majors? Now they're a scant three games over .500 (37–34), and six teams in the AL have better records. One of my favorite Red Sox fans e-mailed me tonight, her message consisting of two words.

"It's over."

Tuesday, June 27

Back in Boston. And looking at my scorebook after the game, I see that, for the first time this season, I didn't make a single extra note, which I suppose is one of the hazards of going to the game with a pretty girl (Susan). However, I did manage to retain enough of my wits to keep score (notwithstanding a few missed substitutions). So I can report that Pete Schourek pitched his best game of the year—seven innings, four hits, no runs—but once again failed to win (so he's still 2–6). I can report that the Red Sox held a 1–0 lead after eight innings, but Derek Lowe gave up a run in the ninth, and the game went to extra innings. I can report that Lowe stayed in to pitch the tenth, and that he gave up a single to the first hitter he faced, and a home run to the second. I can report that Lowe was removed from the game, but the Orioles scored two more runs against Bryce Florie, thanks to Nomar's fielding miscue. And finally, I can report that in the bottom of the tenth, Nomar hit a two-run homer over the Green Monster, but the Red Sox still lost the game, 6–3, and so the Orioles broke their nine-game losing streak.

Wednesday, June 28

Tonight was, I believe, the first time I've ever been truly upset by a baseball game that didn't involve the Kansas City Royals. I suppose the effects of last night's heart-breaker lingered, but I just wasn't in the mood to watch the Red Sox lose another game they should have won. But that's exactly what they did; last night it took the Sox ten innings to lose by three runs, tonight it took them eleven innings to lose by one run.

But at least they were interesting, as once again Jimy Williams spurned his designated hitter in the late innings.

The Sox trailed in the eighth, 6–5. But DH Morgan Burkhart led off the bottom of the frame with a base hit. Burkhart's slower than pond water, so Curtis Pride entered the game as a pinch-runner. I'll spare you further details on Williams's various lineup machinations; suffice it to say, the Red Sox scored twice to take a 7–6 lead, but in the process they lost their DH, with Derek Lowe now occupying the sixth slot in the batting order (they lost their DH last night, too). He blew the lead in the ninth, and when Lowe's spot came up in the bottom of the ninth, Williams sent up a pinch-hitter . . . pitcher Pete Schourek, because all of the non-pitchers had already been used . . . and Schourek singled, thus becoming the first pitcher since 1986 (Tim

Lollar, another member of the Red Sox, was the last), and the fourth since 1973, when the DH rule was instituted, to hit safely as a pinch-hitter in an American League game.

The Sox didn't score, though, and we went to extra innings again. And before it ended, Wakefield was utilized as a pinch-hitter, too. This marked the first time since 1985 that two pitchers were used as pinch-hitters in an American League game, and just the third time since 1973 . . . and Wakefield laid down a perfect sacrifice bunt. Again, to no avail, as Izzy Alcantara followed with a routine fly to center field at 11:27. That concluded a bizarre contest that lasted four hours and twenty minutes, far too long if the end result is little more than bile trying to force its way up one's digestive system.

I did have good company, though, in the person of Tom Nahigian. In fact, I probably wouldn't have been nearly as disappointed with the result if I'd been sitting by myself. But Tom wants the Red Sox to win so badly that I couldn't help but empathize with him. In the top of the fourth, after a fourth straight Oriole reached base without hitting the ball particularly hard, Tom rhapsodized,

> They need a sign,
> they need a break.
> Something. Damn.

Tom grew up, and still lives, in Arlington, about eight miles from Fenway, and he's been coming to this ballpark for thirty years. He was at Fenway on April 29, 1986, when Roger Clemens struck out twenty Seattle Mariners. And he was at Fenway last May when Nomar hit a two-run homer *and* a pair of grand slams, thus driving in ten runs.

"I went to my first game on July fifth, 1970, when I was eight years old," Tom reminisced. "It was a beautiful Sunday afternoon at Fenway, and I still can remember the feeling of being at that game. The Red Sox beat the Indians, eight to four. Mike Nagy started against Rick Austin, and John Kennedy hit an inside-the-park homer. We went as a family. My grandfather's brother John was a big Red Sox fan, and he got the tickets for everyone. Not long after that game, I sent away for autographs, and got back a postcard signed by Yaz and a photo of Tony Conigliaro, rubber-stamped with his signature. I still have them both."

I asked Tom for his favorite Fenway experience.

"Can I give you two?"

Sure, Tom.

"When I was fifteen—it was April fifteenth, 1978—I came to Fenway with my dad and his dad, my grampie, who was eighty-seven at the time. Brewers against the Red Sox. My grandfather was born in Armenia and not really a baseball fan, but I think it made him happy to see his son and grandson enjoying this American game. On this cool, bright, April day, the three of us entered the ballpark on Jersey Street (later renamed Yawkey Way). I remember an ancient usher greeting grampie with great enthusiasm; the usher was old enough to have been working here when Babe Ruth played for the Sox.

"The game moved along, the Brewers scoring two in the top of the first, the Sox answering with two in the bottom of the third. The Brewers chased Sox starter Dennis Eckersley in the sixth, taking a 6–2 lead. The Sox answered with three in the bottom of the sixth. In the seventh, Sox manager Don Zimmer called to the bullpen, and who should emerge but one of the most popular players in Red Sox history, Luis Tiant. El Tiante. All at once, the park echoed with the loud chanting, 'LOU-EE, LOU-EE.' My grandfather got a big kick out of this. El Tiante dazzled the Brew Crew with three innings of shutout relief. And in the bottom of the ninth, the Red Sox rallied for two runs, the winning run coming when Carlton Fisk doubled high off the Green Monster.

"Here's the other one. In 1982, I was attending Boston University, five minutes away from Fenway on foot, and I set a personal high, thirty-one games in one season. In a game against Cleveland in September, the Sox held their first, and last, seat-cushion giveaway. This cushion, suitable for sitting, featured the Red Sox logo. Nothing eventful happened until the fifth inning or so, when a man sitting near the Pesky Pole started banging two of the cushions together, making a racket so loud you could hear it throughout the park. And before long, chaos. Carney Lansford homered for the Sox, and suddenly the field was showered with hundreds of seat cushions. Glenn Hoffman homered, too, and again cushions came cascading from the stands. Sherm Feller, the inimitable public-address announcer, finally said, "'Try *sitting* in the cushions, it's more comfortable that way. Thank you.'"

◆ ◆ ◆

When I got home, there was already an e-mail from my best friend, Jim Baker, waiting for me . . .

> Bosox one whole game over .500 . . . time to look into a new angle on the book. How about THE BEST HOOKERS IN BOSTON? Just a thought.

I responded with:

> Thanks buddy, I'll add that to the list. Sounds better than my best alternative so far, THE RED SOX MADE ME SLIT MY WRISTS.

And then, Jim again:

> Or you could try one of these titles:
> THE RED SOX RUINED MY FUCKING BOOK
> ANOTHER WASTED YEAR AT FENWAY
> WHAT THE FUCK DID I EXPECT? IT'S THE RED SOX

Jim's a funny guy, and tonight I am incredibly thankful that he's my friend.

Thursday, June 29

Wakefield pitched seven innings of shutout ball before running into trouble in the eighth, but by that time the Sox had already scored eight runs, with Brian Daubach well on his way to the best game of his career: five hits in five at-bats, two home runs and six runs batted in.

We heard "Sweet Caroline" after the seventh. The Sox won going away, 12–4, which means they've now won seven games and lost zero when Neil Diamond has graced the sound system. Of course, the dj in the press box rarely plays "Sweet Caroline" unless the Sox are ahead in the late innings, but the song still feels like a good-luck charm.

◆　◆　◆

The Yankees and Blue Jays both won big tonight, so the Sox didn't gain any ground, except on perhaps their self-esteem issues. Here are the standings, with the Red Sox heading off for a seven-game road trip:

	W-L	GB	RS-RA	PYTHAG W-L
BLUE JAYS	44–35	—	443–450	39–40
YANKEES	38–35	3	385–364	38–35
RED SOX	38–36	3 1/2	377–327	42–32

The Yankees are dead on their Pythagorean projection; yes, this is really how "good" they are. The Bombers did finally make a big trade tonight, picking up Indians slugger David Justice. Now, Peter Gammons has been telling us for weeks that the Yankees would eventually acquire Sammy Sosa from the Cubs; it just made too much sense, he told us. Well, that did not happen, and now it's almost certainly not going to happen. Justice may well be a better fit for the Yankees, anyway, as he bats left-handed and came a lot cheaper than Sosa would have. And he's been just as good a hitter as Sosa, at least this season.

The Red Sox, meanwhile, apparently are hoping that Morgan Burkhart can step into the lineup and give them the production they've been so sorely missing; even after tonight's outburst, the Sox rank eleventh in the American League in run production. And as I've written too many times already, you don't win pennants that way.

I'm skeptical about Burkhart, but he's fast become a favorite of the Fenway Faithful. The burly switch-hitter made his major-league debut Tuesday night, and after three games he's collected six hits and drawn four walks. Burkhart's twenty-eight, old for a rookie, and one of the best stories around. Two years ago, he was in the middle of his fourth professional season. Unfortunately for his career prospects at that point, that was also his fourth season in the independent Frontier League, which was (and is) generally populated with players that none of the thirty major league clubs deemed worthy of even a late-round draft pick. Burkhart played for the Richmond (Indiana) Roosters, and won three league MVP awards in those four seasons. They only play about eighty-four games per season in the Frontier League, but here are Burkhart's combined stats for his four years in Richmond, prorated to 162 games:

G	AB	R	H	HR	RBI	BB	OBP	SLG
162	593	155	209	45	163	132	.471	.676

Yup, pretty impressive. But it was Burkhart's final season in Richmond that finally got him a shot in so-called Organized Baseball. In 1998, he hit .404 with thirty-six homers and ninety-eight RBI in just eighty games. So the Red Sox, always on the lookout for cheap ballplayers, signed the burly slugger. He spent the first half of the 1999 season pasting Class A pitchers—at twenty-seven years old, anything less probably would have gotten him a quick return to Richmond—and the second half struggling against Class AA pitchers.

However, Burkhart re-established his reputation with an MVP season in the Mexican Winter League, and opened the 2000 season with Triple-A Pawtucket. He did hit well there—.283 average, seventeen homers, and fifty-four RBI, according to the *Herald*—but not so well that the Red Sox couldn't wait to bring him up.

Now, though, he's finally here. Burkhart's fun to watch. While most hitters set up as far back in the batter's box as they're allowed, Burkhart sets up as far *forward* as he can, so that his front foot is nearly out of the box at the completion of each murderous cut. It's as if he's waited so long for his shot in the majors, he simply can't bear to wait another split-second for the pitch to arrive.

Like I said, Burkhart's a great story.

All that said, I'm not quite convinced he can help the Sox. Burkhart's stats in Pawtucket were not particularly impressive. He's in the majors not because he *earned* a promotion, but because the Sox didn't have any choice, what with all the injuries. Troy O'Leary is on the disabled dist, Trot Nixon is on the disabled list, Darren Lewis is on the disabled list . . . and Jiminy Christmas, lately Jeff Frye's been playing right field!

Friday, June 30

In the air yet again, this time for the seemingly interminable flight to Seattle. Most of my trips this season and every season, even the "vacations," are simply busman's holidays, off to visit some ballpark or another. But aside from a minor-league game in Tacoma this weekend, these next seven days will be completely baseball-less, as the Mariners are on the road and my various Pacific Northwest accommodations don't even have cable TV. I might get on the computer to check the scores (and e-mail) every day or two, but then again I might not.

What I'm hoping is that a week away from the game will, to use a tired phrase, recharge my batteries. I've now seen exactly fifty professional baseball games this season—thirty-six in Boston, six in Seattle, five in New York, two in Miami, and one in Tacoma—and I wonder if I've written everything there is to write about them.

Fifth Inning

Friday, July 7

Vacation's over. And from Monday morning until this morning at the airport, I didn't so much as look at a box score. I haven't gone so long without seeing a box score or listening to a baseball game during the season since . . . jeez, I can't imagine how long it's been. When I was in the Army National Guard, we'd be at some fort or another for two weeks every summer, but I always took a radio and listened to the Royals while huddled in my sleeping bag and gazing up at the stars. When I vacationed in France for two weeks in 1990, most days I managed to pick up a version of *USA Today* that contained at least some baseball news, the standings and abbreviated box scores. I guess it probably hasn't been since 1980—twenty years ago—when I was in a car wreck and spent a few days in the hospital, too groggy to even (consciously) think about baseball, that I completely lost touch with the game for a few days.

So what brought about this latest temporary parting of the ways between Rob Neyer and Major League Baseball?

Yes, a woman. Back in May (as you might remember), I spent some time in Washington State, and while there I also spent the better part of a day with Kristien. Since then, we've spent far too much time e-mailing to and fro. So this last week, my vacation, was supposed to give us a chance to find out if maybe we've got some sort of future. Kristien called it the Rob.com Vacation (I never did ask her whether that referred to my vacation from *being* Rob.com, or her vacation *with* Rob.com).

The first few days of Rob.com Vacation were spent in Seattle, and I did devote

a few minutes each morning to looking at box scores. Nothing serious, just checking to see how the Red Sox and Royals were faring (poorly, in both cases). But then
Kristien and I spent two days and nights in a country cottage, miles from the nearest town, or newspaper. No phone line, so no box scores. Yeah, I could have
sneaked out to the car for a scoreboard show on the radio, but frankly that never
occurred to me, not even on a theoretical basis. For a good forty-eight hours, my
thoughts of baseball were rare, and limited to occasional worries about this book.

Kristien and I returned to civilization on Wednesday afternoon, but the
damnedest thing happened . . . I never did think to plug in my laptop and look at
box scores. In our various walks around Seattle, I did have little pangs of desire
when we passed newspaper honor boxes, but I resisted the impulse to insert two
quarters. Don't get me wrong, Kristien would have been fine with a few minutes of
me perusing the sports pages. I just didn't want to interrupt whatever we were
doing at the moment. And it felt okay.

So maybe Jim's right. Maybe I'm not truly obsessed with baseball, because an
authentic obsessive couldn't live so long with nary a glance at the scores.

◆ ◆ ◆

All right, enough about me. Let's talk about the Red Sox, who still have some problems of their own. Before today, the last I knew the Sox had dropped to four and a
half games behind the Blue Jays. That was after the Sox got swept in Chicago and
looked bad in the process, getting outscored 25–8 and losing each game by at least
five runs. But then Boston traveled to Minnesota and recorded their first four-game
road sweep of the Twins ever. They'd played nineteen four-game series in
Minnesota since 1961, and they'd never swept one, until now.

Presto, back in the pennant race. Here are the standings heading into tonight's
game against the Braves:

	W-L	GB	RS-RA	PYTHAG W-L
BLUE JAYS	46–40	——	478–507	41–45
YANKEES	42–37	1/2	431–395	43–36
RED SOX	42–39	1 1/2	429–379	45–36

Third place ain't much fun, but the truth is that the Red Sox have outplayed
their competition qualitatively, if not quantitatively. The problem is that they're

6–17 in one-run games, worst in the American League. Give them just an average record in those games—say, 12–11 rather than 6–17—and the Sox would boast a four-and-a-half-game lead in the East. And people in Boston would be postponing their October vacation plans.

It's really amazing how many people miss this simple truth. I just read a column that Peter Gammons wrote for ESPN.com a couple of days ago. It runs more than 1,600 words, all on the Red Sox, and Gammons makes some wonderful points about the club's performance this season. Yet he never does mention the Sox record in one-run games, which is the single biggest reason they're not in first place.

But if you asked one hundred baseball fans—or, more worrisome to me, one hundred baseball *writers*—what this means, they'd tell you that the Red Sox are suffering from poor chemistry. Or that the Sox don't know how to win the close ones. It's all bullshit, though. That old saying about "good teams knowing how to win the close ones" is a complete and utter crock. Always has been. Good teams do win the close games, but they win them because they're good, not because they've got some magical, chemistry-related ability to win them. In the 1990s, the World Series winners won 59.9 percent of their regular-season games. Now, the common wisdom would suggest that those World Series winners must have won more than their fair share of the close ones, but did they?

No, they did not. The nine World Series winners of the 1990s won 58.8 percent of their one-run games in the regular season. For all practical purposes, that percentage is, of course, identical to the teams' overall records. One-run games are essentially about one thing. Luck. And the Red Sox' luck has been awful this season.

◆ ◆ ◆

Their luck didn't get any better tonight, either. Pete Schourek gave up five runs (and got yanked) in the second inning, and that was enough to beat the Sox, even though the bullpen combined for seven-plus shutout innings after Schourek hit the showers. The Sox put four runners on base in the bottom of the first but didn't score, thanks to first a double play, and then Bernard Gilkey's strikeout (looking, on a full count!) to end the inning. They scored three runs in the eighth, but again left the bases loaded when Varitek lifted an easy fly to center field. This came, by the way, just a few minutes after John Rocker entered the game—to a cacophony of boos, naturally—walked Ed Sprague, then was lifted after throwing just one pitch—a ball, naturally—to Manny Alexander.

Final score: Braves 5, Red Sox 3. The Blue Jays lost tonight, but the Yankees beat the Mets to take over first place in the East.

I've been incredibly careless all season long, and today it very nearly got me into trouble. This morning, I went to Fenway to buy tickets for the games tonight and tomorrow night. Once I had the tickets, I did what I always do, stuffed them into my shirt pocket and headed back home.

But then I did something that I don't normally do: laundry in the afternoon. Walked into my apartment, stripped off my shirt, and dropped it into the laundry basket. Put on another shirt, and carried the basket down to the laundry room in the basement. Tossed the darks into the washer, along with my four quarters. Back upstairs to read e-mail for an hour. Downstairs to shift darks from washer to dryer. Back upstairs to write e-mail for an hour. Downstairs to retrieve my now-dry clothes.

And it was while pulling my stuff out of the dryer than I found them: two strips of thick paper, five and a half inches by two inches, charred black. My tickets.

I didn't panic, because of course I could always buy two more. But they did cost forty bucks apiece, and while I'm now used to high ticket prices, that doesn't mean I enjoy throwing eighty dollars into the garbage. Or in this case, into the clothes dryer. So I went back to Fenway and threw myself upon the mercy of the court. They were nice about it, too. If you looked at the tickets very, very closely, you could still read them. So the guy at the window, with the help of his supervisor, deciphered my tickets and printed out replacements.

I was happy to keep my seat for tonight. After thirty-six games in the lower deck, I was finally going to sit on the "roof," a four-row level of seats that sits atop the lower deck. Mind you, the roof seats aren't typical "upper deck" seats. In most ballparks, especially the new ones, the upper deck is a long ways from the action, so far from the field that it's fairly rare for a foul ball to even reach the seats. At Fenway, on the other hand, the upper deck is so close to the field that not only do foul balls routinely reach the heights, but three or four times per game they soar *over* the upper deck, headed for parts unknown.

I guess I'm spoiled, though, because as close as the upper deck is, it felt too far away. I did enjoy the different perspective, which is especially useful if you want to know how different hitters set up in the batter's box. Atlanta's Walt Weiss, for example, stands as deep in the box as anybody in the game, with his big toe just touching the back line, like a little boy testing the temperature of the pool water. And then there's rookie Morgan Burkhart, who stands as far *forward* as anybody I've ever seen. When Burkhart finishes his swing, his front foot nearly ends up on the infield grass, which is technically against the rules.

◆ ◆ ◆

Another thing about the roof seats, you've got a better view of things outside of Fenway Park. And this was a great night for a better view, because for most of the second inning, half a rainbow was visible to the northeast, over Logan Airport.

And you know what? It was almost too much. I am so captivated by the beauty of the game on the field, that adding another dollop of beauty approaches sensory overload. What am I supposed to watch? Tom Glavine's subtle artistry, or the primary hues using the sky as a giant coloring book?

Saturday, July 8

The Red Sox looked awful tonight, scoring just one run in eight innings against Terry Mulholland, the Braves' number-five starter and a crafty left-hander whose best years are well behind him. The Sox did collect seven hits, but couldn't manage a single walk, against either Mulholland or his replacement, John Rocker. Meanwhile, Ramon pitched decently, but left in the sixth and the Braves wound up winning 5–1.

Early on, the guy sitting next to me saw my scorebook, asked, "What are you, a scout?"

To which I responded, "Nah, just a nut."

That seemed to satisfy both him and his girlfriend.

The truth is that I'm a little tired of the questions, and not much in the mood for conversation tonight, but at least these two left me alone (before they were ejected from the seats in the fourth inning by the rightful owners). The worst was last night, when a different girlfriend asked a bunch of silly questions, my least favorite of them, "So, are you going to put us in your book?"

I couldn't help but tell the truth.

"Sure, if you do something interesting." Implying, of course, that the couple hadn't done or said anything interesting yet, and wasn't likely to. And they didn't.

◆ ◆ ◆

Troy O'Leary went one for three tonight in his first home game since June 17. This was actually O'Leary's fifth game since coming off the disabled list last Monday, and since then he's eight for twenty with two homers. Considering that he'd hit only five home runs in the first three months of the season, O'Leary's recent performance has to be considered a good sign. He was batting an empty .211—and I mean *empty*— when he went on the DL, and if the Sox are going to have any chance at all this season, O'Leary has to do a lot better than that.

◆ ◆ ◆

I didn't want to be in Boston today.

My first choice would have been New York City, where the Yankees and Mets played the first one-city, two-ballpark, major league doubleheader since September 7, 1903, when the New York Giants faced off against the Brooklyn Superbas.

A few weeks ago, the Mets and Yankees were rained out. Given their schedules, today was the most feasible day for a makeup game. Shea Stadium in the afternoon, Yankee Stadium in the evening, and I really wanted to be at both stadiums for the games. I had tickets lined up, too.

The problem was that the Red Sox hosted the Braves today. And if I were in New York I couldn't be here, thus breaking my perfect record of attending every Red Sox home game. Still (I figured), the doubleheader in New York would make a great story in the book, far better than some humdrum contest between the Bostons and the Atlantas, right?

So I decided to go to New York. Then I decided to stay in Boston. Then I decided to ask somebody else what I should do. I asked my editor. I asked my editor's assistant. I asked a friend who's an editor. I asked my best friend. I asked my best friend's best friend. I asked my best friend's best friend's barber.

The final vote was exactly even. But my editor—right now and for the next nine or ten months, the second-most important person in my life—"suggested" that I stay in Boston. So that's what I did. Thus, while watching the Sox lose to the Braves today, I missed seeing the Yankees take two from the Mets.

Today was a tough day for the Mets (and their fans), and a tough day for the Red Sox (and their fans). Yesterday afternoon the Sox were one game behind the Yankees, but in two days they've dropped two and a half games relative to the Bombers . . . and tomorrow they have to face Greg Maddux.

Sunday, July 9

Today, it happened.

The Boston Red Sox, the Old Towne Team, the Bosox, finally caught a big break. They were supposed to face Greg Maddux, arguably the best pitcher of the last half-century, and one of the better pitchers of this particular season, currently boasting a 10–3 record and a 3.32 ERA. But yesterday in batting practice, Maddux got nailed in the shoulder by a baseball, and today that shoulder was sore. He couldn't pitch today, and he won't pitch in the All-Star Game Tuesday night.

Then again, the Sox might have won this afternoon even if Maddux had been able to pitch, because Tim Wakefield pitched his best game of the season, permitting just two runs in seven innings. Garces and Lowe each tossed a scoreless inning, and the Sox picked up an easy 7–2 victory, thanks to Wakefield and to Garciaparra, who slugged a pair of home runs against Braves starter Kevin Millwood.

The Blue Jays won today, trounced the Expos in Montreal.

With the Atlanta Braves in town, today seemed like the perfect time to see where the Boston Braves used to play. And it's not far from here. After leaving Fenway at the conclusion of today's game, instead of turning left and heading for home, I turned right and headed for Kenmore Square. There, I turned left and headed west on Commonwealth Avenue. And two-thirds of a mile down, I found Nickerson Field, the former site of Braves Field, home of the Boston's National League team from 1915 through 1952.

There was a time when Braves Field and Fenway Park bracketed Boston University like bookends. Whenever I pass this way, walking or riding my bike down Comm Ave, I wonder what it would have been like, to be a B.U. student *and* a baseball fan in those years. According to my watch, it would have been a twenty-two minute walk from the main gates of Fenway Park to the main gates of Braves Field.

Near as I can figure, the only downside would be that the best months, weatherwise, are during the summer vacation. But if you pick your spots, there are certainly some nice days for baseball every April, May, and September. And with two ballparks so close, you'd certainly have plenty of spots to pick from.

Regrettably, those years when both ballparks were home to major-league teams, 1915 through 1952, were mostly lean ones for Boston baseball. The 1920s and

'30s were particularly rough. There's one season, though, when the atmosphere in these parts must have been something else.

Nineteen hundred and forty-eight. On September 23, the Braves clinched their first National League pennant since 1914. Meanwhile, the very next day, the Red Sox found themselves in a three-way tie for first place in the American League with the Indians and Yankees, all of them with 91–56 records.

The Yankees fell off the pace, but on October 4 at Fenway Park, the Red Sox and Indians squared off in a one-game playoff for the A.L. flag, the winner earning the right to face the Braves, two days later, in Game 1 of the World Series, a World Series that had already been dubbed—assuming the Red Sox made it—"the Streetcar Series," as Braves Field and Fenway were merely six stops apart on the Green Line.

In a decision that will forever be second-guessed, Sox manager Joe McCarthy selected Denny Galehouse, rather than ace Mel Parnell or fastballer Ellis Kinder, to start against Cleveland in the playoff. Galehouse didn't have anything that cool, partly cloudy afternoon, and in the fourth inning Indians third baseman Ken Keltner hit a three-run homer over The Wall to give his club a 4–0 lead. The final was 8–3, and the Indians went on to beat the Braves in a six-game Series. (For a wonderfully written and researched account of the playoff game, see pages 264 through 266 in *Red Sox Century*, previously cited.)

W. P. Kinsella famously wrote, "Is this heaven?" "No, this is Iowa." But it seems to me that for a baseball fan in 1948, Boston University would have been heaven.

That was as close as the Red Sox and Braves—who moved to Milwaukee in 1953, and then Atlanta in 1966—ever came to meeting in a World Series. So it was only through the "magic" of interleague play that they finally met in a game that counted for something. I'm not a proponent of the Americans and Nationals mixing before October, but this particular matchup does carry a certain historical resonance (though after all these years I would assume that any such resonance is lost on most of the fans in the stands).

Unlike the great majority of ex-ballpark sites, this one is still used for close to the same purpose as in its glory days. Where once stood Braves Field is now Nickerson Field, the locus of Boston University athletics. What's more, actual remnants of Braves Field remain. The old right-field pavilion has been transformed into a section of stands. And the old main gates into the ballpark, a three-story building with arched entrances, now serves as the Boston University Children's Center, and headquarters for the Boston University Police. There's an open space between this building and the stands, and emplaced there is a large plaque, placed atop a boulder, that reads

SITE OF BRAVES FIELD
1915–1952
THE FANS OF NEW ENGLAND WILL NEVER FORGET THE
EXPLOITS OF THEIR BRAVES
AND THE FOND MEMORIES ASSOCIATED WITH BRAVES FIELD
THREE WORLD SERIES
1948 BRAVES DEFEATED BY CLEVELAND FOUR GAMES TO TWO
1916 RED SOX DEFEAT BROOKLYN FOUR GAMES TO ONE
1915 RED SOX DEFEAT PHILADELPHIA FOUR GAMES TO ONE
MAJOR LEAGUE BASEBALL'S LONGEST GAME, MAY 1, 1920
BRAVES VS BROOKLYN DODGERS, 26 INNINGS, 1–1 TIE,
PITCHERS JOE OESCHGER OF
THE BRAVES AND LEON CADORE OF THE DODGERS
PITCHED COMPLETE GAMES
HOME OF VARIOUS PROFESSIONAL FRANCHISES SUCH
AS BOSTON BRAVES
FOOTBALL TEAM (NFL), BOSTON PATRIOTS (AFL), AND
BOSTON BREAKERS (USFL)
THE LEGACY OF BRAVES FIELD LIVES ON TODAY IN THE FORM OF
NICKERSON FIELD, HUB OF BOSTON UNIVERSITY ATHLETICS
THIS PLAQUE ERECTED AUGUST 6, 1988 BY BOSTON
UNIVERSITY, SOCIETY
FOR AMERICAN BASEBALL RESEARCH, AND NEW ENGLAND
SPORTS MUSEUM

I learned something today! I didn't know that the Red Sox won two World Series here at Braves Field (or if I did know, I forgot). In 1915, once the Red Sox reached the Series they adopted Braves Field as their home park, because Braves Field—just christened the previous August—featured the largest crowd capacity in the major leagues. Indeed, attendance for Game 3 of the World Series was 42,300, a new postseason record. And when the Red Sox captured another pennant in 1916, again they moved to Braves Field for the Series, and again they beat their National League foes (this time the Dodgers) in five games. In Game 2 of that Series, a kid named Babe Ruth went the distance, pitching fourteen innings to beat Brooklyn, 2–1.

Monday, July 10

Late last night, I arrived in Atlanta for the All-Star Game, as a representative of ESPN.com (and I was on the same airplane as Nomar Garciaparra, who, along with Carl Everett and Derek Lowe, will represent the Red Sox).

I could cover more events than I do, but frankly it tends to involve a fair amount of actual work, consisting mostly of (1) tracking down ballplayers for the same quotes that everyone else is getting and (2) writing stories about games that people have already seen. I don't much like "work," which I define as anything that's not fun. Getting generic quotes and writing generic stories ain't much fun.

This time, though, I got the impression from my editor that my career would benefit from a trip to Atlanta. And figuring it might be good for this book, I agreed to go.

So today, I worked. The day before the All-Star Game, every player is installed behind a table in a big banquet room in a downtown hotel, for the sole purpose of answering questions from baseball writers. First the American Leaguers for an hour, and then the National Leaguers for an hour. I asked Derek Lowe about pitching for Lou Piniella, I asked Mike Sweeney if he would like to be a catcher again someday, and I asked Jason Giambi about the development of Terrence Long. Those guys all had something to say, stuff I could use in a "notebook" piece I was putting together for ESPN.com. I also spoke with Jeff Kent and Troy Glaus and Darryl Kile, and they were all a complete waste of time. Kent was boring ("I'm just going out there and working hard."), Glaus bristled at my moderately controversial question (about his relationship with his hitting coach), and Kile simply wished he could be anywhere else in the world (twenty minutes into the session, he was already asking a representative from his union, "Do you know long we have to be here?").

Overall, the players were friendly, and more interesting than I'd expected, but then again, this is a special event. I still think the *Herald*'s Charles Pierce had it right when he wrote, ". . . the reason that so many people have taken to becoming baseball essayists, rather than baseball reporters, is because essayists do not have to deal with the overwhelming number of rude and stupid people who play the game."

Actually, I think that perhaps Pierce overstates his case. In my admittedly limited experience—today, plus a few locker-room interviews over the years—only a few players have actually been rude, and even fewer struck me as downright stupid. But it's strange, discomforting work, hanging around someplace where you're not particularly welcome, and asking half-naked men the sorts of questions that they've answered hundreds of times. For the most part it's drudgery, and I think I'd rather deliver pizzas for a living.

And then this evening, I went to Turner Field for the Home Run Derby. It lasted nearly two hours, and between the heat and the boredom, I actually nodded off a few times. There were brief periods of excitement when Sammy Sosa batted—he finished the night with a record twenty-six homers, some of them gigantic blasts into the upper deck—but the rest of it was mind-numbing. It didn't help that David and I, along with hundreds of other electronic media, were parked in the auxiliary press box, a dark, slightly fetid place well beyond the fence in left-center field.

The most interesting part of my evening came near the end. It was late, and David and I were in the parking lot outside Turner Field, waiting to board a bus that would take us back downtown, where we could retrieve our rental car. As we stood there, I noticed, in another line not far away, two little boys wearing Red Sox T-shirts, and for some reason both shirts had DUQUETTE lettered across the back. This struck me as a little strange, and I pointed out the kids to Dave.

"Yeah, that's Dan Duquette," he said.

And sure enough, standing behind the boys was Boston's general manager, right there in living bland.

Now, what kind of man dresses his little boys in matching T-shirts and then parades them around like animated trophies?

Well, here's something else about Dan Duquette. In the Boston Red Sox Media Guide, Duquette's biography runs exactly 1,224 words.

That's a lot. I went through the media guides of the other thirteen American League clubs, and discovered that the average of the fourteen American League general managers is a shade over 580 words. But that average—or the *mean*, as a statistician would say—is misleading, because two GMs, Duquette and Tampa Bay's Chuck LaMar (1,282 words) seriously skew the average. The *median* of the group—

that is, half the sample is lower, half the sample is higher—is 517 words. After LaMar and Duquette, the next-highest number of words devoted to a general manager is 729, for Chicago's Ron Schueler.

Here's another revealing thing from Duquette's bio in the media guide: "Duquette . . . has constructed one of baseball's best overall operations. The Red Sox system provides a feeder system for the major league club with players rising through the system to the majors such as Nomar, OF Trot Nixon and INFs Donnie Sadler and Wilton Veras."

Huh? You're holding up Donnie Sadler and Wilton Veras as examples of Duquette's player-development acumen? I know that Duquette didn't actually write this crap, but I guarantee you that, as general manager, he read every word of his bio before it went to press. Now, perhaps I shouldn't attempt to engage in armchair psychology in what's supposed to be a baseball book, but it seems to me that all those words, 1,224 of them, in addition to telling us about a man's personal, professional, and charitable accomplishments, might also tell us something about his personality. Something that perhaps he'd rather we didn't know.

Observing him from the other side of the continent, I never really understood why so many people didn't like the Red Sox general manager. But after observing him from four blocks away, I'm starting to understand.

Tuesday, July 11

I enjoyed FanFest. I didn't think I would, but I did.

FanFest is an annual event, takes place every year somewhere close to whichever ballpark is hosting the All-Star Game. Like most things these days, it's essentially a marketing gimmick, with a bunch of companies trying to sell stuff.

As I walked past the vendors' tables, I realized that I have finally outgrown the desire to collect things. No more cards, no more signed balls, no more miniature likenesses of professional athletes molded in hard plastic. Nothing except books.

Yes (I'm thinking), after all these years I'm officially a grown-up.

And then I saw the Hoyt Wilhelm baseball card. Nineteen fifty-three Topps, one of the few Wilhelm cards that I don't already own. Wilhelm's one of only two knuckleball pitchers in the Hall of Fame, and of course I do love knuckleball pitchers. And so after a moment of dickering it was mine, for the reasonable sum of twenty-five American dollars. Okay, so maybe I'm not a grown-up after all . . . but I'll *need*

Wilhelm's '53 Topps when I get around to writing my book about knuckleballers, right? Where else could I learn that in 1951, the rookie Wilhelm's mound appearances fell just three short of the all-time record?

Thus, having convinced myself that I was indeed all growed up, I continued my adultlike stroll between the vendors' tables, looking upon the products with a haughty disdain the result of my maturity . . . and then I saw the baseball signed by a significant number of 1944 Washington Senators. The roster that year included four knuckleballers, and three of them—Roger Wolff, Mickey Haefner, and Johnny Niggeling—signed this particular, circa 1944 Rawlings baseball (missing, unfortunately, the signature of Dutch Leonard, the best of the knuckleballing quartet). The label said $375, and after a bout of spirited haggling—Me: "Any wiggle room on the price?" Him: "I can go to three hundred." Me: "Do you take credit cards?"—I had tangible, spherical proof that I have not growed up at all. At least not when it comes to knuckleball pitchers.

◆ ◆ ◆

At 8:45 tonight, just a few seconds before Randy Johnson threw his first pitch in the 2000 All-Star Game, it hit me: *I can't cheer.* It's been so long since I sat in a press box, going on two years now, that I'd forgotten the rules: no alcohol (don't care) and no cheering (do care). And no singing "Take Me Out to the Ball Game," either. Granted, I'm not actually in the press box proper—like the great majority of the media, I'm in the auxiliary press area, far beyond the left-field fence—but I think the rules here are the same.

I *hate* that. Or maybe I *can* cheer. I'm not sure. If Jermaine Dye takes Tom Glavine deep and I start screaming, what are they going to do? Take away my membership in the Baseball Writer's Association of America? Nope, because the BBWAA won't let me join in the first place (newspaper writers only need apply). I suspect that if I do stand and applaud Jermaine Dye or Mike Sweeney, the only thing that'll happen is the people around me will think I'm a bit daft. And they might report me to the Fun Police, but I can handle those goons.

Regrettably, the extent of the Royals-related excitement was Dye's leadoff walk in the fourth, and even I wasn't moved by that action. If the American Leaguers had taken a late-innings lead, I might have jumped out of my seat. But that wasn't necessary, as the National Leaguers spent the last four frames flailing away helplessly.

And boy, do I love it when the Americans beat the Nationals.

For every day of the baseball season, I'm neutral in the A.L. vs. N.L. debate. On a personal level, I prefer the American League because I don't particularly enjoy watching pitchers (try to) hit. But on an intellectual level, the game does seem to make more sense if every fielder, including the guy on the mound, has to bat. And I misspent much of my youth watching National League games on TV, on WGN (Cubs) and WTBS (Braves). So I got no complaints against the Senior Circuit (as broadcasters used to call the National League).

But once the All-Star break rolls around, I hate the National League. It's not so much that they kept beating the Americans all those years, it's that they were so damned arrogant about it. And about . . . well, about everything. They don't talk about the All-Star Game anymore because it's been pretty even for the last five years or so. But they still talk about the "more aggressive style of play" in the National League, which always drives me nuts. Like you put a guy in an American League uniform and suddenly his testosterone level drops off the table like a David Wells curveball. Please.

Wednesday, July 12

Another flight, another Nomar sighting. This shouldn't be a big surprise, I guess, as there are only so many nonstop flights between Boston and Atlanta. I didn't actually see him this time. I boarded the plane fairly early, and a few minutes later a trio of high-school kids sat in my row, excited because they'd seen Nomar chatting with Mia Hamm in the waiting area. Now he was supposedly sitting by himself in first class, and so the kid next to me asked if he could borrow a piece of paper. I tore a sheet from my notebook, and damn if the kid didn't return a few minutes later with my scrap of paper, now adorned with Garciaparra's moderately legible signature.

I don't profess to know what Nomar thought about on our flight home. Maybe he was thinking about Mia Hamm the entire five hours we were in the air, but I hope that he spent at least a few minutes thinking about the pennant race. I sure was . . .

	W-L	GB	RS-RA	PYTHAG W-L
YANKEES	45–38	——	441–402	45–38
BLUE JAYS	48–41	——	502–523	43–46
RED SOX	43–41	2 ½	440–391	47–37

The last month obviously hasn't been kind to the Red Sox, who have gone from first place to third. But of course, two and a half games isn't a lot of ground to make up, not in the middle of July. And even more heartening is the last column in that table. If we look at the Pythagorean records, the Yankees and Red Sox are virtually even, qualitatively, with the Jays significantly behind.

And by gosh, I can't think of anywhere I'd rather be than New England in late summer, with the Yankees and Red Sox dueling for the East flag. I just can't help myself. I *love* pennant races, always have and always will.

Anyway, this particular three-team pennant race took a significant turn today, as the Yankees swung a big deal with the Cincinnati Reds, acquiring left-handed pitcher Denny Neagle in exchange for four minor leaguers. The Yankees were already considered the favorites in the East, but now they're no-brainer favorites. Defending world champs sitting in first place, and they just added one of baseball's top five or six left-handed pitchers to their rotation? Yep, it's official. The Sox are playing catch-up.

Thursday, July 13

Tonight I sat farther from the field than I usually do, up in the grandstand beyond third base. I was perfectly centered between two supporting beams, so watching the game was like watching a movie, with the posts on the sides, the upper deck on top and the fans below me serving as the borders of the screen.

And if today's game were a movie, the central theme would have been "missed opportunities."

Missed opportunities. They're not native just to baseball fans. Ask a rabid fan of nearly any sports team (except maybe the Yankees, who never seem to miss their opportunities) about missed opportunities, and he can remember them. I still remember a completely meaningless Royals-Rangers game in which every Ranger ground ball somehow sneaked through the infield ("grounders with eyes"), and every Royal line drive veered directly into a defender's glove ("atom balls," as in "right at 'em"). That was a dozen years ago, and I still think about it sometimes even though each of the uniformed participants probably had forgotten that game a week later.

Red Sox fans are going to remember this game for its missed opportunities, doubly so if the Sox wind up missing a postseason berth by just a few games.

Pedro Martinez came off the DL after not pitching in eighteen days, and pitched like he's supposed to (seven innings, ten strikeouts, five hits, and only two runs).

All evening long, the Sox failed to score despite placing plenty of runners on base (seven in the first four innings, including three in the fourth).

What made this all the more painful was the American League scoreboard at the base of the Green Monster (the Yankees were losing to the Marlins in the sixth, eight to three, and the Blue Jays were losing to the Phillies in the eighth, also eight to three).

The Sox did finally score in the seventh, when Morgan Burkhart's two-run homer—his second as a major leaguer and his first at Fenway Park—into the home bullpen tied the game at two apiece.

But in the top of the eighth, the Mets scored an unearned run, with the help of Carl Everett's error that allowed Edgardo Alfonzo to sprint all the way home from first base on Mike Piazza's single. The Sox threatened in their half of the eighth, but were thwarted by first baseman Todd Zeile's diving stop of O'Leary's grounder down the first-base line. If the ball gets past Zeile, Nomar could have jogged home from second base with the tying run. Instead, he merely advanced to third, and died there when Burkhart struck out looking.

It was still 3–2 when the Red Sox came up in the bottom of the ninth. Varitek grounded out to Zeile, but pinch-hitter Scott Hatteberg worked reliever John Franco for a walk (and was replaced by pinch-runner Manny Alexander). A good start for a rally, but unfortunately Franco was yanked in favor of Armando Benitez, a block of a man who throws the ball ninety-five miles an hour. And while he didn't strike out the next hitter, Jose Offerman, he did even better; Benitez got Offerman to hit into a double play. Six to four to three, and the game was over.

But for a few inches here and there—hell, but for a few *tenths* of inches—the Red Sox could easily have won this game. Instead, they lost their first game of the season's second half, and they failed to pick up any ground on their competition. One can only hope that this isn't some kind of omen for the rest of the season.

◆ ◆ ◆

Okay, a confession. I've been cheating. Lying. Obfuscating. Because you know what? The Sox *did* win this game. In the bottom of the ninth inning they started getting the inches, and the tenths of inches.

Not that all of it was a lie. Everything up there is the truth, until the last couple of paragraphs. Offerman didn't hit into a game-ending double play, but he did hit what Mets shortstop Melvin Mora called a "perfect" double-play ball. But Mora bobbled the ball—*an inch for the Sox!*—and all hands were safe. Jeff Frye followed with a fly to center field that moved Offerman to third base. That brought up Brian Daubach, who's come through so many times in the last year. With the count one-and-two, Benitez threw a fastball just off the outside corner—*a tenth of an inch for the Sox!*—for ball two. And Daubach lined Benitez's next pitch over right fielder Derek Bell and into the right-field corner, where it struck the bottom of the padding and just . . . *stuck.* If the ball had hit the padding just a bit higher, it would have bounced back to Bell, who might well have had a shot at throwing out Offerman at the plate. Had it hit short of the fence, it might have come back to Bell, or bounced into the stands, or been interfered with by a fan.

For the first time this season, I cried at Fenway Park. I didn't look around to see if anyone else was crying, too, because then people could have seen the tears rolling down my cheeks. Now that I think about it, though, I'm sure that all the fans around me, most of them with larger emotional stakes in the Sox than I've got, would have been too busy enjoying the moment to notice me.

Friday, July 14

It was a weird night, all the way around.

My friend Pete, a Mets fan, took the train up from New York this afternoon, and we arrived at Fenway a few minutes early for the 7:05 start. What we found was a huge throng of people, wedged into the street and sidewalks along Yawkey Way, between the ballpark and the souvenir shops, like college students stuffed inside a Volkswagen.

Why? Because the gates were closed. And in typical Red Sox fashion, there were no official announcements, no signs, no team employees shouting updates from the office windows above us. Eventually, word did pass through the crowd that a transformer in the area had blown, resulting in a power failure throughout Fenway Park. This didn't really explain why the team hadn't opened the gates— would it really be so awful if we took our seats inside a powerless ballpark?—but like I said, that's the Red Sox for you. Thoughts of the fans, if they come at all, are always last.

So there we stood, in the middle of the masses, until the gates finally opened a few minutes before eight o'clock, and Pete Schourek threw the first pitch at 8:07, almost exactly an hour late.

The game was worth the wait. Mike Piazza hit a couple of titanic homers over the Green Monster. Nomar collected four hits, lifting his batting average to .400 on the nose with a ninth-inning double off the Monster. The bottom of the seventh inning was vividly wild. Jimy Williams came out twice and asked plate umpire Marty Foster to inspect baseballs thrown by Mets reliever Dennis Cook. Shortly after the second of these visits, Scott Hatteberg and Mets catcher Todd Pratt started scream-ing at each other, with both benches emptying. And with his very next pitch, Cook buzzed Hatteberg with an oh-and-two fastball, high and tight. That got Cook a warn-ing from Foster, and two batters later he got an ejection after plunking Everett. With the Sox trailing 6–4 in the bottom of the ninth, Manny Alexander came up with two runners on base and two outs.

Would the Sox do it again? If the noise being produced by the 33,293 in atten-dance was any indication, they thought so. Alas, Alexander's no Brian Daubach, and he struck out swinging, helpless at the sight of Armando Benitez's serious heat.

So we all trooped out of the ballpark, most of us unhappy with the loss, yet still thrilled with the action. Unfortunately, I still had some not-so-thrilling action in my future.

Just as I was about to cross the threshold of Gate E and step onto the sidewalk, I caught a sudden flurry of movement out of the corner of my eye. I looked to my left and understood immediately what had just happened.

A somewhat geeky-looking man, carrying a Mets athletic bag and wearing decidedly unstylish glasses, had just been punched in the face. Blood was dripping steadily from the middle of his brow, and forming a small pool on the cement floor, right next to his glasses, which had apparently been jarred loose, and broken, by the punch. The young man who had dealt the blow—he was wearing a black leather jacket, decidedly stylish short hair, and a sneer as indifferent as a sneer can be—lingered for a moment to admire his handiwork, and then turned on his heel and walked briskly east on Lansdowne.

And I didn't do a damn thing to stop him.

Was it fear that paralyzed me, for the two or three seconds that mattered?

I don't think so, because the prospect of being struck by another man's fist doesn't scare me much.

I've been hit, I mean really *hit*, twice in my life.

First time. I was ten years old, and almost exactly a year older than my brother, Eric. Dad thought it would be good for us to learn how to box. Sounded like fun to us—organized fighting? Hell yeah!—and even in hindsight I think it was a pretty good idea. God knows I could have used some toughening up. Anyway, the old man had each of us strap on a pair of peewee boxing gloves, and then he taught us how to keep our guards up, and jab with the left hand while protecting ourselves with the right hand . . . all that manly stuff. Unfortunately, our first basement sparring session lasted all of, oh, maybe fifteen seconds. Eric faked to my middle with his left, then nailed me with a right cross. And the next thing I know, I'm staring at the ceiling, wondering how the hell big brother got decked. I've always been bigger than Eric, still outweigh him by fifteen or twenty pounds even though we're the same height and roughly the same build. We fought constantly as kids, and Eric never hurt me. He just wasn't big enough or mean enough. But the only time we ever had a fair fight, he knocked me out.

Second time. Fast-forward four years. I'm at the Oak Park Public Library in Overland Park, Kansas—safe territory, right?—and who should sit down across the table from me but Scott: two years older than me, mean as hell, an inveterate bully. Scott had taken a few shots at me before, but never anything serious. This day, it was like we'd never met. I loaned him a few sheets of notebook paper. When it was time to go home, I preceded my friend Chuck outside, lurking around a corner to surprise him. But it was me that got the surprise. Instead of Chuck, it was my favorite bully coming around the corner, and as soon as he saw me, *Wham*, Scott slugged me hard, just under my left eye.

This wasn't another knockout. It was worse. I fell back against the wall, slumped to the ground, and started bawling like a baby that's been hungry for two hours. It wasn't the pain, it really wasn't. Getting hit in the face does not particularly *hurt*. It's worse than pain. It's disorienting as hell, taking you from where you were—wonderful, blessed consciousness—to somewhere different, a place where you don't have any control of your body, your faculties, or your emotions. That's why so many boxers just sort of quit when they're getting beat up, unable to defend themselves. It's not that they lack heart, it's that after taking enough shots to the head, they simply can no longer function as they would like.

But it doesn't *hurt*. And that realization is liberating as hell. After Scott clocked me, I was never afraid of getting hit. From that point, when bullies started up with me, I just went right toward them. And I know it's a cliché, but bullies don't like it when their victims fight back, so all but the toughest move along in search of easier pickings.

So if I wasn't afraid, then what? Why didn't I go after this thug who assaulted someone practically right in front of me. Was it simply an inability to react quickly?

Perhaps, but I haven't always been so slow to react. When I was a senior in high school, I played intramural basketball with all the other kids who weren't good enough to make the varsity. At the conclusion of one game, an opposing player— Dennis, a former teammate of mine on the sophomore football team, and a guy that I'd always got along with okay—belted a casual friend of mine, Matt, who'd been refereeing the game. Dennis ran up behind Matt, and slugged him hard on the side of the head. Matt fell to the ground like he'd been shot, and I was so outraged that I impulsively wrapped up Dennis—who was both stronger and meaner than I—and wrestled him to the ground, screaming at him the whole time.

My anger subsided fairly quickly—I've never been able to sustain a violent rage for long—and when I released Dennis, he sprinted off before the adults in the gym could detain him.

A trifling incident, remembered by practically nobody (perhaps including even Dennis, who got into more serious trouble later, and might not even remember something as mindless as punching a classmate upside the head). But I suspect that Matt will take the pain and humiliation of that moment to his grave, and I know that I will take that moment, when I reacted without fear or hesitation, to mine.

And for many years, I thought of myself as that young man who wasn't afraid, who saw an injustice and did what seemed like the right thing. I never actually did anything like that again, but in the back of my mind (and sometimes in the front), I thought that I would if the occasion arose.

Tonight I didn't, and I suppose it's time to revise the ol' self-image. I'm not really so quick and brave after all. Were I quick and brave, I'd have sprinted after that bullying bastard, tackled him to the asphalt, and hung on until the authorities took charge. Instead, I stood there like a damn parking meter while that bullying bastard ran off into the night, where he would face nothing but his own deficient conscience.

And the victim? He didn't seem to be seriously hurt, although I suspect he wound up with two or three stitches.

And the Fenway fans? I hate to tar them all with the same brush, but there is certainly more violence inside and outside this ballpark than any other I've visited. During the games, people fight in the bleachers. And then after the games, alcohol-soaked men punch other men for no particular reason.

Of course, the great majority of the people at the ballpark don't get drunk, aren't violent, and want little more than to see the Sox win and get home at a reasonable hour. The great majority of the people at the ballpark are just like people at all the other ballparks, but with a bit more passion and a bit more memory.

Saturday, July 15

Last night's game featured enough anger for an entire series, but of course anger often begets violence, and it seems that what happened today might well have been precipitated last night.

In the bottom of the second inning. Everett leads off for the Sox and, as he always does, takes great pains to erase the chalk that delineates the inside edge of the batter's box. The switch-hitting Everett is batting right-handed (against the left-handed Mike Hampton), so it's that box that gets his attention.

When Everett bats right-handed, he erases the inside line and places his back (right) foot quite close to the plate, with a few inches of that foot completely outside the (now-vanished) line defining the box. When he bats left-handed, he erases the inside line and places his front (right) foot quite close the plate, with a few inches of that foot completely outside the (now-vanished) line defining the box. Got all that? The result is that Everett crowds the plate as much as any hitter in the history of the game, and so he's almost impossible to pitch inside.

So in this case Everett is erasing the inside line, then setting up with his back foot nearly touching the plate. Hampton throws a strike, catcher Mike Piazza complains that Everett is setting up illegally, and plate umpire Ron Kulpa steps up and redraws the inside line of the box with his foot. Everett sets up illegally again. Kulpa redraws the line again. Hampton throws another strike. Everett starts jawing at Kulpa. Everett is ejected.

And then things got a little crazy. Everett behaved as if someone had cursed his mama, slapped his kids, and violated his wife. Everett's bout of temporary madness, as strange as it looked, doesn't particularly interest me. Yes, it's just another in a long list of incidents, but what interests me is, what does all this mean for *the game*.

Rule 6.03 of baseball's Official Rules states, "The batter's legal position shall be with both feet within the batter's box. APPROVED RULING: The lines defining the box are within the batter's box."

The rules, unfortunately, do not tell us what should happen to a hitter who refuses to take a legal position in the batter's box. But the umpire essentially is empowered to take whatever action necessary to get the hitter where he belongs. In practice, that usually means a warning that takes care of the problem. But if a player refuses to obey a rule, thus making a mockery of the game, the umpire does have the right to simply eject said player. It never comes to that, though, because very few players are as stubborn as Everett.

After the game, various Red Sox complained to the press that Kulpa enforced the batter's box only because Bobby Valentine or Dennis Cook or Mike Piazza pointed out Everett's indiscretion. Crew chief Randy Marsh, who was at first base on Saturday, did give Piazza some "credit." According to Marsh, Piazza said, "Come on, what's the deal? The guy's standing way inside."

But Marsh also claimed that Piazza's comment was irrelevant. "He doesn't have to make a complaint," Marsh said. "Anytime we see a guy that's standing over the line, we have to tell him to get back in the box."

Sure, Randy. Then why don't you always do it? Everett's been pulling this shit all season long, yet it's not until Game No. 87 that somebody tells him to get back in the box?

There aren't any good guys here. Carl Everett is wrong, both for breaking the rules and for head-butting an umpire. Ron Kulpa and Randy Marsh are wrong, because they shouldn't have waited until this weekend to notice that Everett consistently breaks the rules. It sure would be nice if the umpires enforced the rules, without having to be prompted by self-interested players and managers. It would be nice if the umpires enforced the rules uniformly and consistently.

Here's a start: Any hitter that comes to the plate and starts messing with the lines—back, front, inside, outside—shall immediately be ejected. There is no conceivable rationale for allowing hitters to destroy those lines, and frankly I'm sick of watching them do it.

After all, Everett didn't go berserk because a rule was enforced. He went berserk because a rule was enforced for the first time this season, after eighty-six games of non-enforcement. Throw in what is apparently—let's be blunt—a touch of madness, and you've got a recipe for violence. Call it a crime of passion, but Everett still deserves a lengthy suspension, at least ten games.

◆ ◆ ◆

Yes, there was actually a baseball game played at Fenway Park, though I don't suppose anyone will remember anything that happened after the second inning. Looking at my scorebook, though, I see that the Sox got more than their fair share of breaks: a bunch of bloop hits, and a few ground balls with eyes. What's more, Everett's replacement, Brian Daubach, lofted a fly ball over the Green Monster in the sixth inning, for a three-run homer that made the difference in Boston's 6–4 victory.

Unnoticed in all the hullabaloo was the return of Izzy Alcantara from his two-week exile to the bench, the result of sloppy, lackadaisical play in Chicago. Nestled into the number-seven spot in the order, Izzy singled and doubled in four at-bats.

Fenway Moment: Pete wore his Mets T-shirt to the game, and as we were making our way down Yawkey Way afterward, a burly fellow wearing a Sox cap growled at Pete, in a menacing sort of way, "Ay, bettuh luck next time."

Sunday, July 16

Yesterday, Randy Marsh, first-base umpire and crew chief, said, "I would think Carl would realize what the rule is. It's not like we're making him stand on the outside of the batter's box. If he takes it to extremes, I'll do what I have to do."

Today Marsh worked the plate, just one day after claiming that he would defend the integrity of the batter's box just as Ron Kulpa did.

Carl began his first plate appearance by wiping out the inside line—quite flamboyantly, I might add—and then he set up like he always does, with part of one foot clearly outside the box. Yes, Everett was batting left-handed against the righty Mike Johnson, but all this means is that he breaks the rules with his front foot rather than his back foot. Perhaps unnerved by all this, Johnson walked Everett on four pitches. In his next three appearances, Everett doubled off the scoreboard, homered into the center-field bleachers, and walked again.

And through it all, Marsh just stood behind the plate with his thumb up his ass, flouting the rule as if yesterday never happened.

◆ ◆ ◆

Fucking Yankees.

That was my first reaction—and my second, and my third—when I got home from Fenway, turned on ESPNews, and found out what happened today in the Bronx, where the Yankees hosted the Phillies. Going into the bottom of the ninth, the Phils owned a healthy 6–1 lead over the Yanks; the score had been the same since the fourth, so we had been seeing that score for quite a while on the Fenway scoreboard. Seemed safe.

Except the Yankees scored five runs in the ninth, sending the game to extra innings. And after the Phillies scored twice in the top of the tenth, the Yankees scored three in the bottom of the tenth to win. So what should have been a great baseball afternoon—Wakefield pitches wonderfully, Sox win . . . and Yankees lose—becomes merely a good one.

Monday, July 17

Pitcher Joaquin Andujar famously summed up baseball in (as he described it) one word . . .

Youneverknow.

I thought about Andujar tonight, when the Sox won a game they might reasonably have been expected to lose.

Bottom of the seventh, two outs, runners on first and second. Troy O'Leary due up, and Expos manager Felipe Alou summoned left-handed reliever Steve Kline from the bullpen. And I couldn't believe it when Jimy Williams didn't make a move.

I thought I had everything figured out.

Why wouldn't Williams send up a pinch-hitter for O'Leary? Kline's got a 2.00 ERA this season, and he's held left-handed hitters to a .203 batting average and zero home runs in sixty-four at-bats. O'Leary's hit one home run in seventy at-bats against left-handed pitchers this season.

Well, this time O'Leary hit a one-and-two slider that hung right over the middle of the plate. Hit a hanging slider into the visitors' bullpen. Hit a hanging slider into the visitors' bullpen for a three-run homer. Hit a hanging slider into the visitors' bullpen for a three-run homer that gave the Red Sox a 5–3 lead (and they wound up winning 7–3).

Youneverknow.

◆ ◆ ◆

No book about a ballpark is complete without a note about the food and drink available in said ballpark. Unfortunately, on any given night I'm among the least qualified to write such a note, because I don't eat any sort of meat. No hot dogs, no chicken, no fish, no anything that ever moved by itself.

Anyway, here's what I can tell you about the food at Fenway Park . . .

The pizza's better than most ballpark pizza, plenty of sauce and an edible crust. It's too greasy, of course. When I don't eat before heading to the ballpark, I generally stop and grab a cheese pizza on the way to my seat, but after I finish eating one I almost always regret it. That heavy, oily feeling in the pit of one's stomach will do that to a guy.

The ice cream . . . actually, I have yet to sample the ice cream. For some reason, this particular item is called a "sports bar." So you have these kids roaming the aisles, carrying small cardboard boxes full of these ice-cream bars (but without the usual sticks), calling out, "Spowts bahs, getchuh spowts bah here!" I like ice cream, but I worry about something that's supposed to be frozen, but has been transported to me within a cardboard box. How long has it been out of the freezer? How cold could it be?

The popcorn—sold by young men walking around with boxes tied to a stick—is fresh enough, but most of the time it's too salty (and I like salty popcorn).

Speaking of salty, man are the peanuts salty. However, there's a real benefit to buying a bag of peanuts at Fenway Park, at least if you're sitting in a lower-deck seat anywhere from first base around to third base. That benefit is Rob Barry, who's just about the coolest peanut vendor that every plied the trade.

There are two things that I like about Rob. One, he's incredibly skilled. Skilled at what? Skilled at throwing bags of peanuts, of course. Rob can throw a bag of peanuts twenty-five or thirty yards with a high degree of accuracy. Uphill. Earlier this season, he was briefly suspended by some idiot who works for the concession company, this particular idiot apparently new on the job, and not knowing that throwing peanuts long distances is a venerable tradition here. The other thing I like about Rob is that he's just flat-out cool. As he's making his rounds, he's scanning the crowd. All you have to do is wave, and you're in his memory banks. He'll give you a cursory nod—I see you, buddy, give me a minute to get in range—and then it might be a few minutes until he's close enough. When he's ready, he points at you, and then lets loose, often from long distance. The peanuts generally hit their target right in the numbers; after three months, I think I've seen just one or two bags go seriously awry, usually high by a row or two. After you catch the bag—a bag of peanuts is easier to catch than, among other things, a cold or a Nerf ball—he gives you a thumbs-up with his right hand.

And does Rob then come to collect his money? Nope, that would be a waste of time. He might have three or four other customers between you and him, so it can take a few minutes. But he never forgets a customer, and eventually he'll arrive for his dough. Tip him, and you'll get another thumbs-up as he's walking away.

I actually ran into Rob one night, both of us heading north on Yawkey Way a few minutes before a game. Turns out that during the days, he works at the halfway house next door to my apartment building (and I wondered to myself if the scar on his left cheek was inflicted by an inmate). I told Rob that I liked to watch him work, and he told me, "My dad worked here for twenty-five years, and my sister works at one of the beer stands. I guess you could say it's a family tradition."

Tuesday, July 18

Tonight the Red Sox won again, moving past the Blue Jays (who lost) into second place behind the Yankees (who won). Pedro was Pedro, struck out a dozen Expos in eight innings, and Lowe pitched the ninth to save the Sox' 3–1 win.

Last fall, Roger Angell wrote of Pedro Martinez, "He is, by fact, the great pitcher of our day . . . and he's a gift or reward of some sort for old fans who sometimes turn their gaze away long before the latest home run has begun to bend in its arc and, duh, come back down again."

Pedro can throw a mid-nineties fastball when the mood strikes. But more than the velocity—outstanding but not historic—is what he can *do* with the fastball. Depending on the way he grips the ball, Pedro can make the fastball ride in on a right-handed hitter, or sink. He also throws an outstanding curveball. But what really frustrates the hitters is Pedro's circle change-up. He holds the ball in the back of his hand, presses the tips of his right index finger and thumb together, and throws the ball with an identical motion as his fastball. The ball comes in at a greatly reduced velocity, and often breaks rightward to such a degree that hitters think he's throwing a screwball (in essence, a reverse curve). But he's not.

He's simply got great "stuff," which means that whatever pitch he throws, it's going to move around a lot. It's been suggested that Pedro comes by this movement naturally, as he's got fingers that are not only exceptionally long, but also curve upward, almost freakishly so, from the middle joint to the tips.

Of course, it's not just his arm, not just his fingers. Pedro's got a presence when he's on the mound. You watch him, and you get the idea that he can essentially do *whatever he wants to do.* That's not to say that he's perfect. He's not. But when he's healthy and focused, he just might be the best pitcher who ever lived.

Fenway Moment: There was a blowhard sitting behind me tonight. This didn't annoy me nearly so much as I suspect it annoyed the people sitting next to him, a couple from Canada visiting Fenway for the first time. This guy spent much of the game dispensing various bits of information, some true and some not so true. I tuned out most of it, but I did write down this gem: "You'll be interested to know that eighty percent of the Fenway grass is Kentucky bluegrass. I don't remember what the other twenty percent is."

Wednesday, July 19

I've got a friend named Steve who works in Washington, D.C. I've been wanting to get down to Baltimore and Oriole Park at Camden Yards, for a compare-and-contrast kind of thing, and this week marks the Red Sox' last trip down there this season. Steve lives near D.C. and has access to season tickets at Camden Yards, so he graciously offered me both a seat and a place to stay. The Sox were scheduled to open their series against the Orioles tonight, and I figured I'd fly to Washington this afternoon, we'd drive to Baltimore this evening, and then I'd fly back to Boston early tomorrow morning.

Steve called at 8:30 this morning—well, I was sort of awake—wondering if I might want to delay my visit until tomorrow. It seemed that rain was forecast for Baltimore all day and evening. I told him I'd call the airline and get back in touch with him.

Weather is, as we all know, capricious. Plus, I don't trust anything anybody tells me, unless it's related to something exceedingly technical, like an automobile engine or a computer. Or a stapler. So I fired up my computer and started looking for Baltimore weather reports on the Web.

Baltimore Sun? Rain.

USA Today? Rain.

The Weather Channel? Scattered thunderstorms.

Ah, finally. Like a terminally ill man who keeps going to doctors until he finds one that says he's not actually dying, I'd found the forecast I wanted. *Hey, baseball games are played all the time under the threat of scattered thunderstorms.* Plus, I called Continental and discovered that putting off this trip until tomorrow would cost me an extra three hundred bucks. Even assuming I can write off half of that as a business expense, it still seems like a lot of money just because I'm a little scared of the weather. So I called Steve back and told him that I would, indeed, be showing up at his office this afternoon. And so I did, after flights to Newark and Ronald Reagan Airport, then a cab to downtown Washington, where I found Steve's office.

Steve is only thirty-three, but he's an *adult* in so many ways that I'm not. He works for Latham & Watkins, a huge law firm with sixteen offices around the world, including places like Singapore and Moscow. He's married and has a two-year-old son (plus another bun in the oven). He lives in a big house in Chevy Chase and owns a car.

Steve's office is roomy and has big windows that overlook a vaulted atrium where a number of scenes for the film *Broadcast News* were filmed. On a bookshelf sits the 1988 edition of *The Baseball Encyclopedia*. On a wall hangs a lithograph print of Bill Purdom's painting that depicts Sandy Koufax striking out Harry Bright to end Game 1 of the 1963 World Series.

All this is, I presume, what happens to normal intelligent people who love baseball. They have an office and a family and a *Baseball Encyclopedia* on the shelf and a well-conceived retirement plan. Meanwhile, I've got no office, no family, no house, no car . . . but twelve *Baseball Encyclopedia*s on the shelf. I look at Steve's life—or at least his life with the limited perspective available to me—and I have to fight off the pangs of jealousy. After all, we do tend to want whatever it is that we don't have. I'm sure that there are plenty of people like Steve—maybe even Steve, though I wouldn't ask him to admit it—who envy my life just a bit. The trick is to acknowledge the wonderful things about the lives of others without thinking those lives are better than yours. We generally end up with the lives we've got because we've chosen them, even if we don't remember making the choices that led us to them.

◆   ◆   ◆

We took the Metro from Washington to Chevy Chase, to pick up Steve's car. And then, halfway between Chevy Chase and the ballpark in Baltimore, we heard on the radio that tonight's game had been postponed, and would be made up as half of a day-night doubleheader tomorrow. This presented a couple of problems for me, those being (1) I only brought the shirt and pants that I'm wearing (I do have clean underwear and socks for tomorrow), and (2) changing my flight will presumably cost me some money. There are some positives, too: I get to spend more time with Steve, and I don't have to get up at 4:30 tomorrow morning to catch a 6 A.M. flight. Oh, and the biggest positive of them all, my first-ever day-night doubleheader. Three hours of baseball, three hours of screwing around in Baltimore, then three more hours of baseball.

Steve and I don't really know each other all that well; we've hung out at a couple of SABR conventions, and there's the occasional e-mail exchange. But on the drive back south, I learned that Steve and I have even more in common than I thought. For example, in addition to baseball, we share passions for Woody Allen movies and *Seinfield*. More to the point, Steve seriously considered becoming a sportswriter; in fact, his decision to *not* become a sportswriter was as deliberate as my decision to become a sportswriter was casual.

"I was working for the *Belmont Citizen-Herald* as the assistant editor," Steve remembered, "writing everything from the police logs to obituaries to front-page stories. I wanted to write about baseball, though, so I called up Dan Shaughnessy, who was the baseball columnist for the *Boston Globe*. I called him out of the blue— he didn't know me from Adam—and left a message that I'd like to meet with him.

"He was very nice, returned my call almost immediately, said he was down in spring training but told me, 'When I get back to Boston, you can come over and we'll talk.' So a few weeks later, I went to Shaughnessy's house in Newton, just off the Massachusetts Turnpike. We talked for a while, and he told me about growing up as a young sportswriter. This was in 1990, so he'd probably been covering the Sox for twelve or fifteen years. And I'll never forget what he told me.

"'I love my job, but you gotta be willing to deal with a guy like Dwight Evans, he knows you for twelve years and still treats you like a fire hydrant.'

"Shaughnessy said it was a great job and he seemed to like it, but he told me how tough the hours are, you're on the road half the time, and even when you're home you're working nights and weekends.

"So when I sat down with my rational twenty-three-year-old mind, I asked myself, how many Dan Shaughnessys are there in the world? When you think about it, there just aren't that many of the really good jobs to be had. Twenty-six baseball teams (then), a handful of beat writers per team, and only a few of them are really in the big time. Would I be satisfied being a beat writer for the *Worcester Telegram* when I was thirty-five?

"I might answer that question differently now, but then my answer was no. So instead, I spend my days trying to save the Salt Lake Olympic Committee."

Steve's not really so cynical as you might think from that ending. He knows that he's found himself a good balance: making a good living and enjoying his family, but still finding the time to occasionally write about baseball for publication, and getting to the ballpark six or eight times every season.

Thursday, July 20

You hear stories about leather-lunged Red Sox fans who have a heckle for every occasion, but it turns out that I had to fly to Baltimore to find one of them.

Steve couldn't make the beginning of the first game this afternoon—1:35, official start time (1:38, actual start time)—so I took a train to Baltimore from Washington. On the way, I had something of a jarring experience. For some reason my thoughts turned to home, and for a brief moment . . . for a brief moment, I didn't have any idea where home is. No idea in the world. I've heard baseball players talk about waking up in the morning while on a road trip, and having no idea what city they're in. But until today, I'd never actually experienced anything like that. And I can't say I care to experience it again. As much as I enjoy living in Boston, and traveling around the country to visit different ballparks, this summer's been a bit much. When I was a boy, I'd go for years without traveling at all, and I suppose I'll always be a homebody at heart.

Anyway, today my home is Camden Yards. I settled into my seat just a few minutes before the first pitch, and that's when I was treated to the most vociferous heckler I've ever heard.

This guy's routine might best be described with the running commentary directed toward (or about) a single player. Ed Sprague led off the second inning with a line drive to left field that bounced over the fence for an automatic double. Our heckling friend went into high gear at the sight of Sprague standing on second base.

To the players on the field: "Hey, that's gotta be his first Red Sox hit! Somebody save the baseball for him!"

To Sprague: "Hey Ed, is that your number [44] or your IQ? You know where third base is? I got a road map for ya!"

To any fans within a hundred feet: "There's two guys on this team I can't stand: Darren Lewis and that piece a shit on second base!"

A few minutes later, he turned around and said to the parents sitting behind me, "I'm loud, I'm obnoxious, but I promise you one thing. I'll keep it clean for the little guys. I coach youth hockey back home."

Now, if I were a truly fearless journalist, I'd have tried to make friends with this guy, because I'm sure he'd have given me plenty more material for today's entry. But the truth is that I have little tolerance for people who seem to be so in love with themselves, and talking to the guy didn't even occur to me until late this evening. Hell, I was just hoping he'd leave after the first game.

And he did, but not before watching Ramon Martinez earn an improbable victory. Everett hit a two-run homer in the top of the first, but in the bottom of the inning, Will Clark hit a grand slam off Martinez. Pedro's big brother settled down after that, though, and by the time he departed after five innings, the Sox owned an 8–5 lead. Steve showed up at about that point, and together we saw the Sox cruise to an 11–7 win.

◆　◆　◆

This was a day-night doubleheader, so Steve and I had to vacate Oriole Park for a few hours. We took our supper in a large Chinese restaurant that was completely deserted. Steve lived in or near Boston for six years, and he spent as much time as he could at Fenway Park. While we waited for our food, I asked Steve about Fenway Park. I took some mental notes, but later I asked Steve to e-mail me his thoughts about Fenway . . .

"Fenway was my first home park. I grew up in Columbus, Ohio, home of the International League Clippers, but our closest major league stadium—and "stadium" is clearly the right word—was Riverfront, in Cincinnati, about two hours away, warranting the trip down I-71 only once or twice a year (usually for a scheduled doubleheader, which they still had in those days) through the cornfields and soyfields, past Washington Courthouse (the halfway point, noteworthy for a McDonald's within sight of the highway) and Kings Island amusement park, down into Cincinnati through the hills, toward the river, and then up, up, and up into the red seats, just below the stadium's precipice, where we could see—just barely—Pete and Johnny and Joe dancing far below.

"So when I moved to Boston for college and beyond, Fenway seemed accessible, as easy as going down the street to buy the *Globe* in the morning before jumping on the Green Line to head in to work. And almost as routine was heading back out that Green Line, leaping off the streetcar at Kenmore Square, and ascending with the navy-capped throng into the evening air, smoky with sausage and peppers.

"Every game I saw at my first home park was memorable, in the sense that my memory of Fenway is not a single play, or game, but a collection of them all. But somewhere between the finest moments—from Roger Clemens vs. Nolan Ryan to Pedro Martinez vs. Tom Glavine, from Mike Greenwell hitting for the cycle to Wade Boggs collecting (yet again) his two hundredth hit of the year—what comes to mind when I'm asked about Fenway is a single event, which happened *twice*, one evening during my last full summer at Fenway.

"The matchup itself was unremarkable, a midseason weeknight game against Minnesota, a team clearly without any postseason plans. But still, Fenway itself is an attraction on any night—like a soiree held by a Beacon Hill hostess, you don't much ask or care who else will be there—and my friend and I were relegated to standing-room-only tickets just to gain entry. We soon enough found two open seats a dozen rows behind home plate and sat ourselves down, with a view of the sunset off the Prudential Tower, the dim light bathing the park in a deep green glow.

"Early on, the Sox were threatening, men on first and second, and none out. The next Sox batter hit a sharp grounder to Minnesota third baseman Gary Gaetti, who fielded it cleanly and stepped on the bag, tossed to Al Newman at second, who threw over to Kent Hrbek, beating the not-so-fleet Bostonian by a few steps. The Twins trotted off the field, accompanied by a silent crowd (the kind of silence that follows a waiter dropping a full tray in a fine restaurant), followed by a murmur, as each patron turned to the next, asking, 'Did you see that?' The intermission afforded us all the opportunity to confirm that we had never seen a triple play live, even on TV, but maybe on replays on *This Week in Baseball* or perhaps that new ESPN show called *Baseball Tonight*.

"The talk was still of triple plays and lethargic Boston base-running when the Sox mounted another scoring threat. Then another ground ball to Gaetti, another step on third, another toss to Newman, another relay to Hrbek. Another silence, this one longer. More murmuring, this time louder. Again, no cheering, just talking, comparing notes, wondering if it had ever happened before, twice in a single game. As the next inning started, the centerfield scoreboard told us: the only game in major league history with two triple plays. And against the same team—which still won the game, so we all went home happy, with 33,871 stories to tell. When you ask me, that's Fenway."

The ending of tonight's second game wasn't so happy for any other Red Sox fans who might have been in the stands, as two Sox suffered particularly poor games.

Pete Schourek started, and didn't escape the third inning, having allowed five hits and four walks in his brief stint (the Sox wound up losing handily, 9–4, as Schourek's mound successors didn't fare well, either). This makes four straight horrible outings for Schourek, and the Sox clearly have to make a change, either release the left-hander or put him on the disabled list.

Nomar started the game with a .403 batting average—he went three for five this afternoon—but finished it with a .396 average after going hitless in five at-bats. In each of those at-bats, Garciaparra swung at the first pitch. Of course, he does that all the time, and I continually am amazed that pitchers ever throw their first offering anywhere near the strike zone. But they do, and so he gets his hits.

Lots and lots and lots of hits. In 1997, his first full season, Nomar led the American League with 209 base hits. He missed too many games in 1998 and '99 to lead the league in hits, but last year he did top the A.L. with a .357 batting average. And this year, of course, he's leading the league in batting average again.

What amazes me about Garciaparra is that he does so well even though enemy pitchers must know that he's just aching to swing at the first pitch. It seems to me that pitchers simply shouldn't throw the first pitch near the strike zone, but they often do. And often as not, Nomar takes a good cut. Kirby Puckett liked to swing at the first pitch, too, and he did okay for himself. There are, it seems, a few supremely talented hitters who can get away with it.

When it's Nomar's time to hit, he's like one of those thoroughbreds who has to be wrestled into the starting gate, and then fidgets until they turn him loose. From the moment he leaves the on-deck circle until the time he finishes his plate appearance, Nomar has to be doing something. Before each pitch, he steps out of the box and adjusts his batting gloves. First the left, then the right, then the left again, then the right again, then the left again, then the right again, and finally the left again. And to complete things, he gives the sweatband on his left forearm a quick pat or two.

Then, as Nomar steps into the batter's box, he touches the brim of his helmet with his left hand, then the crown of the helmet. And finally, the feet. After taking his stance, he kicks the ground with the toes of his left foot, then the right, then the left, then the right, and finally the left again (he says he does this to get his feet as far forward in his shoes as possible). Now he's ready to hit . . . and if this pitch doesn't end the plate appearance, he'll do it all again before the next one.

Garciaparra sees approximately 3.2 pitches per plate appearance, which means he'll adjust the batting glove on his right hand approximately two thousand times per season. Hey, whatever works.

A friend tells me that I should, within this book, determine once and for all who's the best shortstop in the world: Garciaparra, Alex Rodriguez, or Derek Jeter. After all, it's the biggest baseball question of our time. Just as baseball fans argued about Mays and Mantle and Snider, today they argue about Garciaparra and Rodriguez and Jeter. It's such a big question, in fact, that I shan't try to explore it with any sort of precision in this book. One could easily write an entire monograph, if not an actual book, about this. However, here's a thumbnail take on the trio . . .

In my mind, Jeter quite clearly doesn't measure up to Garciaparra and Rodriguez. The former's hitting stats fall well short of the latter two, which leaves two arguments for Jeter's legion of supporters: defense and winning. And aside from the wild-eyed blatherings of (mostly) New York media types, there is very little objective evidence that Jeter is an outstanding defensive shortstop. (In fact, a number of analysts argue that he's actually a poor defensive player, but I'm not prepared to argue that point in this space.) As for winning, well of course it's true that Jeter's Yankees have won three of the last four World Series. But it strikes me that he's had a fair amount of help, and I have a hard time believing that the Yanks would have suffered much if Nomar or Alex had been manning shortstop in the Bronx.

So who's better, Rodriguez or Garciaparra? Defensively, neither of them is perfect. Like most power-hitting shortstops, they sport strong arms. Alex looks best when he's making long, twisting throws from behind second base, Nomar looks best when he's gunning down runners from deep in the hole between short and third. Both are prone to the occasional error, and neither is likely to win a Gold Glove. I know it's a cop-out, but I honestly believe that both are adequate defensively; no worse, but not much better.

	AGE	G	AVG	OBP	SLG
ALEX	25	790	.309	.374	.561
NOMAR	27	595	.333	.382	.573

I actually cheated on their ages, but just by a few days. Garciaparra turns twenty-seven in three days, and Rodriguez turns twenty-five next Thursday. So Alex is almost exactly two years younger, despite the fact he's played 195 more games than Nomar, because he earned an everyday job in the majors when he was twenty. Nomar went to college and didn't win the shortstop job with the Red Sox until 1997, when he was twenty-three.

In terms of on-base percentage and slugging percentage, it's practically a dead heat. Nomar does have a slight edge in both categories, but he's benefited from a pretty good hitter's park, maybe a little better than Seattle's Kingdome (where Alex toiled until a year ago), and probably a lot better than Seattle's Safeco Field (where Alex has toiled since the All-Star break last season). Still, it's essentially a toss-up. If forced to choose between the two, I'd take Garciaparra for the next week or the next month. But like almost anybody in baseball, if I could have one of them for the next eight or ten years, I'd take Rodriguez. His two-year age advantage means that he's significantly more likely to wind up with a better career than Garciaparra. To put it simply, Nomar's got a good shot at the Hall of Fame, but Alex has a good shot at becoming the best shortstop since Honus Wagner.

Oriole Park at Camden Yards is often held up as the paragon of the new-style ballpark, and it's probably the best of the crop (though I haven't seen San Francisco's Pacific Bell Park, which people rave about). Back in Boston, WEEI's Ted Sarandis asks callers who want to save Fenway Park, "Have you been to Camden Yards in Baltimore?" And if they respond in the negative, then he tells them they have to see Camden Yards, or PacBell Park, or Jacobs Field in Cleveland before they dare argue for the preservation of Fenway.

Well, I've been to Camden Yards, back in 1992. I had a good time, as I did today, I still think it's the best of the "retro ballparks" built in the last decade. But there was, and is, no magic, no power, no impulse to spend a season in Baltimore writing a book. That's not to say that Ted is wrong. Perhaps many pro-Fenway Bostonians would change their minds after a game at Oriole Park, with its ample seats and ampler bathrooms. I'm just not one of them.

Friday, July 21

Technically, tonight's game at Fenway was sold out. In fact, the best I could do, ticketwise, was a seat well above first base, near the top (Row 12) of the grandstand (Section 15). Grandstand seats aren't so bad if you've got a bit of room, but if you don't . . . well, I got a little nervous when I realized that the fellow who owned the seat to my right was going to be sitting in the seat to my right. You see, Bryan—I introduced myself early on—is a big man, not particularly tall but plenty wide, perhaps too wide for the Fenway grandstand. I mention this not to embarrass him, but rather to be quite clear about what kind of physique really isn't suited to a substantial percentage of the ballpark's seats.

See, he simply couldn't sit all the way back in his seat, as a stringbean like me can. He had to scoot forward five or six inches. But here, so to speak, is the rub. If you're anywhere near six feet tall, you can't just scoot forward six inches, because the seat in front of you is too close. So if you scoot forward, you also have to spread your legs to both sides. The farther you scoot, the more you have to spread. Bryan would apparently have to spread a fair amount and, as we've already seen, the seats are narrow. When you start spreading your legs to the sides, you start getting real chummy with your neighbors. And let's be honest, most men don't want to get that chummy with other men, not for three-plus hours.

I've always been lucky, and tonight my luck held. Maybe the game really was sold out, but Bryan and I wound up having five seats for the two of us. So we did what any two men would do: empty, Rob, empty, Bryan, empty. And despite the space between us, we quickly got to talking, and I learned that Bryan is an insurance underwriter from Bloomington, Illinois, specializing in crops (mostly milo and sorghum). He and a friend left Bloomington yesterday, spent the night in Columbus, Ohio, and then drove through Ontario and Niagara Falls on their way to Boston today.

"We drove around ten times looking for Fenway. We could see it, we just couldn't figure out how to get to it."

That's a pretty typical story, as the area around Fenway Park is no easier to navigate than Fenway Park itself. As one current Boston guidebook says, "The few street signs that exist seem geared to the people who know where they're going, which, given the constant influx of students, visitors, and new residents, means only about 50 percent of the people on the road."

And you get the same sort of feeling at Fenway. It starts when you arrive at the ballpark, where the entry gates don't make any sense at all. Looking at Fenway from above, and going clockwise, there's Gate A just to the left of the plate, Gate E in the left-field corner, Gate C behind the bleachers, Gate B in the right-field corner, and finally Gate D just to the right of home plate. A-E-C-B-D.

Once you're inside, the bleachers are easy enough to navigate, but the rest of the park . . . Well, tonight's game was my forty-ninth at Fenway (including the three last fall), so I know my way around the old gal. But when I sit in the grandstand, for the first inning or two there's always a steady procession of out-of-towners going back and forth around me, trying to figure out which seats are theirs. The row numbers are painted on the steps, but in a way that makes which row is which somewhat unclear. And it's worse in the Loge Box seats, directly beneath the grandstand seats. The Loge Box seats each carry a row number and a section number, like the grannies, but also a box number. And you give a tourist three numbers to deal with, and he'll be as lost as a blind man in an echo chamber.

There's a similar situation down in the Field Box seats. These are, of course, the best in the building, forty-five bucks apiece. But damn, those forty-five-dollar seats can be hard to find. Why? Each "box" is four seats wide, and carries a box number, from Box 9 halfway down the right-field line to Box 82 halfway down the left-field line. The problem is that it can be very difficult to know which box is which. Some of them are clearly—well, somewhat clearly—marked, with a red number atop a white square. Except at least half of the red numbers are illegible, most of the red paint simply worn away by the years and the elements and the shoes.

Let's see, what would it take to fix this problem? I figure some stencils, a couple cans of paint, eight hours of labor . . . Gee, it might cost the Red Sox the grand sum of one hundred dollars. So why don't they do it? I'm not real big on conspiracy theories, but I think the club's management actively wants people to dislike Fenway Park, in the hopes that such dislike will result in more spirited agitation for a new ballpark. So simple maintenance, maintenance that would only help the fans in the stands, is, in a sense, prohibited.

At least, that's my theory. I certainly can't imagine why else nobody's bothered repainting the numbers in God knows how many years.

Anyway, once Bryan found the ballpark, he was in fine spirits.

"This is a dream come true. The first World Series I ever saw was in 1975, and

I've been a Red Sox fan ever since. I grew up in a little town on the Illinois-Iowa border, and in the National League, I follow the Cardinals rather than the Cubs, because in 1973 my grandfather brought me back a Cards hat from St. Louis."

With the game only two-thirds over, Bryan said, "Well, even if the Sox don't win I got to see a little bit of everything tonight." And he was right.

In the bottom of the fourth, in his fifty-third at-bat as a member of the Red Sox, Ed Sprague finally hit a home run. Except nobody thought it was a home run, not at first. When it came off the bat, I thought he got all of it. But then I looked at left fielder Carlos Lee, who was setting up for an easy catch well in front of the Monster. I actually looked down at my scorebook and wrote in a "7" for Sprague. But then a cheer arose, and I looked up just in time to see the baseball settling into the netting, with Lee still set up to make the routine play. It was windy tonight—20 m.p.h. out to left field at game time—but it wasn't *that* windy.

One of the many traditions at Fenway Park is for drunken college students to jump onto the field in the late innings and slide, headfirst, into one base or another before surrendering to the authorities and walking off peacefully. It's been fairly rare this season, but tonight after the top of the ninth, a young man, his ball cap turned backward and looking like he spent a fair amount of his evening hours with a cup of beer in his hands, jumped out of the stands beyond third base and sprinted down the baseline before sliding headfirst into home plate.

O'Leary returned to the lineup on July 3. In fifteen games since, he's batted .433 (26 for 60) with twenty RBI. Tonight O'Leary hit a three-run homer in the first, and singled and scored in the sixth.

Right-handed pitcher Tomo Ohka made his first 2000 appearance with the Red Sox tonight. He pitched one and a third innings of shutout relief, but will presumably slide into the rotation as soon as the Sox need another starter, because he's always been a starter. In 1999, Ohka, a (then) twenty-three-year-old native of Japan who speaks virtually no English, split his minor-league season between Class-AA Trenton and Class-AAA Pawtucket. He started a dozen games at each level, and didn't lose. Literally, he did not lose, going 15–0 with a 2.31 ERA. He pitched briefly in Boston last year, too, but returned to Pawtucket to open this season. And on June 2, Ohka threw a perfect game, just the third perfect game in the 117-year history of the International League. And in an interesting twist, Ohka's catcher, thirty-two-year-old Joe Siddall, retired immediately after that game.

At some point during nearly every game, a beach ball escapes from the bleachers and floats to the grass behind whoever's playing center field. Usually, he just looks over his shoulder while a member of the grounds crew vaults the fence separating the Red Sox bullpen from the field, jogs over to collect the ball, and returns to the bullpen. Tonight, though, Carl Everett didn't want to wait. Somehow he popped the beach ball himself, and stuffed its lifeless skeleton into his back pocket.

Bryan and his buddy are heading to Yankee Stadium tomorrow, so I asked him to send me an e-mail message later, telling me how the rest of his trip went. While it's true that I've lived in Kansas City, Chicago, Seattle, and now Boston, and it's true that I don't know milo and sorghum from Griffin and Sabine, I still feel like Bryan and I are something of kindred spirits, boys from the Midwest rendered slightly agog by the bright lights and the confusing road signs of the big city.

Saturday, July 22

Today my stupid male ego cost me seventy-five dollars.

My luck with tickets ran out this afternoon, though I have only myself to blame. A week or so ago, David Schoenfield, my editor at ESPN.com, told me that he and a pair of coworkers were thinking about coming to a game this weekend. Could I get tickets?

Sure, no problem. I'm Rob Neyer. I can do anything, right?

The game was scheduled to start at 5:05, so a bit before noon I walked over to the ballpark to see if I could cadge some tickets. I found Kevin, but he didn't have anything. He gave me his cell-phone number, told me to check back in an hour or two. I called him at 12:30, still nothing. Finally, at 2:30 I went back to the ballpark and found Kevin again. He still didn't have four tickets together, at least not in my price range. And then—I'm not exactly sure how this happened—I got involved in the scalping business. Kevin told me to go into the ticket office, wait until a particular window was available, walk up, and say, "Jimmy? I'm Scott's friend."

Apparently, these magical words would result in an envelope being passed to me. I would deliver this to Kevin, and among the contents of this envelope would be four tickets I would then be allowed to purchase. Except it didn't work out that way, perhaps because I tend to freeze up in these situations (I'd make a lousy spy). Instead, it went like this:

"Hey Jimmy. I'm Scott's friend."

"What?"

"I'm Scott's friend."

"Oh. How many tickets did he want?"

"He, uh, didn't say."

"All I have is standing room."

"Uh, okay. Thanks anyway."

And that was it. Bereft of tickets, I went outside and immediately ran into Kevin, who asked me what happened. I left out the parts that might have made me sound like a tongue-tied idiot, and I think maybe he bought it. Unfortunately, I was still bereft of tickets on a personal level, and Kevin told me to come back in an hour, at which time he'd have something for me. Of course, that's what they always say. I've dealt with these guys six or eight times now, and I've yet to hear them say, "Sorry, buddy, can't help you today, go talk to that other guy."

But wouldn't you know it? I went back an hour later, and Kevin still didn't have four decent tickets for me. So I finally gave up on him. Walked north on Brookline, over the Mass Pike and to the corner of Brookline and Newbury, the locus of scalping in the hours before a game. Found a guy I'd never seen before, asked him if he had four good ones together. He said he had four "grannies" (grandstand seats) for eighty apiece, and after looking at the top two in his stack, I said I'd give him three hundred for the four of them. Deal.

And boy, was I pissed when I looked at the tickets and discovered that they weren't together, but instead were separated by two sections. One pair was in Section 24, the other in Section 22. In a way, though, this relieved me of one last duty: deciding who would sit where. When you're holding four tickets, it's an issue at the particular point in time when you have to distribute them. But since these four weren't together, I simply told everyone that we'd trade seats during the game, which would allow me to get acquainted with both Sherry and Ashley (I've spent plenty of time with David, plus he's a guy).

Sherry's an editor, Ashley's a publicist, and both of them have led interesting lives (if short ones, as they're both still in their middle twenties). So we had plenty to talk about. In fact, I talked so much that I didn't pay a whole lot of attention to the game. I took only five notes during a game that saw the Sox take a 6–0 lead into the seventh inning, then hang on for an 8–6 victory as the bullpen gave up six runs in the last three frames.

All right, here's where my ego got in the way of my wallet. For some reason, I just couldn't tell Ashley and Dave and Sherry that I had paid seventy-five bucks apiece for their tickets. I felt like I'd failed somehow, spending that much money on a silly old baseball game. If I were really a sharp guy, or really was connected, I would have gotten us free tickets, or at least cheap tickets, right? So when it came time to settle up after the game, I told everybody the tix cost me fifty apiece, which means that in addition to paying seventy-five for my own ticket, I also ate twenty-five apiece for their tickets. Thus, my pride cost me seventy-five dollars.

In the end, though, I really couldn't complain about my day. The Red Sox beat the White Sox (8–6), the Yankees and Blue Jays both lost, and I enjoyed both my half-a-game with Sherry and my half-a-game with Ashley. And what good is money anyway, if you can't use it to avoid feeling foolish in front of young women?

Sunday, July 23

Another day, another visit to my friends the scalpers, because with Pedro scheduled to work this afternoon, Susan really wanted to go to the game.

This time I did manage to hook up with Kevin, half an hour before game time, and he even gave me a pretty good deal: two upper grannies, directly above the Red Sox on-deck circle, $120 for the pair. Such a good deal, in fact, that I didn't lie to Susan when she asked what they cost.

We got our money's worth.

Nobody scored through the first three and a half innings, but the Sox broke the logjam with an unearned run in the bottom of the third when Izzy Alcantara reached second base on shortstop's Jose Valentin's throwing error and then scored on Varitek's single.

Aside from that, White Sox starter Mike Sirotka matched Pedro inning for inning (though not strikeout for strikeout). With the score still 1–0 after seven frames, Susan said, "We need some insurance runs."

I disagreed. As much as I might want the Red Sox to win today, and eventually reach the postseason, my number-one priority is still drama. That's the case whenever I watch a game of any sort, unless the Royals are involved. And how dramatic would it be if Pedro were protecting a one-run lead in the ninth?

And indeed, there was a bit of ninth-inning drama, because the Red Sox—true to both their nature and their recent history—once again couldn't give Pedro much support. A pair of Sox reached base in the fifth, but neither of them scored. And after escaping that jam, Chicago's Mike Sirotka set down the Red Sox in order in the sixth, seventh, and eighth innings.

So when Pedro came out for the top of the ninth, he still had that one-run lead to protect. Chicago's leadoff man, Magglio Ordoñez (here's what my notes say) hit a "routine grounder to SS, took crazy hop and trickled into LCF." In other words, Nomar was in position to field the ball, but something happened, and Ordoñez wound up on second after a good bit of hustle. No problem. This was Pedro's day. Paul Konerko struck out swinging. Chris Singleton popped out to Nomar. Carlos Lee struck out swinging. Game over.

Three hours and thirty-five minutes, 131 pitches, and fifteen strikeouts after he'd begun, Pedro had a 1-0 shutout in the books.

(And yes, three hours and thirty-five minutes is a long time for a nine-inning game that included just one lonely run. As I'm sure you know, baseball games have been getting longer and longer and longer in recent years, with the average game time now approximately three hours. People complain about this all the time, but "people" usually means broadcasters and writers. As a fan, I've never really minded so much. Now that I have to be at the ballpark every night, I know why the broadcasters and writers are always bitching. They don't have a choice in the matter, and they just want to get home, or to a restaurant, or to their hotel room. But if it's not your job, then you probably don't give a damn.)

As I'm sure I've already mentioned, I prefer night baseball, and today I found another reason: "Sweet Caroline" doesn't have nearly the same impact when the sun is out. The last time we heard it, after the seventh inning on June 21, the crowd behaved something like a huge party, and that included singing along with Neil. But people just don't have the same kind of energy in the daylight, and so when . . .

> *Sweet Caroline*
> *Good times never seemed so good*

. . . came blaring out of the speakers after the eighth inning, the great majority of fans just sat where they were: resting, and letting the notes roll over them, like bored Catholics an hour into Mass.

◆ ◆ ◆

I have this theory, never tested, that if you watch a baseball game closely enough, you can see something you've never seen before. Every single time.

That might be a bit of an exaggeration, but today I did see something I've never seen. In the top of the second, one of Pedro's fastballs grazed Paul Konerko's chin and then dropped into the crook of Konerko's right elbow. So Konerko reached down with his left hand, grabbed the ball, and hurled it *back to Martinez* before trotting down to first base. Eventually a trainer came out and toweled away some blood from Konerko's chin, but he was able to remain in the game.

◆ ◆ ◆

Today I learned something about the distribution of Red Sox tickets that I didn't know, primarily because most of the guys who work the ticket windows are generally loathe to volunteer information, or even answer questions with any degree of forthrightness.

I went to the box office to buy single tickets for the games tomorrow and Tuesday night against the Twins. I asked for the "best singles," but there was nothing in the Field Box—the lowest section—only some so-so seats in the upper reaches of the Loge Box. Great seats, but not a great value at forty dollars per. Now, I've been doing this all season—asking for the best single seat when I was going by myself—and it wasn't until today that someone at the window told me, "If you come in the day of the game, you can probably upgrade when the team releases more tickets." I asked when I should check. "The best time is maybe half an hour before game time."

Suddenly, a lot of things made sense. See, every team has to hold back a certain number of tickets, in case (for example) players from either team need some for friends or family or whoever. But some of those tickets are always left over, and at some point the team releases them for sale. From the fan's standpoint, however, these tickets are tricky. First of all, you have to either know exactly when they become available, or you have to get real lucky. Second, I suspect that most of these tickets aren't actually made available to the public at all, at least not through official channels. What I think happens is, the guys who work in the ticket office buy them and then resell them to scalpers for a profit, who in turn resell them to fans for yet more profit.

Remember yesterday when Kevin sent me to the ticket window with those magical code words? I think that I was supposed to be serving as the (unwitting) bagman for just such a transaction.

◆   ◆   ◆

Today, the Mike Stanley situation finally hit the fan.

On July 5, Stanley was placed on the DL with a case of tendinitis in his right shoulder. Stanley hadn't been playing well, and today the Sox designated him for assignment, which means they have ten days to dispose of him in whatever fashion they deem appropriate. According to the *Herald*'s Michael Silverman, Stanley was not informed of this move by Dan Duquette, who's in Cooperstown for Carlton Fisk's Hall of Fame induction. Rather, yesterday Stanley called assistant general manager Mike Port, who told Stanley not to show up at Fenway Park today.

Classy, huh?

Look, Mike Stanley's not a great player. A one-time catcher who now plays first base and DH, Stanley's hitting just .222 this season (though he's drawn his share of walks, and ranks third on the club with ten home runs). But since Mo Vaughn left Boston prior to the 1999 season, Stanley—who arrived in the middle of the '98 campaign—has been considered the team's spiritual leader. After Vaughn left, Stanley even took Vaughn's locker, an honorary corner location in the back of the clubhouse.

So while it's one thing to discard a player like Stanley, it's quite another to discard him with little sign of respect. How could Duquette handle this situation so poorly? Why hasn't he learned, in the nearly nine years that he's held this job (two-plus years in Montreal, six-plus in Boston), how to at least give the *appearance* of caring about his players? These are questions for a mental-health professional, of course, but let me follow up my earlier analysis of Duquette's psyche with some real conclusions.

I think that Duquette is a man on a serious power trip, and I think that he has little interest in the many people he considers his inferiors. This includes his manager, the great majority of his players (the exceptions being, I suspect, superstars like Pedro and Nomar), the fans, and perhaps most of all, those in the media.

How does Duquette keep his job? First of all, with the exception of his interpersonal relationships, he's generally done a pretty good job. The Red Sox have made the playoffs three times in Duquette's six full seasons, and he was smart enough to trade for Pedro Martinez a few years ago. Second, I suspect that he's excellent at kissing the appropriate asses. Red Sox manager Jimy Williams doesn't like Duquette, but I'll bet my left thumb that CEO John Harrington likes Duquette just fine.

I believe that Dan Duquette is a good general manager, but I also believe that he'll never be a *great* general manager. These days, baseball players wield an immense amount of power, at least relative to the old days. And if you're a general manager despised by your players, you're dealing from a short deck.

I also believe that if Dan Duquette were a brave man, brave enough to spend a few years in psychoanalysis, at the end of which he might theoretically have improved his ability to communicate with his "inferiors," then he *might* become a great general manager. But I've seen no indication that he's a particularly brave man.

Monday, July 24
I spent the night in Fenway Park, and the things I saw . . .

But first, the game.

What Twins left-hander Eric Milton did to the Red Sox tonight reminded me a bit of what White Sox right-hander James Baldwin did to the Red Sox on May 9. Here are the two enemy starters' pitching lines in their Fenway gems:

	DATE	IP	H	R	BB	K	PITCHES
BALDWIN	MAY 9	9	3	0	1	8	102
MILTON	JULY 24	8	4	0	1	7	111

The only real difference, of course, is in the innings column, as tonight Milton departed after the eighth with a four-nothing lead, only one Red Sox hitter (Jeff Frye) having reached even second base.

Well, there's one other difference. Baldwin entered his May 9 start with a 5–0 record and a 2.97 ERA; Milton came into tonight's game with an 8–6 record and a 5.36 ERA. Qualitatively, though, assuming both are healthy, there's not that much difference at all between them. Before tonight, Baldwin's career ERA was 5.08, Milton's was 5.10. They're both mediocre pitchers (albeit with live arms) who enjoyed exceptional outings against a team that couldn't hit water if it fell out of a big boat.

In the bottom of the ninth, the Red Sox still trailed 4–0 when Izzy Alcantara stepped to the plate with two outs and a runner on third base. The guy in front of me said, purely for the benefit of those around him, "Izzy, if you don't hit a home run, you're *done!*"

And about a minute later, Izzy drove a one-and-two fastball from Eddie Guardado over the Green Monster, over the netting, and into the night. Third baseman Sean Berry, a veteran playing in his first game as a member of the Red Sox, was the next hitter, and he struck out looking to end the game. For the first time (in eight tries) this season, the Twins beat the Sox.

Now, about the Fenway sleepover . . . Back in May, as you might remember, I went to a game with Dan, who writes for the *Hartford Courant*. In the course of our discussions, I shared with Dan a somewhat labored metaphor, Fenway Park as beautiful woman. As I explained it to Dan, my first visit to Fenway last fall left me wanting more. Lots more. Just as you might first fantasize about simply talking to that beautiful woman you've been admiring from afar, when that finally happens and you discover that she's got a brain to match her looks, you're not satisfied. You want to spend every day with her. You want to fall asleep next to her, you want to wake up next to her. Similarly, I wanted to be at Fenway Park all summer long, fall asleep next to "her" and wake up next to "her." And given my eighty-one-game schedule and the location of my apartment, that's essentially what I've been doing all season.

Well, when that appeared in print there was something of a lurid quality to it—yes, I was misquoted, though not by much—as if I somehow fantasized about making love to Fenway Park. That wasn't exactly what I meant, but of course I took a fair amount of grief from my friends in Connecticut. And then I forgot about it . . . until tonight. I'm not sure whose idea it was, but back in May, Bill Nowlin and I cooked up this crazy scheme to *literally* spend the night with Fenway Park.

But how would we do that? Well, in the course of researching his next book, about the people who work in and around the ballpark, Bill has gotten friendly with various high-ranking members of the cleanup crew, which begins its chores shortly after the last fan exits the ballpark, and generally remains until around five or six in the morning after a night game. He thought that the cleaning crew would give us the cover we needed to avoid getting kicked out of Fenway soon after the game ended.

I initially just figured on staying until the cleanup crew finished up, whenever that might be, but Bill had his heart set on staying in the park until dawn. And he figures we shouldn't have too much trouble avoiding whatever security is here through the night. At least, that's what I thought. When we met after the game, Bill didn't seem quite so optimistic about evading security, but he was still game for the effort.

Haven't you always wondered how a ballpark gets cleaned up? After nine innings, the concrete beneath the seats is covered with filth: half-eaten hot dogs, plastic beer cups (lots of plastic beer cups), Cracker Jack boxes, cardboard pizza boxes, plastic water bottles, plastic soda bottles, and peanut shells. Lots and lots and lots of peanut shells. Next time you see a game, hang around for a few minutes afterward and stroll around your section of seats, just to see how much people leave behind, and what a great variety of garbage there is. And by the next day, it's gotta be gone. All of it.

Well, here's how you clean Fenway Park:

Workers called "pickers" start in Section 33, in the left-field corner. Pickers gather larger items—essentially, everything except small paper items and peanut shells—and fill large plastic garbage bags. When a picker fills a bag, he ties it shut and moves on.

A small group of workers—if there's a special name for them, I didn't write it down—is responsible for the full garbage bags. First the bags are tossed into the nearest aisle, then into ramps leading to the concourse under the grandstand.

Once the bags are sitting in the ramps, men wheeling large, four-wheeled carts collect them. From there, the carts are pushed all the way around the ballpark, to a large trash compactor behind Section 1 in the right-field corner. (As you might imagine, the smell back there is not pleasant, and the dim young man who spends his nights there deserves hazard pay.)

That would just about tell the story, but for the small matter of peanuts. On a typical evening at Fenway Park, vendors sell many thousands of bags of peanuts. Each bag contains approximately forty peanuts. Do the math, and you'll realize that we're talking about a lot of peanuts. Double that number, and you've got a pretty good idea of how many peanut shells—half-shells, actually—are left after a game. That's a hell of a lot of shells, and somebody's gotta clean 'em up.

That's where the blowers come in.

The word "blowers" refers to both the equipment—garden-variety, gasoline-fueled leaf blowers—and the men who operate them.

On this night there were six blowers—three men and their three machines—and they made a hell of a racket. One might imagine that Fenway Park in the middle of the night is a place of peacefulness, an island of green solitude suitable for quiet reflection. It just ain't that way, though, as the cacophony from midnight until the sun comes up is the sort that results in noise ordinances in Southern California.

Bill and I hung out with the cleaning crew for maybe half an hour, both to glean information and to take cover, in case any security guards wanted to know what the hell we were still doing inside the building. And it worked. The game ended at 10:03, and by eleven o'clock there weren't any security personnel in sight. As near as we could tell, the old ballpark was ours for the roaming.

At 12:02, the CITGO sign went dark, thus answering a question that I've had since I moved here; namely, when *does* the CITGO sign shut down? I suppose that midnight is the official target, but someone's clock isn't synchronized to the correct time (my watch is). A few minutes later, Bill and I made our way to the concourse under the center-field bleachers. I had a radio interview scheduled for 12:20, and Bill thought the bank of pay phones out there might be, at this point in the cleaning process, the quietest in the ballpark. And they're also the most isolated, a concern given that we still don't quite know if we're supposed to be here.

A year ago, I talked to a couple of guys who worked at the Astrodome in Houston, and they claimed that late in the evening, after nearly everyone had gone home, a squad of cats were released from a pen in the bowels of the stadium. Their mission? Kill any rodents bold enough to loot the Eighth Wonder of the World. (How these cats were corralled after their nocturnal adventures, nobody in Houston seemed to know, but why let details ruin a great story?)

This story popped into my head shortly after Bill and I arrived under the center-field bleachers. There's a large storage area down there, in which the batting cage and other equipment are kept. And scurrying into that storage area, after we interrupted its meal of pizza crust, went a moderately sized rat. I poked my head through the gate blocking off the storage area, and there he sat next to the batting cage, pondering his next move.

At 12:20, I called ESPN Radio producer Andy Elrick, and at 12:25 I was on the line with host Bob Valvano (one of the best in the business), and we began chatting about current baseball events.

At 12:30 on the dot, two more rats emerged from that same storage area, and trundled across the cement right in front of me, perhaps fifteen feet away. Bob had just asked me a question, but I wasn't able to focus on what he was saying. Instead, I said, "Bob, you'll have to excuse me for a second, but two good-sized rats just crossed my path, so I'm a little distracted."

My furry friends took little notice of me—they just sat there, ruminating—and I quickly regained my composure, finishing the interview as if I were sitting on my couch back home. Well, close.

After the interview, Bill and I still had time to kill. All the time in the world. Time enough to get in trouble, time enough to read a short novel, time enough to drive each other crazy, time enough to fall asleep and wake up having missed something important, like the sun coming up.

Rather than any of those things, though, we went exploring.

First, I wanted to head up to the bleachers. Specifically, I wanted to see, and sit in, the most famous seat in Fenway Park, the seat marking the longest home run in Fenway Park history, struck by Ted Williams against Detroit's Fred Hutchinson on June 9, 1946. According to the Red Sox Media Guide, "The ball landed on top of the straw hat of Joseph A. Boucher, 56, a construction worker from Albany, New York who was sitting in section 42, row 37, seat 21 . . . 'The sun was right in our eyes,' he said . . . 'All I could do was duck . . . I'm glad I didn't stand up . . . They say it bounced a dozen rows higher, but after it hit my head I was no longer interested . . .'"

Reggie Jackson once hit a long home run to right field, and afterward he said, "It was an insurance run, so I hit it to the Prudential Building." Actually, nobody's ever hit a ball out of the ballpark to right field, and in fact nobody's ever hit a ball deeper into the right-field bleachers than Ted Williams did. So the next time you're at Fenway Park, it's worth a trip to the red seat. Make your way to Section 42 after the game, sit there for a moment, gaze at the far-distant plate, and wonder at the power generated by a man—they called him the "Splendid Splinter"—who stood six-three and weighed about 185 pounds.

Bill and I walked around to the other side of the ballpark, where I sat in another of Fenway's singular seats: Section 28, Row 1, Seat 1. What's unique about that seat? Well, Seat 1 is the *only* seat in Row 1 of Section 28. Section 28, above the visitors' dugout, on the third-base side of the diamond, is where the grandstand turns north. So Section 28 is actually a triangle, with Row 1 representing the single-seat, lower point of the triangle. Only in Fenway . . .

From there, we went where fans don't normally go: the bowels of the ballpark, beneath the grandstand down the left-field line. This is where, among other things, the grounds crew stores fertilizer and dirt and paint and everything else they use to keep the field looking the way it does. I poked around inside one storage room that looked like it hadn't changed since 1934, or perhaps even 1912.

It was also in the bowels that we happened across a huge machine, the P/M 2000 Orbital Ice Storage and Dispenser System. Even at this late hour, the P/M 2000, which looks like it's pretty well along in life, is chugging away at its assigned task, with packages of thirty or forty ice cubes cascading to the concrete floor at random intervals, like cubic silver dollars from a cranky slot machine.

After nearly two hours of wandering around to see what we could see, Bill came up with a radical idea. Why not go introduce ourselves to the security guard (stationed just inside the service entrance between Gates D and A)? Yes, he might order us out of the building, but he might also have some good stories—I think that's what motivated Bill, who's collecting such stories—and if he liked us, we'd have the run of the place, and wouldn't have to spend the next four or five hours looking over our shoulders.

I was a bit leery of this idea, but I tagged along like the relative neophyte that I am. And as it turned out, Bill's instincts were right on. We found Brad, a Pinkerton man, sitting in what can only be described as a decrepit little room, little bigger than a closet, and with a view of the service entrance and Yawkey Way beyond. Brad seemed to me to be in his middle or late fifties, a man who is generally well-fed but doesn't drink much. He had a paperback book sitting next to him, and *Star Trek: Deep Space Nine* playing on a small color television set.

Bill's got something of a gift for gab, and so we (mostly Bill) talked to Brad for close to forty-five minutes, mostly about his job. It seems that not much happens from midnight until dawn, other than the occasional intoxicated young man who rattles the big gate just up the ramp from Brad's cage. That is to say, if you don't mind the hours, serving as Fenway Park's sole overnight security guard is pretty cushy work. With Brad's apparent blessing, we struck out in search of more adventure . . .

I do have a mischievous streak, and I did some things that could have gotten Bill and me tossed out of the ballpark on our ears, if not actually arrested. We wound our way to the left-field corner, and I realized that it wouldn't take any particular agility to clamber to the top of the exterior wall, the same wall that becomes the Green Monster once it reaches fair territory. I toyed with the idea of walking along the top and out to the netting to see if any baseballs were still resting there, but Bill talked me down. Later, I realized just what a crummy position Bill would have been in, if I'd fallen from the Monster to the warning track, thirty-seven feet down, and broken my leg, or worse.

What Bill didn't stop me from doing was going on the field, something that could certainly have gotten us in trouble. Mind you, I did stay off the grass, as nobody, but *nobody*, is allowed out there. Anyway, I slid over the wall next to the Sox dugout, poked around in there for a minute—nothing except a few stray paper cups as evidence of the evening's game—and then I walked all the way to the scoreboard at the base of the Green Monster, staying on the dirt along the fence the entire way. Along the way, I came to realize that between midnight and dawn in this place, rats really do abound. As I reached the left-field corner, another rodent emerged from a hole under the fence, scurried right past my feet and along the base of the Green Monster until it reached a hole at the base of the scoreboard door, and disappeared.

By 3:30, Bill and I had pretty much exhausted the wonders of discovery, and we sat down to wait for the sun. A few minutes later, the blowers turned off their blowers—it was break time—and for the first time since 11 P.M., Fenway Park was nearly silent.

At 5 A.M., the skies beyond center field began to lighten, and within a few minutes hundreds of gulls descended on Fenway, the great majority of them fluttering and screeching in the bleachers, where the blowers had not yet chased the peanut shells away.

Dawn came at 5:30 on the nose, and Bill and I left for our respective beds.

I would be back in thirteen hours.

Tuesday, July 25

Today was a big, big day in Red Sox Nation, even without considering yet another humdrum, 4–2 loss to the Twins:

The Yankees destroyed the Orioles tonight, 19–1. The Blue Jays did lose, but now the Sox and Jays are both three games behind the Yanks, and it's starting to get scary again . . . especially when you consider Boston's upcoming schedule. After another game against the Twins tomorrow afternoon, the Sox hit the road for seven games against the Athletics and Mariners, the two best teams in the West.

Yesterday, Red Sox third baseman Sean Berry tied an all-time record:
Shortest Stay with Major League Club, 1 Day
With Trot Nixon coming off the disabled list today, somebody had to go. And
Berry—who went oh-for-four last night in his first and apparently only game with
the Red Sox, and struck out looking to end the game—was the somebody.

The medical reports on Pete Schourek came in today, and they were, uh, not
pretty. Schourek's doctor found bone chips in his left elbow. And a bone spur in his
left shoulder. And a frayed rotator cuff in his left shoulder. Whenever I read about
something like this—actually, I can't remember reading about any pitcher having
three injuries like this—I can't help but wonder, "So why was the guy allowed to
pitch for so long, so poorly?" In his last four starts before going on the DL, Schourek
managed only fourteen innings, gave up 25 hits, and posted an 11.57 ERA. The Red
Sox lost all four of those games, and I'm not sure they had to.

Today the papers reported that Manny Alexander, one of the Sox' exciting
young third basemen (he wrote, fingers dripping with sarcasm) is being investigated
for possession of illegal steroids. It seems that on June 30, batboy Carlos Cowart—
I've sat within a few feet of his station, near the home on-deck circle, many times
this season—was stopped by police. He was driving Alexander's car, and the cops,
after discovering an outstanding warrant, conducted a search of the car. They found
vials of illegal steroids and syringes. Cowart didn't show up for work today, but now
the question is, whose steroids were they? Steroid use is banned by Major League
Baseball, but there's no drug testing in the majors, so the "ban" is essentially meaningless. I predict that absolutely nothing will come of this, other than the
twenty-year-old Cowart, with a string of arrests behind him, losing his job.

And finally, tonight we had our first celebrity sighting of the season. Of course,
famousities are a dime a dozen at Yankee Stadium, but here in the Fens they're
about as rare as a three-dollar bill. In the middle of the sixth inning, though, the following flashed on the big display board beyond the center-field bleachers:

RED SOX
WELCOME
HOLLYWOOD STAR
DANNY DEVITO
TO TONIGHT'S GAME

And then the JumboTron showed DeVito waving to the crowd from his seat in the Roof Box not far from the 600 Club. He was sitting next to Rhea Perlman, and I wondered if she wondered why her name wasn't up there on the screen, since she's the one who costarred on *Cheers* for so many years. (Completely irrelevant aside: DeVito is one of our least-appreciated great character actors. Look at his work in *Tin Men* or *Get Shorty* or *L.A. Confidential* or *The Big Kahuna*, and tell me this guy's not one of the best.)

◆ ◆ ◆

Monday, I speculated that employees in the Red Sox ticket office might sometimes profit by selling tickets to scalpers. Well, yesterday in New York, eight Yankee ticket agents were indicted by a grand jury for just such shenanigans.

Manhattan District Attorney Robert Morgenthau said that so far this year alone, more than $300,000 worth of Yankee and Mets tickets were diverted.

"Ordinary fans showing up at the stadium had virtually no chance to obtain the best tickets available to Yankee games, since corrupt agents were diverting them to scalpers," Morgenthau said.

State Attorney General Eliot Spitzer, whose office ran a parallel investigation, said there was an "unholy alliance between ticket scalpers and those who work in the box offices."

Wow, an unholy alliance. And Sunday afternoon, I was a willing (if somewhat reluctant, not to mention ignorant) participant in one just like it.

◆ ◆ ◆

As I was heading down the ramp to the concourse after tonight's game, I heard a little girl ask, "Daddy, how do they clean up the ballpark when the game is finished?"

I hope that she (or her Daddy) reads this book someday.

Wednesday, July 26

It was the kind of day, for a baseball fan with tickets to the game, that might have resulted in a visit from the Dementors, J. K. Rowling's fictional demons that clamp their jaws over your mouth and suck out every thought of happiness. The rains showed up this morning and still hadn't left by midnight, so as much as the club wanted to avoid having to schedule yet another doubleheader, there just wasn't any way to get this one in.

As if that weren't bad enough, the Sox lost ground tonight, too, as both the Yankees and Blue Jays won. The latest in American League East pennant-race fun:

	W-L	GB	RS-RA	PYTHAG W-L
YANKEES	54–42	—	531–459	54–42
BLUE JAYS	54–48	3	557–597	48–54
RED SOX	51–46	3 ½	502–448	54–43

It's getting scary again. Three and a half games doesn't look like much, but three and a half can turn to six and a half over the course of a weekend, and six and a half in late July or early August is usually too much.

Thursday, July 27

In today's *Herald* appeared an article, written by Steve Conroy, headlined SOX NEED A BOOSTER SHOT. The basic gist, that the Red Sox won't win anything this year if their hitting doesn't pick up, is absolutely correct. It's the rest of the article that's messed up. The accompanying graphic, for example, doesn't tell the story well at all. It's a table right in the middle of the piece, with the heading, AMERICAN LEAGUE TEAM BATTING and the Red Sox stats highlighted in bold face. They're eighth, roughly the middle of the pack, among the fourteen American League teams. But they're only eighth because the men who run sports departments tend to be doddering fools who still worship at the altar of batting average. Yes, the Sox do rank eighth in the A.L. in that particular stat, but they're even worse—tenth—in the only statistic that truly matters: runs scored. Only the Twins, Orioles, Devil Rays, and Tigers are worse than the Red Sox; three of those clubs are bottom-feeders, and the other (Detroit) plays in a great pitcher's park.

That's one problem with Conroy's article. The other is more insidious, because there's no easy fix, and happens whenever baseball writers go to baseball players for answers.

Backup catcher Scott Hatteberg is supposedly one of the more intelligent players on the club, and not coincidentally one of the better interviews. But when it comes to simplistic analysis, he's no better than the rest. Of offense, Hatteberg told Conroy, "I think it's contagious. I think it snowballs—and it can go the other way as far as not scoring runs. It's a confidence thing. I think we can go out there and score some runs and we'll be able to pile them on . . . The secret is to win games. We've got a lot of the core guys that are able to do it . . . We just have to go out and win. We have to play like a team."

But when it comes to clichés, Hatteberg can't touch Garciaparra, who said, "That's baseball. We just have to go out and do the little things, like I've always said. Pitching, solid defense, and timely hitting. If all those things don't come about, you don't win. That's evident."

No, Nomar, no. What's evident is that if you don't hit home runs, you don't win. And right now, your team ranks eleventh in the American League in home runs. Those aren't the little things, those are the big things. And you're not doing them. Or rather, your teammates aren't doing them.

Is the situation hopeless? Absolutely not. A year ago, the Red Sox won ninety-four games despite an offense that finished the season ranked just ninth in the league. But the Sox have to score more runs, which means that (1) a few players will have to improve slightly over the next two months, and (2) once Everett finishes serving his suspension (he did get ten days for his explosion on July 15), he and Garciaparra and Trot Nixon all have to remain healthy for the rest of the season. There is very little margin for error.

◆ ◆ ◆

I will remember, more than anything else, three things about my summer in Boston: Fenway Park, rain, and airplanes. This morning I found myself on yet another of the latter, a Boeing 767–300 on its way from Boston to Denver. Tomorrow night, my brother Eric is getting married—I never thought it would happen to him before me, but what are you gonna do?—and I flew in a day early to see the Rockies and the Dodgers.

This was not my first visit to Coors Field, as I was here for a Mariners-Rockies game back in 1996. It's a nice ballpark, as good as or better than most of the other new ones, thanks to some nice little touches, like the purple row of seats, near the top of the upper deck, that is exactly a mile high. Coors is better than Safeco Field in Seattle, and it's better than Jacobs Field in Cleveland.

I couldn't have been happier with the game. I wanted to see a Coors Field slugfest, and that's exactly what I got: Dodgers 16, Rockies 11.

◆ ◆ ◆

The Red Sox finally made a big trade tonight, and frankly I have no idea what Dan Duquette thinks he's doing.

Leaving the Red Sox: second baseman Jeff Frye and pitcher Brian Rose.

Frye hasn't been a popular fellow in the team offices upstairs, as he joined Nomar in voicing his disgust with the club's treatment of Mike Stanley. Rose looks like yet another talented young pitcher who simply couldn't develop in Boston. There's been a string of them lately, and I'm not sure who to blame.

Joining the Red Sox: second baseman Mike Lansing and pitcher Rolando Arrojo.

Lansing used to be a decent player, but that was years ago. This year, he's batting .206 away from Coors Field. What's worse, he's under contract through the 2001 season, in which he'll "earn" six million dollars, which is about five million more dollars than he'll deserve. Or the Sox can afford. While it's true that Frye was overpaid at $2.5 million this season, there's certainly not a $3.5 million difference between him and Lansing. As Dan Shaughnessy notes in tomorrow's *Globe*, it's probably "not total coincidence that Frye was traded four days after ripping Dan Duquette over the Duke's treatment of Mike Stanley."

Rolando Arrojo posted a 5.18 ERA in 1999 and is even worse this year, at 6.04. According to the official sources, Arrojo is thirty-one years old, but there are people who think that he's actually thirty-four or thirty-five. On the plus side, this is just Arrojo's third season in the majors, so he doesn't make much money at all, his non-Coors ERA this season is 4.94, and Jimy Williams and Joe Kerrigan have gotten a fair amount of mileage from veteran pitchers in recent years.

About the best you can say about Lansing is that he's not a convicted felon.

The scuttlebutt has it that the Rockies would give up Arrojo only if the Sox would also take on Lansing (and his salary). And the Duke fell for it.

Sixth Inning

Thursday, August 3
Being an Account of How I Missed, Among Other Things, the
Longest Game of the Season . . .

When last we spoke, I was on my way to Seattle, home of Kristien and the Seattle Mariners, and soon to be a stopping point for the Boston Red Sox. My plan for the next five days was, I thought, both simple and well conceived. Saturday and Sunday, I would spend with Kristien. Monday morning, Kristien's eight-year-old son Micah would arrive in town after a weekend with his grandparents, and that evening we would enjoy (I hoped) the Mariners–Red Sox game from the comfort of some fantastic seats. Tuesday night, no baseball game for me (even though Tim Wakefield would be pitching for the Sox); instead, the three of us—along with Kristien's mom, Cheri—would attend Cirque du Soleil. And then Wednesday night, my last in Seattle until the middle of September, Kristien and I would return to Safeco Field to see "the greatest pitcher in the world" (as I described Pedro Martinez to her).

Days 1 through 3 of the plan went beautifully. The first two of those days were mostly about Kristien and I making eyes at each other, and thus not really within the purview of this book. So I'll skip ahead to Day 3, at the end of which a little boy enjoyed a baseball game about as much as he could have . . .

Day 3 (Monday)

Cheri and Micah arrived early in the afternoon, and after getting acquainted (me and Cheri) and reacquainted (Micah and Kristien), Kristien, Micah and I headed downtown, hours before the game, with nothing particular in mind. There's a wonderful toy store in Pioneer Square, just a few blocks north of Safeco Field, called Magic Mouse, and that's where we soon found ourselves. Kristien's good at occupying herself, so that's what she did while Micah and I played with various puzzles. Our playtime was cut short, however, when Micah felt the call of nature.

"You need to go now?"

"Uh-huh!"

"Hmmm . . . Okay, I know a good bathroom not far from here."

I said this nonchalantly, but inside I was proclaiming to any and all, "Worry not, small human. Rob Neyer, master of not only Pioneer Square, but of all things Seattle and beyond, shall escort you to the lavatory of your childish fantasies."

So with me feeling quite full of myself, we walked the three blocks to Elliott Bay Book Company, the best independent bookstore in the city. As I walked through the door, Kristien grabbed my arm and asked, "Hey, did you plan this?"

Huh? Plan *what*?

I took a step back and looked at the door, at which she was pointing. There, a cardboard, hand-lettered sign read:

> Tuesday, August 1
> ROB NEYER
> of ESPN.com
> will discuss and sign his book,
> "Baseball Dynasties"

Huh? Discuss and sign *what*?

And then it all came flooding back, like memories of ritual Satanic abuse unlocked by an unscrupulous psychiatrist. Back in April, somebody from Elliott Bay had contacted me about doing a reading/signing. Since I knew I'd be back in Seattle when the Red Sox were in town, we picked August 1. Except I completely forgot about this. In fact, just a few days ago I remembered that we'd talked about it, but I thought they'd blown me off for whatever reason. No such luck, though.

It took a while for the surprise and frustration to wear off, in part because the signing would necessitate me missing our pre—Cirque du Soleil dinner at Zeeks, the best pizza place in the city. But by the time the three of us finished our Chinese food at the Pike Place Market, I was resigned to my fate. And then it was time to head for Safeco Field, where we'd be meeting my friend Scott Stone, with whom I share two season tickets. Scott and my tickets are in the upper deck, but that's not where the four of us would be sitting this evening. Nope. This would be Kristien and Micah's first Mariners game, and I had something else in mind. Back in early April, I went to a Mariners game with Mike Slade (who used to run the company I worked for), and at some point he graciously offered me the use of his tickets when I was in town again. These are truly great tickets, third row behind the middle of the visitors' dugout. And on the aisle, no less.

I wanted Mike's tickets not to impress Kristien—she's not impressed by such trivial things—but because I wanted her and Micah to enjoy the game. And of course it's a lot easier to enjoy a baseball game when you're close enough to hear the bat meet the ball and the ball meet the glove.

Micah's not a baseball fan. He's never really played the game at all, and his experience as a spectator consists of a single Wenatchee Apple Sox game earlier this summer. So I wasn't sure what to expect. Would he get bored and want to wander around the ballpark? (That's supposed to be a major appeal of the new mallparks, they're "fun for the whole family.") Would he spend most of the game asking for various foods and beverages? (I've seen and heard that act far too many times.) Would he get so bored or cranky that Kristien would have to take him home? (I told her I'd pay for a cab if it came to that.)

Answer: none of the above. Micah's a great kid, and baseball's a great game, especially when you're sitting twenty feet from the field. We bought a giant bag of kettle corn on the way to the ballpark, and he was perfectly content. Didn't ask for more food, didn't ask for anything to drink. Perhaps this was because he was having such a great time. The game got off to a rousing start, as Seattle's Jay Buhner hit a grand slam off Ramon Martinez in the bottom of the first. (That was the only hit Martinez would allow in the game, but unfortunately he also issued five walks and was yanked early.) The Sox came right back with three in the top of the second, and after five innings the Mariners owned a 5–4 lead.

Beginning in the fourth inning, Pedro Martinez began to pop out of the dugout during the breaks and look into the stands. I told Micah to yell at Pedro. He did, and Pedro looked right back at Micah, smiled real big, and gave a little wave. Even though Micah has no idea that Pedro's the greatest pitcher in the world, he still got a thrill out of this.

And then during the seventh-inning stretch, Micah was on the big video screen. Dancing. Like a crazy person.

See, at this point in the game, after "Take Me Out to the Ball Game," the PA system plays a pop song—I didn't write down tonight's—and a few guys carrying video cameras train them on the stands, looking for people willing to dance. Well, Micah is always willing to dance, and eventually one of the cameramen found him. And whoever was running the video board must have liked him, because he remained on the screen for a good ten or fifteen seconds. A few seconds in, he saw himself, and of course that just encouraged him to gyrate even more.

The wave from Pedro and seeing himself on the big screen would have been plenty for Micah, but there was more. When the game ended—Sox won 8–5, thanks to Varitek's three-run homer in the eighth and yet another brilliant performance by the bullpen—we stood behind the dugout for a few minutes, though I wasn't sure why. None of the Red Sox players seemed to be carrying baseballs, and anyway Micah was just one of a dozen kids lined up. But we waited nonetheless. And when the relief pitchers reached the dugout, I noticed that Bryce Florie was holding a baseball, and in fact it seemed apparent that he was intent on giving said baseball away. And for some reason, despite the imprecations of all the other kids, Florie pointed right at Micah, so when he tossed the ball on top of the dugout, nobody interfered as it bounced into his glove . . . and then out of his glove. But to complete an incredibly fortuitous evening, the ball trickled into my waiting right hand, and I shoved it right back into Micah's mitt.

And so Micah's experience was complete. I don't think I've ever seen a happier, more jazzed little boy.

I should clarify here that I am not testifying to the magic of a baseball game. I'm testifying to the *potential* magic of a baseball game, a potential magic that is much more likely to be realized if you're lucky enough to have one of the best seats in the house. And yes, I will use this episode to again suggest the improbable . . .

every major league club should set aside a block of great seats, close to the field and not far from a dugout or dugouts, and provide every season-ticket holder with those seats at least once per season.

The next time I ask Micah if he wants to see a baseball game, I'll just bet that his eyes will get real big as he says, "Yeah!" But if we'd been sitting in the cheap seats Monday night, I'm not sure what he would say.

With all this going through my mind, as we stood at the top of the concourse waiting for Scott to catch up with us, I said to Micah, "Now, you know that it won't always be like this, right?"

"Yeah, I know," he replied. But I'm not sure that he does.

Day 4 (Tuesday)
I have long dreaded book signings. This fear dates back to 1991, when I went to a signing by Ian Frazier, who is merely one of the great writers of our time. He was on a tour to promote *Great Plains*, which is one of the very few non-baseball books that I've read more than once. For some reason, his publicist had booked him at a hole-in-the-wall bookstore in Overland Park, Kansas. Granted, this was before the days of a mega-bookstore in every good-sized suburb. Still, whoever put Ian Frazier in this particular store probably should have been asked to find another line of work.

I spoke with Frazier for five minutes, and I was his only company for those five minutes. The lesson here was a simple one: If somebody like Ian Frazier stiffs at a book signing, then what chance would I have?

My fears, as it turned out, were unfounded. There were maybe twenty-five people in the audience (all of them men, including one adolescent), and they seemed genuinely happy to be there. It is, I must admit, an odd feeling to look upon those faces and realize they all belong to people who think I have something important to say. As it happened, there were very few questions about my book (*Baseball Dynasties*), and a whole bunch about the current game. Which was just fine, since I haven't really thought much about *Baseball Dynasties* since it was published in March. One of the things that I've discovered about writing books is that once it's out in the world, it's out of my mind and on its own ("Farewell, my paged friend!").

The original plan called for me to walk to Safeco Field after the signing and continue talking to anyone who showed up. But of course, I'd completely forgotten the original plan; my own plan required that I end the signing by 6:45, and take a cab to Zeeks Pizza, where I would meet Kristien and Micah and Cheri, and from where we would drive to a parking lot in Renton, where the Cirque du Soleil tent is set up.

Or so I thought. When I got to Zeeks, I learned that the tickets that I thought were for tonight are actually for tomorrow night. Yet another Rob Neyer screwup. And it was too late to get to the ballpark, where Wakefield was starting for the Sox. I took it pretty well, but the next morning when I found out what I'd missed, I felt like I'd got my fingers slammed in a car door.

You see, the Mariners and Red Sox played the longest home game in Seattle's franchise history. The game finally ended, five hours and thirty-four minutes after it began, when Mike Cameron led off the bottom of the nineteenth inning with a home run off Jeff Fassero. Cameron's at-bat included seven foul balls, one of them a long drive down the right-field line that went foul by just a few feet.

This game merely reinforced something I realized a few years ago. If you think about going to a game, you should go. If you plan on going to a game and then don't, you'll miss something. Tonight, I should have been there.

Day 5 (Wednesday)

Of course, my Cirque du Soleil screwup had a ripple effect. I missed not only last night's marathon, but also tonight's Pedro Martinez start. So when we finally got home—the circus went later than the baseball game—the first thing I did was check the scores. Honestly, I half expected to see that Pedro had finally pitched his no-hitter, which would have been a tough thing for me to deal with. Tough, as in, I would have spent, quite literally, the rest of my life wishing I'd been at Safeco Field rather than under the big top. Fortunately for my long-term emotional health, he pitched well but not *that* well, a five-hitter to beat the Mariners 5–2, and run his record to 13–3.

If I had to do it all over again, I wouldn't have changed anything at all. The looks of pure joy I saw on the faces of not only Micah, but also Kristien and Cheri, gave me more thrills than even Pedro Martinez could have provided.

A no-hitter notwithstanding, of course.

Friday, August 4

I may now officially proclaim that this season has gone by too quickly. It seems to me like the Royals were just visiting Boston a few weeks ago . . . but it was nine weeks ago exactly, and nine is more than a few.

Last time the Royals were here, I had no compunction about pulling for them. At that point, the possibilities still existed that (1) the Royals might put together a pretty good season, and (2) the Red Sox might, as so many predicted, emerge as the American League's best team, and thus run away with the East flag. Alas, neither of those things happened. So with the Royals going nowhere and the Red Sox fighting desperately just for a postseason berth, the choice here is obvious: I should root for the Sox. Sitting there in our bleacher seats before the game, Susan and I agreed on this.

But I just can't do it, not tonight. I figured this out quickly, in the bottom of the first when Trot Nixon led off with a long fly to center field . . . *C'mon, catch it. CATCH IT . . .* So that's the way it was going to be. I've been living and dying with the Royals for far too long to change my ways at this late date. So it was with a certain amount of disgust that I watched Brian Daubach lead off the eighth inning with a long fly ball that reached the center-field bleachers, not far from where Susan and I were sitting, to give the Red Sox a 5–4 lead with which they would finish the game.

◆   ◆   ◆

Red Sox manager Jimy Williams is a good one. Royals manager Tony Muser is a bad one.

No, it's really not that simple, but I think the cognitive skills of the two can be fairly gleaned from the following, selected comments made by each following this evening's game . . .

Muser: "We had to make a four-run lead stand. We're getting leads and are lacking killer instinct . . . When you're out of a pennant race, players look around and say, 'What's in it for me?' And they kind of fraction themselves from the team. That's what we've got now: a lot of people playing for themselves."

Williams: "When you win, you've got chemistry—when you lose, you've got physics, isn't that right? You can talk all you want to about chemistry—that can take on a life of its own—but chemistry can be created on the playing field."

That's Muser in a nutshell, spouting all that crap about "killer instinct" and blaming the losses on poor attitude rather than poor players or (heaven forbid) poor managing. And Williams, God love him, is at least smart enough to know that chemistry is mostly a bunch of bullshit.

Saturday, August 5

The Red Sox bullpen finally blew one today.

In the bottom of the seventh, Carl Everett—in his first action after the ten-game suspension—crashed a long fly ball off the very top of the Green Monster in left-center field, winding up on second base with two outs. Garciaparra followed with an RBI single to right field, tying the game at four apiece. But in the top of the eighth, Jermaine Dye and Joe Randa both singled off Rod Beck. He was replaced by Rheal Cormier, who gave up a couple more hits, and the Royals wound up scoring three runs in the inning. It was still 7–4 in the bottom of the ninth, and with the Sox down to their last out, Everett hit a solo home run. The next two batters walked, but Varitek struck out on three pitches—the last of them a slider in the dirt—to end the game.

Watching the Royals score three runs in the eighth was a thrill, but I actually had a bigger one that same half-inning. During Joe Randa's at-bat (he singled), a peregrine falcon soared over the center-field bleachers and alit on one of the posts that holds up the netting atop the Green Monster.

In a 1993 issue of *Yankee* magazine—a publication about New England, as opposed to a certain pinstriped baseball team—naturalist Ted Levin wrote, "Boston's Fenway Park—nestled along the Charles River and the Atlantic Ocean—may be the best ballpark in America for watching birds."

Among all the major-league ballparks, this could only happen at Fenway. There are substantial bodies of water nearby, and more important, Fenway is about half as tall as modern ballparks. The birds come because they can.

◆   ◆   ◆

Today, Carl Everett struck again, and I'm not talking about his home run in the bottom of the ninth. It seems that on his first day back, Everett blew up again, this time at his manager.

The *Globe* was, typically, relatively spare with details, but the *Herald*'s Michael Silverman didn't leave much to the imagination. According to Silverman, "The gist of the argument was believed to be that Williams was displeased that Everett had left the Red Sox in Seattle during the recent road trip one day early and flew home to Tampa on Wednesday. Given that Everett wasn't eligible to play in Seattle anyway, this wasn't a huge thing, but apparently Everett didn't ask for the team's permission. And that's a no-no, even if you're a ballplayer making nearly $10 million for seven months work.

Anyway, Silverman reported Everett's reaction as: "I leave for one game and you're all over my ass! I don't need this (expletive deleted). I miss one day and you're going to give me this (expletive deleted) (expletive deleted)? (Expletive deleted) that!"

Filling in the blanks here doesn't take a great deal of imagination. A bigger challenge: trying to figure out if Everett's temper is hurting the team.

Actually, it already has hurt the team, in the form of his recent ten-game suspension. But do Everett's outbursts hurt the "chemistry" of the team, as so many—writers, fans, and players alike—seem to think? It's even been suggested that because the Red Sox' ancient locker room is so small, it's more important for them to get along than most teams. I have no idea if that's true, but I do know that many, many championship teams over the years have included players with tempers, and players who didn't particularly like each other. What's more, Everett played for pennant-winning teams in Houston in 1998 and '99, and after he left the Astros, his ex-teammates raved about him.

It gets back to the same thing. When you're winning, you've got good chemistry. And when you're not, you don't.

Sunday, August 6

This evening, a frequent e-mail correspondent named Scott sent me the following:

> So were you a baseball author, or a baseball fan this weekend?
> Hoping I never have to face that dilemma,
> —Scott

The truth is that I didn't truly enjoy any of the three games this weekend, and what's worse, I'll face this same dilemma in a few weeks, when I'll accompany the Red Sox to Kansas City (we'll be on different planes, of course) for a four-game series. Kristien's meeting me, though, so I'll probably see only two, or perhaps three, of the four games.

I'm not exactly sure where or when, but at some point during today's game I finally crossed the line and wanted the Red Sox to beat the Royals. Actually, it probably happened, at least subconsciously, as soon as I saw Wakefield take the mound to start the game. He pitched quite well, but so did Royals starter Dan Reichert. Kansas City scored an unearned run in the first inning—O'Leary dropped a routine fly ball—and Boston scored once in the sixth, courtesy of Nomar's home run into the center-field bleachers.

In the top of the eighth, the Royals strung together four singles and scored twice. In the bottom of the ninth, the Sox strung together three singles . . . and didn't score at all. Lansing led off with a line drive off the Green Monster, and got thrown out trying to stretch his single to a double. From the stands, Lansing looked safe, but it was still a stupid thing to try, given the score. And it looked all the stupider when the next two hitters singled. Take away Lansing's daring, and the Sox have, at worst, the bases loaded with nobody out. Instead, it's two on and one out. Ricky Bottalico trotted in from the bullpen, retired Nixon and Daubach, and the Sox had lost.

So now they've lost two of three to the crummy Royals, while the Yankees were losing two of three to the excellent Mariners. Officially, the Sox didn't lose any ground these last three days, but they really did, missing a great chance to make up a game or two in the standings. They've got more good chances in August, with six games against Anaheim, six against Tampa Bay, seven against Texas, and three more against Kansas City. No cream puffs in the bunch, but all beatable teams. The Sox really need to make some sort of move this month, because September brings opponents like the Mariners, Yankees, Indians, and Athletics. And the Indians series, because of those rain-outs back in April, will include five games in three days.

As for the Yankees, it's not too early to start thinking about them. They're here September 8, 9, and 10, and then the Sox travel to New York for a single makeup game on the eleventh. Those four games—assuming, of course, that the Sox are still within striking distance of a postseason berth—promise to be absolutely insane, probably the biggest games of the season for both clubs.

◆　◆　◆

Today the *Globe*'s Bob Ryan writes of the Red Sox' ballpark plans: ". . . they are circulating a ballpark design that would perpetuate the nonsense of the left-field wall, a freak of real estate that has skewed performance evaluation for sixty-six years and . . . has had as much to do with the team's inability to construct a championship team as any other single factor."

Ryan exaggerates.

While Fenway Park has long been blamed for the franchise's failure to win a World Series, I believe that that's an outdated concept. For many years, Fenway was perhaps the best hitter's park in the American League. As Bill James once wrote, "The Red Sox perpetually overrate their hitting and underrate their pitching and defense. The pitchers, shuttled into and out of 12–9 games like the white chips in a penny ante poker game, lose their rhythm and their confidence, while for everyday players, Fenway makes stars out of ordinary ball players."

Bill composed those convincing words in 1979, and while I doubt if Bob Ryan (or Dan Shaughnessy, who also blames Fenway for the eighty-two-year World Series drought) are familiar with Bill's work, they still subscribe to the theory.

Unfortunately, it's an outdated theory.

In 1979, a typical Red Sox game at Fenway Park included fourteen percent more runs than a typical Red Sox game away from Fenway Park.

In 1989, a typical Red Sox game at Fenway Park included eleven percent more runs than a typical Red Sox game away from Fenway Park.

In 1999, a typical Red Sox game at Fenway Park included seven percent more runs than a typical Red Sox game away from Fenway Park.

The trend is, I would suggest, fairly obvious: relative to the rest of the American League, Fenway Park has become less favorable to the hitters over the last twenty years. But as some of you know, single seasons are not necessarily representative; that is, the sample sizes are not necessarily large enough for us to draw an accurate conclusion. So in the interest of precision, let's look at three-season periods. In the chart below, "HR" refers to the effect Fenway had on home runs, relative to other American League parks, and "Runs" does the same for runs. A "100" means that the park was neutral, while a "105" means that the park inflated the statistic in question by 5 percent. Got it?

YEARS	HR	RUNS
1977–79	120	129
1987–89	108	99
1997–99	92	102

Clearly, Fenway Park is *not* a haven for sluggardly sluggers, not anymore. In the 1970s, Fenway was the best hitter's park in the American League, both in terms of home runs and overall run production. By the late 1980s, however, both categories were down. And from 1997 through 1999, Fenway's actually been tougher than the typical American League park, at least in terms of home runs. And while I haven't listed the numbers here, lately it hasn't been a great park for right-handed power hitters, who presumably are able to take advantage of the Green Monster's coziness, either.

What's interesting is that Fenway's actual dimensions, the distances from home plate to the various fences in both fair and foul territory, haven't changed since World War II. However, many other things about the ballpark *have* changed.

In 1982 and '83, luxury suites were constructed atop the roof down the left- and right-field lines.

In 1988 and '89, the infamous 600 Club, containing 610 plush seats and a fancy restaurant, was constructed above the grandstand behind home plate, and a new press box was built atop the 600 Club.

In 1992, a metal roof was installed above the left- and right-field roof seating.

Unfortunately, it's difficult to draw any strong, direct correlations between these alterations and Fenway's hitting environment. It's clear that something happened, but it's not clear what that something was, or when.

The most striking difference, statistics-wise, is in the home-runs column. In the 1970s, Fenway was one of the two or three best home-run parks in the American League. But in the late 1990s, it was actually one of the worst.

You might wonder, if Fenway's not a good home-run park, then why is it still a decent hitter's park, simply in terms of run production? The answer is simple. Fenway remains a fine park for batting average and doubles. This is due to a number of things, but I typically cite a small amount of foul territory (the smallest in the majors), and the excellent visual hitting background.

But while I can't fully explain the effects, or non-effects of the various alterations, it's pretty clear that Fenway should no longer be described as a great hitter's park. It's a good one, but certainly not good enough to significantly distort the performance of either Red Sox hitters or Red Sox pitchers. I believe this is due, primarily, to the other American League ballparks. Nine A.L. ballparks were either constructed or significantly altered in the 1990s, and the majority of them have been more favorable to the hitters than those they replaced.

So while Fenway might be almost exactly the same as it's been for half a century, it's become a better pitcher's park in recent years *relative to the other ballparks*. And if Fenway is now fairly neutral, "penalizing" neither the hitters nor the pitchers to any great degree, then how can we blame it for the front office's personnel decisions?

We can't. Or at least we shouldn't.

I do agree with Bob Ryan about one thing, though. Here's what he wrote today about plans for a new Red Sox ballpark that apes a number of features from Fenway: "The Red Sox have seriously discussed painting one of the bleacher seats in the new park red, to commemorate the 1946 Ted Williams home run that hit a man on the head and broke his new straw hat. How sick is that?"

Pretty sick, Bob. Pretty goddamn sick.

◆　◆　◆

With the Sox gallivanting across the continent yet again, let's take another look at the top of the American League East standings, through today's action:

	W-L	GB	RS-RA	PYTHAG W-L
YANKEES	59–47	—	584–516	59–47
RED SOX	56–51	3 1/2	542–501	57–50
BLUE JAYS	58–55	4 1/2	620–661	53–60

The tyranny of Pythagoras reveals itself once more, as the Yankees are dead on their projection, and the Red Sox are just a game off. The Blue Jays continue to outperform their projection, but the gap has gotten smaller and will likely continue to shrink. It's still hard to take Toronto seriously as a pennant contender.

And the Wild Card standings?

	W-L	GB	RS-RA	PYTHAG W-L
ATHLETICS	61–49	——	643–594	59–51
INDIANS	57–51	3	607–554	59–49
RED SOX	56–51	3 ½	542–501	57–50
BLUE JAYS	58–55	4 ½	620–661	53–60
ANGELS	57–55	5	598–593	56–56

There's good news here, and there's bad news. The good news is that, on a fundamental level, the Red Sox have performed virtually as well as their competition for a Wild Card spot. Pythogorean-wise, the Indians and Athletics are ten and eight games over .500; the Red Sox are seven games over.

The bad news is that the Sox are three and a half games behind in this race, too. What's worse, they've got to get past two teams for the Wild Card, rather than just one for the A.L. East title. And both of those teams, along with the Yankees, are probably better, which of course is the biggest problem of all.

Tuesday, August 8

Hung around the apartment all day, sleeping and tidying and working. At 5:30, finally decided to get cleaned up and hit the town, which in my case usually means a walk to Barnes & Noble and then Thornton's Fenway Grille, home of big salads and almost uniformly attractive waitresses.

My walk to Kenmore Square and then back to the Fenway neighborhood does, of course, take me past Fenway Park coming and going. And on the way back, I did what I often do. I lingered for a moment along Yawkey Way, dragging my left hand over the old bricks, running my fingers along the brass baseballs that border the Tom Yawkey plaque near Gate A. And it was then, as I grudgingly walked away from the ballpark, that I realized, *I really do love this old building.*

With this realization came another.

I don't want to be in Boston when the Red Sox aren't.

I am incredibly fortunate, in that I have relative financial freedom and—aside from the shackles imposed by the baseball schedule—few limits on my time. So why should I be here this weekend, when I'd rather be in Seattle?

◆ ◆ ◆

Hell of a pitcher's duel tonight in Anaheim.

Or rather, it was a hell of a "Pedro duel," because Pedro Martinez's mound opponent tonight was a twenty-three-year-old righthander named Ramon Ortiz, and nicknamed "Little Pedro."

Before tonight's game, I found a preseason scouting report that says Ortiz is "[c]ompared by many scouts to Pedro Martinez because they're both short Dominicans with fine stuff . . ."

But it goes far beyond that. The two look almost exactly alike when they pitch from the windup. Martinez and Ortiz begin their deliveries differently; Ortiz brings his hands above and behind his head, while Pedro's never get higher than his neck. But from that point, they're virtually identical from mid-delivery through follow-through.

And tonight the results were virtually identical, too, with both pitchers permitting few hits while tossing complete games:

	IP	H	R	ER	BB	K	PITCHES
BIG PEDRO	8	3	2	2	0	9	112
LITTLE PEDRO	9	2	1	1	2	6	112

During last night's TV broadcast, Sean McDonough raved about Angels center fielder Garret Anderson. But while McDonough may not understand that the undisciplined Anderson is a poor hitter, he apparently does understand that the undisciplined Red Sox are, as a group, poor hitters.

Varitek led off the top of the fourth, at which point the following exchange took place between broadcasters Sean McDonough and Jerry Remy:

Sean: Jason Varitek swings at the first pitch of the fourth, and hits it to left-center. Erstad, just shy of the track, makes the catch. One pitch, and one out. And Jerry, we've seen this Red Sox offense go through many stretches this year where they haven't done very much collectively, but this is becoming one of the worst. All of a sudden, the Red Sox have slipped to eleventh in the American League in runs scored, and they're dropping fast.

Jerry: A lot of first-ball swinging, too, it seems like. There are a number of guys throughout the lineup that like to jump on that first pitch, and they're not getting a lot of situations where they're getting themselves into hitter's counts.

Exactly. And then in the ninth . . .

Sean: Pedro Martinez, all he can do now is look on and hope that finally the offense will break through against Ramon Ortiz, who's allowed one run on two hits, hasn't allowed a hit since the fifth inning . . . First-ball swinging, Varitek, a foul ball for strike one . . .

Jerry: We'll have to see if there's any pressure on Ortiz here, working into the ninth inning in a 2–1 ballgame. It's almost like you're obliged to maybe take a strike against him, see if maybe he gets himself in trouble. Walks somebody.

Sean: The Red Sox just don't do that. In this situation, you see it over and over again, behind late in the game, almost all of them go up there and swing at the first pitch.

Varitek wound up fouling out to the catcher.

Nomar swung at the first pitch, hit a weak grounder to first base.

Everett took strike one, eventually fouled to Glaus on a two-one pitch to end the game.

And so the Sox had been two-hit by a pitcher who came into this game with a 6.16 ERA.

◆   ◆   ◆

Pedro's now lost four games this season. He's allowed nine runs in those four games, and in those four games the Red Sox have scored three runs. *Three.* Sean McDonough pointed out that Martinez could easily be undefeated—17–0!—but it does work the other way, too. Or at least, that's what I thought. Surely Pedro's gotten a few wins despite pitching poorly, right?

But he hasn't. Pedro's now started twenty games this season, and only one of those starts might be considered even close to poor. On June 25 in Toronto, he allowed five runs—thanks to three homers—in six and two thirds innings. He went on the disabled list after that game and hasn't allowed more than two runs in a game in his six starts since rejoining the rotation on July 13.

Wednesday, August 9

Desperately tired tonight, but I stayed up until almost one in the morning and listened on the radio as the Sox beat the Angels, 4–2. Derek Lowe pitched the eighth and ninth to earn his twenty-fifth save.

Lowe is a good object lesson in why it's stupid to make pronouncements in May about what a player's stats will look like in September. On May 5, I made a big to-do about the way that Jimy Williams was using Lowe, quite often for more than one inning at a time. But whether due to fears about Lowe's health or because of Hipolito Pichardo's emergence as a quality middle reliever (or both), for the last few months Williams has been using Lowe in the conventional fashion.

Here's the chart that I ran back on May 5, describing Lowe's stats to that point, and what they projected to through the end of the season (remember, a "long save" is any save consisting of two innings or more):

	SAVES	IP	LONG SAVES
DEREK LOWE	6	18	5
PROJECTED THRU 162	40	117	32

That was then; this is now. Here's the same table, but with stats through tonight's game, in which Lowe recorded his twenty-fifth save with two scoreless innings:

	SAVES	IP	LONG SAVES
DEREK LOWE	25	64	7
PROJECTED THRU 162	36	94	10

Lowe recorded five long saves through May 5, but only two more in the three months since.

Friday, August 11

In the air again and reading this morning's *Herald;* the featured topic in the back pages is the lack of support Pedro Martinez has received from his teammates.

As I may already have pointed out once or twice, the Red Sox have scored very few runs this season when Martinez was the pitcher of record. Among the forty-seven American League pitchers who have thrown enough innings to qualify for the ERA title, Pedro ranks forty-first with 4.27 runs of support per nine innings.

Here's what Scott Hatteberg said about his club's failure to score when

Pedro's pitching: "I think there have been times when it has been a lackadaisical thing for us, because we know we'll only have to score a few runs to win when he pitches. But a lot of times, the credit has to go to the other pitcher, because Pedro brings out the best in a lot of guys. Those pitchers know, 'We may not score a run tonight, I've got to be at my best.'"

Interesting theory. Strangely enough, yesterday I ran across another interesting theory while flipping through *The Bronx Zoo*, Sparky Lyle's diary of the 1978 season. On June 7 of that season, Ron Guidry beat the Mariners 8–1, running his record to 9–0. Apparently the Yankees scored plenty of runs when Guidry pitched, leading Lyle to say, "Billy [Martin] has an interesting theory that when Gid is on the mound, our hitters feel less pressure and hit better than they do for the other pitchers. They know he's only going to allow a run or two, so they relax at the plate and hit better."

So you have one major leaguer saying that hitters don't perform as well because they don't think they have to, and you have another major leaguer saying that hitters perform better because they think they don't have to.

It's all bullshit.

Let's look at Pedro's basic stats, along with his run support, over the last four seasons:

	W-L	ERA	SUPPORT
1997	17–8	1.90	3.54
1998	19–7	2.89	5.43
1999	23–4	2.07	6.03
2000	13–3	1.59	4.27

If there's a discernible pattern there, I'm certainly not seeing it. In 1997, Martinez pitched brilliantly and was rewarded with the National League's Cy Young Award, but he went "just" 17–8 thanks to lousy support from his Montreal mates. In 1999, Martinez pitched brilliantly and was rewarded with the American League's Cy Young Award, and went 23–4 thanks to great support from his Boston buddies.

Did the Red Sox hitters not realize, in 1999, that Pedro Martinez was the greatest pitcher in the world? Did they need this most recent off-season to comprehend his greatness? Were Scott Hatteberg and his fellow hitters holed up in their basements all winter, staring at Pedro's 1999 stat line until they understood what it meant?

I doubt it.

And then there's ESPN's own Joe Morgan. I like Morgan because he *says* things, things that jump right at you. About half of them are brilliant and half of them make no sense at all. The best-ever example of this may be found in Morgan's autobiography:

> The two most overrated stats in all of baseball are batting average and earned run average. I measure a player by his run production: Slugging percentage and on-base percentage actually tell you more about run production than batting average . . . *[Exactly right, Joe!]* . . . With pitchers, the same division occurs with earned run average and wins. It doesn't matter what a guy's ERA is, what counts is how many wins he has. Say a guy goes through a season with a 2.98 ERA but has a losing record. What that tells you is the guy pitches well enough to lose. A pitcher's job is to bring home the bacon, not to hold down his ERA.

Exactly wrong, Joe!

And I don't think that Morgan would *really* argue this point with me. Here are three pitchers, all with essentially the same records:

	W-L	ERA
TIM HUDSON	12–4	4.74
ANDY PETTITTE	13–6	4.21
PEDRO MARTINEZ	13–4	1.46
JAMES BALDWIN	13–4	4.16

Take Morgan's logic to its ridiculous extreme, and you might conclude that Hudson, Pettitte, and Baldwin are all doing their "job" about as well as Martinez. But is anyone out there so foolish as to believe that's the case? Hudson is 12–4 *not* because he's pitching particularly well, but rather because the Athletics have scored 7.8 runs per nine innings for him. Martinez is 13–4 *not* because he doesn't know how to "bring home the bacon," but rather because the Sox have scored 4.3 runs per nine innings for him.

None of it means anything. The performance of hitters has virtually everything to do with who's pitching *against* them, and virtually nothing to do with who's pitching *for* them.

Seventh Inning

Monday, August 14

I spent the weekend in Seattle and took a chance with a return flight that wasn't supposed to land in Boston until 4:30 this afternoon. If the flight was delayed, I might not have made it to Fenway in time for tonight's game against the Devil Rays.

Things worked out for me, though, as they usually do. My flight actually reached Boston a half hour early, and I was in my apartment before five. There, a message waited somewhat impatiently: Susan had an extra ticket for the bleachers tonight.

It would be a strange evening. As happens so often here—or at least, as so often happens here this particular season—a steady drizzle fell through most of the game. Pedro started for the Sox, and he struck out five Devil Rays in the first two innings. But in the third, light-hitting Miguel Cairo cleared the Green Monster, down the left-field line, for a three-run homer. His first home run of the season. His first since July 20, 1999. That's a hell of a warning sign, and Pedro left after the fourth with a stiff shoulder. As usual, though, Boston's bullpen performed brilliantly, three relievers combining for five scoreless innings.

Meanwhile, the Sox scored three runs in the sixth, thanks to three Tampa Bay errors. And that's where things stood heading to the bottom of the ninth. Billy Taylor, not exactly the Devil Rays' best pitcher, came in from the bullpen . . . and plunked number-nine hitter Darren Lewis. Lewis stole second base and then moved to third on Trot Nixon's fly ball to right field. Varitek struck out, though, leaving Lewis on third base with two outs.

Due next: Carl Everett, then Nomar Garciaparra. Devil Rays manager Larry Rothschild ordered up an intentional walk for Everett, which made a fair amount of sense given that (1) Everett switch-hits, and (2) both first base and second base were open. Rothschild's next move, however, didn't make much sense at all to me.

He ordered up another intentional walk to Garciaparra.

I believe that walking the bases loaded is generally an asinine strategy, and especially when there are two outs.

If the winning run, in the person of a home-team base runner, is on third base with fewer than two outs, there are any number of ways he can score. A fly ball to the outfield will likely score him. So will a routine ground ball, which means the infielders have to play closer to the plate than normal, with hopes of holding the runner at third, or throwing him out at home. So the typical strategy, with a runner on third base and fewer than two outs, is to walk the bases loaded, pull the infielders and outfielders in, and hope for a strikeout, a pop-up, a shallow fly ball, or a grounder right to an infielder.

Ideally, the defense gets an out or two (as necessary) and then resumes its normal positions, from where it's most likely to prevent a game-ending base hit.

Again, that's with a runner on third base and fewer than two outs.

But there's a big problem with loading the bases; it results in an immense amount of pressure on the pitcher to throw strikes. If, after throwing four—or in this case, eight—balls on purpose, he throws four balls *accidentally*, the game is over, and in somewhat humiliating (for the pitcher) fashion. That's why you'd rather *not* load the bases unless the situation absolutely demands it.

Of course, all of the above fails to take specific batter-pitcher matchups into account. Billy Taylor throws with his right hand. Everett's a switch-hitter, so he batted lefty against Taylor. With both first and second base open, walking Everett didn't really cost the Devil Rays much, aside from a certain margin for error with the next two hitters.

But when the Devil Rays walked Garciaparra—a right-handed hitter—they left themselves with no margin for error, none at all.

So the bases were loaded, by design. And up stepped Rico Brogna, who had pinch-run for Daubach in the eighth. Brogna's a left-handed hitter, and Taylor has always had big problems with left-handed hitters. Since 1995, he's held righties to a

.220 batting average, but lefties have pasted him for a .307 average with good power. And that difference was particularly pronounced in 1999.

Brogna joined the Red Sox on August 4, supposedly to give the club another RBI man in the lineup. In his nine games since, he's three for sixteen with one RBI. Jimy Williams won't play him, and there have been murmurs of a "slow bat." This night, though, Brogna's bat was just fast enough. Taylor, throwing all fastballs, ran the count to two balls and two strikes. Then Taylor tried to surprise Brogna with a back-door slider. Brogna wasn't surprised at all; after the game, he said he'd been looking for the breaking ball.

Sitting in Row 7 of Section 35 in the bleachers, Susan and I had a perfect view as bat met ball, and ball described its path over second baseman Cairo, through the wind and the mist, over right fielder Jose Guillen, and finally over—*just barely over*—the bullpen wall.

Grand slam.

Sox win. Sox win. Sox win.

◆ ◆ ◆

Rico Brogna is what we'll all remember about tonight, but he wasn't the only New England hero on the field. Lou Merloni made his 2000 debut in the Red Sox lineup, and singled in two at-bats (with a pair of sacrifice bunts). Merloni's a huge favorite here; every time he comes to the plate, or makes a play at third base, a healthy percentage of fans bellow, *Looooooo!* ("No honey, they're not booing.")

And why? Because Lou Merloni hails from Framingham, Massachusetts—almost exactly twenty miles due east of Fenway Park—and Red Sox fans do love their home boys. What's interesting is how he got here.

Back in 1993, the Sox selected Merloni, who'd been attending Providence University, in the tenth round of the June amateur draft. Early on, the organization realized he wasn't going to be a star, so they groomed him as a utility man. Merloni slowly climbed the ladder in that role, and he reached Fenway Park in 1998. He split his 1999 season between Boston and Pawtucket, and didn't perform particularly well for either club.

The Sox released Merloni last November, and he signed with the Yokohama Bay Stars of Japan's Central League. Merloni struggled terribly in Japan, and recently he drew his release from Yokohama, having batted just .213, with one home run and three RBI, in forty-two games.

After returning to the States, Merloni signed a free-agent deal with the PawSox on July 31. And after hitting .410 in eleven games at Pawtucket, he's back home in Boston. And he's got a hell of an opportunity. With John Valentin out, here's how the four other third-base candidates have fared this season with Boston:

	G	AB	R	RBI	OPS
VERAS	49	164	21	14	577
ALEXANDER	67	140	17	11	558
SPRAGUE	33	111	11	9	599
BERRY	1	4	0	0	000
TOTALS	150	419	49	34	572

Wow. Those totals are almost unbelievable, like the product of some sick Yankee fan's mind. But they're the real thing, all right. That 572 OPS (on-base percentage plus slugging percentage) would be poor for a group of shortstops, but it's absolutely horrible for a group of third basemen. And Duquette really doesn't have any excuse for this foolishness. Valentin tore his ACL on May 30 (after missing most of April with a different injury), and there's no reason for the Sox to have suffered through this group of miscreants for the last two and a half months, just hoping that one of them would learn how to hit. Veras is too young, Sprague is too old, and Alexander's simply too untalented. And the Duke should have known this, and done something about it.

Well, now he has. Sort of. Merloni's not a great player. In fact, he's not really a good player. He's twenty-nine, and he brings a career 673 OPS into this season. I do think Merloni's a little better than that—he's played significantly better with Pawtucket over the years—but he's no All-Star. That said, the Sox certainly can't do any worse than those four guys in the chart. If he gets off to a decent start, any kind of start at all, Framingham Lou is going to go straight from Bay Stars cast-off to Red Sox mainstay.

◆   ◆   ◆

Merloni took the roster spot formerly held by Izzy Alcantara, who was placed on the 15-day disabled list with what the Red Sox are calling a "lumbar strain of the lower back." The Sox say that Alcantara hurt himself yesterday when he caught Ed Sprague falling into the dugout. Lately Alcantara has done little more than waste a roster spot. He started at DH in Seattle on August 1 (and went hitless in four at-bats), but batted just once in the ten games since. But he'll likely be back in Boston when the rosters expand in September.

Tuesday, August 15

Once again, I grabbed a great seat just a few minutes before game time, wound up sitting in the third row behind the visitors' on-deck circle.

Jeff Fassero pitched his best game in quite some time. He did get in serious trouble early, but allowed just one run, and settled down enough to strike out ten Devil Rays in six innings before departing. Fassero took the loss, though, as again the Sox couldn't muster enough big hits. They scored one run (in the seventh), and left thirteen runners on base. Particularly painful were the fifth, eighth, and ninth innings, in which the Sox stranded a total of six base runners, the game ending when Bernard Gilkey drove a fly ball to deepest center field.

Final score: Tampa Bay 3, Boston 1. And we really can't complain because of what happened just twenty-four hours ago. Still . . .

Wednesday, August 16

Missed a few batters tonight, thanks to yet another bout of absentmindedness. Susan called me today, asked if I could tape *Survivor* for her. I've never actually seen the show myself, but if you believe the ratings, I'm certainly in the minority. Anyway, at 6:30—twenty minutes before I left—I put the tape in the VCR, set the cable box to Channel 4 . . . and then I completely forgot to start the machine. Stuff like this has been happening to me all summer long. It's as if there's room in my head for only two things: baseball and Kristien. Everything else—appointments, book signings, remembering that my scorebook's sitting in a seat pocket on the train—doesn't seem to have a prayer.

Actually, all this fits in with a theory that I came up with (or stole), that goes like this . . . Humans evolved slowly over many thousands of years, and so did our brains. This slow evolution worked out pretty well, as long as the rates of change in our various societies weren't too speedy. But then, all of a sudden comes first the Industrial Revolution, and now the Digital Age. And sometimes I wonder if maybe our brains haven't quite kept up with all the decisions we're supposed to make every day. I mean, we're able to make them, but it seems to me that something might be getting lost along the way, whether it's our health or our attention spans or whatever.

Anyway, that's my story and I'm sticking to it.

I tried to call a guy I know, but he wasn't home. So I finally decided to just go home and start the VCR myself. One problem, though: how to get back in the ball-park. At every exit, there's a big sign that reads, PASS OUT AND RETURN CHECKS NOT PERMITTED. This dissuaded me for a moment, as I'm easily cowed by rigid authority. But my shame at having forgotten a promise won out, and I went to a ticket-taker at Gate D.

"Can I leave and get back in?"

"How come?"

"I left something at home, I live just down the street."

"All right, let me see yer ticket."

And then he scribbled his name (coincidentally, Rob something) on the back of my ticket stub, the date ("8–16"), and an indecipherable something else.

So I jogged home, hit the Record button, and jogged back. In the process, I missed the top of the second inning (in which the Devil Rays scored a run), the bottom of the second (in which the Red Sox didn't), and three batters in the top of the third.

It was a good win for the Sox tonight. They trailed 2–0 until the sixth, when Troy O'Leary tripled to the triangle with two outs, then scored on Daubach's single.

You'll rarely hear Neil Diamond unless the Sox are winning, but tonight we heard "Sweet Caroline" after the bottom of the seventh, even though the D-Rays still led, 2–1 . . .

And the times did get good. Tampa Bay upped their lead with a run in the top of the eighth, but the Sox came back with three in the bottom of the eighth, and Lowe made the lead stand up, closing out Tampa Bay with three straight ground balls in the ninth. The Sox are still perfect when Neil sings.

Lou Merloni took over at third base on Monday night, and tonight Jose Offerman came off the disabled list. The odd man out? Ed Sprague, who's been released after batting .216 and driving in nine runs in thirty-three games. And I can't help but think how happy that heckler in Baltimore must be tonight.

Thursday, August 17

Just as Monday night's will be remembered—at least by me—as "the Brogna game," tonight's will live in my memory as "the Lansing game."

Since joining the Red Sox on July 28, Lansing had been hitting .231, with four walks and *zero* extra-base hits in seventeen games and 65 at-bats.

Nevertheless, in the bottom of the eighth inning, with left-handed reliever Mike Venafro on the mound, two runners on base, and the Sox trailing the Rangers 6–2, Williams called upon Lansing to pinch-hit for Brian Daubach. Cleanup hitter Brian Daubach.

Baseball's a funny game, though. Lansing rifled a grounder past third base and into the corner, and wound up on second with a two-run double. A moment later, he scored, too. That made it 6–5 Rangers, and Lansing—fortunately, as it turned out—stayed in the game to play second base. The Rangers made it 7–5 in the ninth, setting the stage for high drama in the bottom of the ninth.

Varitek led off with a grounder to second base. One out.

Hatteberg walked (on a full count!), and was replaced at first base by Darren Lewis.

Garciaparra drove a ball to deep right field . . . where it was caught. Two outs.

Offerman singled to right field (Lewis moving to second), and was replaced by Rico Brogna (a powerful testament to just how gimpy Offerman's been lately).

Gilkey hit an easy grounder to shortstop Royce Clayton . . . who fumbled the ball *just* long enough for Gilkey to beat Clayton's throw by half a step.

Rangers closer John Wetteland might have been rattled by Clayton's error, or he might not have been rattled. Either way, his next pitch plowed into Carl Everett (who had struck out in his three previous at-bats). That plated Lewis and left the bases loaded for . . . Mike Lansing, again.

At this point, the fans in Fenway were in a state of mass hysteria. If you'd polled them—hell, *us*—somewhere in the neighborhood of 90 percent would have guessed that the Red Sox were going to win, though the "odds" were clearly against such a thing.

But with the count one ball and one strike, Lansing hit Wetteland's next pitch high off the Green Monster in deep left-center. Brogna trotted home to tie the game, Gilkey sprinted home to win it, and I cried.

Not the big, racking sobs that might accompany the loss of a loved one. And not tears of joy, at least not in my case. Rather, they were the tears of release.

◆   ◆   ◆

It was reported after the game that the Red Sox set a team record by leaving fifteen runners on base. If that's true, somebody needs to come up with a new system for counting runners left on base. See, they left thirteen on base through eight innings. They won the game in the bottom of the ninth.

So how do you get fifteen?

You count Everett and Lansing, happy as clams as they stood on their respective bases and watched the winning run score, as having been "left on base." And that's perhaps the silliest thing that any statistician will ever be asked to do.

Friday, August 18

Jim Baker arrived in Boston late last night, for a weekend of games at Friendly Fenway Park. Jim was a Red Sox fan in the 1970s—the Sox were his American League team, the Mets were his National League team—and talk of tearing down Fenway sickens him. "I look out on this outfield," he says, "where Jim Rice and Fred Lynn and Dwight Evans once roamed, and I shake my head."

The Red Sox scored four runs in the first, two runs in the third—in the process, they caught about a million breaks—and then they hung on. Tomo Ohka pitched his best game yet, permitting just one run in seven innings, but things got a little scary in the ninth. With the Sox up 6–1, Cormier came in to mop up. He apparently does not skillfully perform such lowly chores, however. After a fly-out and three straight hits, Jimy Williams summoned Lowe from the bullpen. He gave up a two-run double to the first batter he faced, but then struck out Bill Haselman and Royce Clayton to end the game.

◆   ◆   ◆

Twice in three nights? Yep . . .

> *I've been inclined*
> *To believe they never would*

Times were good for the Red Sox in almost every way. Ohka's performance tonight is obviously a good sign. Oakland got hammered in Detroit, and there were some wonderful doings in the Bronx, where the Yankees took an 8–3 lead over the Angels into the ninth, only to blow it before losing in the eleventh. So the Sox are now just one game behind the Athletics in the Wild Card standings, and three behind New York in the East.

Saturday, August 19

Sometimes, everything does go according to form. Here's today's pitching matchup:

	W-L	ERA
MATT PERISHO	2–5	6.33
PEDRO MARTINEZ	13–4	1.59

Pedro pitched brilliantly and Perisho didn't, the end result a 9–0 laugher for the Sox, who scored all nine of their runs in the first four innings, four innings that also saw sixteen Boston base runners. All this action scared me, because Jim and I had another ballpark to get to. Way back in May, when Jim was planning his trip to Boston, he checked the schedules for the various minor-league teams in New England (Jim's the thorough sort). As it happened, the Pawtucket Red Sox—or as they're known around here, the "PawSox"—were scheduled for a six o'clock start tonight. So once the Red Sox decided on an early-afternoon start—today's tickets read: "Game Time 1:15 or 5:05 p.m."—we started making our schemes for two ballparks in a single day.

Most evening baseball games, of course, begin at 7:05 or thereabouts.

Not in Pawtucket, though. Saturday nights, they start at six o'clock, for reasons that make sense if you think about it. Six o'clock starts are great for families—and that's the market for minor-league teams, much more so than the big-league clubs—but not so great for nuts trying to see two games in two cities in one day.

According to Yahoo! Maps, the trip from my apartment building to Pawtucket's McCoy Stadium would take fifty-six minutes. However, that number did not take into account post-game traffic in my neighborhood. Nor did it take into account confusing directions or confusing street signs in Pawtucket (this is, after all, New England). So we figured on needing at least an hour to reach Pawtucket, and at least another fifteen or twenty minutes more to find the ballpark, locate a parking spot, and make our way to the seats. We'd make it, I figured, if we could be on the road by 4:45.

And like I said, things weren't looking good early, what with all those base runners. After the fourth, however, things moved along nicely: only nine base runners for both teams combined, and no runs at all. The game lasted two hours and forty-six minutes, actually a bit less than the American League average. Jim and I were back at my apartment at 4:28, Susan showed up a few minutes later, and at 4:49 Ken Borah, a friend of Jim's, arrived. Ken was the key piece of the equation, because he's the one with the car.

I really, really wanted to get to McCoy Stadium on time. Bret Saberhagen was scheduled for a rehab start, and he's been one of my favorite pitchers ever since 1984, when the then-gawky, twenty-year-old rookie broke in with the Royals. Last March, Saberhagen talked about pitching for the Red Sox in May. He's spent the entire season trying to come back, though, and has made a few starts in the minors but probably won't ever pitch in Fenway this year.

We didn't quite make it, mostly because the directions were confusing and so were the signs in Pawtucket. I got dumped at the Will Call window (why do they call it that, anyway?) and picked up our tickets, but I still had to wait until those guys parked the car and walked back to the ballpark. Eventually, though, my excitement got the better of me. I entered the ballpark and found a vantage point, but sprinted back to the gate between each batter to meet Jim and Susan and Ken. So I missed only a couple of batters, and my compatriots finally arrived in time for the top of the second inning.

Saberhagen pitched reasonably well, five hits and two runs in five innings (before giving way to Paxton Crawford, who didn't).

The most impressive thing about McCoy Stadium? The Team Store. Not only is the PawSox souvenir shop big (bigger than souvenir stores in major league ballparks that I've visited), it's *busy*. I've simply never seen such a thing at a minor-league park. After the game I picked out a red PawSox T-shirt, and had to stand in line for ten minutes to give them my money.

Actually, the most impressive thing about McCoy Stadium was the number of people filling it up tonight. Attendance was announced at 10,209, and exemplifies one of the most striking things about baseball in this country, which is that *people love this game*. Every year, Organized Baseball—that is, the minor-league teams subject to the rules dictated by Major League Baseball—sets a new attendance record. But that doesn't even count all the fans flocking to the independent leagues, which have been sprouting up all over the Republic like friendly weeds. My friend Pete Fornatale argues that Major League Baseball is incredibly lucky. Because even as they're pricing out middle-class families with exorbitant ticket prices, they've got not only a farm system for young players, but also a veritable farm system for young (or poor, or young and poor) fans.

Sunday, August 20

I sat out in the bleachers this afternoon with Susan, and Jim was in the grandstand behind third base with Marci, a friend of ours who arrived in town this morning.

Jeff Fassero pitched brilliantly for four innings, not a single Ranger reaching base. Then the wheels fell off in the fourth, leading a fan behind me to say, "Fassero should be a reliever, the guy can't pitch more than three innings." And the way things have been going lately for Fassero, I would tend to agree. Meanwhile, the Sox hitters didn't do much with Texas starter Doug Davis, who came into the game with an unspeakable ERA (but not unwriteable: 8.02). They loaded the bases with nobody out in the first inning, but scored just once. They didn't score again until the eighth. At some point—I didn't note exactly when—a fan growled, "Aw, Jesus Christ. Bullshit. Play the game here." And that fairly summarized the Sox' performance, or lack thereof, in this game, at the end of which they'd been hung with a 6–2 defeat.

◆ ◆ ◆

The Saga of Izzy continues. Supposedly suffering from a strained lower back, and thus in Pawtucket on "injury rehab," Alcantara hit a two-run homer last night when we were there. And this afternoon, he homered again and doubled.

It's amazing what MLB lets teams get away with.

Fenway Moment: In the top of the seventh, Rusty Greer stole second base on what looked like, from the bleachers at least, an extremely close play. A nearby fan bellowed at second-base umpire Dan Iassonga, "C'mon, blue! Head out of the ass, let's go!"

Monday, August 21

Today I took the Fenway Park tour. Been meaning to do it for months, but it took the kick in the pants of Jim's and Marci's visits to actually get me going. So at 10:45 this morning, the three of us met Susan at Gate D. An hour earlier, I'd purchased tickets for all of us—the tours do occasionally sell out—at five bucks per. As it turned out, nobody ever took our tickets. I suspect that the Sox really don't care about the nominal amount of money the tours generate, but charge admission just to keep the riffraff out.

Anyway, at the stroke of eleven o'clock, a smarmy young man led us through Gate D and up a series of ramps to the press box, and the 600 Club, where we all took seats facing the field. I've been meaning to view a game from the 600 Club all season, but now that I've been there, I don't really feel the need anymore. It's essentially a bar/restaurant, with a dress code and seats like those you'd find in a new movie theater. The 600 Club is, of course, completely enclosed by glass, so sound is piped in from microphones installed just above the field. Seems to me a horrible way to experience a baseball game, but it's not a bad place at all to experience a relatively brief talk on the history of Fenway Park, because everything's in plain view from there.

From there, we made our way back downstairs and onto the field. We were allowed into the home dugout. I sat on the bench, picked up the phone, and someone on the other end gruffly answered, "Yeah, this is Jimy Williams, what can I do for ya?" I think it was somebody out in the bullpen having some fun with me, and I should have said something like, "Get Kinder and Radatz"—two Red Sox relievers of the fifties and sixties—"warmed up if Pedro walks this guy!" But I was so shocked to hear a voice on the other end of the line, I simply hung up the phone.

Next, we walked, counterclockwise, along the perimeter of the field—nobody, and I mean nobody, is allowed on the grass—until we reached the Green Monster. This was everyone's favorite spot for photos. I looked through the cracks in the scoreboard, at the various inscriptions scrawled by scoreboard operators and ballplayers over the years. Our guide let us linger along the warning track for a good ten minutes before hustling us along the fence, and into the seats just short of the visitors' dugout. (All of this would, I suspect, have been significantly more thrilling for me if I hadn't already explored Fenway's nooks and crannies during my overnight stay, exactly four weeks ago.) And from there, we were led to the concourse and (with apologies from our guide) to the interior entrance to The Lansdowne Shop, the team's souvenir shop (which pales in comparison to its unofficial counterparts along Yawkey Way).

(A reader of my column, Chris, e-mailed with an interesting piece of advice about the Fenway tour. He says that when your guide dumps you off, instead of proceeding like lemmings into the Lansdowne Shop, you can make a beeline for the seats behind third base. Chris and his friends simply sat in the box seats for an hour, watching batting practice, and nobody bothered them.)

To complete the old-ballpark experience, we piled into Susan's car and drove to Nickerson Field (long-ago home of the Boston Braves), which of course I had seen before, and then to the site of the Huntington Avenue Grounds, which I had not. Now in the middle of the Northeastern campus, just a few miles from the Fens, the Huntington Avenue Grounds served as the Red Sox home field from the franchise's inception, in 1901, until they moved to Fenway in 1912. We parked the car on Huntington Avenue . . . and had no idea what to do next. We knew that a statue of Red Sox great Cy Young stood on the grounds somewhere, but that's all we knew. I finally went into an administration building, where a receptionist had no idea of the whereabouts of the bronze Mr. Young. She did, however, connect me to the Athletics Department, and a woman there was able to guide me to the site of the old field. As it happened, we were just a few hundred feet away. There, nestled between four buildings and halfway hidden behind various sorts of shrubbery, stood ol' Cy himself, bent over with his glove hand on his left knee, his right hand holding the ball behind his waist.

Jim had his camera, and so we all posed for photos next to Cy, bent over and peering in for the catcher's sign, just as he was.

◆ ◆ ◆

After our visit to Cy Young, Jim left for his home in Texas, leaving me in the company of Marci for tonight's game. Like me, Marci keeps score at the ballpark, which led the guy sitting next to me to say, as we were scribbling down the lineups, "All right, I gotta ask. Do you two work for a sports magazine or something."

I get these questions a lot—"Are you a scout?" being another popular query— and they've become fairly tiresome. So lately I've taken to saying something like, "Nah, I'm just a fan with a mild case of obsessive-compulsive disorder." This usually serves to stifle further conversation, which is my knee-jerk desire when somebody thinks that if you're keeping score, you must be a professional, or a geek. With Marci sitting on the other side of me, though, I just mumbled something about keeping score because it's fun. Whatever.

I keep score because it results in a tangible document of my experience. Some experiences deserve documentation more than others, and tonight's game deserved documentation about as much as any experience I've had. The fact is that if tonight's events were not commemorated in my scorebook, *in ink*, then I might not quite believe what I did, indeed, see with my own eyes.

The game moved along quickly, as most of the hitting action was concentrated within a few half-innings. The Sox took a 2–0 lead in the third, but left the bases loaded. The Angels tied the game moments later, in their half of the fourth, and went ahead 5–2 in the sixth when rookie Adam Kennedy smashed a three-run homer into the Sox bullpen. A couple of close and questionable calls went against the Angels, the first of which led manager Mike Scioscia to file a protest (which has absolutely no chance of being upheld).

Thanks once again to the amazingly dependable Red Sox relief corps (and the second of those questionable calls), the score was still 5–3 heading to the bottom of the ninth, by which point Marci and I had moved down to the third row behind the home dugout (a fair number of fans left after the Sox failed to score in the eighth). This left us in perfect position to watch one of the more dramatic endings to a game during this season.

O'Leary led off for the Sox and bounced out to second base. Gilkey followed with a hot grounder, but right at shortstop Kevin Stocker. That brought up Varitek. Never the most patient of fellows, Varitek nonetheless walked on four pitches. That brought up Brian Daubach. Rarely at his best against left-handed pitchers—Daubach entered tonight's game with a .248 career batting average against lefties—he nonetheless lofted a fly ball into the visitors' bullpen, for a game-tying home run.

Yes, I just soft-pedaled one of the more dramatic moments in the Red Sox season to this point. Fortunately for all of us at Fenway tonight, there was plenty of drama to spare.

With the game now deadlocked at five runs apiece, and the crowd's mood fast approaching mass delirium, Mark Petkovsek trotted in from the bullpen and struck out pinch-hitter Trot Nixon. Made him look silly, too. The tenth inning passed fairly uneventfully, perhaps a necessary respite between the ninth just passed and the eleventh to come.

Angels third baseman Troy Glaus led off the eleventh with a double down the left-field line. Bengie Molina moved Glaus to third base with a routine sacrifice bunt. With the lefty-hitting Adam Kennedy due next and the righty-hitting Ron Gant on deck, I figured Jimy would order an intentional walk for Kennedy. I had a great view into the Sox dugout, though, and I didn't see anybody holding up four fingers.

I did see, however, Williams giving some signs to Varitek behind the plate, and this reminded me that visions of a squeeze bunt must be dancing around in the heads of everyone wearing a baseball uniform. And the more I thought about it, the more sense it made . . . light-hitting second baseman at the plate; pitcher (Derek Lowe) who throws a lot of low strikes; tight, tiring ball game . . . and sure enough, on a one-oh count Kennedy did drop down the bunt, and Glaus sprinted home with the lead run. Ron Gant then grounded out to Lowe, but the Angels owned a 6–5 lead.

As you've probably guessed, the Sox weren't finished. Not by a long shot.

Nomar Garciaparra led off the bottom of the eleventh with a four-pitch walk. The Angels brought in lefty Mike Holtz to face the left-hitting O'Leary. Everybody was expecting a bunt.

But when the corner infielders are charging for the bunt, *go ahead and swing away.* There are more than a couple of reasons for this, but the two that immediately come to mind are (1) the pitcher's not trying to do anything fancy, so the hitter will quite likely get a fastball in the strike zone, and (2) a hitter that swings away with not only the first and third basemen charging, but also the second baseman moving to cover first base, must derive a huge advantage with all that extra space in the infield. Oh, and I almost forgot; eschewing the bunt means you're *not* giving the defense one of your precious outs.

I don't generally make much noise when I'm at the ballpark. But sometimes, when I'm sitting close enough to the field and my blood gets to boiling with indignation, I let loose like any other blowhard fan. And after O'Leary squared around on the first pitch and took it for ball one, and then squared around again and took a strike, I couldn't control myself any longer . . .

Swing the bat! Let him swing the bat!

To the frequent dismay of my mother, I have a loud voice, and while Jimy Williams and Troy O'Leary certainly didn't hear my imprecations, I'm fairly certain that third-base coach Wendell Kim did. That made me feel good about myself, as did the backward, (and what I took to be) approving looks from the fans sitting between me and the field. But what really made me feel good was that the Sox took my advice (whether they heard it or not). O'Leary did swing the bat, and drove a single to right field that sent Nomar all the way to third base.

Bernard Gilkey was due next, but Scott Hatteberg pinch-hit instead. And looking like a left-handed version of Jeff Bagwell—legs spread apart and half-squatting, like an undersized sumo wrestler—Hatteberg coaxed a six-pitch walk out of Hasegawa. That loaded the bases and brought up Jason Varitek . . . who lasered a sharp one-hopper directly to Kennedy—yes, him again—who threw a strike to Angels catcher Molina, thus forcing Garciaparra, and then Molina fired to first base to retire Varitek by more than a step. Mo Vaughn then threw across the diamond to third base, where O'Leary was sliding in safely. What Marci and I *didn't* see, not until we watched *Baseball Tonight* nearly two hours later, was that Vaughn could easily have ended the game by transforming the rare 4–2–3 double play into an even rarer 4–2–3–6 (or 4–2–3–6–4) *triple* play. Manny Alexander, for reasons known only to himself and God, didn't take off for second base with the crack of the bat. Rather, he was perhaps a third of the way to second base when Vaughn threw to third.

I'm not faulting Vaughn. He did have a slight chance of getting O'Leary at third base, and he'd have lost that chance if he'd taken a peek at Alexander. And there really wasn't any reason for such a peek, because most major-league ballplayers would have been well on their way to second base. Alexander wasn't, but fortunately for him nobody noticed until it was too late, and he did reach second safely.

So now it's second and third, two outs, and Brian Daubach's up, once again in the position to make people forget that he's not really good enough to be playing regularly for a team with postseason aspirations. And with the count one-and-two, Daubach dumped a medium-sized blooper into short left field. In a normal ballpark that's an automatic single and the game's over, but of course this isn't a normal ball-park. It's Fenway, where the left fielder seemingly plays in the shadow of the shortstop, and Anaheim left fielder Orlando Palmeiro had a fighting chance to make a sensational play. He didn't quite make it, though, coming up a foot or two short with his dive, and his desperate throw plateward wasn't nearly in time to keep Alexander from scoring the winning run to move the Sox into a tie atop the Wild Card standings.

When the Red Sox win, the PA system almost immediately blares forth with "Dirty Water," a No. 11 hit for The Standells back in 1966. The song is usually little more than pleasant background accompaniment for our slow, congested journey toward the exits. But after a dramatically happy conclusion—and tonight marked the Red Sox' third walk-off victory in their last eight games—a good percentage of the fans hung around to sing . . .

I love that dirty water . . .
Oh, Boston you're my home!

I've never sung along, just don't feel like I've been here long enough. But if
you're a baseball fan, you haven't lived until you've heard thirty-thousand-odd New
Englanders sing their triumphant song of victory.

Tuesday, August 22

I've done a lot of stupid things this summer—losing my scorebook, missing a flight,
buying Cirque du Soleil tickets for the wrong night—but my Season of Stupidity
reached its nadir tonight. Or so I hope.

Last week, I bought two tickets at the box office for tonight's game, one for me
and one for Marci. At least that's what I thought I was doing. When I handed my
ticket to the ticket-taker at Gate E, he tore off the stub but then stopped me.

"Hold on a minute. This ticket is for last night's game."

And it was. It was indeed. So was Marci's. I've been screwing up details all season, and I'd apparently done it again. Fortunately, we'd gone to the ballpark earlier
than I usually go, which gave us time. When confronted with something that
demands a sudden change of plans, especially if it's the result of my own stupidity,
I like to sit down for a minute and think. Now, it shouldn't have taken more than
about ten seconds to realize we'd have to get our tickets from a scalper, but it took
me my normal minute. Fortunately I was carrying a fair amount of cash because,
unless we wanted to sit in the bleachers, that's what it would cost.

If you're buying tickets from a scalper you don't know, please take the following pieces of advice to heart, or at least print them out and take them to the
ballpark next time you're without tickets for a sold-out game:

Have a seating chart handy, and *make sure* you examine the tickets closely before
handing over any money. Because *most* scalpers—not all, but most—will lie to your
face if it'll get them an extra five or ten bucks. And they'll enjoy every second of it.

If at all possible, transact your business alone. I know you don't want to leave
your date standing on the sidewalk, or parked on a bar stool somewhere. So if
you're at Fenway, you might want to gently suggest that she (or—let's be politically
correct just this once—*he*) browse for a few minutes in one of the souvenir shops
on Yawkey or Lansdowne.

And yes, I came by both of these suggestions the hard way. I mean, I already knew them, but apparently not well enough, because tonight I had to learn each of these lessons all over again.

I'd already been to see Tommy, and I knew he didn't have anything good. So Marci and I walked along Brookline toward Kenmore Square, with me holding up two fingers. This wasn't going too well—in the summer months, even Tuesday nights are a hot ticket, especially with the Sox still in contention—and I got to worrying just a bit. Finally, though, we found someone who could "help." He was a short, squat, rectangular fellow in his early forties, and when I asked him if he had a couple of good ones, he responded, "Yeah, fourth row behind the on-deck circle. But I don't have 'em. Here comes the guy now."

And sure enough, walking toward us was another scalper, younger and taller. When he got within talking distance, Rectangle Man said to him, "Hey, these guys want to buy those tickets."

The little guy didn't seem like the most confident fellow in the world, and I got the idea that he wasn't experienced in this line of work. And his boss seemed a bit impatient, telling him, "*You* can sell 'em." So he did.

First, I asked to see the tickets. Row DD. Now, I may still be something of a Midwestern rube, but after nearly five months in Boston, I sure as hell know that DD doesn't mean the fourth row, and I said so.

"Yeah, that's what I said. Fourth row of the upper box."

Okay, now we're getting somewhere. How much?

"I can give 'em to ya for one-fifty."

That's too much.

"Hey, you've got this beautiful lady with ya tonight, why worry about a few bucks?"

Divide and conquer. Marci wasn't helping, either. She was reaching for her wallet, tugging at my sleeve and saying that she had money.

I have plenty of money. It's not about the money, it's about not enriching these predatory weasels any more than absolutely necessary.

But as soon as they had Marci on their side, the game was up. Divide and conquer.

(Lest anyone get the wrong idea, I should mention here that Marci might be the smartest person I've ever known. Tonight after the ball game, we played

Trivial Pursuit. I've always been pretty good, have lost maybe five or six times since 1984. Well, Marci utterly thrashed me. Twice. More to the point, she's a world-class scientist. She just doesn't have much experience dealing with Fenway sharpies.)

Anyway, then I did something stupid. People are streaming by on both sides, cars full of homebound commuters are whizzing by on the Mass Pike below, Marci's clearly impatient with me, and I can't blame her because I'm still pissed at myself for having bought tickets for the wrong game.

I peeled off (what I thought were) seven twenty-dollar bills and a ten, and we had our tickets. I was, I'm ashamed to admit, a little peeved at Marci, and she didn't seem particularly thrilled with me at that moment, either. What should have been a nice, relaxing trip to the ballpark had turned into something else. Oh well, at least we finally had valid tickets, and just enough time to get inside for Tim Wakefield's first pitch.

But then, just as we were about to enter Gate E, I felt someone tugging at my shirt. As I was turning to discover the unwelcome sight of Rectangle Man again, I heard, "Hey, you didn't give me enough money."

Huh?

"It was supposed to be one-fifty, you only gave me one-thirty."

I had no idea if he was telling the truth—in retrospect, it's hard to imagine a scalper going to all this extra trouble just for an extra twenty—but this guy seemed like such a scumbag that I didn't trust him. I was fully prepared to trade his old tickets for my old money, and start the process anew, even though the game was going to start in about five minutes.

But then Rectangle Man was gone, as quickly as he'd appeared. I don't know if he decided that my $130 was enough, or if perhaps he spotted one of Boston's finest in the vicinity. He was a jittery little fellow, and I don't think it would have taken much to scare him off.

One final and unpleasant surprise awaited us. We found our section and our row, only to discover that I had Seat 9 and Marci had Seat 12. As for "behind the on-deck circle," of course that was a lie, too. These seats were in Section 31, well down the left-field line. Still fine seats, and fairly close to the field, but certainly nowhere near anybody's on-deck circle. We were able to sit together, though; I took Seat 12 and Marci, Seat 11, with the men owning Seats 10 and 11 shifting down one.

All this made me appreciate Tommy more than ever, because for all his faults, he behaves like a man running a business. Yes, it's an illegal business in more ways than one, but it's a business nonetheless. He's got an office (his car), he's got an employee (Kevin), and he knows his customers. Most of the other scalpers don't run businesses; they run scams. I've now bought tickets twice from other scalpers, and both times I got screwed.

Neither Marci nor I were in particularly fine spirits when the game started, and our moods were not greatly improved when it ended. Wakefield started for the Sox, and got blasted for eight runs in four and a third innings. The Sox touched Angels starter Kent Mercker for nine hits and three walks in the first four innings, but they scored only four runs. And from the fifth through the ninth, just one Boston hitter reached base. Final score: Angels 11, Sox 4.

Wednesday, August 23

After five straight games with company (and good company), I was ready for an evening of relative solitude, and that's just what I got tonight. Officially, 32,958 fans attended the final game of the Angels series, but unofficially the number was maybe a third of that, because, thanks to a two-hours-and-fifty-three-minutes rain delay, the contest didn't even begin until 10:06. Those of us who stuck around—actually, I spent nearly all of the delay in my nice dry apartment—were rewarded with a victory for the home team. Tomo Ohka tossed five quality innings, and once again the bullpen shined, this time with four shutout frames. That was enough to beat Ramon Ortiz, who out-dueled Pedro Martinez in Anaheim a few weeks ago. And at 1:03 in the morning, Derek Lowe retired Orlando Palmeiro to seal the Sox' 5–3 victory and earn his twenty-ninth save.

Despite the lateness of the hour, I wanted to linger. At the game's conclusion, the Red Sox announced that attendance reached two million tonight. They did it in just sixty-three games, the franchise's quickest ever. The previous best was sixty-four games, at which point they reached two million in both 1990 and 1991. Not bad for a broken-down old ballpark that's supposedly unfit for human habitation.

So it's sixty-three games in the books, which means I've only got eighteen more (barring, of course, a somewhat unlikely postseason berth for the Sox). The impending conclusion of the baseball season saddens me every year, but I suspect it will be worse than usual this time around. The end of the season means an end to my love affair with Fenway, and it also means I'll have to get serious about finishing this book; neither prospect is particularly appealing.

◆ ◆ ◆

If the Red Sox had lost tonight, the evening would have been a complete disaster. The Yankees blew a big lead, but beat the Rangers with a run in the bottom of the ninth. The Royals blew a big lead, and lost to the Blue Jays. The Indians beat the Athletics. So the Sox didn't gain ground on anybody tonight, the only positive being that they're now in sole possession of second place in the Wild Card standings.

Speaking of standings, here are some now:

A.L. EAST

	W-L	GB	RS-RA	PYTHAG W-L
YANKEES	69–54	—	700–595	71–52
RED SOX	66–57	3	613–559	67–56
BLUE JAYS	66–61	5	709–737	61–66

Three games seem like nothing, and they seem like everything. While it's true that a three-game deficit can be wiped out in three days, it's also true that most teams with three-game leads in late August eventually do finish in first place. Tonight during the rain delay, I tuned in WEEI to monitor the situation. Ted Sarandis was discussing with his listeners, among other things, the Wild Card. Specifically, Ted wanted to know if fans were pleased with its existence.

Every caller said virtually the same thing: "All I know is that without the Wild Card, the Red Sox wouldn't have much chance of getting into the playoffs."

A common sentiment, and I'm probably old enough to stop being annoyed when people form opinions based on short-sighted self-interest. But there was something missing from this discussion, so I tried to call the station and add that something. WEEI is not only the Red Sox' flagship station, but it's also *the* sports-radio outlet of New England. And Ted is perhaps *the* most popular radio personality in Boston. So I wasn't able to get through . . . until I realized that I have more power than most listeners.

I simply called Ted's producer, Chris, and asked if perhaps I could interject something. Chris and Ted have both treated me wonderfully since I arrived in Boston, and this time was no exception, as I got hustled onto the air within a few minutes.

And my point was this . . . Yes, the Wild Card is good for the Red Sox' postseason chances, but it's caused many of us to lose sight of the single best thing baseball has to offer: a winner-take-all pennant race between division rivals. New England should already be crackling with anticipation of the Red Sox–Yankees series in three weeks, but the Wild Card "race" has dampened the atmosphere considerably. When the scoreboard on the Green Monster shows the Yankees taking a lead, or falling behind, there's almost no reaction in the stands. You might hear somebody say, "Damn, the Yankees are ahead," or "Hey, the Yankees are losing."

But what I want to hear is an audible reaction throughout the stands. Perhaps that's never something that would happen, at least not before September. But I do think that people would be paying more attention if the only path to the World Series went through the Yankees. The four games between the two clubs in September will be incredibly exciting. But how exciting would they be if both teams *needed* to beat the other?

What's more . . . but wait a minute, first let's look at the Wild Card standings through tonight's games:

	W-L	GB	RS-RA	PYTHAG W-L
INDIANS	66–56	—	695–631	66–56
RED SOX	66–57	0 ½	613–559	67–56
ATHLETICS	66–59	1 ½	710–689	64–61
BLUE JAYS	66–61	2 ½	709–737	61–66
ANGELS	65–62	3 ½	672–665	64–63

Looking at the last column here, the Indians and Red Sox seem to be the class of the group, with the Athletics and Angels, fundamentally, little better than .500 teams, and the Blue Jays still overachieving. Oh, and notice that only the Jays have a difference of more than two games between their actual and Pythagorean records, and the Indians, Sox, and Angels are all within one. You might be thinking that there's really no point in showing the Pythagorean stuff at this point in the book, but I'm bound and determined to convince anyone reading this that teams don't have some magical ability to win baseball games. Rather, they win because they score more runs than their opponents, and that's true whether you're the Yankees or the Twins.

Okay, back to problems with the Wild Card . . . Yes, the race is certainly competitive. And yes, interesting. But it's competitive and interesting only because none of the Wild Card contenders are particularly good. Or to put a more positive spin on things, it's competitive and interesting only because a number of teams are somewhat better than average. The Wild Card race is *not* particularly interesting over in the National League, where four teams—the Braves, Mets, Giants, and Diamondbacks—are apparently fighting for three postseason berths (the Cardinals have the Central pretty well locked up).

Essentially, the American League Wild Card is a battle among also-rans. And it's hard for me to get excited about the Red Sox as the best second-place team, even though I desperately want to spend a few October evenings in Fenway Park.

Thursday, August 24

The Red Sox make just one trip to Kansas City this season, and I've been planning to follow them there since March. It just happened that, as the schedule worked out, Pedro would indeed be pitching in Kansas City tonight; and I would be meeting Kristien there, for her first-ever visit to what someone once labeled "Flyover Land," i.e. everything between the coasts. I met Kristien at the airport, and as we drove the rental car into the city, she was somewhat shocked to see green things. Trees, grass, all of it. I couldn't quite get her to admit this, but I think that Kristien thought the entire middle part of the country was essentially a large, light-brown desert.

We showed up at Kauffman Stadium about thirty minutes before the game; I figured we could buy good seats outside the park, or if that failed, buy a couple of not-so-good seats at the box office. After a few minutes of standing around with two fingers in the air, I was approached by a kid, probably about to start his senior year in high school, with a couple of box seats available. The kid wanted twenty-five bucks . . . for both of them. The face value was thirty—fifteen bucks apiece—so that's what I gave him. In Boston, fifteen bucks gets you a bleacher seat. In Kansas City, fifteen bucks gets you a Field Box seat; tonight ours were in Row V, directly behind the Royals dugout. A comparable seat, in terms of distance from the field, costs forty dollars at Fenway. And it's not just the tickets that are cheaper. After four months of Fenway, walking around Kauffman left me with a distinct sense of reverse sticker shock. The peanuts are cheaper, the soda pop is cheaper, the pretzels are cheaper . . . a pizza costs about the same, but it's a bigger and a better pizza.

I wanted Kristien to see *the* Pedro Martinez, and so she did . . . but not until the second inning. In the first inning, she (and I, and the other eighteen thousand-odd people in the stands) saw some *other* Pedro Martinez. A Pedro Martinez whose fastball wasn't so fast. A Pedro Martinez whose change-up didn't change so much. A Pedro Martinez who gave up *six hits and five runs* in just the one inning. And then he gave up another in the second, when Mike Sweeney hit a long home run into the Red Sox bullpen.

And then, as sudden as a Kansas thunderstorm, that Pedro Martinez was gone, replaced by the Pedro Martinez I wanted Kristien to see. He struck out Jermaine Dye to end the bottom of the second, and then allowed one base runner (who was immediately erased by a double play) over the next six innings. Meanwhile, the Red Sox fought back against Royals starter Mac Suzuki, who somehow managed to walk seven Sox in three-plus innings. The score was 6–6 after four frames, and that's where it stayed until the tenth, when the Sox scored three runs. The Royals answered with a run in their half, but left a couple runners on when Derek Lowe retired Jermaine Dye to end the game.

This was my first visit to Kauffman Stadium, my "home park," in a few years. And in all honesty, I can't say that I care much for it anymore. It's comforting in its way—I especially like the giant scoreboard beyond the center-field fence, which hasn't changed one iota since I saw my first game here, twenty-four years ago—but after five months of Fenway, Kauffman strikes me as a giant, slate-gray eyesore. Like a lot of 1960s- and '70s-era ballparks, it's not so bad when the team is good and the stands are full. But when the team is mediocre and the stands are mostly empty—as has been the case for the last decade or so—it's hard to rouse much passion for what's happening on the field unless you *really* love the Royals.

Saturday, August 26

No baseball for me and Kristien yesterday. Instead, we spent the day in Chase County, Kansas, which has the distinction of being (a) the subject of William Least Heat Moon's opus, *Prairyearth* and (b) one of the hottest places in the country this weekend. When we arrived in Cottonwood Falls, the county seat, a downtown bank sign informed us that the temperature was 106 degrees.

It was cooler than that in Kansas City today, but not by much. The game started late because of a college football game played across the parking lot at Arrowhead Stadium this afternoon. Still, when Brian Meadows threw the game's first pitch at 8:06, the thermometer read 93 degrees. No breeze, but plenty of humidity. To her credit, Kristien didn't complain once, which of course made me love her even more than I already did.

Wasn't much of a game tonight. Just as Pedro got hammered in the first inning on Thursday night, Royals starter Meadows gave up four runs in the first inning tonight. And like Pedro, Meadows settled down after that, but this time he didn't get the support that Pedro did, and the Sox wound up on top, 5–3.

Monday, August 28

Kristien flew home to Seattle yesterday, but my flight doesn't leave for Boston until this afternoon, which gives me all morning with a rental car and nowhere particular to be. So I did something that I've been wanting to do for years, spend more than a few minutes exploring the site of Kansas City's old Municipal Stadium, where the Kansas City Monarchs played from 1923 through 1950, the Kansas City Athletics from 1955 through 1967, and the Kansas City Royals from 1969 through 1972.

It's gone now, replaced by a vacant lot and the Municipal Stadium Community Garden. What happened at old Municipal Stadium? Well, among other things:

On June 12, 1939, Lou Gehrig played his last baseball game, an exhibition against the Kansas City Blues, a Yankees farm club. Gehrig batted once, grounded out weakly to second base, and left in the third inning.

On April 12, 1955, the Kansas City Athletics beating the Tigers, 6–2, in the first Major League Baseball game ever played in the city.

On April 8, 1969, the Kansas City Royals played their first game, beating the Twins, 4–3 in twelve innings.

On December 25, 1971, the Kansas City Chiefs lost to the Miami Dolphins, 27–24, in what was, and remains, the longest game in NFL history.

I learned all that, and more, from a sign at the corner of Twenty-second and Brooklyn, just a few blocks south of Arthur Bryant's Barbecue, which *The New Yorker*'s Calvin Trillin once famously described as "the single best restaurant in the world."

As interesting as that sign was, however, I found myself fascinated by another,

adorning the Bibleway Pentecostal Church on the opposite corner. Lettered by hand
with a brush and black paint, it read:

> ARE YOU AT YOUR END?
> "STRESSED" "DEPRESSED"
> "DISCOURAGED"
> HAVE YOU TRIED ALL YOU KNOW?
> JESUS CHRIST IS THE ANSWER
> TODAY
> DAY SERVICES HELD DAILY MON
> 10:00—1 PM
> ALL ARE WELCOME
> PASTOR R. WILKINS
> COUSELING BY EMERGENCY APT.

Yes, "counseling" really was misspelled. And though I didn't reproduce them
here, Pastor Wilkins's office *and* home phone numbers were listed at the conclusion
of the message. I'm not sure why this fascinated me so. I'm not particularly stressed
or depressed, or even discouraged. At the moment, though, I guess it struck me that
the living, breathing people inside the Bibleway Pentecostal Church are probably
more interesting than the ghosts I'd like to imagine still haunt the site of old
Municipal Stadium. From time to time, I wish I could occasionally write about something other than baseball, and today was one of those times.

I flew "home" this afternoon, and the cab deposited me at 111 Park Drive at 7:08, just
in time for me to see the first pitch from St. Petersburg, where the Devil Rays were
hosting the Red Sox. It wasn't a happy evening for the Sox, as they dropped a 5–2
decision to the worst team in the American League.

Tuesday, August 29

Most 8–0 games aren't particularly exciting, but the boys over at ESPN called this
one "perhaps the wildest game of the year," and perhaps it was.

The story this evening might be summed up thusly: Devil Rays hitters spent most of the game trying to get a hit off Pedro Martinez, and Devil Rays pitchers spent most of the game trying to hit Brian Daubach.

First, Brian Daubach . . . but wait a second, this story begins with Martinez, too. Gerald Williams led off the bottom of the first, and Pedro quickly got ahead in the count. But then he came inside with a fastball, and it struck Williams—who dives toward the plate as the pitch arrives—flush on his left hand. Williams began to walk toward first base, alternating stares at Pedro with stares at his stricken hand . . . and then he sprinted toward the mound. He got off one punch that missed, and then Sox catcher Jason Varitek tackled him. A general melee followed, with first baseman Daubach and third baseman Lou Merloni in the middle of a big pileup on the mound.

Williams eventually took his spot on first base even though he'd been ejected, and it took another five minutes for the umpires to convince him to leave the field, during which time Rays manager Larry Rothschild got thumbed, too.

And then for some reason, the Tampa Bay pitchers took every opportunity to put fastballs into Daubach's ribs. In the third, Daubach narrowly avoided a high-and-tight pitch, and got plunked with the next one. Rays starter Dave Eiland was immediately ejected. In the seventh, Rays reliever Cory Lidle threw a pitch behind Daubach. Lidle was ejected. His replacement, Tony Fiore, threw an inside pitch to Daubach and then hit him with his second pitch. Fiore was ejected.

Jimy Williams finally took pity on Daubach and lifted him for a pinch-hitter. (Daubach, it turned out, had been injured all along, as he'd wrenched his left elbow in the fracas back in the first inning. And Merloni suffered a mild concussion in the same fray.) After the game, the Devil Rays accused Daubach of throwing sucker punches during the first-inning fight, but I watched a replay of the "incident" at least ten times, and I didn't see him do anything particularly untoward. The pitchers who plunked Daubach will undoubtedly be suspended (as will Williams), but they were just following orders from Rothschild, who later said of Daubach, "The only problem was that our pitchers kept missing the guy."

And the guy who started everything? Pedro Martinez, after beaning Gerald Williams, set down twenty-four straight Devil Rays. Innings two through eight, no Tampa Bay hitter reached base.

And then, catcher John Flaherty.

Whatever John Flaherty has accomplished (not much) or will accomplish (quite likely, not much), Red Sox fans will always remember him for a line drive to right-center field, in the bottom of the ninth inning on August 29, 2000. Hell, given the elephantine memory of Sox fans, Flaherty might even get booed the next time he appears in Fenway, as Gerald Williams certainly will. Flaherty hit a fastball and he hit it hard, a drive to right-center that neither Everett nor Nixon had a real chance at catching. (In the *Herald*, Jeff Horrigan demeaned Flaherty's hit by calling it "an opposite-field single," but it was a legitimate line drive.)

The next three Devil Rays went down in order—Miguel Cairo ended the game with a bullet directly at Garciaparra—and Pedro had a one-hitter and his third shutout this season.

So it's still been more than thirty-five years since a Red Sox pitcher threw a no-hitter, the last coming on September 16, 1965, when Dave Morehead tossed one against the Indians at Fenway. (The Sox have themselves been no-hit four times since 1965.) How does this thirty-five-year drought compare to the other major-league clubs? Excluding recent expansion teams,

METS	NEVER
PADRES	NEVER
RED SOX	1965

The Mets were born in 1962, the Padres in 1969, which means that only the Mets have gone longer than the Sox without having one of their pitchers throw a no-hitter. This can be partly attributed to Fenway Park, long one of the ballparks most conducive to hitting. Still, given the presence in Boston of either Roger Clemens or Pedro Martinez since 1984, it's a bit surprising that nobody's done it since '65. I sincerely thought that Pedro would throw a no-hitter this season (if only for the benefit of my book), but time is running out.

Thursday, August 31

August was the month. August was the month the Red Sox were going to make their move, go for the gusto, grab the brass ring, blah blah blah. From August 4 through August 30, the Sox played teams against which they had a pretty clear edge. And with a tough September ahead, they needed to make hay against the also-rans.

The Sox went 14–12, and that ain't hay.

With that in mind, here are the standings as we enter September, which, with apologies to T. S. Eliot, certainly has the potential to become the cruelest month for Red Sox fans.

A.L. EAST

	W-L	GB	RS-RA	PYTHAG W-L
YANKEES	74–56	——	743–631	75–55
RED SOX	69–61	5	647–594	70–60
BLUE JAYS	70–63	5 ¹/₂	743–758	65–68

As it happens, today I received an e-mail from my editor, David Schoenfield, asking if I could provide a quick analysis of the American League East pennant race, to run with the thoughts of other ESPN.com contributors. Here's what I sent David:

> The A.L. East race? It's all over but the shoutin',' sports fans. The Yankees open September with a nice fat five-game lead over the Red Sox, which would be bad enough . . . but the Red Sox have a killer schedule the rest of the way. Two games against the Athletics, three against the White Sox, four each against the Mariners and Tigers, and *eight* against the Indians. Of Boston's 32 remaining games, only seven might be considered against potentially weak opponents: one game against the Twins, and three each against the Devil Rays and Orioles.
>
> If you're really paying attention, you might have noticed that four games are missing from the above analysis. No, I didn't forget that the Red Sox still have four games against the Yankees, and you can bet that neither the Red Sox nor the Yankees have forgotten. Three games at Fenway, September 8, 9, and 10, then a makeup game on the eleventh at The Stadium. There'll be plenty of shoutin' in both ballparks, but the Red Sox need to do some winnin', too. Given their September schedule and their relative lack of talent, the Sox might need to win all four games just to have a decent chance at the East pennant.

Yeah, I know the Red Sox could win five straight while the Yankees are losing five straight, and *poof*. . . just like that, they're tied. The math is simple, but so are the odds, and the odds are greatly against the Sox making up five games in thirty-one days. The Wild Card, fortunately, is a different story . . .

WILD CARD

	W-L	GB	RS-RA	PYTHAG W-L
INDIANS	70–60	—	750–681	71–59
RED SOX	69–61	1	647–594	70–60
BLUE JAYS	70–63	1 ½	743–758	65–68
ATHLETICS	69–63	2	710–689	68–64
ANGELS	65–62	3 ½	672–665	67–66
TIGERS	66–66	5 ½	668–669	66–66

The Indians got blasted tonight, 14–7 by the Rangers. With all these clubs bunched together, one certainly can't suggest, with a straight face, that the Sox are *likely* to win the Wild Card. But it is fair to say that they've got about as good a chance as anybody.

◆　◆　◆

Perhaps I should have led off today's entry with THE BIG NEWS . . . Yes, the Red Sox have finally . . . actually, let me quote the *Globe*'s Bob Hohler: "In his unrelenting—and yet unfulfilled—quest to add consistent punch to the Red Sox' lackluster lineup, general manager Dan Duquette . . . tried again, this time picking up Dante Bichette, one of the most productive hitters in baseball for much of the 1990s."

Gee, that depends on what you mean by "most productive." It's true that Bichette piled up some big numbers; from 1995 through 1999, he averaged 128 RBI per season. But Bichette spent those seasons playing for the Colorado Rockies, and his home stats in, first Mile High Stadium, and then Coors Field, dwarfed his road stats. This year, playing for the Cincinnati Reds, Bichette hit only sixteen home runs in 125 games. Dan Duquette's explanation of the deal? "We've been looking for a veteran presence to help our lineup and Dante is a proven RBI man who's been one of the leading run producers in the major leagues since 1995."

The Providence Journal's Michael Byrnes had perhaps the final word on this season (even though the season's not final) when he said, "If I looked at the complete record of Red Sox transactions over the last few years, without knowing who the GM was, I would have guessed that the Red Sox got a new GM sometime between the Everett and Sprague trades." And Duquette's evaluation of Bichette is perhaps the best example. If the man running your favorite team starts tossing out terms like "veteran presence" and "proven RBI man" and (worst of all) "run producer," you should be very afraid, because usually that means he's just acquired a sluggardly slugger who doesn't get on base nearly enough.

And wouldn't you know it, that description fits Bichette to a T.

My friend Art Martone wrote, "Trading for Dante Bichette would seem to be a desperate measure. But these are the very definition of desperate times."

True. But desperate enough to give away Chris Reitsma, a twenty-two-year-old right-hander who is one of the Red Sox' best pitching prospects? Desperate enough to assume the remainder of Bichette's contract, which will pay him $6.5 million *next* year? I wouldn't have made the deal. I would not have, as Duquette himself described the deal, "mortgag[ed] part of our future, obviously." The Red Sox' chances of reaching the World Series, let alone winning it, simply aren't good enough to warrant such foolishness. And what makes this truly pointless is that the Red Sox already have players who can give them approximately what Bichette will . . . but they won't use them. Here are the combined major-league stats for two ex-Red Sox currently playing for Pawtucket, along with Bichette's numbers this year:

	G	HR	RBI	OBP	SLG	OPS
PAWSOX PAIR	34	4	18	.410	.440	850
BICHETTE	125	16	76	.353	.466	819

"PawSox Pair" is Izzy Alcantara and Morgan Burkhart, each of them currently exiled to the International League for no apparent reason. Are they really as good as Bichette? Perhaps not. But they're certainly close enough that it's damn near impossible to justify spending a good pitching prospect *and* all those future millions for what is only a marginal upgrade.

If nothing else, though, the Sox are getting a player who wants to be here.

"I said to myself, 'Please let it be Boston,'" Bichette said. "It's a place I've always wanted to play. I met my wife at a Gold's Gym beyond the Green Monster. I've had a lot of luck there."

The Sox are going to need a lot of luck, too, because they haven't significantly improved the team that actually plays the games. With a month left in the season, this isn't exactly like rearranging deck chairs on the *Titanic*. But it's not far off.

Eighth Inning

Friday, September 1

Tonight it was balmy. And not relatively balmy, but actually balmy, as in 86 degrees at 7:07, when Rolando Arrojo got things started. Arrojo's been up and down since joining the Sox a month ago, and tonight he was up: seven innings, five hits, one run. The game was scoreless through five innings, but the Sox bats came alive in the sixth, and they cruised to a 6–2 victory over the Mariners, who are also battling for a postseason berth.

The Indians won again, so the Sox are still a game out in the Wild Card race. On a happier note, the Athletics and Angels both lost—Oakland succumbed to Toronto's ninth-inning rally, and Anaheim blew an 8–1 lead in Chicago—so at least some of the competition is starting to drop off. It's looking more and more like a two-team race between the Red Sox and Indians, and in mid-September they'll face off at Fenway for five games in three days, three days that might well decide who gets to keep playing after October 1.

Saturday, September 2

Today's tilt was supposed to start a few minutes after one o'clock, but it rained all morning and into the afternoon, so the game didn't get going until a few minutes after three. Earlier, I made my way to the press box, for a pregame interview on KIRO, the Mariners' flagship station back in Seattle. After the interview (mostly about *Baseball Dynasties*), I got to talking with Dave Niehaus, a Pacific Northwest institution who's been broadcasting M's games since the club was born in 1977. I didn't even have to ask Dave what he thinks about Fenway Park. He asked me what I was doing here this summer, I told him, and then he started gushing.

"I love this place, just love it. There's so much history here, and you've got that weird corner in right field, the triangle in center, and of course the Green Monster . . . I've told my wife, if I die before they tear this place down, I'd like to have my ashes buried under home plate."

Now that, my friends, is a testimonial.

I chatted with Dave until they kicked me out of the booth, and then I headed back home, as the rain wasn't letting up and it was apparent that baseball wouldn't be played on this site anytime soon.

◆   ◆   ◆

As I usually do when I'm at home waiting out a rain delay, this afternoon I turned on WEEI to see what the idiots were saying. And while cohost Larry Johnson might not be an idiot, he didn't disappoint my temporary craving for foolishness, saying, "Anybody who thinks we don't need a new ballpark, all you have to do is look at that picture in the *Globe* a couple weeks ago, with Jason Varitek pushing a broom, trying to sweep the water out of the dugout."

Actually, what that picture tells me is that the dugouts should have better drainage, which I'll bet could be accomplished without spending more than half a billion dollars on a new ballpark.

◆   ◆   ◆

I made it back just in time to see Ramon Martinez take his last few warm-up tosses. As it turned out, the Sox would have been better off with a rain-out, as badly as everyone did want to get this one in.

The last time Martinez pitched, on July 31 in Seattle (I was there), he walked five Mariners and gave up a grand slam, recording just three outs before getting yanked. The next day, the Sox placed him on the disabled list with what they called "a knee contusion" but was probably nothing. Today, going against the same Mariners, he pitched well, if not brilliantly. He did walk four hitters in five-plus innings, but he also allowed only two hits, and left in the sixth with the game still scoreless. The bases were loaded at the time (thanks to two of those walks plus an HBP), but Pichardo retired Carlos Guillen on a foul pop, and then—with the Fenway Faithful on their feet—he struck out Mike Cameron swinging.

Dante Bichette went two-for-four last night—both of his hits were ground-ball singles—but tonight we saw the real Dante Bichette. First at-bat? Strikeout, swinging. Second at-bat? Strikeout, swinging. On three pitches in the dirt. Third at-bat? Foul-out to the third baseman. On a two-and-oh count. That one really hurt, because the next hitter, Troy O'Leary, smashed a hanging change-up over the center-field fence for the Red Sox' first run. That was in the seventh, and tied the game at one apiece. The tie didn't last long, though. Edgar Martinez led off the top of the ninth with a home run over that same center-field fence, and Seattle tacked on a couple more runs. In the bottom of the ninth, the Sox got the tying run to the plate in the person of O'Leary, but he lofted a high fly to right field to end the game.

◆ ◆ ◆

This afternoon I saw the Boston fans at something close to their best, and something close to their worst.

In the top of the sixth, with the game still scoreless, the Mariners loaded the bases against Ramon Martinez, and Hipolito Pichardo trotted in from the bullpen. Carlos Guillen swung at Pichardo's first pitch and lifted a high foul to Merloni at third base. That brought up center fielder Mike Cameron, and after his second strike, everybody in the ballpark stood up to exhort Pichardo, who responded by punching out Cameron on a mighty swing.

That's the best.

The worst?

In the top of the ninth, my favorite knuckleball pitcher struck out Alex Rodriguez and Edgar Martinez, two of the greatest right-handed hitters of our time, on three pitches apiece. Unfortunately, not many other fans were still around to enjoy it. Wakefield replaced Rich Garces just after Garces gave up a two-run double to scrub Brian Lesher (who also cracked an RBI triple today, in his first major-league game this season). Lesher's double gave the Mariners a 4–1 lead, and a hefty percentage of the crowd headed for the exits.

What's up with that? Since when is a three-run lead insurmountable? Did everyone really have someplace they needed to be at 6 P.M. on a Saturday evening? Or has everyone already given up on this season?

Sunday, September 3

This morning I was at Gold's Gym and—probably just a few feet from where Dante met Mariana!—I ran into my first truly bad luck of the season. I'm not sure what they call the exercise that I was doing, but I do know that it involved my arms and my lower back, and when I stood up, the aforementioned lower back hurt like hell. More exercise didn't help, so I gingerly walked home. I think I strained my lower back, something that happens to me every two or three years. If I were an elk right now, I'd be the first one culled from the herd by wolves.

I wouldn't normally bore you, Gentle Reader, with such a pedestrian complaint. But as it turned out, tonight's game happened to be the one during which I finally occupied one of those seats in the right-field corner, not far from Pesky's Pole, where you're facing directly toward the center fielder rather than even the general vicinity of the infield.

Fortunately, a couple of things happened to ameliorate the pain: It was a pretty quick game, and I almost got to see a no-hitter.

Tomo Ohka, so good in recent weeks, got roughed up for a couple of runs in the first inning, but he didn't give up anything else before exiting after the sixth. Meanwhile, his counterpart on the Mariners, Paul Abbott, was even better. Mixing up his low-nineties fastballs with his low-eighties sliders, Abbot didn't allow a hit through four innings, at which point I finally noticed (you just don't think "no-hitter" when Paul Abbott's on the mound) the zero in the hits column for the Sox.

To that point, the closest thing to a Red Sox hit came in the second inning, when O'Leary drove a fly ball to deep center field, where Stan Javier hauled it in. There was another close call in the fifth, when Rico Brogna lined into a double play, but Abbott still had his no-hitter after seven frames. Meanwhile, the M's padded their lead just a bit, to 3–0, with a run off Rod Beck in the seventh.

Jason Varitek led off the eighth and sent a fly ball that was caught by right fielder Charles Gipson, not far from where we sat. Next up: Rico Brogna, in the lineup only because Daubach is still nursing a sore left elbow. It was Brogna's first start since August 15, and entering his eighth-inning at-bat, he was batting just .167 (five hits in thirty at-bats) since joining the Red Sox on August 3.

Long story short, Brogna bounced a single up the middle, just past the diving Alex Rodriguez.

Finally, something for Sox fans to cheer!

After Brogna's hit, Abbott completely lost it. Pinch-hitter Midre Cummings lofted a fly ball to deep center, and then Hatteberg walked on a full count. Lefty reliever Arthur Rhodes was ready in the bullpen, and I was so sure that Mariners manager Lou Piniella would remove Abbott that I actually made the appropriate markings in my scorebook. But after a long conversation, Piniella stuck with Abbott . . . who walked Nixon on a full count, too.

That loaded the bases, with Garciaparra due next.

Mariners closer Kazuhiro Sasaki was in the pen, and for the second time in five minutes I assumed a pitching change that didn't happen, as Piniella called on Jose Paniagua rather than Sasaki. At the time, I just couldn't understand the move at all. I know that Sasaki's the closer and usually doesn't pitch until the ninth, but couldn't he record four outs instead of three?

There were a couple of things I didn't know. First off, with a home run the only disastrous outcome at the moment, Paniagua's probably the better choice. He'd allowed just four home runs in sixty-eight innings this season (and five in seventy-eight innings last season), while Sasaki has permitted ten round-trippers in fifty-one innings.

The other thing I didn't know is that Sasaki has thrown more than one inning in a game *just once* this season. A thirty-two-year-old rookie from Japan, Sasaki has pitched in fifty-five games this season, but virtually never more than one inning at a time. This kind of workload is fairly common for left-handed relief pitchers, often called upon to retire just one hitter. But even in today's world of specialty relievers, it's rare for a closer to have his workload regimented to this extent.

Anyway, Paniagua did his job, retiring the slumping Garciaparra—who's hit safely just once in his last fourteen at-bats—on a routine fly to right. And after Alex Rodriguez hit a two-run homer in the top of the ninth, Paniagua remained in the game and retired the Sox in order to end the game.

So the new-look lineup—cleanup hitter Dante Bichette at your service, ma'am!—has totaled one run and four hits over the last two games.

◆ ◆ ◆

Tonight I sat with Mark Haubner, a friend from Seattle and a fellow ESPN.com employee. Mark went to college in western Massachusetts and loves baseball, and so of course he has "a Fenway story," too . . .

"I remember that night in the Fenway bleachers as if it were a nondescript 1991 game against the Toronto Blue Jays. Which it was.

"I recall the Red Sox' opponents because, that night, the bleacher denizens started a rhythmic, rolling, oh-so-politically-incorrect chant of . . .

"'White does Carter up the ass, doo-dah, doo-dah,

"'White does Carter up the ass, oh duh-doo-dah-day

". . . and pointing from center field (Devon White) to right field (Joe Carter) while swaying as one, for the full effect. As if that lovely tune weren't enough, a rather inebriated fellow behind us would periodically break into this 'song': 'Hey hey, the Red Sox, they're the best goddamn team in the land.'

"The first time we heard it, we laughed heartily. The tenth time we heard it, we were annoyed. And by the fortieth time we heard it, we were singing along."

◆ ◆ ◆

Aside from sharing with me that somewhat disturbing story, Mark served an important role tonight. He was the only one in the stands—or at least in our particular neighborhood—to notice that the Red Sox almost certainly must be the first team in the history of Major League Baseball to feature a righty-lefty mullet tandem in the bullpen.

For anyone who doesn't know what the hell I'm talking about, a mullet is a man with short hair on the sides, but long hair in the back (if I've piqued your curiosity, there are all sorts of websites devoted to this strange beast). For a number of years, the best example in baseball was Randy Johnson, but this season he's sporting a conventional length in back. So that leaves Rod Beck, Boston's rotund relief man. He's been a mullet ever since he reached the majors, nine years ago. So you gotta give the guy points for loyalty, if not style.

And then today the Red Sox called up twenty-nine-year-old Sang-Hoon Lee from Pawtucket, and he showed up sporting a blond-dyed *and* mulleted head. (Actually, Lee pitched to four batters on June 29, but nobody noticed.) Even better, tonight Beck pitched the seventh inning, and Lee followed Beck and pitched the eighth and ninth. And that's how Mark Haubner, alone among we cognoscenti, realized that, while we didn't get to see a no-hitter, we did get to see something pretty spectacular. As Mark said, "Wow, the Red Sox are going to go righty-lefty with the mullets!"

Wow indeed, Mark. Wow, indeed.

Monday, September 4

If you like good music when you're at a ball game, Fenway Park's not the place for you. Once you get past "Center Field," always played when the Sox take the field before the first inning, the selection generally includes a long string of forgettable pop songs. But before today's game, somebody got it right.

First, Aaron Copland's "Fanfare for the Common Man."

Next, the Foo Fighters' "My Hero."

The occasion? Today, the Red Sox retired 27, worn by catcher Carlton Fisk from 1969 through 1980. In Game 6 of the 1975 World Series, Fisk hit the most-viewed home run in the game's long history, and earlier this summer he was inducted into the Hall of Fame.

The Red Sox, alone among major-league teams, have always had incredibly rigid standards for the retirement of numbers, which explains why, before today, only four numbers were placed along the facing above the grandstand in right field: 1 (Bobby Doerr), 4 (Joe Cronin), 8 (Carl Yastrzemski) and 9 (Ted Williams). Those standards are

- ◆ Membership in the Baseball Hall of Fame
- ◆ At least ten years of service with the Red Sox
- ◆ A career that ended with the Red Sox

Or at least, those *were* the standards. They've been bent, if not snapped in half like a twig beneath a bulldozer. Because Fisk did not "finish his career with the Red Sox," not really. After leaving the Sox with great animosity after the 1980 season, Fisk signed with the Chicago White Sox, for whom he played until 1993. He played more seasons with the White Sox (thirteen vs. eleven), and significantly more games (1,421 vs. 1,078).

But as Dan Shaughnessy wrote today, "The Boston brass claim Fisk finished his career with the Sox because they gave him a cheesy job last spring."

That cheesy job is, according to the team's media guide, "Special Assistant to the General Manager." Of course, Fisk is nothing of the sort, and I'd be surprised to learn that he has spoken to Dan Duquette more than once or twice all season.

Bending the rules for Fisk will undoubtedly result in arguments being made for Jim Rice (who's not in the Hall), among others. But Fisk is something of a special case, because he grew up in Charlestown, New Hampshire. As Red Sox fan Mark Starr told Peter Golenbock in *Fenway: An Unexpurgated History of the Red Sox*,

> The most important aspect of Carlton Fisk was that he was home-grown. Remember, this isn't California. We're provincial up in New England, and we don't produce that many ballplayers.

Today, I saw it from the center-field bleachers; Section 36, to be precise, where I sat with Susan and her friend Sandy. The ceremonies honoring Fisk were supposed to start at approximately 12:30, and the actual game at around 1:15. Of course, things didn't exactly work that way. What with the three proclamations—including one from "Her Excellency, Jeanne Shaheen, Governor of the State of New Hampshire," along with congratulations from Boston mayor Thomas Menino and Massuchusetts governor Paul Celluci—and Fisk's victory lap, and statements from various Red Sox functionaries, there was no way this game was going to start before 1:30. Fortunately, Fisk, who rambled on forever in Cooperstown at his induction cere-mony, limited himself to a six-minute speech today. And at 1:48, Pedro threw his first pitch of the afternoon.

While waiting for the game to start, I thought about what it might be like, to be primarily remembered, as Fisk is, for one solitary moment, a moment that came nearly twenty-five years ago. Of course, this happens to writers all the time. It's cer-tainly possible that my first book, published last spring, will always be considered my best. Thirty years from now, I might be at a SABR convention, and people might still be wanting to talk about *Baseball Dynasties*, even though I will (presumably) have written many other books in the interim.

The difference, I suppose, is that Fisk *knows* that he'll always be remembered for something that happened when he was twenty-seven years old. It's the lot of a professional athlete. A writer, on the other hand, harbors hopes that he will, for as long as he's alive, continue to produce work that might meet with critical and/or popular acclaim. Still, I have to think that Fisk must be tired of talking, over and over again, about something that happened in 1975.

◆ ◆ ◆

After the eighth:

Sweet Caroline . . .

At that point, the Sox held a 5–1 lead, with all five runs coming in the third inning, the big hit Jose Offerman's "triple" that should have been scored as an error for Mariners center fielder Mike Cameron, who camped under Offerman's long fly and then fell on his ass. The M's got their run in the seventh, when Cameron homered over the Green Monster. Aside from that, Pedro was mighty stingy. He allowed just six hits in his eight innings, and Lowe pitched a scoreless ninth.

◆　◆　◆

In Toronto, the Athletics thrashed the Blue Jays, 10-0, as Mike Stanley continues to make Dan Duquette look bad. Here are Stanley's stats since the Red Sox released him, along with a few right-handed bats that have joined the club since then:

	G	AB	HR	RBI	OBP	SLG
STANLEY	25	82	3	15	.392	.476
SPRAGUE	33	111	2	9	.293	.306
GILKEY	26	77	1	9	.333	.377
BICHETTE	4	15	0	0	.250	.200
BERRY	1	4	0	0	—	—
LANSING	31	106	0	10	.246	.217

This just hasn't been Duquette's year. In eighty-two at-bats with Oakland, Stanley's got as many home runs, and almost as many RBI, as the four new Red Sox acquired as right-handed "bats" have compiled in more than 200 at-bats. Granted, Stanley can't play third base (like Sprague did) or right field (like Gilkey can, though rarely does). But what the Red Sox have needed, all season long, was a right-handed bat, and Stanley would probably have performed that job better than any of the stiffs with which Duquette tried to replace him.

I threw in Lansing just for laughs. He's a right-handed hitter, too, but also a middle infielder so not really comparable to Stanley. Still, Lansing has been so pathetic that the Sox played Donnie Sadler at second base tonight, and Sadler might see plenty more playing time if he can give the Sox anything at all offensively.

In that same game, David Wells took the loss for the Blue Jays, and in the process essentially locked up the American League Cy Young Award for Pedro Martinez. Here were their stats before this afternoon's action:

	GS	IP	K	BB	W-L	ERA
WELLS	29	194	142	30	19–5	3.94
MARTINEZ	24	182	239	27	15–4	1.68

Yes, anybody with half a clue would look at those numbers and vote for Pedro with little hesitation. But there are still a few foolish baseball writers—they're the guys who vote for awards like the Cy Young and MVP—who worship at the Altar of the W, and if Wells were to finish the season with, say, five or six more victories than Martinez, he would almost certainly draw at least some support in the Cy Young balloting. After today's game, however, that's not likely. Here are the latest stats for both pitchers:

	GS	IP	K	BB	W-L	ERA
WELLS	30	195	143	31	19–6	4.24
MARTINEZ	25	190	250	28	16–4	1.66

They both will probably start five more games, and I suppose that if Wells finished with twenty-four wins and Pedro with sixteen, Wells would still draw some Cy Young support. But what's more likely is that Wells will finish with twenty-one or twenty-two victories, Pedro will finish with nineteen or twenty . . . and Pedro will be the unanimous winner of the award.

Tuesday, September 5

This afternoon, I did something that I've been meaning to do all season.

At exactly five o'clock, I took up a station on the north side of Lansdowne Street, and peered up into the bright blue sky. My prey? Baseballs. On the other side of the Green Monster, directly to my front, the Red Sox were taking batting practice; later, the Oakland Athletics would do the same.

Simply put, I wanted to see what happened back here during batting practice.

(I'd also like to know what happens back here during a game, but I've been loathe to give up my seat when there's actual baseball being played.)

So, what does happen? Not much. It's nothing like the scene along Waveland Avenue in Chicago, where a veritable army of crazies fights over every ball that clears Wrigley Field's left-field bleachers.

At my arrival, I counted ten baseballs already stuck in the netting that tops the Green Monster, and by 5:03, three more balls had landed in the netting, but none had soared completely out of the park. As for what happened next, here's a transcript of my tape-recorded diary of the next hour or so . . .

5:20: Haven't seen a ball drop into the netting in fifteen minutes, maybe longer.

5:25: Sidewalk traffic is getting heavy . . . lot of people just getting to the ballpark, walking to the souvenir shops, food places . . . the bleachers open pretty soon. But it's still just me, the old guy, and one other guy. I think he's just hanging out, but he does periodically look up at the net.

5:29: Ball came over the net, slammed into a wall, bounced back into the street, where the guy who was just hanging around grabbed it after it bounced back off the brick wall of Fenway Park. Gotta be quick, apparently . . . I guess the guy who got the ball is associated with Save Fenway Park! He and another fellow just set up a card table on the sidewalk, and sitting atop the table are "Save Fenway Park!" bumper stickers. Aside from those two, there's me, the same guy who's been here since the beginning, a middle-aged man and his son, and, uh, one more . . . which makes, let's see, one, two, three, four . . . five, not including the Fenway Park duo.

5:32: Well, that figures. A ball just hit exactly where I was sitting, directly in front of the parking garage.

5:38: The guy who's been here since the beginning just left, maybe he knows something I don't. That leaves, really, just two of us, plus the Save Fenway guys (who I should talk to, by the way, before I go home).

5:41: Foul ball over the fence, not the netting, bounced off a wall on my side of the street, caromed back off the exterior wall of Fenway, and then rolled back across the street, right toward me. I was sitting down, got up, took two steps toward the ball . . . and tripped over my own feet. One of the Save Fenway guys was going after the ball, but he must have felt sorry for me, because he slowed down and let me grab it . . . Adding to the degree of difficulty is the fact that people are walking by all the time, and like most people I'm, uh, curious about other people. So it's hard to stay focused on looking up into the blue sky above the net for something that may or may not come.

5:50: Still the two Save Fenway guys, another guy who's been here for half an hour, and one other guy, a businessman wearing a tie, who's been standing on the ramp to the parking lot for about ten minutes. That's it, just the five of us.

5:53: A couple of kids just walked by, wanted to know if any balls had come over, and then they wanted to see mine. One of them said that he counted twenty-four balls in the net.

5:57: Haven't seen anything even hit the net since the ball I got, so I'm guessing that b.p. is over.

At six o'clock, exactly one hour after I'd arrived, I realized that nothing else was going to happen, and got up from my sidewalk perch. I did stop and talk to the people manning the Save Fenway Park! Table; they're familiar with my work, which made breaking the ice easy enough. Mostly, we commiserated about the unwillingness of the media—both print (*Herald* and *Globe*) and radio (WEEI)—to give anything like fair coverage to the issues surrounding the old ballpark and the proposed new one. Unfortunately, nearly all of the newspaper writers are lined up squarely behind a new ballpark, and nobody at WEEI will even invite anyone from Save Fenway onto the air, which perhaps shouldn't be a surprise, as WEEI is the Red Sox' flagship station (you can draw your own conclusions). I dropped $23.36—all the money in my pocket—into the donation jar, and then I went home, found a blue pen, and printed along the edge of my new baseball's stitching:

9-5-00 5:41 P.M. FROM THE BELLY OF FENWAY PARK

So it's not like Wrigley Field at all. In fact, if you're interested in acquiring a baseball at Fenway Park, I can virtually guarantee you one. I suggest taking a spot on the sidewalk at approximately 4:30 before a night game, and waiting. Assuming that you're generally one of five people with the same goal for the ninety-odd minutes of batting practice, you've got a great shot at getting a ball.

◆ ◆ ◆

The Sox might not have peppered Lansdowne Avenue with baseballs during batting practice, but they did quite well once the actual game started. In the first inning they batted around, and scored seven runs, the last four of them coming when Manny Alexander (of all people!) hit a grand slam, a high fly into the netting down the left-field line. They cruised to a 10–3 victory over the Athletics. Pete Schourek, making his first start since July 20, earned the W with five and a third innings of solid work (two hits, one walk, six strikeouts).

◆ ◆ ◆

When the Red Sox dumped Mike Stanley in July, Nomar Garciaparra predicted, "It's going to hurt our team more than it's going to help us. I'm sure he's going to be picked up somewhere and come back and kick our ass."

Well, today Stanley got his chance. After getting a nice round of applause from the crowd in the first inning, Stanley hit a fly ball to deep left field, where O'Leary made a leaping catch against the Green Monster. But after striking out in the fourth, Stanley finally got some measure of revenge in the sixth, when he lashed an RBI double, and eventually came around to score.

Wednesday, September 6

I had a great seat tonight, seven rows behind the far corner of the Red Sox dugout. And in some ways it was a great game; I made sixteen notes. Rolando Arrojo lasted only three innings, though, and by the end of the eighth, perhaps half of the seats were empty, even though the home team trailed by only two runs. That's how it ended, the Sox losing 6–4 when Jose Offerman struck out with a runner on base in the bottom of the ninth.

◆ ◆ ◆

The Indians won again. That's four straight, eight of ten, and fourteen of nineteen. Cleveland's schedule does start getting tough this weekend—they host Chicago for three games, Boston for three, and then travel to New York for four—but then, so does Boston's. With tonight's result at Fenway, the Red Sox and Athletics are now tied for second place in the Wild Card standings, both three games behind the Indians. The Yankees blew a ninth-inning lead in Kansas City, so the Sox are still six games out in the East.

Thursday, September 7

I went to the game with Jason. Among other things, Jason is twenty-six, and a devout Libertarian; hails from Peoria and cheers for the Cubs; doesn't eat soup, or the great majority of vegetables; is an accomplished jazz drummer, but works just occasionally; and lives in Back Bay, one of the more expensive neighborhoods in this country, though he's got no visible means of support. Jason's also incredibly clever, and he's got an amazing gift for amusing me. (Jason's formula for determining whether or not a woman is too young to date: "Your age divided by two, plus seven.") So I let the kid hang around . . . I'm kidding, of course. Jason's been doing some research for me, off and on throughout the season, and I feel guilty that this is only our second game together.

Actually, we were supposed to be at Fenway back on July 26, to see the Sox play the Twins, but the weather didn't cooperate. For the sake of the Twins, who play in Seattle tomorrow night, this makeup game started at 1:05 (or at least within a couple of minutes; nothing ever starts on time around here). And by 1:15, the Sox were in big trouble, because Ramon Martinez suffered his usual first-inning problems. The first three Twins singled to load the bases. The fourth struck out. And the fifth, David Ortiz, hit a grand slam, just to the fair side of Pesky's Pole. The sixth, Corey Koskie, also hit a baseball into the right-field stands. Ramon retired the next two hitters in good order, but the Sox trailed 5–0 before they even had a chance to bat.

But as they've done so often in Ramon's starts this season, the Sox came back. Including those last two hitters in the first, Martinez retired sixteen of the next seventeen Twins that he faced. Meanwhile, the Red Sox got busy, especially in the fourth inning when they scored five times and wound up with an 11–6 victory. Jose Offerman, so ineffective all season, probably because he really hasn't been completely healthy, hit a pair of solo homers.

Friday, September 8

As I crossed Peterborough Street on my way to the ballpark tonight, my nostrils suddenly perked up . . . "Could that be *(sniff sniff)* a pennant race that I smell?" . . . Alas, 'twas no such thing. A few more steps, and I realized it was the McDonald's at the corner of Jersey and Boylston. And while the atmosphere around Fenway was certainly charged, as it always is when the Yankees visit, it was lacking that certain something that would have been here if the gap between first place and second place were two games rather than six.

The pitching matchup tonight? Tomo Ohka for the Sox, (the despised) Roger Clemens for the Yankees. It was Clemens's first start at Fenway since last October, when he got blasted in Game 3 of the American League Championship Series. That chilly evening remains, for a large percentage of Red Sox fans, the favorite memory of the 1999 season. Tonight, though, Clemens's performance bordered on brilliant. Eight innings, five hits, two walks, seven strikeouts . . . and zero runs. The Sox threatened a couple of times—Merloni tripled with one out in the third, Nixon led off the sixth with a double—but they couldn't buy a key hit.

Meanwhile, Ohka pitched pretty well himself. He left with one out in the seventh, however, the Sox trailing two to nothing. It was still 2–0 in the top of the ninth, when Bryce Florie jogged in from the bullpen with Yankees on first and third, and one out. Clay Bellinger, the number-nine hitter, bunted the ball back to Florie, who threw home in time to nab Jorge Posada trying to score from third. But Florie walked Jose Vizcaino to load the bases, and then Derek Jeter lashed a two-run single. In my scorebook, I wrote a note, "To the exits, I say!" as a hefty percentage of the Red Sox fans—of course, there were a fair number of Yankee fans in attendance, and they hung around for the end—headed home.

Most of them, however, didn't exit soon enough to miss what happened next. ESPN.com's "Game Log," the bare bones that represent the events that occurred on the field, describes what happened next in the simplest terms . . .

Thompson grounded out to third.

Those five words come nowhere near, nowhere *near*, describing what actually happened next.

Florie's first pitch to Thompson—in the game after pinch-running for Paul

O'Neill in the eighth—was a fastball down the middle. Thompson, a journeyman who came into this game hitting .219, shot a line drive up the middle. *Right* up the middle. The baseball struck Florie just below his right eye—of course, I couldn't exactly see this from my seat, but I saw the replay on TV a couple of times before deciding I'd seen enough—and then the baseball ricocheted over to third baseman Merloni, who tossed to first for the out. An exceptionally "easy" out, in a way, because Thompson was so horrified at what he'd done that he took only a few steps toward first base before stopping and staring at Florie, crumpled at the base of the pitcher's mound.

The ball left Florie's hand at ninety-one miles per hour, and it came back to him at a velocity of something greater than one hundred miles per hour. Stop for a moment, and think about that. We worry about hitters getting struck with baseballs, but hitters are virtually never hit directly in the head by hundred-mile-an-hour fastballs. That's what batting helmets are for.

Pitchers have no chance. Their momentum prevents them from taking any sort of meaningful evasive action, so if they don't have time to get their glove up, they're sitting ducks.

Anyway, Florie took this one flush. Later, we learned that he suffered three different fractures around the eye socket, and damage to his retina. He'll undergo eye surgery tomorrow, and there will be more surgeries in his future. Florie will live, but nobody's willing to guess whether or not he'll pitch again.

Like so many things that happen to the Red Sox, this one sent everyone to the history books, if not their memories.

On June 30, 1975, at Fenway Park, Orioles third baseman Tony Muser, who hit maybe a dozen line drives in his entire miserable career, happened to hit one straight up the middle, where it caught Red Sox pitcher Dick Pole flush on the right cheek. Pole wound up losing 90 percent of the vision in his right eye. Today, Pole says, "I don't use that as an excuse. I wasn't a very good pitcher."

However, Pole did come back in 1976 and pitched decently, going 6–5 with a 4.33 ERA in thirty-one games. But in 1977, Pole landed with the expansion Seattle Mariners, and over the next two seasons he won eleven games, lost twenty-three, and posted a 5.74 ERA. Those were his last two years in the majors, and today he's a pitching coach for the Indians.

And then there's Tony Conigliaro, who—as I noted earlier in this book—was severely beaned by Jack Hamilton in 1967.

On a personal level, I feel worse for Florie than I would for any other pitcher, because it was Florie who tossed a baseball to Micah, at Safeco Field back on July 31. If this were almost any other ballplayer, I wouldn't take any special interest in his recovery, though of course I would hope for the best. But because this particular ballplayer completed a wonderful experience for my favorite little boy, I'll be pulling for Bryce Florie to come back and pitch again.

Saturday, September 9

There's no such thing as a "must win," not at this point in the season. But the Red Sox formula for success seems to be, "We'll win all the games Pedro pitches, and we'll try to win around half of the rest of them." The problem is that even Pedro doesn't win all of his games, and he didn't win today . . . thanks to one errant pitch.

The Yankees didn't collect their first hit until the fourth, or their second until the sixth. In the seventh, though, Tino Martinez led off with a single. Pedro retired Dave Justice and Jose Canseco on routine pops, but then he walked Jorge Posada on a full count. That brought up number-eight hitter Scott Brosius, who has done very little since being named MVP of the 1998 World Series. Martinez started off Brosius with a pair of change-ups; Brosius swung at both, and missed. Pedro then threw a couple of cut fastballs; Brosius laid off both of them, even though the second might well have been called a strike. It wasn't, though, and soon the count went full. Brosius guessed change-up, Pedro threw change-up, and Brosius lofted it over the Monster in left, for a three-run homer and a 3–1 lead.

And in the ninth, with a man on base, Jose Canseco blasted a Tim Wakefield knuckleball into orbit—434 feet, they said. That put the Yanks ahead, 5–1, and made moot the Sox' two-run rally in the bottom of the ninth.

Realistically, the Sox were already out of time in the East race, but now they're eight games behind the Yankees. And even the most optimistic New Englanders, assuming they can perform simple mathematical functions, should give up on a pennant this season.

Fenway Moment: I was out in the center-field bleachers today, and of course that's where most of the craziness occurs at Fenway. There was very little physical violence in the bleachers today, though. Maybe it was just too hot—83 degrees and sunny at game time—or maybe Sox fans have simply become dispirited by recent events. Still, if you don't mind a certain measure of vulgarity, the bleachers were the place to be.

Behind me were two brothers, one rooting for the Sox, the other for the Yankees. In front of me, a couple of parents and two small boys.

After Brosius's homer, another Yankee fan six rows below us stood up and began bellowing. Shirtless and moderately obese, he turned around and gestured, obscenely, at somebody giving him a hard time.

Behind me, the Sox lover screamed down, "Fuck you, you fat fuck!"

To which his brother replied, nearly as loudly, "Hey, cool it, there's fuckin' kids around here!"

Fenway Moment II: Speaking of fans interacting with one another, at one point a Sox fan simply shouted, "Yankees suck!"

To which a Yankee fan responded, halfway under his breath, "Yeah, they suck all the way to the World Series."

Sunday, September 10

It was, as Susan wrote in my scorebook, "a sad, mellow day in the bleachers, very unlike the usual Yankees–Red Sox matchup."

What a difference a day makes. Before yesterday's game, the Red Sox trailed the Yankees by seven games. Yeah, that's a huge lead at this point in the season, but still . . . Pedro wins on Saturday, and the Red Sox beat Randy Keisler—scheduled to make his major league debut—on Sunday, and then a Sox victory Monday night at Yankee Stadium means a miracle is still at least in the realm of possibility, the land of reality, the kingdom of feasibility.

But of course, Pedro didn't win on Saturday. And with a miracle no longer even remotely on anybody's mind, the energy level at Fenway Park today was but a fraction of yesterday's. I sat out in the bleachers again, this time with Susan, and where yesterday the cops might have been called into action a dozen times and removed double that many rowdies, today Boston's finest were summoned once or twice, and they escorted perhaps five unruly fans from the grounds.

The Red Sox didn't beat Randy Keisler, either. He allowed one run in five innings, Dwight Gooden allowed one run in four innings, and the Yankees won 6–2, completing their first three-game sweep in Boston since 1991.

◆ ◆ ◆

The Indians were rained out this afternoon, but Oakland and Toronto both won, and suddenly the Red Sox are fourth in the Wild Card race:

	W-L	GB
INDIANS	76–63	—
ATHLETICS	75–66	2
BLUE JAYS	75–68	3
RED SOX	73–67	3 ½

The Yankees, of course, are reputed to have crushed Red Sox postseason hopes many times. If the Red Sox are Wile E. Coyote, the Yankees would be Acme. And while I would rather have avoided treading upon that old ground in this book, the events of the last four days fairly demand some historical perspective.

In 1949, the first-place Red Sox entered the last weekend of the season with a one-game lead over the Yankees. So with the two clubs scheduled for a pair of contests at Fenway Park, a single Boston victory would clinch the pennant. They didn't get it, because the Yankees won both games, 5–4 and 5–3 (and the next week, they beat the Dodgers in the World Series).

In 1978, on July 19 the first-place Red Sox owned a fourteen-game lead over the Yankees. No team in American League history had ever come back from a fourteen-game deficit, yet that's exactly what the Yankees did. On September 7, still trailing the Sox by four games, the Yanks arrived in Fenway Park for a four-game series. And in what will forever be remembered as "the Boston Massacre," the Yankees swept the Sox four straight by the combined score of 42–9. The Sox then lost five of their next six (including two in New York), but rebounded with a dozen wins in their next fourteen games. After 162 games, the Red Sox and the Yankees were tied, and the East pennant came down to a one-game playoff at Fenway Park. I imagine you know the rest of the story; suffice it to say that in New England, Yankee shortstop Bucky Dent still has a middle name that begins with the letter *F*.

In 1999, the Red Sox and Yankees met in the American League Championship Series. The Sox won just one game (pounding Roger Clemens in a Game 3 that sent the Fenway Faithful into a paroxysm of maniacal glee). Sox fans remember the two calls blown by umpires, but aside from Game 3, the Yankees outscored the Sox by a huge margin (22–8).

In 2000, the Yankees swept a three-game series at Fenway Park, putting a huge dent in the Red Sox' postseason hopes. That said, we don't know yet if these last three games will be decisive or not; the Sox might end up six or seven games behind not only the Yankees, but also whoever ends up winning the Wild Card.

Suddenly I'm wondering what all the fuss is about. Is this about two baseball teams, or about two cities? Because from what I can tell, the Yankees have only gotten in the way of the Red Sox four times in the history, now exactly a century long, of the American League. At its heart, I suppose the animosity comes from one simple fact: since Boston sold Babe Ruth to New York in 1920, the Yankees have won twenty-five World Series . . . and the Red Sox have won none.

Still, you think about it, and four times—1948, 1978, 1999 and (arguably) 2000—in fifty-three seasons (and none before that) doesn't seem like an awful lot.

The next time you're in Boston, try telling that to a Red Sox fan.

Monday, September 11

Back on June 12, the Red Sox and Yankees were rained out in New York, and tonight was the makeup game. I was there, using the same tickets that I didn't get to use back in June.

Visit Yankee Stadium and Fenway Park, and it's quite apparent just how different they are. However, even a blind man can get a sense of the dramatic contrast between the two parks. All he'd have to do is listen to the music played at the beginning of the games, and the music played at the conclusion of the games.

The music at Fenway Park has, as its foundation, a sort of provincialism, some of it self-deprecating and some not.

This season, the following people or groups of people have performed the National Anthem at Fenway Park: Kevin Maloney of the Worcester Fire Department; Claire Smith (violin) and Scott Chaurette (cello) of Boston; Colleen Ferry of Chelmsford; Julie Mittleman of Boston . . . well, you get the idea.

The Yankees, needless to say, don't allow Vinnie of Queens or Kathleen of New Rochelle to sing the National Anthem. At Yankee Stadium, most games are preceded by the following announcement: "And now, the legendary Eddie Layton will play our National Anthem." Layton's been playing the organ at The Stadium since 1967, or nearly as long as I've been alive. (Of course, Layton's got nothing on Bob Sheppard, now in his *fiftieth* season as the club's public-address announcer.)

So first we hear the National Anthem. And then, approximately three hours later, the game ends and there's more programmed music.

In New York, it's Sinatra (or sometimes Minelli) singing "New York, New York." Every game, win or lose.

In Boston, it's the Standells singing "Dirty Water" after each Red Sox victory (after a loss, the speakers fall sadly silent).

I don't guess this needs much analysis, but the message in each song fairly mirrors the attitudes of the natives of the two cities.

New York?

> *I want to wake up in a city*
> *That never sleeps*

Translation: "This is the greatest city in the world! (And don't you forget it, pal.)"

And Boston?

> *Well, I love that dirty water,*
> *Oh, Boston you're my home.*

Translation: "We may live in a shit-hole, but by God it's ours and we love it."

That's not to say that Boston is a shit-hole. In many ways, Boston's more livable than New York. The point is that Bostonians do tend to suffer from a serious inferiority complex when it comes to New York, whether they'll admit it or not. And this is true, perhaps *especially* true, when it comes to their baseball team.

◆ ◆ ◆

Okay, so it's far too late for the Red Sox, at least when it comes to winning the East. However, they did retrieve a bit of their lost dignity tonight, and also picked up a half-game in the Wild Card standings on idle Cleveland, by beating the Yankees 4–0. Rolando Arrojo tossed seven and one third shutout innings, and Lowe finished up perfectly.

I was at Yankee Stadium with Allen Barra (the most successful freelance writer on the planet), his wife, Jonelle, and their eight-year-old daughter, Maggie. They're all Yankee fans, which just goes to prove that nice people really *can* love the Yanks. I asked Allen what he thinks about Fenway Park, and he answered, somewhat cryptically and with a gleam in his eyes, with a quote from Edward II: "The only problem with Scotland is the Scots."

Allen also came up with the only explanation anyone's offered for the surreal sights and sounds of "Cotton-Eyed Joe," which afflict the senses during the seventh-inning stretch during each game at The Stadium. According to Allen, "It's merely one of Steinbrenner's many ploys to keep us off-balance."

Tuesday, September 12

I was up until nearly two in the morning, writing my column for ESPN.com. And then I woke up at 5:30, just a few minutes ago, the memory of a dream still fresh in my mind . . .

I find myself outside a ballpark, a ballpark that looks much like Fenway. But this ballpark is not located in Boston; rather, it's surrounded by parking lots, an island of bricks in the middle of an asphalt sea. (Come to think of it, the setting looks much like Kauffman Stadium back in Kansas City, bricks notwithstanding.) There's a game in progress, but I apparently have no interest in attending. Instead, my sole purpose here is to track down foul balls, which come flying out of the ballpark at regular intervals. The baseballs first hit the pavement, then bounce high into the air and in unpredictable directions, at which point I, and a few other men my age, scramble after these wayward fouls. I am successful once or twice, but the hunt continues. Eventually, one ball careers down a hill, and I'm the only one who bothers chasing it. I catch up to the baseball twice, only to have it skip over my foot and on down the hill. Realizing the futility of my efforts, I sprint to the bottom of the hill, and this time I'm waiting to corral the ball when it reaches me. Walking back up the hill with my prize, I notice that it's just about the worst-looking baseball I've ever seen. The leather panels have peeled back from the yarn-wrapped core, and someone's attempted, with little success, to repair the damage with transparent tape. And the panels, where they are attached, aren't stuck to each other with red stitching, but instead with red shoelaces.

And that's when I woke up.

Freudians, start your engines.

Wednesday, September 13

Back in Seattle for (1) a friend's wedding, (2) the chance to spend more time with Kristien, and (3) also to see the Royals, who finished a three-game series against the Mariners tonight. Again I was torn. The Royals are the Royals, but the Mariners are fighting for their postseason lives. The M's have somehow managed, in just the last few weeks, to fritter away most of a seven-game lead in the West, and entering tonight's action the Athletics were only one game off the pace.

Anyway, we saw a wonderful game at Safeco Field tonight, the Mariners beating the Royals 2–1, thanks to an umpire's blown call at the plate in the bottom of the eleventh inning. I brought along Kristien and Micah, and I was able to convince Kristien to let Micah stay for the end, even though he has school tomorrow morning. Hey, how often do you get to see a close play at the plate climax an eleven-inning game? And anyway, the kid was having a blast. As Harry Caray used to say, "You can't beat fun at the ol' ballpark." Or in this case, the new ballpark.

Safeco Moment: After a questionable strike call on a Mariner, a fan near me squawked at plate umpire Marvin Hudson, "I know a good optometrist at Sears!"

Like I probably said earlier in the book, this ain't exactly Fenway.

Monday, September 18

The Sox were idle today, but the Athletics and Indians both won. In fact, Indians right-hander Bartolo Colon nearly no-hit the Yankees, which would have been a fairly big story, given that the Bombers haven't been no-hit since knuckleballer Hoyt Wilhelm turned the trick back in 1958. Colon finished with a one-hitter (the one hit being Luis Polonia's single up the middle in the eighth inning).

The Yankees' loss makes little difference to the Red Sox, who now trail New York by seven games in the East. While two weeks ago the Sox were still marginally a part of the American League East pennant race, now they're not. So that means it's the Wild Card or bust, and my money's on bust. Here are the latest Wild Card standings:

	W-L	GB	RS-RA	PYTHAG W-L
INDIANS	80–66	—	858–750	82–64
ATHLETICS	80–67	½	851–769	80–67
RED SOX	78–70	3	718–684	77–71
BLUE JAYS	78–71	3 ½	789–832	71–78

The Sox were, if only briefly, just a game behind the Indians last weekend. Now they're three behind Cleveland and two and a half behind Oakland. And while it's plenty difficult to make up three games in two weeks on one good team, it's simply damn hard to make up three games in two weeks on two good teams. The Sox' position isn't quite untenable, not yet. But it's getting there.

Ninth Inning

Tuesday, September 19

What if tonight's game is postponed? The Indians already are scheduled to play every day the rest of the season, including day-night doubleheaders tomorrow and Wednesday that would preclude a makeup game Wednesday or Thursday. The Red Sox are off next Monday . . . but they certainly can't play the Indians that day, because Cleveland is already scheduled for a bizarre three-team doubleheader: first they host the White Sox in the afternoon, and then the Twins that evening.

So if the weather doesn't cooperate tomorrow night, there would be two options. One, the Red Sox and Indians could play a *triple*-header Wednesday or Thursday. I don't believe this has ever happened in the major leagues, but it's not unknown in the minors; in fact, it happened earlier this season. Still, it's hard to imagine Major League Baseball or the Players Association okaying such a thing. More likely, MLB will simply wait until the end of the season and hope that the missing game doesn't make a difference in the standings or the postseason seedings. If it does, the Indians and Red Sox would presumably play on October 2, the day after the scheduled conclusion to the regular season. The only real problem with that plan? If the makeup game resulted in a tie in the Wild Card standings, there would have to be a playoff game the next day, which would mess up the postseason schedule.

◆ ◆ ◆

This afternoon, I rode my bike to the post office, to pick up my mail of the past week. On the way back, I decided to swing by the Star Market on Boylston, pick up something for supper tonight. The Star Market's not far from my apartment, three short blocks up (to Boylston), one big block over (to Kilmarnock). I don't go there often, though, because the checkout lines are too long, plus there's a 7–Eleven about thirty steps from my back door. It's amazing how long a person can live on the fare available at 7–Eleven. I do, however, occasionally make the long trek to Star Market when I'm feeling the need for a bit of variety in my diet.

Anyway, as I was about to hop my bike over the curb, I noticed something in the gutter, a bedraggled blue hat, lying there just like a discarded sock or an empty soda cup.

As it often does, my curiosity got the better of me. Yeah, I felt a little self-conscious plucking "garbage" from the street . . . but what the hell? And when I picked up this garbage, I found that it was exactly what I'd hoped it was: a Red Sox cap, weather-beaten but still in perfect working order . . . and already adjusted to fit my head perfectly. I've been thinking about buying some sort of Red Sox hat all season, but it just never felt right. You don't just show up in a new city and suddenly start wearing the colors of the local team, or at least I don't (I was in Seattle for three years before I owned a Mariners cap). In a way, I wanted my Red Sox cap, if I got one, to be like my last dog; I wanted it to find me, rather than the other way around.

So this just felt right. Like I said, it's weather-beaten, as if it has been worn on more than a few fishing expeditions far into the North Atlantic. But the fancy red B, outlined in white, is still bright as can be, just like the Red Sox have worn since 1946.

This one found me, and it fits. So I'm keeping it.

And I wore it to the game tonight. Sat in Row 25 of the bleachers with a bunch of Boston College students, one of whom, Ryan, e-mailed me the other day to offer a bleacher seat. I get offers like this from time to time, and I must be growing up, because I actually accept a fair number of them these days. It wasn't so long ago—last year, actually—that meeting strangers made me nervous, but now I just figure that if someone's a baseball fan and wants to meet me, how bad can they be?

Anyway, Ryan and his three buddies—Steve, Kevin, and Dave—are all juniors at Boston College. Ryan's from Brooklyn and he's a Mets fan, which means he fits in quite well with all the Yankee-haters around here. I asked Ryan for his best Fenway story, and he came up with a pretty good one . . .

"In the fall of my freshman year, I came to see the Yankees play the Red Sox. I was rooting for the Sox because I can't stand the Yankees. My seats were right on the right-field line, behind the Pesky Pole. I was sitting next to a somewhat rotund and, eventually, quite inebriated Sox fan. Throughout the game he was screaming obscenities at Paul O'Neill, and this only increased after O'Neill homered for the Yanks. It was obvious that Paulie could hear the guy but, ever the professional, he never looked over. After Scott Hatteberg hit a grand slam to give the Sox the lead in the latter innings, the fat guy continued to scream at O'Neill. Through some lapse in concentration, Paulie finally looked the guy's way . . . and was greeted with a double flip-off that would have gotten perfect tens even in the bleachers at Yankee Stadium. O'Neill, obviously upset with himself for allowing the guy to get the best of him, just shook his head with a certain measure of disgust. And as poetic justice would have it, O'Neill led off the next inning with a shot into the bleachers to tie the game. And the Yanks would eventually win on Jeter's second home run of the night."

Ryan recounted this tale during an eleven-minute rain delay in the top of the seventh. It was 74 degrees at game time, but the temperatures dropped and it was either misting or raining for the entire game, so it seemed quite a bit cooler than that. By the time the real rains finally came in the seventh, the Sox led the Indians, 7–3, thanks in part to Nomar's two-run triple and (a moment later) Bichette's two-run homer, a titanic blast over the Green Monster and onto Lansdowne. The Indians did score a run a few minutes after the game resumed, but Beck and Lowe shut the door on Cleveland in the eighth and ninth, and the Sox had one of the four victories they so desperately need in this five-game series.

As I said, Bichette's home run cleared both the Green Monster and its shawl-like netting, and I would assume that it cleared Lansdowne Street, too. (Very few home runs actually land on Lansdowne, because of the angle involved. If a fly ball clears the net, it will typically strike one of the buildings on the other side of Lansdowne, and then carom back to the street.)

I have written very little about the Green Monster to this point in the book, and for that you've got my apologies. If you made it this far, you might have been thinking I never would discuss baseball's most famous barrier. I had my reasons for the delay. Or rather, my reason: I was hoping to add something to the literature, the answer to a question that, to my knowledge, has never been satisfactorily answered . . .

When did the Green Monster get its nickname?

Unfortunately, despite the best efforts of Jason Brannon and the good efforts of Rob Neyer, I'm not much closer to the answer today than I was last March. I simply don't know when or how the nickname gained currency. However, here's what I do know about the Green Monster . . .

In 1933, a young millionaire named Tom Yawkey bought the Boston Red Sox. The following winter, per Yawkey's orders, Fenway Park was essentially rebuilt. Among the changes was a new left-field wall. The old fence was twenty-five feet high. The new fence was composed of a concrete barrier, eighteen feet high, topped with nineteen feet of railroad ties, bolted together and covered with a thin skin of tin. Thus, thirty-seven feet worth of wall.

Two years later, for the 1936 season, the Sox added a twenty-three-foot netting to the top of the wall, to protect the windows of businesses on the other side of Lansdowne Street.

In the 1940s, the upper twenty-five feet of the fence were completely covered by three colorful signs. From left to right: Calvert whiskey (a well-dressed owl saying, BE WISE. CLEAR HEADS CHOOSE CALVERT); Gem Blades (a skimpily clad woman on the phone, telling someone, OK, IF YOU AVOID 5 O'CLOCK SHADOW.); and Lifebuoy (a happy fellow in a shower, accompanied by the words, THE RED SOX USE . . . LIFEBUOY HEALTH SOAP). These were not signs. These were gaudy, colorful, attention-grabbing billboards featuring, among other things, an owl hawking whiskey, and they're worse than anything you'll find in a ballpark today.

But when fans arrived in Fenway Park for Opening Day in 1947, they found a transformed left-field fence. The signs had been painted over, leaving the wall bare, save for the American and National League scoreboards that had been at the base of the wall since 1934.

In 1976, the Monster was replaced! After the '75 season, which ended when the Red Sox lost Game 7 of the World Series, the old Monster was cut up and sold, with the proceeds going to the Jimmy Fund. The new Wall—the one that's still there—is constructed of steel and Styrofoam, resulting in something much like Formica.

At the same time, the lower portion of the Wall is padded—Fred Lynn had been injured crashing into it during the World Series—and the scoreboard is moved rightward twenty feet. And for some reason, the National League portion of the board is lopped off.

On December 22, 1992, the U.S. Patent and Trademark Office issued Registration No. 1,742,345 to the Boston Red Sox for "Green Monster" for use on clothing. In response, three brothers named D'Angelo filed suit against the Red Sox and their vendors, alleging that they, the D'Angelos, had been using "Green Monster" on their own souvenir clothing since 1985. At this writing, the case has not yet been resolved.

Backtracking a bit . . . In 1934, the number 315—as in feet—was painted at the base of the wall in the left-field corner. For more than six decades, nobody believed that number, but the Red Sox refused to change it. The original blueprints listed the distance as 308 feet. In 1975, the *Boston Globe* used aerial photography and measured it as 305 feet. In April 1995, the *Globe*'s Dan Shaughnessy simply walked onto the field and measured it himself. The result? Three hundred and nine feet, and three inches. About a month later, Red Sox groundskeeper Joe Mooney measured, and when the Red Sox took the field on May 12, 1995, the old number had been replaced with a new one: 310.

Just prior to Opening Day in 1997, Shaughnessy wrote, "They are 25 feet tall and they are hideous. You can see them from the Massachusetts Turnpike, from Lansdowne Street, and from Section 9, Row 12, Seats 1 and 2. You can probably see them from the top of Mount Wachusett if you have a telephoto lens.

"They are three giant fiberglass Coke bottles and they are strapped to a light tower that rises from the top of Fenway Park's historic Green Monster."

Dick Bresciani, then, as now, the club's Grand High Poobah of Spin, explained, "We didn't want a neon flashing bottle. Nothing obtrusive . . . This is a major change at Fenway Park. And we think it might add excitement for kids to see a ball hit off the Coke bottle."

Right. Spoken like a true flack, Dick.

Speaking of which, here's what the Red Sox Media Guide says about those Coke bottles (I have italicized the truly offensive parts):

> **March 19, 1997:** Unveiling of a 25-foot Coca-Cola contour bottle design atop the LF Wall light tower signifying the Red Sox' and Coca-Cola's partnership and *their commitment to fans, commu-*

nity and Jimmy Fund through the "Monster Refreshment" program . . . The program *has ensured ticket price savings for fans*
and significant contributions to the Jimmy Fund for each Red Sox
home run hit over the left-field wall or one that hits the Coke
bottle . . .

Those Coke bottles are still there, and they're still hideous.

(One thing I've learned this year is that whenever the Red Sox start talking
about their commitment to the fans, you should make sure your bullshit detector is
operational. Because you're going to need it.)

Oh, and the color? It would be nice if you could walk into any hardware store
and pick up a gallon of Monster Green, but unfortunately it's not quite so easy to
find. There actually is something called Monster Green, but it's custom-blended by
John Smith, a commercial painter from Wilmington, Massachusetts.

So there you have it, a history of the Green Monster. But like I said, we're still
missing some important information. Namely, when did people start calling it that?

That's a damn good question. According to documents from the aforementioned court case, a judge ruled, "There is no dispute that 'Green Monster' as a
nickname for Fenway Park's left-field wall probably originated with the Boston
press in the late 1940s and long ago passed into common usage."

No dispute, huh? In the 1940s and '50s, the left-field wall was typically referred
to as "the Fence" or "the Fenway Fence." By the 1970s, "The Wall" had replaced "the
Fence" in common usage. I examined every page, all 588 of them, in the autobi-
ographies of both Ted Williams and Carl Yastrzemski—one or the other manned left
field at Fenway from 1946 through 1978. In Williams's book, *My Turn at Bat*, he men-
tions "the wall" three times, but no "Green Monster." In Yastrzemski's book, *Yaz:
Baseball, the Wall, and Me*, he references "the Green Monster" four times . . . and
"the Wall" *fifty-nine* times.

The earliest reference we could find is from 1968, when Will McDonough wrote
in the Red Sox Official Program and Scorecard of Fenway Park's unfriendliness to
pitchers: "Since it was constructed in 1912 with it's [sic] weird 'Duffy's Cliff'—a 10 foot
embankment leading up to the base of what has become the now equally famous
'Green Monster' in left field—pitchers have cursed it."

So that's it. Jason and I can only trace "Green Monster" back to 1968. I'm fairly certain the term appeared earlier than that. We just can't find the damn thing.

There's a popular saying about the Green Monster: "The Wall giveth, and the Wall taketh away." In other words, for every pop fly that drops into the netting for a homer, there's a line-drive double (or single!) off the Monster that would have been a home run in any other ballpark. And of the two most famous hits in Fenway history, one gaveth to the Red Sox, and one tooketh away. In 1975, of course, Fisk won Game 6 of the World Series with his twelfth-inning homer down the left-field line. He had plenty of distance on the ball, but in a ballpark with typical dimensions, Fisk's drive almost certainly would have gone foul before reaching the pole. Three years later, Bucky Dent hit a routine fly ball that didn't stop carrying until it had dropped into the netting; in any other ballpark . . . well, Red Sox fans know the rest.

Wednesday, September 20

This afternoon, a death rattle could be heard emanating from Friendly Fenway Park, as the Red Sox lost a game that most of us thought they had to win. Though nobody ever expresses it quite so bluntly, the hope has always been that Pedro would win all of his starts, and the rest of the pitchers would win about half the time. Do that, and at the end of the season you're in the playoffs. But now the Sox are so far behind the Indians that the Pedro-plus-.500 formula isn't going to be enough.

Of course, it wasn't supposed to happen this way. The Sox won yesterday. They were supposed to win today—after all, *Pedro was pitching*—and then they'd just need to win two of the last three games against Cleveland to get back in the race. Easy as pie, right? Especially when one considered that Pedro's opponent this afternoon would be Steve Woodard, who woke up this morning with two wins, ten losses, and a 6.34 ERA (250 percent higher than Pedro's).

As he has more than a few times this season, Pedro got off to a rocky start. The first three Indians singled, and the fourth hit a sharp grounder to Garciaparra. Only one run scored and, as he has more than a few times this season, Pedro pitched almost flawlessly after his early struggles; following the three hits, Martinez retired seventeen straight Indians.

And as he has too many times this season, Pedro was not rewarded with a victory. He left after the eighth inning, the Red Sox still trailing one to nothing, and he must have been at least a tad frustrated beneath his stoic exterior. Certainly, Jimy Williams was frustrated; in the top of the eighth, he got ejected after arguing vehemently—kicked dirt all over home plate, the whole act—with plate umpire Richard Rieker over a blown call that wound up costing the Sox nothing (except the presence of their manager in the dugout). Certainly, the Fenway Faithful were frustrated; when Varitek grounded out weakly to end the sixth, there were scattered outbreaks of booing throughout the ballpark. True, Varitek had looked particularly bad—in his two previous at-bats, he'd grounded out to first base, and struck out—but the fans really were booing the entire lineup, which to that point had managed but three hits off Woodard. The people at Fenway Park know their stuff—especially in September, when there aren't as many tourists here—and so they knew that Woodard's been terrible all season long. Losing is one thing, but losing to a guy with a 6.34 ERA?

Derek Lowe came out to pitch the ninth, and he was greeted by a home run from Kenny Lofton that just sneaked fair, down the right-field line. That run would wind up meaning something, as the Sox eked out a single run in the bottom of the ninth. Brian Daubach, who's come through so many times in pressure spots since joining the Sox last year, struck out swinging on a full count with runners on first and second, and Pedro had lost for the sixth time. In those six losses, the Sox have scored—ready for this?—the grand total of seven runs.

On a happier note, Martinez did lower his ERA to 1.78. And since today marked Pedro's last home start—he's scheduled for one more start, in Chicago next Tuesday—it's appropriate to put his season in some sort of historical perspective (more pleasant, to be sure, than analyzing the demise of the Sox' pennant hopes) . . .

As Christian Ruzich pointed out on the SABR-L message board, Pedro's on pace to set major league "records" for both largest gap between his ERA and his league's ERA, and lowest ERA relative to his league's ERA.

YEAR	LEAGUE	PITCHER	ERA	LG ERA	DIFF
2000	AMERICAN	PEDRO MARTINEZ	1.68	4.96	3.28
1999	AMERICAN	PEDRO MARTINEZ	2.07	4.86	2.79
1994	NATIONAL	GREG MADDUX	1.56	4.21	2.65
1995	NATIONAL	GREG MADDUX	1.63	4.18	2.55

1997	AMERICAN	ROGER CLEMENS	2.05	4.57	2.52
1930	NATIONAL	DAZZY VANCE	2.61	4.97	2.36
1996	NATIONAL	KEVIN BROWN	1.89	4.22	2.33
1931	AMERICAN	LEFTY GROVE	2.06	4.38	2.32
1997	AMERICAN	PEDRO MARTINEZ	1.90	4.21	2.31
1995	AMERICAN	RANDY JOHNSON	2.48	4.71	2.23

I know that's a monster of a chart for a book such as this, but I really wanted to get the No. 9 guy in. A distinguished group, no question. Aside from Kevin Brown, all seven pitchers in the table are, or likely will be, Hall of Famers. One thing that does worry me a little is the lousy mix of eras here. Two pitchers here toiled in the early 1930s, and the others all posted their stats since 1994. I don't know how to explain this, exactly, but it's probably no coincidence that pitchers have been dominating in the same era in which we've seen Mark McGwire and Sammy Sosa cranking out home runs at record rates. It's apparently a good time to dominate your competition.

Okay, I hope that you (and my editor) will indulge me once more, as I'd like to run one more big table. Another, slightly more logical way of comparing pitchers from different eras is to look at their ERA as a percentage of the league ERA. For example, Walter Johnson posted an American League–best 2.72 ERA in 1924, and Lefty Grove an American League–best 2.70 ERA in 1935. Those figures are virtually identical, nothing separating them except perhaps one earned run. However, the American League ERA in 1924 was 4.23, while the A.L. ERA in 1935 was 4.46. So Johnson's ERA was about 64 percent of his league's, and Groves's was about 61 percent.

Yes, it's a fairly crude tool—we're not considering the effects of the pitchers' home ballparks, or their durability, or the fielders behind them—but it's nevertheless instructive. Well, here are the top ten in "relative ERA"—their ERAs as a percentage of their league—this century:

YEAR	LEAGUE	PITCHER	ERA	LG ERA	PCT
2000	AMERICAN	PEDRO MARTINEZ	1.68	4.96	33.9
1914	AMERICAN	DUTCH LEONARD	0.96	2.73	35.2
1994	NATIONAL	GREG MADDUX	1.56	4.21	37.1

1968	NATIONAL	BOB GIBSON	1.12	2.98	37.6
1913	AMERICAN	WALTER JOHNSON	1.14	2.93	38.9
1995	NATIONAL	GREG MADDUX	1.63	4.18	39.0
1906	NATIONAL	MORDECAI BROWN	1.04	2.62	39.7
1912	AMERICAN	WALTER JOHNSON	1.39	3.34	41.6
1999	AMERICAN	PEDRO MARTINEZ	2.07	4.86	42.6
1985	NATIONAL	DWIGHT GOODEN	1.53	3.59	42.6

A better mix of eras here . . . well, sort of. The only season between 1914 and 1985 is Bob Gibson's 1968, which gives me a little more respect for that famous performance than I had before. What this tells me is that, for whatever reason, it was more difficult to dominate in that seventy-year span, and only Gibson was able to do it. Not Grove or Seaver or Marichal, or even Koufax.

Three pitchers appear twice: Walter Johnson, Greg Maddux, and Pedro Martinez.

Five or six years ago in the *Wall Street Journal*, Allen Barra and I argued that the two top candidates for Greatest Pitcher Ever were Johnson and Maddux, but it seems to me that Martinez will, with a few more great seasons, take his place in that discussion. Assuming, of course, that he hasn't already.

Martinez has won only 124 games in his career. That's clearly too low for Hall of Fame consideration, let alone the title of Greatest Pitcher Ever. But you know, a fair number of analysts—ex-players, mostly—will argue that Sandy Koufax deserves that appellation. Well, consider that (1) Koufax finished his career with 165 victories, and (2) he doesn't appear on either of the above lists, not even once, while Martinez appears a total of five times.

I will take from this season, more than anything else, the simple memory of having seen eighty-one games in the world's greatest ballpark. But runner-up in the memory derby will, I suspect, be the pleasure of seeing Pedro Martinez pitch thirteen times in what *might* be the greatest season any pitcher ever had.

Fenway Moment: When Daubach struck out to end the game, the guy sitting behind me came up with the following, which I present here as verse . . .

Typical Red Sox.

Keep it close.

Tear your heart out.

Stomp on it with a cleat.

◆ ◆ ◆

Tonight's game was No. 100, including a couple of Triple-A games (one in Tacoma, the other in Pawtucket). I have now attended exactly one hundred professional baseball games this season.

Now, one hundred baseball games might not be a lot for a baseball writer; in the old days, baseball beat writers might well see every game his team played, or close to that. Even today, when the writers aren't asked to work nearly as hard as they once were, a typical beat writer might be at the ballpark for upward of 125 games.

But I still consider myself a baseball fan more than a baseball writer, and one hundred games for a fan is an awful lot. I'm not done, either. Two more against the Indians tomorrow, a three-game series against the Orioles this weekend, and then I'm off to Chicago for two Cubs games at Wrigley Field, and a game or two at Comiskey, where the White Sox will be hosting the Red Sox. That'll run the count to 108 or 109, with more likely to come in Seattle, where I'll be for as long as the Mariners are alive in the postseason (assuming they make it, which doesn't look as likely today as it did two weeks ago).

A dream come true.

Nevertheless, I wouldn't be heartbroken if Game No. 100 were also my last. I'm not *sick* of baseball, not at all. I don't think I've ever been sick of baseball. Even after nearly six months of eating, drinking, and dreaming baseball, if there's a game on TV, that's what I'm watching. I think I'm just a little tired of being at the ballpark, where I can manage only a minimal amount of "work" (i.e. writing). And frankly, watching the Red Sox in their death throes, even at Friendly Fenway Park, is not the most pleasant way to spend a week in late September. This weekend, for example, I'd rather be back in Seattle, where the Mariners and Athletics will be fighting each other for the American League West pennant.

At least I had a great seat tonight, as—for the first time all season—I spent the entire game squatting in a seat that wasn't mine.

Our story begins yesterday afternoon, when I visited Fenway to purchase tickets for tonight's and tomorrow night's games (I already had tickets for this afternoon and tomorrow afternoon). There are eight ticket windows, and above each is a round light fixture. If the bulb in a fixture is lit, the window below is manned. Anyway, when one of the lit windows opened up—there was a line, as there always is on a game day—I shuffled over and found myself across from a middle-aged, somewhat scruffy fellow I'd never seen before. This worried me a little, as I've been dealing with the same two guys all season: one young pale fellow with slick hair, the other a young black man, his body composed of spheres.

Anyway, I asked for my usual—"Your best single, please."—for both games, but the best he could do was a couple of grandstand seats. Row 9, no less. Oh well, I thought to myself, I can always come back tomorrow night and trade up, like usual. I didn't bother looking at the tickets, just stuffed them in my pocket, like usual. So imagine my surprise when I returned to the ballpark at seven o'clock, found my favorite ticket guy (young and slick), only to discover that the ticket I wanted to exchange was for *this afternoon's game*, and so now worthless, since this afternoon's game had been completed a couple of hours earlier.

I explained the mixup, but by the time Slick had talked to his supervisor, who authorized a replacement ticket, it was 7:05 (the scheduled game time, and two or three minutes before the typical actual start). Worse, now they wouldn't let me trade up because the new ticket was a "comp," and trading up from a comp ticket is *verboten.*

My replacement ticket wasn't a bad one, a grandstand seat thirty-three rows behind the Red Sox on-deck circle. I've sat in the infield grandstand plenty of times, and the view is just fine (unless, of course, you're behind a post). But I felt like I'd somehow been cheated out of a Field Box seat, and so I didn't want to sit in the grandstand, not on a perfect September evening, not with only five Fenway games left after tonight. So I did what I could have done almost every game this season. I used my twenty-eight-dollar ticket to get inside the ballpark; then I found an empty seat just a few rows behind the dugout, and then I spent nine innings sitting there. Easy as pie.

From that great seat, I saw (1) the Red Sox lose a one-run game that they needed to win, (2) Cleveland's double-play combo, Omar Vizquel and Roberto Alomar, put on a defensive circus the likes of which I've never seen, (3) Trot Nixon hit just his second home run since the All-Star break, and (4) one of the strangest plays I've ever seen, so rare that it deserves further description.

Top of the fifth, Sox leading the Indians three to nothing. With two outs and nobody on, rookie pitcher Paxton Crawford hit rookie outfielder Bill Selby with a pitch. Kenny Lofton singled on the very next pitch, sending Crawford to second base. Vizquel walked, loading the bases. Roberto Alomar singled, scoring Selby and Lofton. Then Vizquel and Alomar worked a double steal so easily that Hatteberg didn't even bother throwing. Crawford walked Manny Ramirez on a full count, and got pulled in favor of Rheal Cormier.

Now, Crawford's sudden collapse was interesting in its own, not particularly unique, way. But it's Cormier that people will remember tomorrow. With Jim Thome at the plate, the Red Sox have been employing an extreme shift: second baseman Mike Lansing sets up closer to first base than usual, shortstop Garciaparra plays on the first-base side of second base, and third baseman Merloni takes up residence where Nomar usually stands. This serves to thwart the extreme pull-hitting Thome, but also makes it impossible to keep the runner at third base—in this case, Vizquel—anywhere near the bag. So with a one-and-one count on Thome, Vizquel sprints toward the plate. And scores, before Cormier even has a chance to attempt a throw.

Straight steals of home are rare; there were only four in the major leagues in 1999. And straight steals of home without even a throw? You might go your whole life and never see one.

◆ ◆ ◆

Are the Sox done? After today's sweep, the headline on Steve Buckley's column in the *Herald* read, "Sox fans, it's all over." Buckley wrote, "Now, whatever happens the rest of the way is pretty much beside the point. It's over."

And I think he's right. The Sox now trail the Yankees in the East by six and a half games, and here are the Wild Card standings:

	W-L	GB
INDIANS	82–67	—
ATHLETICS	82–68	1/2
BLUE JAYS	80–71	3
RED SOX	79–72	4

The Sox do have one more shot at this thing. If they could sweep the Indians tomorrow, they'd trail Cleveland by only two games, and if the A's and Jays both oblige with losses . . . well, hell, anything's possible, right?

Thursday, September 21

Rolando Arrojo picked a lousy time for the worst start of his career. He struck out leadoff hitter Kenny Lofton and then retired Omar Vizquel on a grounder to second base. But the next seven hitters?

Walk

Walk

(Steal)

Walk

Double

Double

Walk

(Double Steal)

Single

The first three walks came on full counts; the last took only four pitches. Catcher Einar Diaz finished Arrojo's day, twenty-two minutes after it began, with a two-run single. Arrojo's replacement, Steve Ontiveros, gave up an RBI single to Lofton before getting Vizquel to end the inning with a fly to right field.

After one-half of one inning, the Red Sox trailed 7–0. If it had been a friendly game of Ping-Pong, they'd have been skunked. But baseball ain't Ping-Pong, and the Sox scored two runs in their half of the first, then six more in the third, the key blow coming when Troy O'Leary drove a pitch over the wall in the right-field corner, for a three-run homer.

The Sox scored another run in the fifth, and then they hung on for dear life. The Indians loaded the bases in the sixth, but didn't score. The Indians scored once in the eighth, but left two runners on base. And in the ninth, the Indians got two runners on base with two out, but four hours and four minutes after Rolando Arrojo (now long forgotten) threw his first pitch, Derek Lowe struck out Roberto Alomar to end the game.

◆ ◆ ◆

I went home between games to check e-mail and get an early start on tomorrow's column. Jim called, and at one point he asked if following the Red Sox to such a great degree has become "work."

"Yeah, it has," I told him. "Especially these last two days, when it seems like I'm always at the ballpark. And it doesn't help that the Sox have lost twice in torturous fashion, and half the fans are pissed off."

Baseball, however, is remarkable in its ability to rejuvenate one's spirit (assuming, of course, that one loves the game, or at least likes it).

At the ticket window a few minutes before the evening tilt, I was able to upgrade from a grandstand seat—a pretty good grandstand seat, but still a grandstand seat—to one of the best seats in the house, in the third row (and on the aisle!) behind the visitors' on-deck circle. On the way in, I ran into Wally the Green Monster, and gave him a high five. I generally eschew this gesture—as Jim says, "The high five is what white guys do when black guys do something good."—but you gotta make an exception for Wally (who graces a T-shirt that I sent Micah a few months ago).

I settled into my seat, the skies clear and the temperature highly comfortable, and looked to the mound, where my favorite pitcher limbered up.

Work? Hardly.

◆　◆　◆

One thing about Fenway Park: there are hecklers in the expensive seats.

This is not the case in most ballparks. In Seattle, for example, nobody in the good seats is going to really let loose. The same is true in Kansas City. Not at Wrigley Field in Chicago, though. I suspect there's a strong correlation between heckling from the good seats and age of ballpark.

Anyway, with Wakefield getting knocked out in the sixth, and the Red Sox hitters fairly quiet until too late—the Sox wound up losing again, 8–5—I derived most of my enjoyment from listening to the people around me screaming at various Indians.

One fan to Manny Ramirez, who sports artificially blond hair: "Manny, who does your hair? *Who does your hair?*"

Two fans loudly discussing Roberto Alomar . . .

"Alomar's smaller than I thought."

"That's what his wife said."

One of those same fans, to Sandy Alomar . . .

"Hey Sandy, did you always play with your brother? Did he pitch and you catch?"

And finally, late in the game when it became fairly apparent that the Red Sox were going to lose: "Roberto, if we don't make the playoffs, *beat* the Yankees. Just beat the Yankees. I *hate* the Yankees."

And lose, they did. With the Sox having already lost twice to the Indians, this game didn't seem particularly important. Still, a win would have been nice. Instead, the Sox trailed 8–1 after seven innings, and their four late runs weren't nearly enough. The Wild Card is still wide open . . . but not for the Red Sox . . .

	W-L	GB
INDIANS	83–68	—
ATHLETICS	83–68	—
BLUE JAYS	80–72	3 ½
RED SOX	80–73	4

Four games behind the leaders. Fourth place. Now it would take a miracle. At least.

Friday, September 22

Tonight, Susan and I sat up on the roof, only my second time up there this season. The view's not bad, but the tickets are seriously overpriced (forty bucks), apparently because one doesn't have to commune with much riffraff up there. There's not much action, either. Here's about as bad (or good, depending on your perspective) as it gets on the roof . . . Carl Everett pinch-hit for Mike Lansing in the eighth and struck out swinging. Behind us, a young adolescent started yelling at Everett.

Boy: "Carl Everett stinks!"

Mom: "That's enough."

Boy: "He's a poor sportsman!"

Mom: "That is *enough!*"

A capacity crowd saw the Red Sox, perhaps drained from just having played four games in two days (I certainly was drained from watching four games in two days), fall meekly to the Orioles, 3–1. Only five Sox reached base, and none after the fourth, as Baltimore starter Sidney Ponson retired the last eighteen batters he faced.

On a happier note, with everybody swinging the bats—the teams totaled three walks—the game was mercifully short, just two hours and seventeen minutes. Given that those aforementioned four games averaged more than three and a half hours, two hours and seventeen minutes felt like nothing.

Saturday, September 23

I ran out of pages in my scorebook last night. But just as Bob Carpenter promised me on the phone earlier this week, today's mail brought a new scorebook.

I might have written this back in the spring, but an empty scorebook is just *full* of possibilities. I imagine it must be something like an empty canvas to a painter, a block of granite to a sculptor, a big, empty house to an interior designer, a full head of thick hair to a stylist. I leaf through the pristine pages, with space for *one hundred baseball games*, and my imagination is tickled by what might eventually fill these pages. A no-hitter? Game 7 of a World Series? A four-homer game for Alex Rodriguez? None of these, probably, but that's why a new scorebook is so magical to me. I don't *know* what's going to happen. *Nobody* knows. I only know that every game will be different, and every game will contain something worth seeing.

I look at the old book, empty just five and a half months ago, and there's such a richness there. Here's Opening Day at Fenway Park . . . there's Carl Everett leading off the ninth with a walk-off homer . . . Pedro Martinez striking out seventeen Devil Rays in one game (and losing to Steve Trachsel!) . . . Brian Daubach beating the Blue Jays, well after midnight, with a three-run homer in the bottom of the eleventh . . . Pedro and the Rocket battling at Yankee Stadium, in perhaps the best game of the season . . . Billy Koch hitting 100 on the radar gun at Fenway Park . . . the Yankees beating the Red Sox at Fenway, 22–1 . . . the Red Sox beating the Yankees on my birthday, and moving into first place (if only for a few days) . . . my first All-Star Game . . . Carl Everett battling temporary insanity, and losing . . . my first sight of the Montreal Expos . . . Nomar Garciaparra lifting his batting average to .400 in Boston, then to .403 in Baltimore . . . an overnight stay at Fenway Park, wherein I made a number of rodent friends . . . Mike Lansing hitting two-run doubles in consecutive innings, the second of them climaxing a four-run, game-winning rally in the bottom of the ninth . . . a game that didn't start until 10:06 and didn't end until 1:03 in the morning . . . Tim Wakefield striking out Alex Rodriguez and Edgar Martinez, two of the finest right-handed hitters of our time, on six pitches . . . Carlton Fisk's number retired . . . the Sox beating the Twins 11–6 after being down 5–0 in the first inning . . . four games at Fenway Park in two days . . . the Sox beating the Indians 9–8 after being down 7–0 in the first inning . . . and perhaps most bizarrely of all, the first lefty-righty mullet bullpen combination in the long history of the game.

Not bad for one scorebook, but maybe not all that exceptional, either. There is an incredible variety of experiences available at the ballpark, if one cares enough to pay attention.

And today, I broke in my new book with a thrilling victory for the Sox. The Orioles scored twice in the seventh to deadlock the score at six runs apiece, and it stayed that way until the tenth. Orioles rookie Chris Richard led off with a single and wound up scoring to give the O's a 7–6 lead . . . and then things got interesting. Nomar led off the bottom of the tenth with a walk, and O'Leary followed with a line drive off the center-field wall. Wendell Kim, aggressive as always, waved Nomar home; the relay throw beat him, but Baltimore catcher Brook Fordyce couldn't quite corral the one-hopper. So Nomar scored, and O'Leary moved to third on the play. Both Merloni and Hatteberg were intentionally walked, thus loading the bases with nobody out. Varitek pinch-hit, and lined out to second. Daubach, who's succeeded in so many situations like this one, fouled out to the catcher. Would the Sox blow another September game?

Nope. On a full count, Nixon coaxed a walk out of Orioles closer Ryan Kohlmeier, and O'Leary trotted home with the winning run. It's far too late for the Sox' pennant hopes, but winning always beats losing, especially when you're at the ballpark.

◆   ◆   ◆

With this season—or half-season—of discontent nearly complete, things have finally come to a head between Jimy Williams and Dan Duquette.

There have been a number of bones of contention between the two—Jimy wanted to keep Mike Stanley, the Duke wanted to release him; Jimy wanted to release Izzy Alcantara, the Duke wanted to keep him—but the primary instrument of antipathy has been Carl Everett.

As you might remember, back in early August Everett cursed Williams, at some length, in the Red Sox locker room, in plain sight of whichever players and reporters happened to be hanging around. The next day, when Duquette was asked if Everett would be disciplined, the Duke replied, "It's been addressed. It's a work in progress. Any behavior that's not conducive to winning will be addressed by the team. The team encourages behavior conducive to winning."

When Duquette was asked if he was doing enough to support his manager, he replied, "The club always supports the manager."

Whatever. Everett was not disciplined in any fashion.

Then came seven weeks of relative calm, but that calm was shattered this week. Thursday afternoon, Everett was penciled into the Red Sox starting lineup, but arrived at the ballpark a few minutes before noon (players were supposed to be in uniform by 11:30), explaining that his nagging quadriceps injury, which had kept him out of the lineup since last weekend, would keep him out Thursday, too. Everett was incensed when he saw his name on the preliminary lineup card, and reportedly yelled to his teammates and coach Tommy Harper, "Can you believe that [expletive]? Last night he [pinch] runs for me, and now he has me in center field. Do you believe this [expletive]? This [expletive] is done."

Not long after that, Williams called Darren Lewis into his office and told Lewis that he'd be starting in place of Everett. Lewis came out, said something quietly to Everett, and then Everett started screaming expletives at Lewis. The two were separated before anything ugly could happen.

Williams's comments before and after the game were restrained, as usual. But he made it clear that Everett, injured or not, should have been at the ballpark earlier. When asked how disruptive Everett's actions were, he answered, "How disruptive? I look at it this way. When you play all these games and you're in the hunt, you shouldn't even have a reporting time. You should get here and want to get here, because you want to play.

"There's no fine for being late in September because nobody's late, especially if you're in the hunt."

For his part, Duquette made great pains to stress that, once again, no disciplinary action would be taken against Everett.

That led Red Sox beat writer Gordon Edes, in his *Globe* column yesterday, to absolutely blast Duquette, leading his column with the following: "Jimy Williams, a man of dignity being treated shamefully by his employers and his All-Star center fielder, has every reason to resign as manager of the Red Sox. Today would not be soon enough.

"That would be a fitting parting shot to an imperious general manager, Dan Duquette, who yesterday sent a clear message that Carl Everett is now in charge of the team."

Williams did not resign, at least not yet. Today, however, he did offer a few understated comments, saying, "If I was a general manager, I'd certainly back the manager. If you can't back your manager, you probably need to get rid of him and get someone you can back. When you separate your team with one player and it's basically going against the thoughts of the manager and the focus of the team trying to win, it becomes very difficult."

There are two reasons why Jimy Williams is still managing the Boston Red Sox. One, Williams is under contract for next season, and if he resigns, he forfeits his $1.1 million salary for the 2001 season. Yes, he could almost certainly find another job, but if he resigns before actually having another job lined up, the Sox could prevent him from taking another job. And two, Duquette doesn't want to fire Williams, because if he does he'll take a horrible beating in the press.

Actually, there might well be a third reason, that being Jimy's integrity. When asked about resigning, Williams said, "I'd never do that. That is wrong. You finish what you start. I've always tried to preach that to my kids. We're still mathematically in [contention]. How could I leave these players? I think too much of them. I can't do that."

So here we sit, with the manager and general manager again playing chicken. Neither wants to work with the other, but both are as stubborn as they come. And who loses in all of this?

The team and its fans. Because no matter who's right and who's wrong, it's no good when your manager and your general manager are continually working at cross purposes.

Sunday, September 24

Barring a major miracle, today's game was my last at Fenway Park this season . . .

I leave earlier than usual, and I try to pay more attention than usual. Out my door, and left onto Jersey Street. There's the Brown Sugar Cafe on my left, then the 7-Eleven where I did so much of grocery shopping this season, and then, just before

Queensberry Street, the Jersey Street Laundry. Another block to Peterborough, and a great view of the Prudential Center straight east. Another block to Boylston, and I sprint ahead to get the WALK sign. One more block to Van Ness, and suddenly Yawkey Way is thick with fans and people wanting to sell things to fans.

I tried to sell my editor on a scratch-and-sniff section at this point, but he wouldn't go for it. So you'll just have to settle for some of the sounds from along Yawkey Way . . .

Hot Dogs! Sausages! Chicken! Steaks! Soda!
Nomar, Pedro, sunglasses!
Yessir, what can I getcha? Hot dog, sausage, steak, chicken.
    Help someone!?
Step right in! Sausage, steak, chicken, hot dogs!
    Wrap 'em up, take 'em to the game.
        Look at the grill, folks, everyone's different!
PEA-nuts, CA-shews, PIS-TA-chios, RIGHT down heeeerre!
Yessir, chicken teriyaki, hot dogs, chicken, steak.
Hey, we got the good stuff! All-beef hot dogs!
RED Sox, souvenirs, hats pennants jerseeeeys!
Hey, we got no waiting here!
Next!
Program and scorecard, only two dollars. Last chance!

At 12:57, eight minutes before game time, I walked into Fenway Park for the last time this season, wishing that it didn't have to end.

◆ ◆ ◆

Meanwhile, the Red Sox hitters looked like they couldn't wait for their last home game of the season to end.

The Sox played their first home game of the 2000 season under gray skies, and that's how they played their last one, too. Granted, it was relatively balmy this afternoon—74 degrees at first pitch, as opposed to 46 degrees back on April 11—but the temperatures were in direct opposition to the mood in the stands, and presumably in the home team's dugout. Though the Sox began their first home stand with a 2–4 record, we still had high hopes for them (everyone has high hopes in

April, whether we'll admit it or not). The Red Sox won that first game handily—it seems like forever ago to me, but unless you're a really slow reader, it probably doesn't seem at all that long ago to you—and in fact, after winning their second home game, too, they never fell below .500 again. People were happy that day, chilly as it was, because at that point anything still seemed possible.

Today, though, all that seemed possible was a single victory, something for the fans to remember through the long, baseball-less winter, the way middle-aged men sometimes return to that game-winning jump shot they made when they were seventeen.

The Red Sox, though, seemed to have something else in mind. Through the first seven innings, Sox hitters totaled five hits, zero walks . . . and fifteen strikeouts. Thirteen of those strikeouts were of the swinging variety. An optimist would suggest that the Sox were aggressive, a pessimist would suggest that they suffered from impatience, and in this case I would tend to agree with the pessimist. Four of those strikeouts concluded with an attempt to check the swing. It was almost as if they were thinking, "Okay, so I want to swing at everything and get the hell out of town, but I probably shouldn't be so damn *obvious* about it."

Until the seventh, no Sox hitter reached even second base . . . and then they caught a few breaks:

Nomar led off with a middling ground ball to the left side of the infield, where Orioles shortstop Melvin Mora made the play but didn't have time for a good throw. That's one break.

After O'Leary struck out (for the third time in three at-bats), Merloni dumped a blooper single into left field, Garciaparra stopping at second base. That's two breaks.

Hatteberg followed with a proverbial made-to-order double-play grounder, directly to shortstop Mora. But just as he did back on July 13 when he was playing for the Mets, Mora botched the play for no apparent reason. That's three breaks, and the bases are loaded with just one out.

But pinch-hitter Midre Cummings struck out, and so did Rico Brogna (now batting .156 since joining the Sox, with one homer in forty-five at-bats; granted, that one homer was a game-winning grand slam). Duquette's brilliant acquisitions come through again.

Mussina left the game after escaping that jam (which was no fault of his own). It was kind of a shame because, with those fifteen Ks in seven innings, he still had an outside shot of matching Roger Clemens's all-time record of twenty strikeouts in a game. Mussina had thrown 107 pitches, though, and earlier in the season Hargrove had taken some heat for overworking Mussina. So out he came.

In terms of drama and heartbreak, the seventh inning didn't have nothin' on the eighth and ninth.

With one out in the eighth, Offerman doubled off the wall in the right-field corner, just missing a home run that would have tied the game at one apiece (as usual, the Red Sox pitchers kept things close; Tomo Ohka allowed just four hits and one run in seven-plus innings). Mike Lansing pinch-ran for Offerman, and with two outs he still stood on second base, with Nomar due at the plate and O'Leary on deck.

Now, as every single fan of the Red Sox or Indians remembers all so well, last October, then-Indians manager Mike Hargrove was faced with a similar situation in Game 5 of the American League Division Series. First base open, Garciaparra batting, O'Leary due next. Not once, but twice. The first time, in the third inning, Hargrove ordered the intentional walk, and O'Leary followed with a grand slam to give the Red Sox a 6–5 lead. The second time, in the seventh, Hargrove again ordered the intentional walk, and again O'Leary followed with a home run, this one a three-run blast that gave the Red Sox an 11–8 and, eventually, the series-clinching victory.

At the time, I blasted Hargrove in my column, arguing that the intentional walk is nearly always a poor percentage move. And that's true. But today, when Hargrove again passed Garciaparra in favor of O'Leary, things were different. First, this year's O'Leary isn't last year's O'Leary. In 1999, he posted a .495 slugging percentage. This season, he was slugging .407 after his first three at-bats tonight. And second, last year there were right-handed pitchers on the mound to face O'Leary, who bats left-handed, both times in Game 5. This year, Hargrove followed the intentional walk with a walk of his own, to the pitcher's mound, from where he summoned left-hander Buddy Groom, who's murder on lefty hitters, from the bullpen.

And Groom made O'Leary look silly, running the count to two-and-oh before inducing a soft grounder to the mound. Just another rally killed by the Great Troy O'Leary.

That would be O'Leary's last Fenway plate appearance of the season, but his teammates still had one more rally to kill. Bottom of the ninth, score still 1–0, Everett pinch-hits for Manny Alexander and walks. Hatteberg sent Everett to second base with a sharp single to right-center field. That brought up Donnie Sadler, assigned a simple mission: Lay down a sacrifice bunt, and move the runners to second and third. Sadler, who should probably bunt every time up no matter what the situation, nubbed the ball softly toward the pitcher's mound. Orioles closer Ryan Kohlmeier, yesterday's goat, rushed in to field the bunt. And fell down. All hands safe, bases loaded, and nobody out.

After nearly three hours of what looked like voluntary futility—I'm not saying that it *was* voluntary, just that it looked that way—the Red Sox were suddenly going to win. Snatch, in a proverbial way, victory from the jaws of defeat.

To that end, Jimy Williams called on Brian Daubach to pinch-hit for Brogna. Both are left-handed hitters, but of course Brogna's been awful this season, both before and after arriving in Boston, and he'd looked bad in his three previous at-bats.

Daubach lofted a Kohlmeier fastball to left field. Coming off the bat, it looked like Daubach certainly would have enough distance for a game-tying sacrifice fly. But a stiff breeze, straight out of the north, had just sprung up, and as soon as Daubach's drive gained some altitude, that breeze took control, and the ball landed in the glove of Delino DeShields in shallow left field.

Maybe Wendell Kim sent Bernard Gilkey home from third because DeShields is a novice left fielder, or maybe he sent Gilkey home from third because he didn't notice the wind, didn't notice that by the time he caught the ball, DeShields was practically standing in the infield. Or maybe he sent Gilkey simply because he is, after all, "Wendell the Windmill."

Whatever the reason, Kim did send Gilkey, and DeShields did uncork a perfect throw home, and Gilkey did get called out at the plate from here to there, completing a 7–2 double play. Then Trot Nixon hit a routine fly ball to center field—medium center field, deep enough to score Gilkey from third base, had Gilkey still occupied that valuable piece of high ground—and Home Game Number 81 was history.

◆   ◆   ◆

Today I resigned myself to a home truth: I stink at catching foul balls.

In the bottom of the second, Hatteberg fouled a ball in my direction. I looked up, and the ball was coming right at me. I stepped out into the aisle. It landed two steps below me and bounced right over my right shoulder and back into the grandstand.

This was my third failure in the last few months to make a relatively easy play, hence my resignation. Unless a bunch of other people screw up and a baseball falls into my lap, I'm not getting one. To console myself, I decided to buy one last bag of peanuts from Rob Barry. Now, catching a bag of peanuts isn't a major accomplishment—I've seen Rob Barry throw scores of bags to pre- and post-pubescent boys and girls, and so far both groups are fielding close to a thousand—but the male ego is a fragile thing, and today mine needs all the help it can get.

If you want the real deal with Rob Barry, though, you have to bide your time, wait to stand up and get his attention until he's a long ways away but looking in your general direction. In the top of the sixth, I finally saw my chance. Rob was down in the Field Box seats behind the plate, heading up the aisle toward the walkway. I was three sections toward third base, and maybe a dozen rows higher. I stood up, gave him a little wave, and he did what he always does when he sees you: just a slight upward movement with the head. The epitome of cool. And when he reached the walkway, he wound up and fired a perfect strike, from sixty feet away. I wound up leaving half the peanuts in the bag—I wasn't all that hungry in the first place—but by God I caught the damn thing.

With that important mission accomplished, I applied myself to a more important pursuit . . . Today I have to say good-bye to Fenway Park.

I've always been lousy at good-byes, and if I don't know how to gracefully say farewell to people, what the hell am I supposed to say to a ballpark? I didn't have any idea. In the meantime, I went to say good-bye to Bill Nowlin, sitting in Box 123 with his nine-year-old son, Emmet. We chatted for the two minutes between the bottom of the eighth and the top of the ninth, and then I headed up to see Liz and her husband, Jim. As it happened, they were sitting close to me, in Section 22 near the top of the grandstand.

We talked about the Sox for a few minutes, and Liz concluded with, "I still think the Red Sox will win the World Series in my lifetime."

Yeah, so do I.

"That's what my grandfather said, too."

Is he still alive?

"No."

I returned to my seat for the bottom of the ninth, because I wanted to be "alone" with the old ballpark when our season together ended. When the Red Sox loaded the bases, though, I turned and looked back at Liz, who grinned a big grin.

"Wow," I thought, "we're going to come back and win this thing," and I imagined that Liz was thinking much the same.

As we've seen, it didn't happen. But I wasn't bitter, or even sad. Knowing that good people, people like Bill and Liz—not to mention Susan and Art and Jason and Andy and Steve, and a score more who helped make this baseball season so pleasant—share my passion for this game . . . well, today that knowledge brought me a certain contentment that transcends wins and losses. As long as places like Fenway Park exist, there will be someplace for people like us to go, and forget about life's complications, if only for a few hours. And today, many of us took our sweet time in leaving this particular place. Twenty minutes after the last pitch, there were still a few hundred of us wandering from section to section, staring out at the field and wishing April weren't so far away.

Back in the middle of the eighth inning, whoever controls the sound system engaged in a sentimental gesture that I'm glad I didn't have to invent . . .

Sweet Caroline
Good times never seemed so good

I fell in love twice this season, with a ballpark named Fenway and a woman named Kristien. And I, who have always struggled to meet people, made a bunch of new friends.

Nope, I never thought the good times would be so good.

Extra Innings

Coda

Improbably enough, the Red Sox weren't officially knocked out of the pennant race until the season's final weekend. Their loss on September 24, coupled with the Yankees' 6–3 victory over Toronto, dropped the Sox seven games behind the Yankees. The Bostons still had six games to play, the New Yorkers eight (though they would not play the eighth unless necessary), so the best the Red Sox could do was tie the Yankees, and that would only happen if the Red Sox won the rest of their games and the Yankees lost the rest of theirs. According to my friend David (who's significantly more adept with numbers than I), the chances of that happening, based on the standings the morning of September 25, were approximately 0.00335 percent. Or to put it more prosaically, about 1 in 29,850.

And you know what? An inch here or there, and it could have happened.

The Yankees lost to the Tigers on Monday, and then they lost to the Devil Rays on Tuesday, Wednesday, and Thursday. The Red Sox beat the White Sox on Tuesday, Wednesday, and Thursday (I was at Comiskey Park for that one). The Yankees lost again Friday night, this time to the Orioles . . . but it didn't matter, because before the Yanks finished losing their fifth straight, the Red Sox had dropped an 8–6 decision in St. Petersburg. This one would have been tough even without the postseason ramifications, as the Sox blew an early four-run lead, the game ending when Trot Nixon struck out in the ninth with two runners on base. And so on Friday, September 29, at exactly 10:09 Eastern Daylight Time, the Boston Red Sox were finally and officially eliminated from postseason possibility.

Saturday, the Sox won and the Yankees lost their sixth straight. Sunday, the Yankees lost their seventh straight. The Sox lost, too, as a sextet of pitchers worked two or fewer innings for Boston, and only four regulars populated the lineup. The result? A 3–2 defeat. But if the game had meant anything at all, Pedro would have started, all the regulars would have played, and the Sox just might have forced the Yankees to play one more game. Had they lost that one (a makeup game against the Florida Marlins tentatively scheduled for Monday), the Yankees and Red Sox then would have met in a one-game playoff for the American League East pennant, at Fenway Park.

Like I said, an inch here or there. The Yankees, of course, would eventually win the World Series—I was at Shea Stadium for Game 5, my 114th game of the season, in which the Yanks clinched their third straight championship—while the Red Sox didn't win a damn thing. But was there really that much difference between the two clubs? The Yankees finished the regular season with eighty-seven victories, the Red Sox with eighty-five.

Two wins. An inch here or there.

(Jeez, I'm starting to sound like a Red Sox fan.)

Of course, that last comment was a digression into Subjective Land, or at least it might have seemed that way. Let's return to Objective Land for a moment and run the final American League East standings (contenders only):

	W-L	GB	RS-RA	PYTHAG W-L
YANKEES	87–74	——	871–814	85–76
RED SOX	85–77	2 1/2	792–745	86–76
BLUE JAYS	83–79	4 1/2	861–908	77–85

Yes, the Red Sox actually finished a half-game ahead of the Yankees in the Pythagorean "standings." Of course, a half-game is nothing, it means even less than those two and a half games by which the Yankees aced the Sox in the *real* standings. I do think it's fair to suggest two salient points, though. One, the Yankees did not play fundamentally better than the Red Sox during the regular season. And two, if the Yankees didn't have the financial freedom—not to mention the baseball acumen—to acquire David Justice and Denny Neagle in the middle of the season, the Red Sox would quite likely have won the American League East and—who knows?—possibly the World Series.

◆ ◆ ◆

Nomar Garciaparra, sitting atop the world with a .403 batting average on July 20, fell far, far short of the magical mark. After going hitless in two straight games against the Yankees on September 8 and 9, Garciaparra's average stood at .357, and suddenly he was in danger of losing the batting title to Toronto's Carlos Delgado. But Garciaparra went three for three on September 10, beginning a twenty-game hitting streak that left his average at .372 at season's end. He thus became the first right-handed hitter to win two straight American League batting titles since Joe DiMaggio in 1939 and '40.

◆ ◆ ◆

Derek Lowe finished with a rush, saving eleven games from September 11 through the end of the season. He wound up with forty-two saves, tied for the American League lead with Todd Jones, and Lowe's 2.56 ERA was tops among A.L. relievers with at least a dozen saves. But the Sox rotation was so unstable this season that management is reportedly toying with the idea of making Lowe a starter again, even though in nineteen career starts, he was 2–10 with a 6.80 ERA.

◆ ◆ ◆

On October 6, Red Sox CEO John Harrington wrote at redsox.com, "I am announcing today that I have decided to put the Yawkey Trust majority ownership interest in the Boston Red Sox up for sale. My goal is to have a new owner, preferably a diehard Red Sox fan from New England, identified and possibly in place for next season."

In his letter, Harrington noted, among other things, "our timetable for opening the [new] park in 2004 looks very unlikely." (Remember, a year ago the Sox were talking about opening their new park in 2003.)

Optimists suggested that the Sox might have a new owner by Opening Day next spring, a new owner with very deep pockets, so deep that he'd be able to make up any financing shortfalls with the new ballpark.

Realists suggested that, given the huge number of expected suitors, it's ridiculous to expect new ownership before next season. What's more, it's unrealistic to think that a new owner, no matter how rich he might be, will spend any more of his own money on a new ballpark than he has to.

And the beat goes on.

◆ ◆ ◆

On October 25, the Red Sox relieved Wendell Kim of his duties. They offered him the proverbial "another job within the organization," which he immediately declined. In Peter Gammons's ESPN.com column, he reported after the season that thirty-seven Red Sox base runners were thrown out at home plate. That probably isn't a record, but it certainly sounds like one.

Five days later, the Sox fired hitting coach Jim Rice, too. I have no idea how effective Rice has been—his first three years here, the Sox scored plenty of runs, his last two they did not—but it won't make a lick of difference who the hitting coach is if Duquette doesn't get some *hitters*.

In their inimitable way, though, the Red Sox covered their collective ass by offering Rice "the opportunity to be elevated to join fellow Boston greats Ted Williams and Carl Yastrzemski as a Red Sox Organization Instructor."

◆ ◆ ◆

On October 28, a number of Boston city councilors blasted the existing ballpark plan, currently estimated to cost in the neighborhood of $650 million (and sure to go higher, as these things always do).

There are thirteen city councilors, and no plan can go forward without the approval of nine of them. According to the Associated Press, "Several councilors said the plan is so flawed that the only remedy is to choose another site—an idea the city administration and team already have rejected after examining more than twenty potential locations."

For now, I'll conclude this subject with the words of Stephen King on the demise of old Fenway Park . . . "I've got this ace in the hole in the back of my mind that it will never happen because Boston is so goddamn corrupt that it'll be forty or fifty years before they grease enough palms."

◆ ◆ ◆

On October 29, the date on which the Red Sox *might*, but for a few inches here and there, have hosted Game 7 of the World Series, it snowed in the Fens.

It snowed.

◆ ◆ ◆

On October 30, The *Boston Globe*'s Stephanie Ebbert wrote, "The uncertainties surrounding the ballpark project and the Yawkey Trust's decision to sell the team have many observers contending that the financing plan approved by the legislature will die a quiet death. The lobbying efforts have been half-hearted, and city councilors, once led to believe that their support was vital to the project, are now wondering whether they will ever vote on it."

◆   ◆   ◆

On November 13, I was walking to the post office in Kenmore Square and noticed a flotilla of TV vans parked on Lansdowne Street. When I got home, I discovered that they were there for a press conference, wherein Pedro Martinez talked about winning his third Cy Young Award, and second straight. Martinez, just like last year, was a unanimous choice.

◆   ◆   ◆

On November 25, the Red Sox announced that their ticket prices, already the highest in the major leagues, would make an astronomical jump in 2001. The best box seats? They're going from forty-five to fifty-five dollars. The next level, the modern plastic seats? They were forty dollars last season, and they're also jumping to fifty-five dollars. And the grandstand seats, which were a relative bargain at twenty-eight dollars? They're going up 43 percent, to forty dollars. Bleacher seats, which last season could be had for sixteen or fourteen bucks, are going to twenty and eighteen.

The timing of the announcement—the day after Thanksgiving—certainly was no accident. As Dan Shaughnessy wrote in the *Globe*,

> Really, guys. The day after Thanksgiving? Friday afternoon on the slowest news day of the year?
>   . . . Once again the Red Sox have raised ticket prices—a bold move in the wake of their train-wreck finish. But they also timed the announcement hoping you wouldn't notice.

Shaughnessy has a gift, a gift which isn't always on display but certainly was in this particular column. As he correctly noted later on, the Red Sox raise their ticket prices every year for one reason, and one reason only: because they can. At the same time, Dan Duquette posted "holiday greetings" at www.redsox.com, including the following:

As we've said before, a high payroll does not guarantee a playoff spot, but we agree that keeping pace financially is crucial in order to remain competitive while operating with economic responsibility. Hence, this year's ticket price increase is intended to help us remain competitive, especially playing in baseball's smallest ballpark and facing baseball's challenging economic climate, as the industry's salaries have doubled in the last five years. We are committed to keeping our product affordable and we are pleased to say that watching the Red Sox play at Fenway Park remains the best professional sports value in New England.

You probably don't need me to tell you this, but there's more bullshit in that single paragraph, written in Duquette's inimitable style, than you'll find in a sports bar on a Friday night, or (if you prefer your metaphors more literal) in a holding pen at a bovine breeding facility. As Shaughnessy wrote, "That's what's great about Fenway: It's an asset for ticket sales, but the Red Sox manage to characterize it as a liability." And of course, there's Duquette's laughable reference to the franchise's commitment to "keeping our product affordable."

Amazingly enough, people will continue to pay, whether an evening at Fenway Park is "affordable" or not. Yes, the price increase will turn off some fans. But there certainly are enough corporations (remember, it's a tax write-off), tourists, and diehard Red Sox fans to fill thirty-three thousand seats every night next summer. And a year from now? We'll be reading about another price hike, and if Duquette's still in power, it may well be announced the day after Thanksgiving—if not on Christmas Eve. Red Sox fans can think of it as the Duke's special gift, the kind that he's best at delivering.

◆   ◆   ◆

In the course of tying up some loose ends, I asked Jason to contact the Red Sox and see if they'd give us a complete list of those who performed the National Anthem at Fenway this season. Jason worked on this for a few weeks, and finally he threw up his hands and sent me the following e-mail . . .

Hey. I called Dick Bresciani, the PR guy at the Sox, about getting a list of Nat'l Anthem singers. It was unreal. He acted as though I was the Justice Department asking for a list of foreign donors.

During our conversation, he asserted the following:

That he wasn't sure they had the list.

That he wasn't sure the singers would want their names published.

That your publisher would have to submit a letter explaining what we want and why we want it before the Red Sox would hand it over to us.

Early on, Bresciani asked (with a tone of great suspicion) why you'd want this list. I told him that your book was basically a diary of your time here in Boston, going to Fenway, and that you'd note a couple of things about all the games. He wondered why you'd want all 81 singers, as you couldn't have gone to all 81 home games. I told him that you did, in fact, go to all the home games. He said, "You mean he watched them on TV?" I told him no, that you *actually attended* every game, and some of the Sox' road games, as well.

"What, he's going to write who sang the national anthem? *That's a book?*"

Bresciani was incredulous, and I'm not sure he believes you actually went to *any* games.

So the long and the short of it is, they're probably never going to give us the list. This fucking seals it. This, and reading the headlines about the Sox wanting "community input" into their ballpark plans. In my view, anything the Red Sox say publicly should be considered with extreme skepticism.

Later,

Jas

I suppose I could call Bresciani myself, assure him that I really am writing a book, and maybe drop the letters *E, S, P,* and *N* into the conversation (that usually does the trick). But I don't really need all eighty-one singers, and I think it makes for a better story if I let Jason's experience with the front office stand as the final word on the subject. The cover of the December issue of *Boston Magazine* asks the question, "Is This the Most Obnoxious City in America?" I don't know about the city—most everybody's been nice enough to me—but I think that Dan Duquette and his lackeys just might qualify for some sort of award.

Shortly after the World Series, my editor at ESPN.com asked me to write an article about Fenway Park for a special series they would be running in early November. With their permission, I'd like to reprint that column here (with a few minor changes), because it does fairly summarize my feelings about Fenway Park . . .

> When it comes to the fate of Fenway Park, I believe that I have something of a unique perspective, as I'm one of the few people in the world—team employees notwithstanding—who attended all eighty-one Red Sox home games of the 2000 season. I've been there in the rain and the sun and the heat and the cold, and I've sat in nearly every sort of seat. I've snagged a foul ball off the bat of "Nomah," and I've stood on Lansdowne during batting practice, on the lookout for titanic home runs. I've even spent a night inside Fenway, from dusk to dawn, just me and the clean-up crew and the rats and the Green Monster. So while I'm certainly no New Englander, not after just six months, there's little of New England's home ballpark that I've not experienced.
>
> And I'm telling you, the day that we lose Fenway Park, we lose something special that can never be replaced. Because as vigorously as Red Sox management strives to destroy the old ballpark's unique atmosphere by playing canned music (most of it horrible) between innings, and posting billboards wherever the space can be found, Fenway remains the single best place on the planet to watch a baseball game. I've been to the great majority of major league ballparks—this year's additions notwithstanding—and I can tell you that on their *best* days, Safeco Field and Oriole Park at Camden Yards and The Ballpark in Arlington might provide *half* the experience that Fenway Park does.

Do baseball fans from all over make *pilgrimages* to Arlington, Texas? Do they walk around Safeco Field slowly, gawking while committing their surroundings to posterity with a camcorder? Do they buy hundreds of tickets, every day from Memorial Day through Labor Day, for tours of Camden Yards?

No, they don't do any of these things. But I've seen fans do all of these things, and more, at Fenway Park.

So what does Red Sox management crave? Yup, yet another version of Safeco Field (less the retractable roof), with perhaps a generous helping of Camden Yards thrown in to satisfy the traditionalists among us. Yes, the Red Sox *say* a new ballpark will retain the intimacy of Fenway Park, but I'm telling you that it's not going to happen. Nobody's done it yet, not anywhere else, and the preliminary designs released by the Sox certainly don't show a surfeit of architectural imagination.

Red Sox general manager Dan Duquette loves to say that a new ballpark will be "for the fans." Really? Which fans are those? Most of the seats in a new ballpark, while certainly more comfortable, will also be significantly farther from the action on the field. And while there will be more of them, the "additional" seating will almost literally be closer to Boston Harbor than home plate. Oh, and don't think they'll be any cheaper. Red Sox tickets are the most expensive in the game, and that certainly will not change.

Of course, there's the "competitiveness argument." A new ballpark will be better for the fans because the fans want to see the Red Sox win a World Series, and with greater revenues will come more victories. Perhaps. But as long as the Red Sox reside in the same division with the Yankees, this will be something of a fool's game. As the logic goes, the Red Sox need a new ballpark in order to compete with the Yankees. No, the Sox won't ever be able to match the Yankees' financial resources, but they can at least close the gap, right?

Sorry, folks, but it won't work that way. In 2001, the Red Sox
will likely have a payroll somewhere in the neighborhood of $90
million, while the Yankees will be closer to $120 million (or more).
But you see, the only thing limiting the Yankees is the knowledge
that $120 million will probably be enough. If the Red Sox suddenly
found another $15 million from, say, a new ballpark, don't you
think the Yankees would themselves find an extra $15 million—or
$30 million, or $40 million—of their own?

Of course they would. The Yankees, because of the immense
size of their local TV revenues, will always have a huge financial
advantage. It's merely a question of how much George
Steinbrenner puts in his pockets, and how much he plows back
into the club. And as the Red Sox get richer, Steinbrenner's pockets will simply get poorer as the Yankees maintain their financial
edge by any means necessary.

So I reject the competitiveness argument. Given the price of
tickets and the large, enthusiastic fan base, there's no reason for
the Red Sox to cry poor. No, they'll never have the Yankees'
money, but that's true no matter what the status of their ballpark. If they can't compete with the Indians and Athletics of the
world, that's Dan Duquette's fault, *not* the ballpark's.

Yes, I know that Fenway's seats can be uncomfortable, especially for tall fans, or fans who might weigh a bit more than they'd
like. And I know that Fenway's bathrooms are a bit ramshackle
and cramped, if not downright revolting by the seventh inning.
And I know that there aren't many seats (though I've never had
much trouble finding one for myself).

But Fenway Park is a special place, a sort of time machine
that allows us to imagine what baseball was like when Ted
Williams galloped around in left field, when Lou Gehrig sent tow-
ering fly balls into the right-field bleachers, when Carlton Fisk hit
the most-replayed home run in baseball history. Yes, it can be
uncomfortable place . . . but have we become so spoiled, so cod-

dled, so insulated that we cannot cope with three hours of discomfort, in exchange for three hours in a time machine?

Okay, so I'm no longer even halfway objective about this subject. Love will do that to a fella.

◆ ◆ ◆

On December 13, the Red Sox signed free-agent Manny Ramirez to an eight-year deal for $160 million. With that single move, Dan Duquette transformed a city of ill-contented baseball fans into a hotbed of enthusiasm. That evening, I walked to the Barnes & Noble in Kenmore Square, and noticed a number of TV trucks parked alongside Fenway Park. "Ah," I thought, "there must be a press conference tonight." And on my way back home, I peeked over the Green Monster and saw the scoreboard above the center-field bleachers . . .

THE
BOSTON RED SOX
WELCOME
MANNY
RAMIREZ
TO
FENWAY PARK

Just a few minutes later, MSNBC's Brian Williams said of Al Gore's concession speech, "By all accounts, he knocked one over the Green Monster."

◆ ◆ ◆

When I first saw Jason after the World Series, I asked him what he thought about the season's finale. Jason's generally quick with a quip, but this time he spurned cleverness.

"I hate the fucking Yankees."

With all due respect to the greatest sports franchise in history, at that particular moment I had to second that emotion. Because the Yankees beat the Mariners in the American League Championship Series, I was in New York, rather than Seattle, during the World Series. And it was in New York—Penn Station, to be precise—that I somehow managed to lose my laptop computer. Within that computer, embedded on the hard drive, were the most recent files comprising the manuscript for this book. I had not, I am embarrassed to admit, backed up those files in nearly two months. So what had seemed a daunting task—finishing this book in about five weeks—suddenly seemed like an impossible one, thanks mostly to my carelessness but partly to the fucking Yankees.

That I did finish the book is a testament to four things: the lucky return, four days later, of my aforementioned laptop; the patience of my friends and family; Jason's hard work; and the desperation of an aspiring author who has already spent his advance. Oh, I almost forgot the fifth thing: my lucky Red Sox cap, rescued from the gutter in September and perched atop my head in November as I labored to write or revise three thousand words every day for thirty days.

So thank you, lucky Red Sox cap. To show my gratitude, I shall, from this day forward, wear you only on special occasions. World Series games, for example. Or visits to Fenway Park, the greatest ballpark in the world.

Rob Neyer
The Fenway
Boston, Massachusetts
January 19, 2001

Printed in the United States
1243600006B/243